THE SEARCH FOR
ANNE
PERRY

JOANNE
DRAYTON

HarperCollins*Publishers*Ltd

Author's note

Every effort has been made to identify the photographers of images contained in personal collections. If a photographer has not been identified, please contact the publisher with details, and acknowledgement will be made in any reprint or future edition of this work.

Published by HarperCollins Publishers Ltd

First published in Canada by HarperCollins Publishers Ltd in a hardcover edition: 2012
This trade paperback edition: 2013

Joanne Drayton asserts the moral right to be identified as the author of this work.

HarperCollins books may be purchased for educational, business,
or sales promotional use through our Special Markets Department.

HarperCollins Publishers Ltd
2 Bloor Street East, 20th Floor
Toronto, Ontario, Canada
M4W 1A8

www.harpercollins.ca

Library and Archives Canada Cataloguing in Publication
information is available upon request

ISBN 978-1-44341-783-9

Printed and bound in the United States
RRD 9 8 7 6 5 4 3 2 1

For Suzanne Vincent Marshall
&
thank you to my mother
Patricia Drayton, an old girl of CGHS,
whose special interest in this story helped to make it happen
&
Meg Davis and Kate Stone,
whose generosity and intelligence
have been unfailing.

The rest is for and about Anne Perry.

CONTENTS

Acknowledgements 9

Prelude 11

Chapter One 16

Chapter Two 51

Chapter Three. 86

Chapter Four 122

Chapter Five 156

Chapter Six 189

Chapter Seven 225

Chapter Eight 258

Chapter Nine 290

Postscript 324

Endnotes 329

Select Bibliography 339

Index 345

ACKNOWLEDGEMENTS

'... you played a large part in putting "an entirely different perspective on the events, more sensitive to the human frailties of those involved & more respectful of them & their personal integrity" ...'

letter from Marion Perry to Nancy Sutherland,
quoting Brian Easton's comments, c April 1995

I have had the great privilege of meeting and working on this project with a number of special people in Anne's life. I would like to thank them for their insights and unstinting support: Meg Davis, Meg MacDonald, Jonathan Hulme, Don Maass, Kim Hovey, Susanna Porter, Ken Sherman, Diana Tyler, Emmanuelle Heurtebise, Lora Fountain, Diane Hinds, Doris Platt, Mike Ducker, Tim Webb, Dagmar Wolfinden, Elizabeth Sweeney, Jane Pimblett and the people of Portmahomack who shared their experiences of Anne, especially David Wilson, Sandy and Liz Morris at the Castle Hotel, Peggy and Abbie (for the walk), and the congregation of the Mormon Church in Invergordon for their hospitality and warmth.

My understanding has been substantially deepened by the poignant recollections of women who knew both Juliet and Pauline as schoolmates — Margaret Luisetti, Brenda Blake, Jan Spang, Marjorie Smart, Margaret Dacre, Caroline Maze, Patricia Drayton and Sonja Mornin — and by talking to Beth Webster (Dr FO Bennett's secretary), Gerald Lascelles and Emeritus Professor Russell Stone.

I am especially indebted to the counselling staff of Westlake Girls High, especially Alison Horspool, who talked with me at length about teenage girls, and to then principal Alison Gernhoefer, who was especially supportive, and to Kate Luisetti, Sue McBride, Megan Davidson, Murray Douglas and Nicola Scott.

My research has been assisted and informed by Philippa Drayton, Mark Hangartner, Dr Peter Lineham, Dr Bruce Harding, Jane Barrington, Tonia Geddes, Laura Reeve, Patti Gurekian, Rebecca Perkins and Sarah Lightman, and by fascinating people met along the way, especially Patricia and Terence Young and Brad and Katherine Side. I would like to thank Oliver Sutherland and his family for granting access to Nancy Sutherland's Parker–Hulme papers in the Macmillan Brown Library at the University of Canterbury. I am grateful to the staff of the following institutions for their co-operation and assistance in accessing archives, images and information: Alexander Turnbull Library; Archives New Zealand; Auckland Libraries (Special Collections); Christchurch City Libraries (Special Collections); Christchurch *Press*; Macmillan Brown Library (University of Canterbury, Christchurch); the MBA author file archive (London); and *New Zealand Herald*.

My grateful thanks go to UNITEC, which has been remarkably helpful and encouraging of this project. I would like to thank members of the administration, the library and academic and allied staff who have kindly supported me in my writing of this book. I am grateful especially to Leon Fourie, David Hawkins, Marcus Williams, Tanya Eccleston, Gina Ferguson, Susan Eddy, Alastair Campbell, and to Mary-Louise Browne and Mitch Harris for their suggestions and support.

My sincerest thanks to former publishing manager Lorain Day and to managing director Tony Fisk, for their vision in taking this project on, and to Vicki Marsdon, Sandra Noakes, Louise Vallant, Eva Chan and all the staff at HarperCollins who worked on this book. I am especially grateful to editors Kate Stone and Anna Rogers. Thank you for your sure and steady support, and for your criticism, encouragement and inspiration. Thank you also to Teresa McIntyre and Liz Stone for their careful proofread. Thanks to Vincent Reynolds for his classic design. At HarperCollins in Hammersmith, London, I would like to thank David Brawn for arranging an amazing lunch with Susan Opie and for his steadfast encouragement.

Some special friends and family members have helped the project along the way. I offer my heartfelt thanks especially to Jennifer Marshall and David Beves (for letting us stay in their flat in London), Bradley Fafejta (for his photography skills), Linda Tyler, Andrew and Shirley Whillans, Mike Small, Judy Barton, Paul Drayton, Chrissie Thomas and Guy Drayton; and for the love and patient support of our children, Jeremy Thomson, and Katherine and Jason and Megan Lovelock.

PRELUDE

Meg hurried back from lunch. It was Thursday afternoon and the next day was her last in the office for two weeks. The weather was warming, and she and her partner, Pim, were going to Wales for their summer holiday. The lunch break had been a chance for them to quickly buy some lamps for their new home together. The day was hot and the streets fumy and noisy, with the hum of London traffic intermittently punctured by screeching sirens. The MBA Literary Agents Ltd office, on the corner of Fitzroy and Warren streets, was in a skinny, grey-brick building with white facings, a brown door with a large brass door handle, and a solid black iron railing. Butted against it on one side was a garish little coffee shop, and above the brown door long, thin windows were stacked in pairs; in all, it was three storeys high with a tiny flat on top.

The office was open-plan, so coming through the door was to become immersed in the clack of keyboards, the screech and whirr of the fax machine, the ringing of telephones, and the relentless buzz of other people's conversations.

As Meg sat down at her desk, Sophie Gorell Barnes told her that a journalist from New Zealand had rung and would call back. Although this was odd — agents usually chased journalists — Meg gave it little more thought.

Two hours later, her telephone rang again. The woman on the end introduced herself as Lin Ferguson. Surprised to learn that Meg knew nothing about the Parker–Hulme case, she proceeded to tell her about two teenage girls, Pauline Parker and Juliet Hulme, who had murdered the former girl's mother in Christchurch in 1954. Then she said breathlessly, 'And, I think Juliet Hulme is your client, Anne Perry.'

Meg exploded with laughter. It was too ridiculous for words. How could Juliet Hulme possibly be her author of 20 bestselling books, the matronly, 'matching bag and shoes' 55-year-old Anne Perry? Finally she recovered enough to say, 'Come off it — I think you've got the wrong woman.'

'Yeah. I guess I must have. Never mind,' came a crestfallen voice from the other end, and the line went dead.

Meg recounted the conversation to everyone else in the office, and they all had a 'fantastic laugh about the whole thing'.

'It's incredible,' Meg gasped.

'Yeah,' agreed Sophie, laughing. 'If you had really committed murder ... you'd become Jane Asher and be, like, "queen of cakes". You'd become Delia Smith and be the "doyenne of cuisine". You wouldn't go and write grisly Victorian murder mysteries.' The next morning, 29 July 1994, the telephone rang again and it was Lin Ferguson.

'Actually,' she said, 'I think it *is* Anne, and we're going to publish the story in the Sunday papers.'

'Well, *you think* you're going to, but you're going to have an injunction in five minutes, so just stay by the phone.' A furious Meg decided to ring Anne immediately, then their lawyer.

'Look, I'm really sorry to bother you,' she began her telephone call to Anne. 'You know how I have to ask you if we're going to involve a lawyer? I think we're going to need to do that.' She quickly outlined the 'ridiculous story' that Lin Ferguson had told her. 'Can you believe it? There's a film being made about this murder, and some people have got hold of this crazy idea that it's you ... But we're going to get an injunction.'

Meg's words hit Anne Perry like the first wave of an atomic explosion. She felt physically sick. It had happened at last, the one thing in the world she feared the most. For a while she was almost senseless, listening but not hearing, the room receding and her head pounding like a drum. 'I'm sorry, but you can't ... You can't refute it — because it's true.'

There was a sharp intake of breath at the other end of the line. 'I'm going to phone you back from a more private phone. I'm going to call you back in ten minutes.'

Ruth Needham, glancing up from her desk and noticing the expression on Meg's face, shot off to Diana Tyler's cupboard, poured a large Scotch and brought it back for her. Meg emptied the glass, steadied her nerves, then climbed the narrow staircase to the hush of MBA's attic flat to ring Anne at her home in Portmahomack, in the Highlands of north-eastern Scotland.

'OK, I still love you. Now, you have to tell me about this.' And so for the first time they had a proper conversation about Anne's past, and things began to fall into place. The gaps in Anne's life that Meg had wondered about, the late teenage years that evaporated in sickness, the furtive glossing-over of certain matters, the way Anne had always made questions disappear as if by sleight of hand — all this Meg had put down to Anne being Anne, but now she realized that it meant a whole lot more. Collecting herself, she began to strategize.

'What we need is a lawyer to manage the press for us. This is going to be big and we need expert advice.' She told Anne to sit tight and talk only to her mother and her closest friend, Meg MacDonald. As soon as she got off the telephone, Meg rang their lawyer, who immediately gave her the contact details for Lynne Kirwin, a publicity agent who would help limit the media fallout.

Lynne Kirwin recommended a plan that she hoped would contain things and reduce the trauma for Anne. 'Anne will have to do an interview for the [Daily] Telegraph, [as that's] the paper in the UK where other journalists get their facts from. We'll have one interview there telling the whole story, and Anne doesn't need to talk to anyone else — we'll just kill it dead right there.'[1]

In this 'huge crisis', should Meg continue with her holiday plans to Wales, or cancel everything and go up to Portmahomack with a 'shotgun picking off journalists and fielding phone calls'?[2] Finally, she decided to trust Lynne's reassurances and go to Wales. If she had realized what was going to happen, she might well have changed her mind. As it was, Anne rang her every day she was away. Meg and Pim spent their first week at a bed-and-breakfast in an old farmhouse. There was only one public telephone, in the hall, and the good-natured staff would serve Meg's cooked breakfast there, while she stood with the receiver in one hand and a fork in the other.

Anne was terrified she would lose everything — her friends, her career, her income and her house. Would it be a repeat of the past, with the same vilification? 'Am I never to be forgiven?'[3] She worried about her brother, Jonathan Hulme, and about the impact on his wife and young children. She feared, too, that the ordeal of having the past raked up again would kill her mother, now known as Marion Perry, who was then 82 years old and in poor health and living a kilometre or so away at Arn Gate Cottage. But when Anne went to tell her mother the news, Marion showed herself to be stronger than anyone could have imagined; she stood by her daughter in steely fashion. There was something cool, self-assured and calculating about Marion. In her day, her coiffed hair, perfect presentation and glamorous looks had hushed party conversation and stopped men mid-stride. Even in old age, something of the coquettish grace and elegance survived. She was clever at reading people, and past humiliation and social disgrace had made her more astute and determined not to give up the life she and her daughter had rebuilt. 'There's no place for tears. If there's any crying, it's to be done much later,' she instructed Anne, and sent her back to her semi-restored stone barn 'to draw up a list of friends and … do battle'.[4] Anne, who would not remember much of what she did during this time, sat down and worked out the people she should see in person, and those she must telephone.

Afterwards she had a conversation which remains vivid in her memory, and which she describes as the hardest thing she has ever done. She rang her friend and contemporary Peggy D'Inverno, proprietor of the village post office and general store, and asked her to come to the house. Anne told her that she and another schoolgirl had killed a woman in New Zealand in 1954, and that it would be all over the newspapers in the morning. This was the first time in 40 years that she had told her secret to anyone beyond her most intimate associates.

That evening she went to see the minister of her local Mormon Church in Invergordon and told him everything. She wept uncontrollably. They prayed together, and the minister predicted that she 'would not lose a single friend'.[5] Her faith was a consolation, but the task ahead was daunting. She had got to know people during her five years in the quiet provincial backwater of Portmahomack. How would they feel about her now? If they felt uncomfortable about her living in the village, she resolved to leave.

On 31 July, the story broke in the *Sunday News* in New Zealand, under the headline: 'Murder She Wrote! Best-Selling British Author's Grisly Kiwi Past Revealed'. Anne opened her curtains the morning after to see that 'her driveway was a sea of journalists from Australia and New Zealand, who had just got on the first plane [to the United Kingdom] and were now pointing with huge telephoto lenses', and that television crews were wandering over her property.[6] Day and night the telephone ran hot with tabloid journalists soliciting her comment. One journalist who woke her swore 'on the life of his child' that he would not send the story out until it was approved, all the while faxing the article to his newspaper.

Anne would spend the next three days ringing the people on her list — family, friends and business associates. She would put long-distance calls through to the United States: to her editor, Leona Nevler; her New York book agent, Don Maass; her film and television agent in Hollywood, Ken Sherman; and her publicist, Kim Hovey. She had no idea how any of them would react, and she feared the worst.

CHAPTER ONE

I

To a Londoner, Darsham is unforgivably remote, bypassed even by the area's main road, the A12. Its redemption is the East Suffolk railway line, which clatters across the county's infinitely flat stretches of farmland, linking the ports of Ipswich and Lowestoft. The journey from London takes two trains and too long. The connection at Ipswich is intermittent; the antiquated carriages baking under brilliant blue skies in summer, and in winter breathing draughts of freezing air that whip ankles, knees and necks. Darsham Station is a mile from the village. In cold and rain, it is a damp, dreary trip between fallow fields; in the warmth, it is a delight of soft, sweet air and narrow country lanes edged with wild flowers and lush hedgerows.

This is an ancient part of England, with a history so old it stretches back to the margins of memory, where myth and legend merge with fact. Just a little way down the East Suffolk line, near Woodbridge, are the mounds that mark the grave sites of Sutton Hoo. Here, an early medieval Anglo-Saxon king, believed to be Rædwald — the legendary leader of East Anglia who died in about 624 — was buried in a ship that was intended to carry his immortal soul to its rest. Mounds mean something more in Suffolk, and so does the soil that has sustained human habitation for 700,000 years. Who knows what other ancient treasures are buried in the earth around Darsham? Whatever the answer, it has certainly proved a fertile site for the imagination.

The area has also been a rich hunting ground, especially in the eighteenth century, when game graced banquet tables and killing it was an aristocratic sport. There are reminders of the animals of the hunt in the village still. The name Darsham comes from the words 'Deores Ham' (home of the deer), and the local pub is The Fox. Of the half-dozen surrounding agricultural properties, White House Farm, with its home dating back to 1750, is probably the most illustrious. It has changed hands just a few times over the centuries. In the village there is a shop, a post office, a school, some tradesmen, a few small businesses (including a pottery and a tile factory), and two ghosts.

This is a modest ghost population for such an old place. One, known as Mandy, dances terrifying country jigs; the other, dubbed the Window Dweller, is believed to be a manifestation of the harrowed soul at Thomas Farriner's bakery who inadvertently lit the Great Fire of London in 1666. There have been nocturnal sightings of the Window Dweller since the seventeenth century, when its smoky presence was detected against the glorious stained-glass window of All Saints Church.

It was in Darsham, in the far reaches of Suffolk just a few miles from the North Sea coast, that Anne Perry decided to bury herself on her return to England in 1972. It was an escape but also a planting of her imagination in home soil. For nearly five years she had lived in Los Angeles, that glitter city with its lights, billboards, huge buildings and cosmopolitan buzz. Although she had gone there to find herself and realize a dream, it had proved a fruitless search. She had moved from job to job, never settling, never finding her place. Then, almost at the same time as she lost her job, she learned of her stepfather Bill's precarious health.

When she first went to California in January 1967, it was to take up a position as nanny with a family in Moraga outside Oakland, across the bay from San Francisco.[1] She arrived to find them in turmoil. The wife, who had died suddenly, had 'lain on the linoleum floor of the family room for hours ... before they bothered to notice she was dead'.[2] The children, three sons aged eight, five and three, were unhappy and obstructive, and Anne felt uncomfortable, alone and physically isolated. 'We were miles away from any public transport. I was totally islanded in a pretty grim situation.'[3] She found her escape with the neighbours, Ray and Chlo Barnes, a couple whose faith in the Mormon Church was unshakeable. They were kind and nurturing when Anne was vulnerable and depressed.

For years she had been considering alternative religions, and options within Christianity, but nothing fitted, or filled the gap that, if she focused on it, was an all-consuming abyss. This new faith was simple enough, but it answered everything. 'Mormons believe we are all children of God, and that the fall from perfection is part of life.'[4] Imperfection was not aberrant, emanating from something inherently evil, but everyday and ordinary.

She did, however, stumble over the Mormon version of Creation. Ray Barnes told her to pray about it. 'He said, "Don't try to argue about Creation or whatever — ask God." When I woke up in the morning, the room was full of light.'[5] This epiphany was beautiful and reassuring, and the threshold of a new beginning. The Mormon Church gave Anne permission to be normal. It was her true release from prison. She could be a child of God if she were a Latter-Day Saint, so she became one.

But there remained a huge hurdle: she would have to tell the officiating pastor about her past. How would he respond? Would she be rejected? What difference would it make to the way they treated her? She felt stripped bare again, ugly and exposed. What he told her, though, became seared in her brain: her sins could be 'washed out of the Book of Remembrance in Heaven'. This is how she remembered it much later for Robert McCrum: 'If you have something you [are] ashamed of, you want it washed away, and if you repent, it can be.'[6]

Forgiveness and salvation were the Mormon Church's big-picture promises; the fine print involved no smoking, no imbibing of alcohol, tea or coffee, 10 per cent tithing, the wearing of very strait-laced clothes and passion-killing underwear called 'garments' day and night, and polygamy. To Anne, who had lived a restricted life, these matters seemed insignificant. She rapidly became enmeshed in the community of the Church; its strict structure became hers. There were regular social functions, special days of remembrance, fasting once a month, plus a marathon three-hour church service on Sunday (their day of rest). The drab life she had lived as a nanny began to drift into the background. Within a year, however, she bade a sad farewell to the Barneses, who had become like a second family, and relocated to Los Angeles. They promised to keep in touch, and did so.

Representatives from the massive Mormon Temple on Santa Monica Boulevard in Hollywood were there to meet Anne when she arrived. She took a 'Beverly Hills apartment on the wrong side of the tracks in a street lined with jacarandas', and become a limousine dispatcher and an insurance underwriter. No job was ever more than the means to an end and an income, however.[7] Although living became a purpose in itself, a voice in her head kept nagging her to become a writer. But her frenetic life gave her neither the time nor the opportunity. So when she heard that her stepfather, Bill, was seriously ill she felt called to go home, not just to support her mother, but also because she hoped to silence the voice.

When Anne arrived back in England she initially stayed with Marion and Bill at Watford, but then unexpectedly she found herself able to purchase a property. Her father, Henry Hulme, now Chief of Nuclear Research at the Atomic Weapons Research Establishment at Aldermaston, gave her a lump sum of £8,500, along with a monthly allowance of £100. With this money she bought a rundown abode in Darsham, made up of two small farmworkers' homes 'knocked together and in a row of five or six tiny terrace houses called Fox Cottages'.[8]

Stolid, steady Darsham was cultural whiplash after Los Angeles. Her winterless Californian life was swapped for four distinct seasons, at least one of which brought driving wind, rain and sometimes snow to a rustic residence that never completely excluded the weather. The thick walls were damp and full of holes, the plumbing and wiring precarious, there were no stairs, mice rustled and squeaked audibly in the thatched roof, and you could send a cricket ball from one corner of the room to the other simply by placing it on the floor — it would be 'travelling at quite a speed by the time it got diagonally across'.[9] She camped on-site for months, spending her nights in a sleeping bag and doing most of the renovations herself. Fox Cottages was far from perfect, but it was hers, and so was the meagre unearned living that accompanied it.

Los Angeles had enchanted Anne as a child, and later she had loved it for its gaiety, its licence, its *anonymity* — and for its crazy, irrational investment in the American dream — but it was not conducive to writing. In five years she had composed just a few short pieces from ideas that had never taken root. In Darsham she could write for the best part of the day and do part-time and occasional work to eke out her allowance. This, she felt, was her last chance, and she was determined to take it.

⚘

Ironically, for someone who treasured anonymity, Anne was a conspicuous newcomer in this out-of-the-way place. A globe-trotting ex-Londoner, with precise upper-class diction and arresting good looks, she stood out in Darsham. At 34, she could turn heads with her elegant, long-legged gait and thick, rich, shoulder-length auburn hair. Her features, if not refined enough to be those of a great beauty, were made inconsequential by her eyes. Grey-blue, aquamarine, they changed in colour like the sea, and they could pierce a person with their astuteness while remaining fathomless.

And then there was her manner. Trivial conversations either made her glaze over or try too hard to appear interested. On the other hand, she was apt to turn a casual chat into a high-flying philosophical discussion. Intense, intelligent and covetous of brilliant facts, she stashed away historical information and aphorisms to bring out later in clever conversation. She was widely read, with a disarming propensity to quote from memory unnaturally long swathes of GK Chesterton, James Elroy Flecker, Rupert Brooke and Shakespeare. Her capacity to judge the moment and the audience was not always perfect, though.

If Anne Perry was a little aloof, sometimes distant even, away in her imagination, she was nonetheless sincere. But it was a larger-than-life sincerity, bigger than any normal situation required. If she had shared more of herself with people, they would have seen that her earnestness was consciously adopted and was galvanized by pain.

There was something fleet of foot and fearful about her. She never talked about her past or opened up about the stockpile of childhood memories that form such an important part of friendship. A direct question about her background could freeze her like a deer, before she bolted under the cover of some vague response. She was more than just different; she was downright mysterious. But this was accepted.

Perhaps Anne Perry might have been more of a known quantity if she had not been a Mormon in traditionally Church of England Darsham. She arrived in the village with her community of Latter-Day Saints close by. In fact, they lived and worshipped at Lowestoft, just a few miles up the East Suffolk line. And the Mormon Church supported Anne again when she moved to Darsham: living proof that every Mormon soul counted.

In fact, the Mormon Church in East Anglia had been anxiously counting souls since its shaky beginnings in the 1840s, when its progenitor and great patriarch, Thomas Price Smith — a short, stocky, zealous man who walked 112 kilometres between villages and slept rough in all weathers in barns and under trees — began spreading the word. He was a fervent campaigner for God, but God was just as ambitious for him.

Thomas Smith climbed both the earthly and the sectarian ladders of success, beginning as a poor farm labourer earning just 10s to £1 a week, and finishing as a wealthy and cherished father of the Mormon Church in Utah. After a short time, in his early twenties, as a labourer in Norfolk, Smith became a preacher in the Wesleyan Church. Not long after his wife died in 1835, he broke away from the Wesleyans, taking 550 members of the congregation with him to form the United Brethren. In 1840 he encountered the Church of the Latter-Day Saints and led enormous numbers of the United Brethren to convert to Mormonism.

This may seem an unbroken, almost corporate, rise to glory, but it was not without its setbacks. As Ron Larter has written in his biography of Smith, his 'effort to take the restored gospel to virgin grounds … was beset with personal challenges, physical suffering and emotional anguish'. His wife died, as did some of his children, and there was an unsettling degree of local hatred towards this upstart sect. The progress of Smith's church was jealously watched by the ministers of other denominations. He was accused of being a false prophet, a fake turned flock-rustler, a stealer of souls. There was suspicion and hostility, too, from other laities. Crusading zealots from 'true churches' took delight in disturbing the Mormon peace. 'Meetings were sometimes disrupted with banging, bell ringing, rattling tin kettles, jeering and shouting. Stones were thrown at the door of … meeting places and small riots rose up.'[10]

But the Saints marched on, and so did Thomas Smith, to Utah in 1851. It is out of this history that the Mormon Church at Lowestoft sprang. And it was here that Anne found sanctuary and a spiritual home.

⚘

The port and resort town of Lowestoft is the easternmost point in the United Kingdom. Its name, tempered over time, comes originally from marauding Vikings, for whom this coast was their first sight of land. And while the sea has brought foes, it has also nurtured livelihoods. The fishing industry was a huge employer, and, even after those jobs declined, its sandy beaches brought tourists; and beneath its waters, in the seabed, was the hidden treasure of North Sea oil.

However, it was not fishing, tourism or oil, but the naval base that brought Invergordon-born Meg MacDonald to Lowestoft. She was following her husband, and the journey — first to Devon, then to the open sunlit lowlands of Suffolk — was something of an escape from the grey, dour intensity of the Scottish Highlands, her adventure having begun when she left her working-class family home at the age of 17. Meg was pretty, with blonde hair and large blue eyes, and had a generous, forthright personality that was appealing and could be charismatic.

In spite of a hole in her heart and other congenital health problems, she married young and had five children in quick succession. But the sudden, unexplained death of her third child, Peter, when he was just a few months old, tore her apart. She could not cope with the cruelty of it, and her husband had no answers. They fought, argued and became strangers. Meg MacDonald would find the answers she sought in the beliefs of the Mormon Church, and there she met Anne. In many respects they could not have been more different, yet they shared an essential need to cope with grief, and to find a friend.

⚘

Anne wrote relentlessly. It was something she felt compelled to do, and the process so consumed her and filled her imagination that she barely noticed the days and the seasons roll by. She wrote manuscript after manuscript. There was one that recreated early medieval England using Arthurian legend; there were stories about the Crusades, the English Civil War, the French Revolution; there was a science-fiction thriller, and an allegorical fantasy that kept shape-shifting in various incarnations between her head and the page.

This last was a religious allegory about the journey of the spirit. She forced it into the fantasy genre, but because it was really a philosophical, emblematic tract containing the ethos and beliefs of the Mormon Church, it refused to gel as a piece of fiction. In fact, nothing gelled. She received one rejection slip after another. Each time a publisher's letter arrived thanking her for sending them her manuscript and regretfully declining it, the disappointment was numbing. She would telephone her mother and stepfather for consolation.

The other thing that kept her going was her faith. Deeply embedded in Mormonism is the buttressing puritan belief that good things will come to those who work for them, and that rewards will materialize in God's good time. So she worked on. Two things gave God a helping hand, or perhaps they were part of His mysterious plan. A repeated criticism from publishers was Anne's lack of a good plot. The writing was rich and sensual, and the characters often evocative and convincing, but the plots were flabby, ill-defined and endless. The solution, which came from her stepfather, was astonishingly simple: 'Why don't you write a murder mystery set in the time of Jack the Ripper?'

The Ripper story had fascinated people the world over since 1888 with its entrée into the macabre mind of a murderer and the compulsions of serial killing — and the fact that the identity of the killer remained undiscovered. Then there was the potential for nineteenth-century costuming, the Victorian detail and the romantic allure of the period: it was a perfect fit for a history buff like Anne. But it was the plot-trimming strictures of the detective form that Bill recommended which would give crucial definition and shape to her writing.

Had she not been in tiny Darsham, Anne might have missed the second thing that changed her life. Writing was isolating her, but her absent-minded detachment from ordinary village life was no mystery for

Maggie Elliot, a writer who had moved in next door. She understood the loneliness, the dedication it took to write, and the deep depression that followed rejection. She made a suggestion. Anne had been making her own approaches to publishers, but Maggie knew of a very good literary agency in London. Why didn't she approach them? So, in late January 1977, Anne penned her first letter to Diana Tyler, the senior partner of MBA Literary Agents Ltd:

> I enclose herewith the manuscript of a science-fiction/thriller novel which I hope you will consider handling on my behalf. I have your name from Maggie Elliot, who is my next-door neighbour; I believe she is writing to you under separate cover. I look forward to hearing from you favourably, but if you are unable to handle it, please return it to me at the above address.[11]

She was accustomed to disappointment and did not expect much. The answer that came back was mildly reassuring, her first ray of hope. Under instruction from Diana Tyler, Anne's case was picked up by Canadian-born Janet Freer, a young writer who was making ends meet by doing agency work. 'Let me say at the outset that I do think it needs cutting,' Janet wrote back:

> but on the other hand, I enjoyed it and feel that it is certainly publishable. I am very much in two minds as to whether it would go better as a thriller or a Science Fiction novel. Instinctively, I feel it is more a thriller, because the Science Fiction element isn't really all that strong.[12]

Janet Freer resolved to send Anne's manuscript to Elizabeth M Walter, the Crime Club editor at Collins.

Hopeful now of making progress, Anne worked on and completed a new project that was the incarnation of Bill's good advice. The relationship with MBA was still new and formal. 'Dear Mrs Tyler,' Anne wrote on 1 June 1977, 'I enclose the manuscript of another thriller, this time late

Victorian, with quite a bit of romance in it. I hope you will also feel able to handle this.'[13] MBA liked it and was quick to move. Janet Freer telephoned Anne, full of positive comments. 'Dear Ms Freer,' Anne wrote in response, 'Thank you for your telephone call today, it encouraged me greatly and I feel like working hard again.'[14]

This second manuscript that Anne Perry submitted to MBA was *The Cater Street Hangman*. 'I don't have a character unless I have a face for them,' Anne has said.[15] She might almost have been looking in a full-length mirror when she found the face and physical appearance of Charlotte Ellison. In Charlotte's long auburn hair, grey-blue eyes, pale skin, tall statuesque figure, and ample and often proudly displayed bust there is more than something of a match for Anne.

Thomas Pitt is another matter. On his visits to the home of the upper-class Ellison family in Cater Street, Charlotte eyes him sideways with the same contempt Anne might well have felt. 'He came into the morning room, filling the doorway, coat flapping, hair untidy as always. His affability irritated Charlotte almost beyond bearing.' His tatty scarf is wound once too often around his neck, and his pockets bulge with a provision kit of essential detection hardware that includes a length of string and two marbles. Pitt is from the wrong side of the tracks, or rather the estate, because his father is a gamekeeper — and one unjustly accused of poaching estate game and deported to Australia.

This history provides Pitt with two things: a posh accent because he has been educated with the son of the house, and a drive to right injustice. It was an ideal combination, perhaps, for an ambitious working-class man in a late Victorian English police force that was changing from a hierarchy dictated by nepotism and privilege to a professional organization.

Anne had her two main characters, and she would set her story in London and build her plot around a murder within a family. The family is Charlotte Ellison's, and the victim is her older sister, Sarah. The Ellison household is ruled over by Charlotte's papa, Edward, a true Victorian patriarch. She can steal only glimpses of the newspaper, because it is considered inappropriate reading for a young lady. This means she must either flout the house rules by appealing to Dominic, Sarah's husband, or discreetly slip into Maddock's pantry and read the newspaper there.

The news, as always, is terrible. It is 20 April 1881 and Benjamin Disraeli has just died: 'Her first thought was to wonder how Mr. Gladstone felt. Did he feel any sense of loss? Was a great enemy as much a part of a man's life as a great friend? Surely it must be. It must be the cross thread in the fabric of emotions.' Anne Perry opens with this powerful reflection on friends and enemies, and continues throughout the novel to make searching and profound comments about human behaviour. She explores power and sexual inequality, incisively giving the most misogynistic lines to the women who police patriarchal boundaries. Class difference and poverty, and lack of education and opportunity are considered, too. She shows how greed and callousness may cause human deprivation, but also how this is maintained by those who turn their backs or live in unfeeling ignorance.

Anne is most cuttingly critical, however, of the hypocrisy of established religion. There are few characters more abhorrent than the pompous Reverend Prebble, who is called on to minister to grief-stricken friends and family after a series of apparently random garrottings of young women whose flesh and clothes are ripped in a sexually perverse manner. Prebble, who believes that women and sexuality are evil, is callous and inhumane. His poor wife, Martha, convinced by his fundamentalist reading of Genesis, is filled with self-loathing and hatred.

Initially, the murderer selects victims from the downstairs staff, then from among the daughters of gentry, including Sarah. Her death catapults the Ellisons into a new world of revelation and suspicion. Pitt's investigations uncover secrets that will leave no one unscarred. It is an agonizing process, and Pitt feels for the family.

In conducting his interviews, he finds himself increasingly attracted to the independent and forthright Charlotte, who is waking up from a protracted infatuation with her brother-in-law, Dominic. Suddenly Charlotte finds herself suspecting Dominic and even her father of her sister's murder. At first she openly despises Pitt, but she comes to realize that his slovenly working-class persona is only superficial, and that it is the person inside who counts. This epiphany is the beginning of her maturing as a character. And at the end of the novel she agrees to jump the social divide and join Pitt in penury as the wife of a detective.

After sending all Anne's manuscripts to Thomas J McCormack, president of St Martin's Press in New York, Janet Freer received this response in October 1977:

> I confess that in going through the other scripts here we have not yet come across any that ignite us the way that Cater Street did. Perhaps rather than keep you and the author waiting any longer, we should simply make an offer on Cater Street alone at this stage.[16]

He suggested an advance of US$3,000, 7.5 per cent for the first 5,000 copies and 10 per cent thereafter, and an 80/20 split; St Martin's would hold world rights. He offered to send a contract immediately.

His message of confirmation was warm and reassuring:

> I'm sorry to say that The Cater Street Hangman remains the only one on which we can offer a contract. This is not nearly so discouraging to us as it sounds because I realize that Cater Street was the last manuscript that Ms. Perry completed and I like to think two things: First, that the writing of the earlier manuscripts taught her her craft and the second, that she has also discovered her genre — and possibly the historical era at which she will be most comfortable.[17]

Janet Freer was delighted. She was so relieved that Anne had a contract at last that she did not think to quibble over terms. She had already discussed with Anne the unlikelihood of St Martin's taking the other scripts, so neither of them was surprised by the outcome. Besides, Tom McCormack was right: Anne had honed her skills on her failures and she had found her genre. Janet Freer asked him to return the rejected manuscripts, and added enthusiastically: 'Anne has reached Chapter 4 on the sequel to Cater Street and is talking of completion around the end of February ... she is using the same characters as in the first book and she tells me she has ideas for three or four more.'[18]

Before the book came out, Anne supplied St Martin's with an author photograph for the back cover. She had some shots taken professionally at a studio. It was a new experience, she was anxious, and the photographer did nothing to make her feel at ease. While she waited for the pictures, she saw a film on television about Edith Cavell, the English nurse who was executed by a German firing squad in the First World War.

> Being put out in the yard and refused a blind-fold and she was shot and she looked less scared and more composed than I did in those photographs. I thought: 'This is dreadful. She looked better the second before she was shot' ... [I looked like] a rabbit in the headlights.[19]

So she threw out the professional photographs and sent instead some amateur snaps.

Anne, now 39 years old, had 'waited so long to get published', then suddenly, within a few months, her dream had come true.[20] She was 'absolutely delighted'.[21] She had found a literary agent, a publisher and now, at church, a friend, for it was around this time that Anne met Meg MacDonald.

Selling her manuscript would not greatly alter her financial situation. In fact, it did little more than replace the part-time work for which she now had no time. Her agreement was that St Martin's would publish one book a year, but this would produce only slim pickings. So she was truly grateful to the artful Meg, who had a canny survivor's intelligence and could make a little go a very long way. Meg remembers their family get-togethers:

> We were as poor as mice — poor, poor, poor. We had nothing, we had *nothing*. She would come on a Sunday and we'd have the one big meal of the week. The fire in the winter would be roaring up the chimney ... We'd pool our food ... to make sure we had one really big decent meal for the children — together — and we'd have a great day. She'd sit on the floor, and Lorna [Meg's daughter] would brush her hair, hour after hour after hour ... Lorna used to brush her hair forever ... [Anne had]

it up in a bun, she used to put it in a coil [which] she [would] loosen on a Sunday when she came home from church and then let the pins out and Lorna would just sit there and brush it.[22]

Meg's family life became Anne's, and when Meg's husband left she was 'the children's second mum', a surrogate parent.[23] She would get down on the floor and play with them, listening to their stories, sharing their plans and schemes. Few adults can re-enter the fantasy worlds of their childhood, but Anne seemed to do it effortlessly, as though the pathway back was undisturbed and the door never barred by adult concerns.

Meg, on the other hand, was responsible for her children's corporeal well-being. The marriage break-up was a time of emotional turbulence and change for the family in which their everyday world was turned upside down. Abruptly they had to shift into a council house, which was incredibly 'grotty'. The children took one look at it and burst into tears, crying 'We want to go home', but Meg knew there was no longer a home to go to.[24] So she created a new life that focused on the children, their friends, their pets, their play; Anne was the other adult in it; and its cornerstone was the Mormon Church.

A worn, tired council house was transformed into something desirable by Meg's practical skill. The inside was cleaned, painted and papered. Outside, she organized work parties to clear an overgrown wilderness of brambles and weeds. She planted trees and a kitchen garden, then stocked the place with a menagerie of animals. As well as chickens, 'they had rabbits, they had guinea pigs, they had the dogs and the cats and the goldfish in the pond [inside], they had the other pond outside. They had everything they wanted … They had fun … They were warm, they were secure, they could invite their friends … it was a "safety" place for them.'[25]

In a life centred on children, Anne was Meg's adult company and she supported her through the acrimony and recriminations of the divorce. The Mormon Church saw women as mothers, homemakers and helpmeets to their husbands. Meg's divorce broke a sacred covenant, and her self-sufficient female-dominated world defied convention. This sat uneasily with her, and probably would have with the Church if it had been tested.

Meg's ex-husband contributed little to the support of their children. Even though she grew their own fruit and vegetables, and Anne would drive over on Sundays in her beaten-up old car so they could pool their resources, finding enough money to cover expenses was always a battle. The salve was their friendship.

⚗

Anne devoted every working hour to her writing. In the year-and-a-half since submitting *The Cater Street Hangman* to MBA, she wrote two more manuscripts. She was in a pleasant state of intoxication about her success, but also anxious to keep her focus: 'Thank you for ... being so patient with me,' she wrote to her agent Janet Freer in May 1978. 'About Mr McCormack's letter, there is no need to send me any of it, unless you feel it is something I need to know and don't; I would rather not hear, unless I require the information!'[26] When things worried her she would talk them through with Meg and sometimes her mother.

Anne's breakthrough had caused a stir of excitement in the Perry household. Bill felt like the founding father of a writing revolution, and Marion took up her old role of copyeditor and casual critic with new fervour. In fact, she read everything Anne wrote chapter by chapter. 'I called my mother, and she will probably finish Charlotte III this weekend. It is a good thing she read it carefully, because I had overlooked a few errors. She will post it to you immediately after.'[27]

St Martin's Press was pleased with the manuscripts it received, or at least pleased to know they were coming and with enough variety within the detective fiction formula to be compelling. This was the reassurance the firm needed to invest in Anne's career: consistency in standard and supply. Tom McCormack was visiting London from New York, and Janet Freer contacted Anne to see if she would like to meet him. Initially she declined the invitation, but then had second thoughts. 'I've decided to stop being so chicken,' she wrote at the beginning of February 1979.

I would like to know when Mr McCormack comes to London. If it's possible I would like to meet him, even if only for a few minutes? He is the first person, after you, to give me a real chance, and it would be nice to say hello and thank you.[28]

This was exciting enough, but nothing it seemed could top the arrival in March of bound galley proofs for *The Cater Street Hangman*, which was due out in August.

However, by the time hardback copies of *Cater Street* were widely available on bookshop shelves, St Martin's had already sold the paperback rights for this book and *Callander Square*, the next in the series, to Fawcett for an advance of US$7500 each. Hope Dellon wrote to Janet Freer with the exciting news: 'this should give the series a tremendous boost, and I hope you and Anne will be as delighted as we are'.[29] What they liked especially was the strong role in the stories played by Charlotte Pitt. On a visit to London, Hope Dellon said this to Anne, as she recounted to Janet:

> I mentioned to Anne at dinner that it might be a good idea for her to continue the series (either with a revised version of the third book I saw or with a new story — preferably one that emphasized Charlotte's personal involvement in events), and the idea seems better than ever. Do you know if Anne has had any thoughts about this?[30]

Feminism had generated room for a fully functioning female detective. In the early decades of the twentieth century, women were on the margins of the genre: wifely, like Dorothy Sayers's Harriet Vane, Ngaio Marsh's Agatha Troy, and Margery Allingham's Amanda Fitton; elderly, like Agatha Christie's gossiping sleuth, Miss Marple; or fashionably imprudent, like Christie's Prudence Cowley of the Tommy and Tuppence series.

These characters were traces of oestrogen in a testosterone-driven field. But by the 1970s the world had changed, and detective fiction needed to change, too. In 1979, the year *The Cater Street Hangman* was published, artist Judy Chicago completed *The Dinner Party*, a collaborative installation piece that was a massive triangular table with 39 place-settings for great women who had been the makers of myth and history over the centuries. Among the more contemporary spots were those for poet Emily Dickinson, writer Virginia Woolf, and artist Georgia O'Keeffe. *The Dinner Party* was a powerful symbolic statement at the end of a decade that had redefined thinking about the roles and place of women in Western society. Now women protagonists needed to drive plots and define action, not act as adjuncts, victims or shrews. It was a perfect pairing: Hope Dellon and St Martin's saw the market opportunity, and Anne created, in Charlotte Pitt, a female character who spoke to readers in the closing decades of the twentieth century, but lived in the twilight years of the nineteenth, and did so in a genre renowned for being straitjacketed. *The Cater Street Hangman* had at its core the explosive implications of murder on a family — the suspicion, the revelation of infidelity, the death, the grief, the shame — which were at the heart of Anne's own story. She knew them intimately and could tap into them easily.

Her first book burned brightly because of its immediacy, but subsequent stories would need a new central dynamic if the series was not to extinguish itself. *Callander Square*, the next novel Anne threw herself into, opens with the discovery of the bodies of two newborn babies. It is the long-shadowed end of a mild, misty autumn day when Pitt arrives at the small garden in the centre of the square. The crumbling hole, already begun by a pair of unlucky gardeners, reveals the bloody bones of one tiny corpse, then another.

This sad discovery sets off the customary chain of events that involves the doctor, the ambulance, the morgue and an autopsy. This is infanticide, but everybody who lives in fashionable Callander Square knows that infanticide matters only when the mother counts. Gossip says that the mother is a servant girl employed by one of the grand houses, who has secretly killed her infants because she cannot support them, or because she fears the shame and retribution that pregnancy out of wedlock brings.

Callander Square introduces a class-ridden world of political marriage, of young trophy wives frozen by icy convention in loveless matrimony to wheezing, desiccated old lechers, or to pompous, mendacious men who cheat on their spouses. But not every upper-class male is a cad.

There is General Brandon Balantyne, whose ethics are as impeccable as his military résumé. 'What the hell do you believe in, man? Have you nothing left but comfort?' he asks of his morally bankrupt neighbour, Sir Robert Carlton. The exhumation of the infant bodies is followed by the revelation that, if the children had lived, they would have been destined to a life disfigured by disease. Their mother was infected with syphilis and the skull of one baby was horribly deformed.

The story unravels in two strands. One is the official inquiry headed up by Pitt, and the other is an amateur operation directed by his inquisitive wife. Charlotte's entrée into high society has been blocked by her impolitic marriage. She no longer moves in these circles. But her sister Emily does; in fact, after her marriage to George, she is now Lady Emily of the distinguished Ashworth dynasty. It is partly by feigning interest in war that Emily gets Charlotte a job copying out the centuries-long military history of the Balantynes:

> Actually warfare bored her to tears; but she must make some intelligent remark. 'How very important,' she replied. 'The history of our men of war is the history of our race.' She was proud of that, it was an excellent observation.

Working as a secretary for General Balantyne will provide Charlotte with an ideal vantage point from which to detect suspect behaviour.

Emily and Charlotte become a female detection duo that all but dominates the telling of this tale. It is Emily who finds the grotesque body of Helena, her mummified hands still gripping the ropes of an outdoor swing, and it is Charlotte and Emily who help Pitt reveal the murderer's identity and the awful predatory selfishness of certain upper-class males. If they had today's historical perspective, Charlotte and Emily would know that they were part of a phenomenon known as the New Woman. Their actions contravened the male-dominated strictures and rhetoric of late Victorian society, and they rebelled against discrimination and inequality embedded in law and convention.

But with the exception of a little boredom, Charlotte and Emily are happy in their heterosexual ménages at opposite ends of the social scale. Pitt, especially, is a loving husband and he will make a caring father. The eagerly anticipated birth of their first child makes a poignant conclusion to this story of infant mortality. '[Pitt] thought of Charlotte's face, full of hope for her new child, and prayed that it would be whole, perhaps even that it would be a girl, another stubborn, compassionate, willful creature like Charlotte herself.'

'Charlotte III', as Anne called it in her letter to Janet Freer, was titled *Paragon Walk*, and continued the theme of lasciviousness among the aristocracy, with a little of the occult thrown in. It opens with Inspector Pitt at the mortuary, affected by sour chemical smells and the sickly sweet odour of death, but overwhelmed by the sense of loss and waste as he stares down at the body of 17-year-old Fanny Nash. She is an upper-class girl who has been raped and murdered on Paragon Walk. What kind of rapist stalks this elegant, tree-filled area of Regency roads and parks? Whose instincts could be base enough to bring down an innocent? Or is she an innocent? These are the questions this inquiry must answer, and no one knows better than Pitt that investigations are not pleasant, things are never the same afterwards, and 'there [is] always hurt'.

Emily once again secures Charlotte's crucial access to the world of upper-class murder. In the cut and thrust of polite conversation Anne demonstrates one of her great strengths as a writer. It is her use of conflict in social situations to create humour, venom and ritual cruelty that is so clever. The competition is as fierce as lawn tennis at Wimbledon, only the match is played with tea and cucumber sandwiches served on fine china. But Charlotte's incendiary personality soon reveals the prejudice and pretence beneath the brittle etiquette. She is stunned by what she hears at an elegant luncheon:

'Are you saying that Fanny somehow invited her attack?' Charlotte asked frankly. She felt the ripple of amazement in the others and ignored it, keeping her eyes on Miss Lucinda's pink face ...

'Well, really, Mrs. Pitt, one would hardly expect such a nature of thing to happen to a woman who was — chaste!'

Not only does Miss Lucinda Horbury think Fanny provoked and therefore probably deserved her attack, but she assumes, as do her companions, that men have different sexual proclivities and therefore should be less stringently judged. Miss Horbury also suggests that Fanny's rape and murder might amount to a disgrace or slur on her poor brother and his family:

> 'Disgrace!' Charlotte was too angry even to try to control her tongue. 'I see it as a tragedy, Miss Horbury, a terror, if you like, but hardly a disgrace.'

This sexually unequal world might be dominated by men, but in Anne's stories disenfranchised women often use its power vicariously to disable and sometimes even destroy their female competitors. Sexual competition between women is a principal theme of *Paragon Walk*, as Fanny's sister-in-law Jessamyn Nash and Selena Montague vie for the illicit attentions of a 'beautiful Frenchman', Paul Alaric. Their power lies in attracting and entrapping men by their sexual allure; their victory lies in telling people about it 'preferably one by one and in the strictest confidence[.] Success without envy was like snails without sauce — and, as any cultivated woman knew, the sauce is everything!'

As the investigation into rape, murder and sexual misconduct proceeds, it is viewed by a range of people acting and speaking from their positions in a rigidly hierarchical society sharply divided by class and gender. Anne's detective seems to be an obvious exception. If Charlotte is a New Woman, then surely Pitt is a New Man, but he is also a man who has married above his class. Their class difference is time-honoured and profound in its effect on the balance of their relationship. Charlotte brings with her the knowledge of upper-class custom, along with the power and prestige of her family connections. If Pitt is not overtly grateful, then he at least knows the value of her contribution.

Equally, Charlotte and Emily are less than purely altruistic campaigners for women's rights. Their consternation begins with their *own* sense of frustration at being cosseted, shut away from the events of public life, politics and men. Charlotte and Emily are central characters but, unlike Pitt's, their actions are not legitimized by established authority, so, although their motives may be blemish-free, their methods are highly suspect. They lie without a conscience — and exceedingly well — and assume false identities and other people's clothes with the least encouragement. Because they are breaking codes and conventions, their operations are more covert than Pitt's and therefore sometimes more dangerous.

Paragon Walk ends with a terrifying encounter with black magic. In a locked garden, broken into by Emily with a handy hairpin, Charlotte and Emily find a pentacle mapped out in stones. Black robes, green horns ... this explains the monstrous apparition that Lucinda Horbury saw through the window. Neither wants to believe in such things, but they have the distinct feeling that others do. A second door to a rectangular room off the garden opens easily. Black carpet, black curtains, green designs, robes with scarlet crosses stitched upside down — this is a coven of devil worshippers and the source of at least some of the evil stalking Paragon Walk. The pair are rescued from a dark demise by the mysterious Paul Alaric. As they make their escape through the garden of 'bitter herbs', Charlotte asks him:

'Is there no such thing as black magic?'

'Oh yes.' He pushed the door open in the hedge and stood back for them to go through. 'Most certainly there is. But this is not it.'

⚭

Anne was asked to send her agent a profile for publicity purposes. The winter of 1979 was unusually cold in Darsham. 'I was going to type at least the magazine bit,' she wrote to Janet Freer in February, 'but the gales & the snow have cut off the electricity — so I've no typewriter!'[31] She sent a biographical snippet that she had already written for a church magazine:

Sister Perry was converted to the Church while living in California twelve years ago. She has now returned to England where she lives in

the country twenty miles from Lowestoft. She teaches Sunday School
and holds the positions of Cultural Refinement Teacher in Relief
Society, and the Cultural Arts Activities Adviser for the ward.[32]

No detail was given on her early life, childhood or education; no parents or
partner were mentioned. It was as if Anne's life began with her conversion
in California, and this was not entirely a deception. Her private life in
Darsham was centred on the Church.

The Relief Society for which she was a cultural refinement teacher
was the official women's organization of The Church of Jesus Christ of
Latter-day Saints. It began in Nauvoo, Illinois, in 1842 when a group
of women met in Sarah Kimball's home to establish a society to sew
clothes for the workmen building the Church's local temple. The group
fostered fellowship among women members, and after 'the Relief Society
was revealed to the Prophet Joseph Smith as a fundamental part of the
gospel' it became a symbol of female collaboration with the ecclesiastical
arm of the Mormon Church.[33] The society retained its conventional,
rather saccharine views of women and motherhood. Meetings promoted
liturgical and cultural education as well as service projects, but the core
concern was the Mormon family. Marriage and homemaking were primary,
and visiting teachers gave lessons in home craft and home management.
The society's motto is 'Charity never faileth', and it is to the credit of the
Lowestoft branch that they found a place for two not-so-conventional
women. Anne shut herself away and wrote at least eight hours a day,
six days a week, about murder, rape, sexually transmitted diseases, and
devil worship, and about strong women defining themselves in a male-
dominated world. Meg was a single mother who surrounded herself with
a hurly-burly of children and animals.

Despite their close friendship, the tension Anne radiated made Meg
wonder if there was more to her than she was letting on. Her instincts
were confirmed by Anne's explosive reaction during their Bible studies
to the story of King David sending Uriah the Hittite into battle so he
could abscond with Uriah's wife Bathsheba. Uriah carried the treacherous
letter from David to Joab, the commander of his army, that said 'set Uriah

in the forefront of the hottest battle, and retreat from him, that he may be struck down and die' (2 Samuel 11:15). To Meg, it seemed a strange thing to get upset over, given all the malevolence and glorious death, destruction and dry bones described in the Old Testament. But David's betrayal of the principled Uriah, who refused comfort and rest while his fellow soldiers lived in tents, was one of the most conspicuous cases of white-collar crime in the annals of Judeo-Christian history. David used his power and authority to kill an honourable man so he could take his wife. The hypocrisy stung her. Anne's universe was far from black and white over ethical issues. In fact, if she had a mandate at all it would be to encourage the acceptance of complexity and diversity, but she drew the line at the double standard that allowed David, an ancestor of Jesus Christ, to be depicted as one of the greatest leaders and most righteous holy men of the Bible — and be a murderer as well. The action might be robed in kingship and obscured by battle, but to Anne it was simply an act of violence motivated by lust. It might have made a perfect murder-mystery plot, and in Anne's writing it would become one. But what justice was there in any theological perspective that condoned it?

And as it happened, God agreed. He sent the prophet Nathan to reprimand David. At the end of a tricky conversation about rich men and poor men and flocks of sheep, David saw and accepted his guilt and Nathan pronounced God's punishment. David's life was graciously spared, but the child he had conceived with Bathsheba in adultery was struck down with illness and died, and his remaining years were marred by war and the infidelity of his wives. Perhaps David found his consolation in the visionary and sometimes confessional poetry of the 73 psalms attributed to him:

I acknowledged my sin to You,
And my iniquity I have not hidden,
I said, 'I will confess my transgressions to the Lord,'
And You forgave the iniquity of my sin. (Psalm 32: 5, 7)

The more Anne tried to explain to Meg how the story of David and Uriah made her feel, the more red-faced and upset she became. Then it just came out: Anne told Meg that when she was 15 she and a friend had murdered her friend's mother. It was a tragic, stupid mistake that she would do anything to change. She had accepted her guilt and been punished for her crime, and now she just wanted to move on and write. The Mormon Church had helped her to forgive herself by promising God's forgiveness, but it also made another miraculous pledge: it had guaranteed the entry into the Kingdom of Heaven of her victim. The assurance is that anyone who has been baptized and accepts the message of the Gospels is certain of salvation. If either one of these conditions has not been met in life, it can be conferred by proxy at a Mormon temple after death.

Although Anne's confession to Meg was cathartic, she was also frightened of how it might change their friendship. Would Meg see her differently now? Could the trust between them survive? How would Meg feel about Anne being around her children? Her friend's humane and reasonable reaction came as an immense relief to Anne. Meg thought about the woman she had come to love and admire, and knew that person had not changed. She felt she could not hold Anne responsible for the crazy, unhinged act of a teenager; she knew exactly how twisted and strange that time could be — 'There but for the grace of God go I'. There was, though, a lingering sense of curiosity and she would have liked to ask more, but Anne was so visibly distressed that she could not.

⚔

The Cater Street Hangman, which came out in August 1979, *Callander Square*, published in early 1980, and *Paragon Walk*, put out in 1981, had almost immediate success. *Alfred Hitchcock Magazine* offered Anne the accolade that 'she had no peer'; *Ashbury Park Press* called *Callander Square* 'a novel that is immediately gripping and holds the reader's interest to the final sentence'. Anne's writing was described as 'witty, shocking and compassionate', and in May 1980 the *Pasadena California Star News* commented that 'we could use more Inspector Pitt stories from Anne Perry. They are as enlightened as they are entertaining.'[34] If there had not been so many failed attempts to get published, Anne might have been lured into the false belief that she was an overnight success.

Critics and readers alike relished her 'juicy soap opera' approach, along with her meticulous descriptions of dress and period. You could all but hear the swish of silk and smell the stench of the rookeries (London slums) in her writing. Anne could make both the workhouses and the grand houses come alive. A few mildly dissenting voices felt there was 'rather too much gore and sin (black magic too) implausibly crammed into a single street', but even that critic thought her 'blend of social comedy and murder mystery seems to be firming up quite nicely indeed'.[35]

The triumphs continued. Janet Freer received notification from Hope Dellon that they had sold the Italian rights for *The Cater Street Hangman* to Mondadori for a flat fee of $2,683.20. Anne was thrilled. She had jumped the divide into a foreign language, and Italian was a language she had made a considerable effort to learn in her youth.

Now Anne felt she could not afford to stop. In fact, her punishing work ethic was accelerated by success. She worked on a fourth book in the Pitt series, and refined a structure for her religious allegory. The response to her outline by Nan Talese at Simon & Schuster was remarkably insightful:

With women in the Mormon Church now objecting to their silent role, with their wanting more authority and recognition within the Church, I think the main character could slowly come to realize her own need to be heard. Then COME, COME YE SAINTS could be the saga book intended, incorporating the story of the founding and persecution of the Mormon Church in America (a fascinating story!), but by making the heroine grow in her own assurance and awareness of what she can contribute to society and the Church, Ms Perry will have a book of splendid character and story as well as one that speaks to the contemporary mind ... The problem with the proposal is there are so many characters, not one of whom really stood out, and the plot was so complex that it was very difficult to become involved.[36]

When Hope Dellon read the manuscript of 'Come, Come Ye Saints', she was similarly disposed, but less charitable. Anne's Mormon novel, as she called it, 'still doesn't work for us; despite all the drama of the material, it seems to fall a bit flat, with heroes and villains too sharply delineated'.[37]

St Martin's liked the balance of characters and trajectory of the Pitts, however, and wanted to keep these books on its list. For *Paragon Walk*, it had given Anne an advance of US$2,000, but both author and agent now found this insufficient in view of Anne's success. The publisher's new offer was 'an advance of $3,500, payable half on signing and half on publication, against royalties of 7.5% on the first 5000 copies and 10% thereafter'.[38] There was considerable debate, however, over how many Pitts St Martin's was prepared to publish annually. Anne found the income from one book a year almost impossible to live on and she was capable of producing more, so Janet Freer began pushing for a commitment to two a year. 'Nothing definite from Hope Dellon yet,' she wrote to Nancy Colbert, a literary agent based in Canada; 'her problem seems to be that Anne is too prolific (we should all have such problems) and I've spent hours on the phone to Fawcett, because books are just not to be found anywhere'.[39]

It was a classic case of a clash of interests. Janet Freer, acting for Anne, wanted to increase her client's income and her own commission, but St Martin's was reluctant to flood the market with Anne Perry titles. Janet Freer firmly believed 'when Tom McCormack first bought CATER STREET he said he was thinking in terms of two books a year'.[40]

But 1981, with the publication of *Paragon Walk* and *Resurrection Row*, was the only year that this happened while Anne was with St Martin's. *Resurrection Row* was one of Anne's gorier journeys into the depths of the human psyche. The plot revolved around the digging up of month-old dead bodies and their deployment and discovery at various locations around London. Lord Augustus Fitzroy-Hammond's cadaver makes its first appearance bent over the reins of a hansom cab.

Swathes of thick, sulphurous fog swirl around the theatre district as an excited audience pours out of *The Mikado*, a new Gilbert and Sullivan opera (and a favourite of Anne's). Sir Desmond and Lady Gwendoline Cantlay have left their carriage at home, deciding instead to take a cab.

Their elation from listening to wonderful music is rapidly dissipating in the bone-chilling evening air and they cannot wait to get home. Sir Desmond steps out onto the street to hail the first cab that looms out of the mist. The horse appears head-down and directionless, the driver is slumped in a high-collared greatcoat. As this aimless vehicle comes alongside, Sir Desmond pulls at the driver's coat and is mortified as the figure spills onto the footpath at his feet. Asleep? Drunk, more like. But on closer inspection he finds the man is dead, and, worse still, has been so for a disgustingly long time. 'Even more dreadful than the livid, puffy flesh was the sweet smell of putrefaction, and a crumble of earth in the hair.'

Lord Augustus is reburied but then exhumed once more to make another posthumous appearance at St Margaret's Church, this time on a bench seat. Lord Augustus's second wife, daughter and irascible, poisonous mother arrive early for the Sunday service. In living memory no one but a Fitzroy-Hammond has ever sat in the family pew, so the old lady is furious when she spots an interloper slouching in a coat with the collar flicked up. She raps her stick on the floor and demands that her daughter-in-law, Alicia, intervene. When Alicia touches the man he falls sideways, revealing Augustus's decomposing face staring blindly up at her from the wooden bench.

Working down the social ladder, Lord Augustus's death-defying performance is followed by those of William Wilberforce Porteous and Horrie Snipe. *Resurrection Row*'s storyline is shallower and more bizarre than Anne's insights and rich, evocative writing deserve, but the detective novel is a popular form that easily encompasses a spot of strategic sensationalism. Once again Anne uses a palatable, appealing genre to deal with an uncomfortable subject. In this book it is the plight of the desperately poor, and especially the children, who make up a quarter of London's population.

A liberal-minded political lobby group led by Somerset Carlisle and including Charlotte's brother-in-law, Dominic Corde, is working to improve conditions for the poor. The latter is taken to see the squalor at Seven Dials, one of the city's worst slums:

The room was large and low, gaslit; one stove burned in the corner. About fifty or sixty men, women, and children sat unpicking old clothes, sorting rags, and cutting and piecing them together again. The air was so fetid it caught in Dominic's throat, and he had to concentrate to prevent himself from vomiting.

Child literacy and improving the lot of the poor would become constant themes in Anne's writing.

Initially, Pitt considers whether Lord Augustus's body might have been dug up by resurrectionists — grave robbers who sell bodies for medical research. This is unlikely, though, because cadavers are now legally available. Then he debates the idea of necromancers, Satanists or perhaps someone with a terrible grudge. Or is it a ruse to cover a killing? It is Dominic Corde who considers what motives might be strong enough to make someone commit murder, and here Anne gives her own insight: 'Actually to kill someone, you have to care desperately over something, whether it is hate, fear, greed, or because they stand in the way between you and something you hunger for.' Anne's insights in her novels frequently offer vistas of her own life and psyche. In *The Cater Street Hangman*, Emily concludes, concerning her father's infidelity, that 'one can overlook one mistake, especially if it happened a long time ago. One cannot forget something that has been repeated over and over again.' This is how Anne saw things. She took solace from never committing any kind of crime again, and by living an almost monastic life defined by Mormon law and driven by the will to achieve as a writer. Such an approach allowed her to see the murder she had committed as a distant, aberrant act, and to see the woman she had become as the person she really was.

In *Paragon Walk*, Emily muses on comments made by the evil-mouthed narcissist Fulbert Nash: 'Perhaps they were old secrets he was referring to; everyone had something of which they were ashamed, or at least would very much prefer to keep from their neighbors.' Anne had thought about murder from every angle, and she knew well its destructive potential. Her life had been dismantled by it. She knew that the secret she kept from all but a handful of people could blow her world apart.

⚛

In the summer months of 1981 Anne undertook her first author's tour, to the United States and Canada in June and July. It was largely self-funded, but a small contribution did come from St Martin's, which had booked her a two-night stay at New York's Gramercy Park Hotel for the nights of 1–2 June. From there, she was to take a bus up to Toronto, where Nancy Colbert had booked her into the Windsor Arms in the centre of town. 'How delightful that you are coming to Toronto!' wrote Nancy in April 1981.[41] It was in Toronto that Anne had the great pleasure of casually seeing a woman buy one of her books. The other ambition fulfilled on this trip was to 'cover the Mormon trek to Salt Lake [City]'.[42]

For a publisher, Anne was a dream author. She was uncomplaining, ardent and enthusiastic about the detection genre and the stories she wrote, and had a remarkably empathetic, human touch. She approached her bookshop visits with the same focus she brought to her writing, signing books willingly and listening to those who wanted to talk about why her writing was important to them. She had the stamina for early morning starts, and because of her Mormon 'dos and don'ts' never suffered from hangovers after a night in the bar. When she spoke publicly she was highly articulate, and her moral world appealed to North American readers. Regardless of the degree of degeneracy, corruption and occasionally even decomposition she created or dug up, there was always an ethical solution reached via a pathway of principled decisions.

In the United States and Canada, Anne's Englishness had some of the exotic appeal contained in her books. Her readers loved the snobbish, abject Victorian England she re-created. This was the Old World many of their ancestors came to the New World to escape, and it was with some satisfaction that they read about the horrors of workhouse slums and an unimaginably turgid class system. A review of *Paragon Walk*, published in the *San Diego Union* not long before Anne left England for her tour, summed up why people bought her books and came to see her as a celebrity.

The Victorian era, with its surface virtues, submerged vices and wall-to-wall hypocrisy, is a fascinating field for the novelist and no one tells it better than Anne Perry … As usual, Perry captures the texture of the times and the flavor of its people expertly and provides us with a suspenseful thriller in the bargain.[43]

Anne's North American trip was followed weeks later by a tour to Europe. She found the travel and meeting people energizing. Although she was reserved, Anne had a gregarious aspect to her personality that craved human interaction and social energy. Writing was a solitary and confining task and one she was accustomed to, but she relished the chance to break out of it for a while. 'It took about 6 weeks after her return to England before she touched ground,' wrote Janet Freer to Nancy Colbert in September 1981:

> Now, of course, she can hardly wait to get back. I think what she was not expecting was that there would be people in North America who actually knew who she was and the fact that she was lionized came as quite a surprise, so coming home where nobody has even heard of her is something of a letdown. Trouble is, she wasn't really there long enough to get used to [the downsides] with being a celebrity, so she hasn't really come round to appreciating her contrasting Suffolk village.[44]

⊗

It was not long after this, however, that Anne came down to earth with a crash. The consequences of extensive travel on a limited budget were dire, and MBA always seemed to be chasing St Martin's on her behalf for payments. She had waited and waited for the rest of her royalty advance for *Resurrection Row*. There were a number of letters between MBA and St Martin's written on her behalf, including one from Janet Freer in June: 'Please could you forward us the money immediately since Anne will be desperate for money when she gets back.'[45] Anne's income lurched between feast and famine. Lump-sum cheques came in, but payments were not consistent or regular like a salary, and St Martin's insisted on keeping the 90-day stand-down period between manuscript submission and their taking up the option. Hope Dellon was unambiguous about their position:

We feel it's essential to retain the wording from the PARAGON WALK agreement that gives us a period of ninety days after acceptance of the final manuscript before we have to exercise our option. As we all know Anne is an extremely prolific writer, and we need at least the breathing space between submissions that the PARAGON WALK contract provides.[46]

This arrangement suited St Martin's, but every time Anne packaged up a manuscript to send to Janet Freer, she knew she not only had to allow time for Janet to edit and work on it before forwarding it to St Martin's, but also for a further anxious 90-day wait before she knew whether it would be published. Writing for her was not a fulfilling hobby: it meant her economic survival. If St Martin's chose not to publish, she was in serious trouble. Then there was the issue of the world rights. The immediate, if relative, success of Anne's books suggested she might become something of a phenomenon. Certainly her standard was consistently high and her rate of production prodigious. There was now an uncomfortable realization at MBA that they were missing out on money and the opportunity to control the global expansion of Anne's books. 'I'm afraid I've made one bad, basic mistake about Anne Perry,' Janet Freer wrote to Nancy Colbert.

I allowed St Martin's Press world rights. It seemed like the right thing to do at the time, because Anne had written about ten previous books, none of which had found a publisher, and it was very much a take it or leave it situation with St Martin's. What nobody could have possibly known at the time was that Charlotte would take off.[47]

As a result, in March 1982, Janet Freer asked Nancy Colbert to help them find someone new. 'Both Anne and I agree that it is, perhaps, about time that she and St Martin's parted company ... Anne has asked me to say that while she is in Canada she would welcome the opportunity for any promotional book signing or lecturing.'[48] Janet herself was planning to return to Canada, and her departure from MBA would coincide nicely with Anne's next trip.

Two months later, in early May, Anne was settled in a tiny bedsit apartment on 303 Davenport Road, in the centre of Toronto. It was sunny, comfortable and five minutes' walk from Nancy's office and two doors away from where Janet was staying. 'I am now roughly settled in and everything is going very well indeed!' Anne wrote to Diana Tyler:

I have met with the most extraordinary kindness all over the place! I have been lent: sheets, pillows & blankets by Nancy: tape recorder & radio by the man who is head of public communications for the Church for the whole of Canada.[49]

Anne loved her time in Toronto, and it began to feel like a second home.

When she returned to England she was introduced to Christine Park, her new agent at MBA. 'It really was a pleasure to meet you today,' Anne wrote in early October. 'I am most encouraged and will get to the Revolution as soon as I can — I hope within 2 or 3 weeks.'[50] Anne was working on manuscript revisions of the next Pitt novel, *Rutland Place*, and a stand-alone historical novel set during the French Revolution. She had been mulling over the latter idea for some time, but her priority at this stage were her bread-and-butter novels. 'I have now had a chance to go over the revised manuscript for RUTLAND PLACE,' Hope Dellon wrote to her in November, 'and I want to thank you for all your good work; I do think you have made the book considerably stronger.'[51]

Anne's setting for *Rutland Place* is a signature aspect of the series. As in her previous Pitts, the story is located at a specific site on the *London A–Z*, where a small community is closely connected in a matrix of relationships that incorporates the upstairs-and-downstairs strata of the grand houses, and usually stretches out to the slums. The murders, the suspects and the villains — plus more than a few red herrings and plenty of greed, ambition, lust, hatred and fear — are all contained within this topographical concentration.

By narrowing the setting and confining the number of characters, Anne creates a world not unlike that of the English 'cosy'. Her square, walk or place functions like a village within a metropolis. The 'cosy' form was defined in the work of such detective doyennes as Agatha Christie, Dorothy Sayers, Ngaio Marsh, Margery Allingham and, more recently, PD James. The trick with their stories, as with Anne's, is to try to guess the perpetrator of the crime before the detective. The difference between Anne's work and that of Golden Age crime fiction is that in the 1920s and 1930s there were limits to what society felt comfortable discussing. Protocols existed in life and in fiction, and some depravities were simply out of bounds for a popular novel. The criminal operated in the same moral paradigm as the detective. Reading a murder mystery with a port after a Sunday roast was more about solving an intellectual puzzle than venturing into the darkest reaches of the human psyche. Modern readers, however, demand stories that pierce institutional veneers and probe individual psycho-sexual behaviour.

Rutland Place deals with the inflammatory subject of incest, which is possibly easier to cope with because of the historical frame. Although Anne's books are set in the nineteenth century and the dress and demeanour of the characters separate them from present-day life, the issues she deals with have an authenticity that ensures they resonate with contemporary readers. If she had not managed this, she would probably never have been published. Stories involving major social taboos are difficult to tell.

In *Rutland Place*, Charlotte's mother, Caroline, is disturbed by the fact that she has lost a locket containing a picture of a man she admires who is not her husband. She feels perhaps it has been taken and that someone is watching her. This is the sad story of a Peeping Tom who meets an ugly end because what she discovers means she cannot be permitted to live.

But it is in the deepening maturity and complexity of Pitt's character that the novel offers its greatest satisfaction. Pitt is beginning to demonstrate an incisiveness and empathy that make him more sophisticated and compelling. Murder quickens his interest, but he also understands that it is an awful 'double tragedy — not only for the victim and those who cared for her, but for the murderer also, and whoever loved or needed or pitied the tormented soul … [For] society was cruel; it seldom forgave, and it never, ever forgot.' Pitt thinks his methodical way through the minutiae of investigation, but also through ethical issues and dilemmas that are sometimes Aristotelian.

The backdrop to these activities is his socially unequal but loving marriage. It troubles him that he has brought his wife down in the world and altered her forever. 'Now that she had moved from Cater Street and left her parents' home,' he thought:

> she had absorbed new beliefs … she had forgotten many assumptions that used to be natural to her as they still were to her parents. She had changed, and he was afraid that she had not realized how much — or that she had expected them to have changed also.

The guilt he feels, and his perceptive understanding of Charlotte, adds another dimension to him as a sympathetic character. It is hard to imagine Lord Peter Wimsey, Albert Campion or Roderick Alleyn being as sensitive or attuned to their wives.

II

As usual, the manuscript for *Rutland Place* arrived in Watford for Marion to read. The scripts of Anne's books were 500 double-spaced pages long, so proofing them was a minor marathon, but Marion was relieved to see her daughter had found her calling. Marion always checked the dedication page: *Paragon Walk* had been 'for my mother'; *Resurrection Row* 'to MEG for all her help'; and *Rutland Place* 'with love to my father … [and] gratitude to the city of Toronto'. She was pleased with the unspecified dedication to herself, but concerned about Anne's growing public profile.

'Have you ever considered that you are perhaps being too adventuresome?' she would say occasionally.[52] There were publicity photographs of Anne in circulation and biographical snippets that might link her to the murder in New Zealand, such as the entry in the index of contemporary authors that gave her stepfather's surname, her birth date and her mother's name as Marion Perry (*née* Reavley). All this had the potential to cast the media spotlight once more on Anne, Bill, Marion and her ex-husband, Henry — and the mere thought of this froze her to the core.[53]

Marion recognized in the Charlotte and Thomas Pitt relationship something of her first marriage to Henry Hulme, but theirs had had the social inequality without being a union of souls. She was born Hilda Marion Reavley on 30 January 1912, in the village of Alnwick in Northumberland, and was raised in that self-possessed, straight-backed English sensibility that belongs not to place or financial standing, but to class. She had ancestors with a local manor house that dated back to the fifteenth century. Her father was a Cambridge-trained Presbyterian minister, and the life she led was one of perfect diction and style. She trained as a teacher, but was brought up for marriage and its attendant social rounds.

By comparison, Henry Rainsford Hulme was the son of a trader, a Lancashire fine leather goods merchant. Born on 9 August 1908 in the village of Ormskirk, not far from Southport, he was a child of prodigious and electrifying intelligence. Educated at Manchester Grammar, he matriculated at the age of 13 with a scholarship to Cambridge, where he became a brilliant mathematician. He graduated with honours in mathematics from Gonville and Caius College in 1929, received his PhD in 1932, and went on to study for a year at the University of Leipzig under renowned quantum physicist Werner Heisenberg. From 1933 to 1938 he was a Fellow of Gonville and Caius, and from 1936 to 1938 he lectured in mathematics at the University of Liverpool.

When the two met, Henry was tall and almost waif-like, with an absent-minded, bespectacled stare that was redeemed by his unexpectedly clever, offbeat sense of humour. Despite his tinder-dry manner, he had a social range that allowed him to be ribald in male company and erudite and refined at a conventional gathering. Hilda had the confidence he lacked. Glamorous and sophisticated, she was able to inculcate in him the correct behaviour and the right values, and introduce him to her set. She had the pedigree and he the intelligence, and when they married in 1937 it seemed a perfect pairing.

CHAPTER TWO

I

In January 1983, Anne received the exciting news from Hope Dellon that the reprint rights for *Rutland Place* had been sold to Fawcett, which the previous year had been bought by Ballantine, a division of Random House, the biggest English-language general-trade book publisher in the world. Fawcett's list was transferred to Ballantine Books and Fawcett became the official arm of Random House's mass-market mystery programme. As a result, Anne was offered a new deal: an 'advance of US$5000 against royalties of 8% to 125,000 and 10% thereafter'.[1] Although this was promising, Nancy Colbert's machinations in Canada to get another publisher had produced nothing. And, more seriously, a manuscript had gone missing.

Anne was frantic, and her floor-pacing anxiety was transformed into a lingering sense of frustration when she discovered what had happened. The manuscript, which she had left with Nancy Colbert to look over before leaving Canada the previous August, had never been forwarded to St Martin's Press. Nancy, acting as her agent, had held onto it with a view to soliciting new interest. She did not see this as a problem, as Hope Dellon had told her that the books were arriving at a rate they could hardly handle, anyway. The hiatus, however, was too long for Anne. It interrupted her cash flow and her momentum with St Martin's. In March she sent a letter finishing their arrangement:

I feel that the problem of communicating over such a great distance is making our working relationship too difficult to be happy for either of us, so after *Bluegate Fields* I would prefer to work directly through MBA in London, where we can speak to each other so easily on the telephone, and I can go in person for consultations from time to time. Thank you for the work you have done on *Rutland Place*, and for your personal friendship while I was in Toronto.[2]

This did not end Anne's difficulties, but it lessened the opportunity for mix-ups in the future. She was still precariously short of funds. There seemed no resolution to the problem of finding another publisher, so, taking up the reins as Anne's principal agent once more, Christine Park set about improving her conditions with St Martin's. She had three main strategies.

In September she wrote to St Martin's with the intention of increasing the availability of Anne's books, especially in Canada where her popularity seemed to have taken off.

I understand from Anne that Diana Cooper-Clark, who teaches English and Humanities at York University, Toronto, would like to include Anne's work on this year's syllabus but is being blocked by the lack of availability.[3]

This was followed by another letter, sent the same month to Hope Dellon, tackling the matter of Anne's upfront income. '[Anne] has always earned out her advance and at times done considerably better than this.' Christine felt she needed more encouragement from the publisher, and she recommended an 'increase in the advance for BLUEGATE FIELDS to $4,500'.[4] Christine's next move was more radical still. Anne had recently returned from a second self-funded promotional trip to the United States and Canada. While in New York she had met Hope Dellon and talked of launching a parallel detection series. She had returned to Darsham in 'buoyant spirits', believing Hope was as committed to the proposition as she was. As soon as she could, she sent Hope some exploratory writing. It was Christine's job to follow up and close the deal.

Anne is happy to do some more work on it, indeed whatever you suggest, but is very eager understandably to get this second series off the ground, using as you suggest a pseudonym. Also the next in the Charlotte series is in the office, let me know when you would be ready for me to send it over.[5]

It was hard to see Hope Dellon's response to their initiatives as anything other than negative. St Martin's had no intention of reprinting hardcover editions of *The Cater Street Hangman*, now that the paperback was widely available through Fawcett. This had been explained in August, and St Martin's had no intention of budging. Also, St Martin's did not like anything that had been sent to them other than the Pitt titles. In January 1984, Hope Dellon turned down Anne's latest historical manuscript, 'Most Violent Ways', and her new detection series with detectives Digby and Ridgeway. 'I thought the idea of this series had considerable charm,' Hope explained to Christine, 'but I'm afraid the book didn't quite work for us ... In the end, we didn't honestly feel we could launch the new series with the kind of enthusiasm it deserves.'[6]

St Martin's *did* increase the advance for *Bluegate Fields* by $500, but confirmation that it would publish *Bluegate Fields* arrived after the 90-day period had elapsed, and the advance was slow to arrive. Christine reminded Hope by letter that Anne was desperately short of money and requested she send the advance 'with due speed'.[7] When it arrived she forwarded it immediately. 'Received the cheque today,' Anne replied. 'Very necessary — Thank you.'[8]

Hopes for a second historical novel — the one set in the French Revolution — were also dashed, as were Christine's efforts to find an English publisher. She sent out the Revolution manuscript, titled 'Lower Than the Angels', with reservations. 'My own feeling is that it would need some re-working and re-shaping perhaps in the balance less detail and more story. But it is, finally, an intelligent and thoughtful book and it would be lovely if you felt it was something you could encourage.'[9] But there was little encouragement for the manuscript or interest in publishing Anne in Britain.

❈

It was a difficult year for Anne. The stepfather she admired, Bill Perry, whose chronic bad health had brought her back to England, was now close to death. 'He was a fine man. The last officer to leave Dunkirk, they say … he was one of the bravest men I ever met,' she remembers.[10] Anne never told anyone at MBA that Bill was her adopted rather than her natural father. She would not tell lies, but she left things deliberately unclear. Explaining the relationship and their surname might have exposed deep hurts and dangerous information. His death would leave a huge hole in her life. She was genuinely fond of him, and he was more of a soul mate and companion to her mother than any man had ever been, standing bravely by Marion through her most terrible moments.

Diana Tyler worried about the impact on Anne of Bill's death. While Christine was away from the office she had fielded a telephone call from Anne that worried her. She left an explanatory note:

> Her father is very ill which is making life very depressing for her. On looking at the contract for BLUEGATE FIELDS I see that the second half of the payment has not arrived and I've written to St Martin's accordingly (letter attached).[11]

Anne's spirits seemed so low that when the staff at MBA had not heard from her for an uncharacteristically long time, Christine wrote to Anne's next-door neighbour, Maggie Elliot, in July:

> Just a short note from Diana Tyler and myself … We wondered if you would be good enough to give the agency a ring, just to reassure us that [Anne] is quite alright and nothing untoward has happened. One cannot help being a little concerned. Perhaps she is just away on holiday or there is some other very simple explanation.[12]

Anne did prove to be away, with a friend and her children who were visiting from the United States, so this was reassuring, but MBA was still concerned and so was relieved when September brought some encouraging news. 'The cheque for BLUEGATE FIELDS has arrived at last,' Diana wrote, 'which I'm sure will be a great comfort to you. I do hope things are a little better ... and that there will be some good news soon.'[13]

It was just a few weeks after this that Bill Perry died. He bequeathed Anne a jade signet ring, which she never took off. She could share her grief with her mother, Meg MacDonald and a handful of others, but only Marion properly knew what his death really meant. 'Very sorry to hear, via Diana, of your father's death,' wrote Christine. 'Must be a very sad period for you ... And not an easy period on the writing either.'[14]

There was Bill's death and funeral to face, and Anne was anxious over the outcome of *Death in the Devil's Acre*. The manuscript had been with St Martin's nearly six months and there had been no decision. She was worried at the very real possibility of rejection, and, while St Martin's procrastinated, Anne's agents were unable to offer the book to anyone else. 'Thank you for your very considerate letter,' Anne wrote to Christine on 23 October, 'it is a hard time, one way and another — but let's hope there will be a break soon.'[15]

At the end of that month, Christine wrote a sharp letter to Hope Dellon expressing her frustration.

I'm really rather surprised that you have let so very long go by without making a specific offer for Anne Perry's DEVIL'S ACRE ... I had understood that an offer was promptly to be on the way. Naturally Anne is getting anxious. Please can you reply to this as soon as possible, preferably by return of post ... Anne has had a hard year with her father dying and one or two other set-backs and so if we can relieve the pressure on DEVIL'S ACRE that will help a little bit.[16]

An offer for *Death in the Devil's Acre* finally arrived at MBA in December. 'What a very long time it has taken for them to come through ... with an offer this time,' Christine wrote to Anne, but she knew the news would lift her spirits and the money before Christmas would be gratefully received.[17]

⚭

There was a growing market, even what could be called a developing fan-base, for the Pitt series in the United States and Canada. It was not hard to become hooked. Like a soap opera it was episodic and the main characters were consistent, but the subject matter was less banal and the intrigue more enthralling. Anne's stories were a time machine. From the safety of their domestic worlds, readers could be transported to a place that was unimaginably foreign yet vividly experienced. In the popular framework of the detective fiction genre she could also challenge readers to think about difficult and morally testing questions.

Bluegate Fields deals with two controversial subjects: homosexuality and child prostitution. The stench of human filth is almost overpowering in Bluegate Fields, and the discovery of a murdered young man in a sewer there nearly turns Pitt's stomach. If it had lain in the drain any longer the barely post-pubescent body would have been consumed by rats. But this youth does not belong to the stinking sewers of Bluegate Fields. He is a child of privilege, his hands unsullied by work and his body untouched by hunger or poverty. His last meal had been 'pheasant and wine and a sherry trifle'. What ravaged him in life was not poverty but the early symptoms of syphilis. 'He [has] been homosexually used,' the doctor tells Pitt after the autopsy.

It is now five years since Pitt first went to Cater Street to investigate the murder of Charlotte's sister, Sarah. Since then they have had two children — Jemima and Daniel, the latter just a few months old. Their home is a sanctuary. After the children go to bed, the Pitts eat a simple dinner around an old stove and share the quiet, contemplative end of a busy day. They have their memories and their plans. This is a communion based on sexual and social egalitarianism. But Charlotte knows Thomas is not a typical man of his time, and on occasion she tortures herself with doubt.

Would he have been happier with someone who left him at heart utterly alone, who never really hurt him because she was never close enough, who never questioned his values or destroyed his self-esteem by being right when he was wrong and letting him know it?

These questions reveal what lies at the heart of this book: the menace of power imbalance in relationships. If it is regarded as an atrocity when it occurs in paedophilia, why is it sanctioned in marriage and by the class system?

Arthur, the murder victim, turns out to be the eldest son of the illustrious Sir Anstey Waybourne. This revelation thrusts Pitt into a social world where his occupation as a policeman makes him subordinate, ranking fractionally above a 'ratcatcher', 'drainman' or minion. Whereas social inequality rankles Pitt, it almost destroys the Waybourne family tutor and Latin master Maurice Jerome, who because of his position is 'forced ... to be always more than a servant and less than an equal, neither in one world nor the other ... constantly and subtly patronized, one minute encouraged for his knowledge, his skills, and the next rebuffed because of his social status.'

Jerome is wrongly accused of the sexual abuse of his young male pupils and the sodomizing and murder of Arthur Waybourne. His sour, self-righteous condescension towards Pitt, whom he regards as inferior, makes Jerome a difficult character to like, but his predicament is unenviable. He is arrested and will be hanged, sacrificed by an aristocratic family to escape the public disgrace of a police investigation. This is corruption, and once again it stems from an abuse of power. To find the murderer Pitt must expose the Waybourne family secrets, but he does so with sensitivity and an understanding of the long-term consequences that Anne understands.

> [Pitt] had seen the damage that the resolution of all secrets could bring; every person should have the right to a certain degree of privacy, a chance to forget or to overcome. Crime must be paid for, but not all sins or mistakes need be made public and explained for everyone to examine and remember. And sometimes victims were punished doubly, once by the offense itself, and then a second and more enduring time when others heard of it, pored over it, and imagined every intimate detail.

Arthur's wasteful death has a parallel in the sticky end of rent boy Albie Frobisher, his polar opposite on the social scale. Both youths are sexually exploited, and their deaths are a result of the self-gratification of predatory older men. Sodom and Gomorrah are mentioned more than once in this book. However, the focus in *Bluegate Fields* on power and its abuse, rather than on homosexuality, leaves Anne free to imply that equal and consenting same-sex associations can have a place in a just and ethical world. Her views on homosexuality are liberal and inclusive. 'Homophobia makes me really angry because of the really fine people I know who are gay, of both sexes ... and they're better people than most of the ones who go after them in many respects — intellectually and spiritually.'[18]

The Mormon Church, however, believes that homosexuality should be condemned in the same way as adultery and fornication. Sexual relations can only legitimately occur between husband and wife, and a Mormon temple marriage is regarded as a union that lasts forever. But Anne does not apply the same criteria. It is part of her personal philosophy not to judge the particularities of people's lives. How can she expect compassion herself if she takes the moral high ground? She also has a special sympathy for people whose lives have been affected by homosexuality, as her own has so indelibly been.

Death in the Devil's Acre, which came out the year after *Bluegate Fields*, is set in 1887, the year before Jack the Ripper's Whitechapel slayings. But instead of women being ritually slain, it is four men, and their mutilations that will have Freudians rushing for their textbooks and the average male clutching his groin. The bodies of Dr Hubert Pinchin, Max Burton, Sir Bertram Astley and Ernest Pomery are all found in compromising locations around the Devil's Acre with their genitals horribly disfigured. With the notable exception of Burton, these are seemingly honourable men who have been viciously castrated by something that appears to have clawed their flesh like a mastiff. Charlotte, however, is not convinced of their integrity:

She had known plenty of 'respectable' people herself. All the adjective really meant was that they were either clever enough or fortunate enough to have maintained an excellent façade. Behind it there might be anything at all.

In order to discover the perpetrator, Charlotte joins Pitt in an undercover operation that takes her once more into the home of the steadfast General Balantyne and his dysfunctional upper-class family from *Callander Square*. She poses again as a single woman, and the gentle general, trapped in an empty marriage, falls in love with her. His sexually compulsive daughter Christina is also caught in an unfulfilling marriage she was forced into after an indiscretion with the family butler, Max Burton, who was dismissed and has become a high-class pimp. Prostitution is a key theme in *Death in the Devil's Acre*.

As Brandy Balantyne explains in a heated conversation with his icy mother, Lady Augusta, there are approximately 85,000 prostitutes in London 'and some of them are no more than ten or eleven years old!' It is not the prostitutes, however, who are under scrutiny here, but the men who use them and the veneer of respectability that disguises their sordid deceits. Christina is the perfect foil for the prostitutes in the novel, because her promiscuity is driven not by financial need but by a sexual addiction. Even her demise is treated with some sympathy, as is that of her unfortunate husband, Alan Ross, whose chivalry prompted him to marry a wife whose appetite he could not satisfy. This intricate story is woven together so each of the key characters' situation and motives are explored, giving greater depth to a potentially shallow narrative.

There was something more searching about both *Bluegate Fields* and *Death in the Devil's Acre*. The hypocrisies and power relationships were less clichéd and melodramatic, and Anne was beginning to use her craft not just to mix a few aberrations and ethical conundrums into a mystery plot, but to deal more consistently and subtly with profound human concerns. Her framework was still Judeo-Christian, and the plot still a struggle between good and evil characters, but the personalities and themes were becoming more complex.

※

Bluegate Fields was published at the end of 1984, and *Death in the Devil's Acre* in 1985, and both were well received by critics. The *Philadelphia Inquirer* found that, in *Bluegate Fields*:

Pitt's compassion and Charlotte's cleverness make them compatible sleuths, as well as extremely congenial characters. Thanks to Perry's extraordinarily vivid sense of the period, we share the Pitts' moral outrage as they investigate the Victorian social underbelly — the workhouses, the sweatshops, the match factories, the poverty, disease and prostitution. It's all terribly squalid, but fascinating and ultimately moving because Perry has the great gift of making it all seem immediate and very much alive.[19]

Critics applauded the authenticity of the worlds she created. In spite of the macabre and sometimes sensational nature of her plots, her Victorian London was real and her dialogue convincing. The special touch she brought was her exposure of hypocrisy and those grand Old World narratives of birth, bloodline and privilege. 'Perry's shrill tone of social outrage occasionally takes the edge off her penetrating views of London's appalling slum conditions,' wrote the *Sun* in Baltimore of *Death in the Devil's Acre*. 'But her sense of irony remains sharp and her drawing-room exposés of the hypocrisies and moral blindness of privileged Victorian society are still very keen.'[20]

The reviews Anne received made her feel that the difficulties were worthwhile, but she tried not to involve herself in the politics of book publishing, which she found distressing and distracting. That was her agent's job. Her strategy was to either avoid or slough off anything that upset her, and to learn from and enjoy the positive critical and personal responses to her writing. When encouraging letters from readers arrived, she answered them with gratitude. She saw that her reputation was growing in North America, but also knew that she was only ever as good as her last book. The effort of writing a book never translated into an adequate income, but she also knew there was nothing else in the world she would rather do. She told her friends there was no Plan B.

Anne pushed forward, because she was driven to, and in the knowledge that success depended not on the inspired genius of an individual story, but on consistency and subtle variation within a repeated formula. When she was working she immersed herself in her writing. At times she became so consumed by it that Meg MacDonald had to instigate regular cottage-cleaning raids.

> My friend and I used to go over once a month because — being Anne —
> she was so busy writing she never saw the house around her, so we would
> go and blitz the cottage for her, spend the whole day cleaning around
> her and then come back, and she [would] come out [with us then] and
> we'd go home.

In her snatches of time off, Anne would go out with Meg and their friend Patsy from church. 'We'd laugh until we were sick, we'd go to the jumble sales — we used to do the stupidest things.'[21]

Not only did Meg provide Anne with friendship and a family, but the overflow of dogs and cats from Meg's menagerie-cum-animal-sanctuary began to populate Anne's cottage, as she explained in a card to Janet Freer:

> My friend Meg has just adopted 3 kittens (mother had 7 & couldn't
> cope!). They are about 3½ weeks old and so beautiful they would melt
> your heart. She is over here today & has brought them with her. They
> need feeding every couple of hours! If I can get a decent photo I will!
> Love Anne.[22]

This was the beginning of many long-term relationships with cats and dogs. Anne loved animals, and treasured being close to the natural world and to the rural rhythms of Darsham.

⚙

Just when she thought things were beginning to settle in her literary career, Anne learned of Christine Park's departure. Christine hoped to do some freelance editorial work, but was planning to concentrate on becoming a novelist. 'After a very happy three years I will be leaving MBA at the end of February,' she wrote to Anne. 'Meanwhile, it has been a great pleasure working with you and getting to know you. And I believe firmly that the work that we have put in together will reap rewards in the long run, over the years to come ... Diana and MBA have your good interests very much at heart, and I am leaving ... with the confidence that you will be well looked after.'[23]

Diana Tyler who, though slight of frame, was a commanding presence with her humour and hard-nosed intelligence, put her best efforts into finding a replacement agent for Anne. Her good judgement and a shrewd understanding of people led her to corral MBA's newest recruit at the Christmas party and ask her whether she felt ready to take on her first client after nearly a year of taking notes, typing and doing the banking.

At just 27, Canadian-born Meg Davis was raw and ambitious. She had been thrilled to get the position as Diana's office assistant, and was hungry to succeed. Diana sensed her drive, but also knew that a period of apprenticeship was required. Anne seemed the perfect person to start with. As a 46-year-old book-a-year author, she was probably the agency's steadiest client. 'At that point nobody really expected she would do anything exciting,' remembers Meg.

Anne would be a really good place for a trainee agent to begin ... It really is kind of like when you go to a riding stables and they give you the horse called Sugar, because the horse won't bolt and there's nothing you can do to the horse that will completely mess up its head — and there is nothing interesting that horse will do apart from just plod along and you can actually learn to ride that way.[24]

Diana explained to Meg that Anne was unmarried and a Mormon, so did not drink alcohol or caffeine, or break other Church taboos, and, apart from being a little fragile and ringing rather too often because she was forlorn, worried or lonely, she was the safest bet they had. Anne's books were as dependable as an annual monsoon. Demand for them was consistent, but was limited by St Martin's decision to release just one title a year. 'As Christine is leaving the agency, anything concerning Anne should now come to me — or, in my absence, John [Parker],' Meg wrote to Hope Dellon in February 1985.[25]

Their pairing seemed right, on paper, but how would the chemistry work in reality? Anne, with her permed auburn hair, was statuesque, a little grand, even formal, although her matronly appearance was at odds with her quirky personality. Meg, on the other hand, was trendy in a leather-jacket-and-jeans sort of fashion. Sharp of mind, she was small, dark-haired, fine-featured and agile. If Anne could be likened to a loping red setter (and she was), then Meg was a quick fox.

Meg's father was an Englishman who, instead of becoming an Anglican monk, had married and settled in Canada. But Meg was even more of a mix of cultures than this would suggest, as she had done a degree in Russian and had visited there; but her passion now was London, and she was as keen to be an agent as Anne was to be a writer. Thoughtful and intense herself, Meg appreciated Anne's philosophical approach. 'Been thinking about our conversation about words,' she wrote to Anne in February 1985, 'you've got me started now! They're not just actions, but also perceptions: the currency of the intellect.'[26] This was her first client and she wanted to impress, and she took on Anne's plodding caseload with quixotic zeal. 'This fascinating, exciting writer, is all mine,' she thought. 'What are we going to do to be a really great success?'[27] Diana, who had suggested they bond by spending time together at Darsham, was annoyed when she discovered that Meg's first visit was just lunch, a quick chat, then back to London that night. Meg, on the other hand, was not so sure she wanted to relinquish her whole weekend for the visit.

Her stays with Anne at Darsham, however, became an established pattern. The change at Ipswich, the rattling two-carriage trip across Suffolk in a draughty train, and the bitterly cold arrival at Darsham station on a Friday night, where Anne would pick her up.

She would give me a salad — a very large salad — at the end [of the trip], and I would think, 'Oh Anne, please, can I have something hot?' But then I cottoned on to the fact that what I really ought to say is: 'Anne this is a *really colourful* salad', and then she'd be happy. I'd shovel down the sweet corn and beetroot … and think, 'OK, well, hopefully I'll be warm in bed eventually.'

On these weekends, they would sit around the cottage if it was wet and miserable outside, or, if it was fine, go on long walks together.

> We would talk about everything. She'd play me Mario Lanza records. We would talk about writing … it was almost like being teenagers again together … we would just really talk about everything.[28]

Sometimes Anne came to London and met Meg at a restaurant close to the MBA office at 118 Tottenham Court Road. 'Many thanks for a very happy and stimulating lunch; I hope your afternoon went off all right,' wrote Meg to Anne in May.

Meg lived with her English grandmother, and sometimes Anne would stay with them when she was caught in town or about to leave for an author tour of the United States, 'because she couldn't afford to stay anywhere else'. The fact that Meg's grandmother fussed over Anne and ladled generous helpings of blackcurrant jam onto her toast in the morning was just fine, but Meg was horrified to find that 'Nana had shown Anne my baby pictures, too, which definitely blurred the personal and professional'.

In the early days they would occasionally meet up with Henry Hulme, who would take them out for lunch. 'We always used to go to a place that had a good salad bar and good ice cream', which was a 'lifelong passion' of Anne's.

> We'd bring him up to date on how things were going with Anne's writing, then he'd wait 'til she went to the loo, fix me with his piercing, pale blue eyes, and ask if I really felt optimistic about her career. I'd take a deep breath, because I felt that if we could just harness the power of Anne's writing, she'd be successful. Then I'd say 'Yes'. But it was always a scary moment, and I always felt that if I were wrong, I'd have him to face in the afterlife.[29]

The highlights of their work together were the contracts they signed. After sending off a finished manuscript and waiting sometimes weeks longer than the three-month period, Meg would get on the telephone and ring St Martin's. 'Have you read it? Do you like it? Do you want to buy it?'[30] St Martin's would take a month or so more to make up its mind and come back to her with a 'grudging offer'. Meg would negotiate the contract within 'an inch of its life'. But in reality there was little room to move. St Martin's refused to commission ahead, and needed to be chased up and courted at every stage, but Anne knew she was lucky to have found an Anglophile publisher in North America prepared to publish her work. Until there was an alternative to St Martin's, there was little to bargain with.

Meg was quick to explore any possibilities. She began by looking into the matter of world rights, hoping there might be some flexibility, but neither Diana nor John Parker was positive about her prospects. 'Here as promised is the cheque for the St Martin's royalties,' Meg wrote to Anne in August.

> It's a very depressing amount, especially since they're keeping us waiting for the paperback money ... I've discussed with Diana and John the possibility of asking St Martin's to let us have the UK rights ... I see their point, but all the same I've asked for a list of publishers [St Martin's] have made submissions to — just to make sure they're doing a proper job![31]

Meg's next strategy materialized during a tea break in rehearsal for an orchestra she played in. She was halfway through a Bourbon cream when it hit her: the problem was Anne's plots. 'At that point [she] was writing one Victorian novel and one unpublishable historical novel a year.'[32] The challenge was to tackle the way Anne structured the plots of the non-detective novels. So far as Meg knew, no one had sat down with Anne and given her detailed editorial notes about her writing. She explained her idea to Anne, who responded enthusiastically:

> Very good to talk to you — & to listen! Here is the chapter in which the Word is discovered & read — hope it moves you to tears — should

have sent a Kleenex with it — in hope! Look forward to getting your notes so I can start with the re-work.[33]

Unfortunately, the tears Meg shed in private were not always the sort Anne was expecting. With renewed hope Anne had resurrected her Mormon novel, with its gargantuan cast of characters, turgid morality and amorphous structure. To the staff at MBA it was the impossible project. For Meg it was the most dangerous part of dealing with 'a horse called Sugar'.

※

At Darsham, Anne's time was greatly constrained by her work patterns. But there were visits from Meg Davis, and always the balance of Meg MacDonald's family life if she needed it. 'Meg Mac's house at Lowestoft is a regular hospital ward! 5 of them ill', Anne wrote to Meg Davis in December 1985. 'Thanks for a lovely lot of conversation — & for trekking all the way out into the wilds!'[34]

The MacDonalds were still in the council house, but by now far more had been done than just the garden and a spot of painting. When Meg's ex-husband had inherited money from his mother, she wrote to him asking to borrow £1,000. With the money she put in new carpets, double-glazing, gas heaters and fires in all the rooms and fresh furniture. 'We dolled the house up for his children, and when the year came up and he wrote me and said he wanted his money back', Meg refused.[35]

Towards the end of 1985, Anne began writing *Cardington Crescent*. After six novels, she once again set her murder in a family directly related to the Pitts. Lady Emily Ashworth, Charlotte's sister, must have felt she was the unluckiest woman in London — first her sister Sarah murdered, and now, in *Cardington Crescent*, her beloved husband George falls victim. The story opens in the rambling ruins of St Mary's churchyard in Bloomsbury. The rotund Mrs Ernestine Peabody has taken Clarence, her wheezing, wilful Pekingese, for a walk. He squeezes around a gate to relieve himself in the churchyard, only to discover a decomposing lump of human flesh wrapped in brown paper, tied up with string and dumped under a bush. The connection between Clarence's grisly find and the Ashworths is one of the book's compelling mysteries. Much of the rest of it is set in the elegant home of Eustace Marsh, located in salubrious Cardington Crescent.

The cast includes: Emily and George; George's great-aunt, Lady Vespasia Cumming-Gould; George's cousin-by-marriage Eustace, his slip of a daughter Tassie, his horrible mother Lavinia Marsh, his painter son William, and William's siren wife Sybilla; and random guest Jack Radley. They gather like the opposing fronts of a perfect storm. The barometer of family integrity is Great-Aunt Vespasia. This is not her first appearance in a Pitt novel; she first makes an entrance in *Paragon Walk*, and would probably have been incidental if Anne had not kept giving her some of the best lines.

To Pitt's pleasant surprise she reappears in *Resurrection Row*: 'he recalled how much he had liked her asperity and alarming candor. In fact, had Charlotte married above herself socially instead of beneath, she might have grown in time to be just such a devastating old lady.' As the series progresses, Vespasia becomes a stalwart of detection, a political activist for child poverty and a supporter of women's suffrage. She is the older woman Charlotte might become and the matriarch Anne would like to be. She defies gravity and age, growing younger and more significant as the series proceeds.

In *Cardington Crescent* she is catapulted into a family crisis when her great-nephew George is murdered. George has been having an illicit affair with William's wife, Sybilla. Emily, overcoming her sense of betrayal, takes on Sybilla, and seems to be winning when George and his faithful spaniel are found dead by the butler. Charlotte arrives immediately to comfort her grieving sister. She sits down on the bed, reaches out her hand to Emily, then slips 'her arms round her and let her weep as she needed to, holding her close and rocking a little back and forth, murmuring old, meaningless words of comfort from childhood'. Anne's mother had done this for her after the murder.

Eustace and Lavinia decide that Emily is the murderer, and if they can manoeuvre things so she appears guilty of George's death they will.

Finding out who really killed George, and later Sybilla, is synonymous with exonerating Emily. The focus of this novel is the institution of marriage. Eustace, boorish, insensitive and rampantly virile, represents everything despicable in the Victorian patriarch. His lecherous eye lingers on ladies' breasts, while his unyielding opinions about the sexual divide leave women eternally subordinate to men. To him, marriage is for political advancement, procreation, continuance of the line and sexual gratification — male, of course. His wife, Olivia, Vespasia's daughter, was pregnant so often she died of exhaustion. 'Eustace, I told Olivia when she married you that you were a fool ... over the years you have given me less and less reason to revise my opinion,' Vespasia tells him.

Eustace cannot work out what the fuss is about. As he explains to Vespasia:

> We raise great men precisely because our women preserve the sanctity of the home and the family ... The fairer sex are designed by God to be wives and mothers; to comfort, to nurture and uplift. It is a high and noble calling. But they do not have the minds or the fortitude of temperament to govern, and to imagine they have is to fly against nature.

Anne had great difficulty with Mormon attitudes to marriage. What position in God's plan did this give her, or any woman who lived outside the conventional corsetry of a Judeo-Christian marriage, made even tighter by the donning of a Mormon garment? *Cardington Crescent* reminds readers that men are financially and legally responsible for women, but that cannot expunge the memory of smug, unlikeable Eustace, or forgive him his fornication with his daughter-in-law, Sybilla.

⚙

On 11 November 1985, Anne sent a parcel to Meg Davis, with a note:

> Actually 11 AM too — Armistice moment! Dear Meg, Thank you very much for telephoning this morning — good cheerful start to the

68

week … Here are the first 4 chapters — including all typos, spelling mistakes & general errors! As usual I look forward to receiving your advice & help to sharpen it![36]

These were pages of 'Thou With Clean Hands', her restructured, revamped historical manuscript set at the time of the Spanish Inquisition. The story was about a young woman to whom some sane, sensible, non-superstitious theology was revealed by God. Because of these heretical beliefs, she is thrown into prison, tortured and tried, and in the process falls deeply in love with the inquisitor, who feels the same way about her. The major problem Meg had with the story was that the heroine was burnt at the stake. All that emotional investment on the part of readers going up in smoke — it would make a better Verdi opera than a novel. Nevertheless, she responded with a raft of editorial notes: 'I dipped a bucket into the well of my imagination and this is what I came up with. Looking forward very much to sparking off some ideas.'[37]

In February 1986, Meg received the manuscript of *Cardington Crescent*. She did some editorial work on it before sending it off to St Martin's, but felt the novel's foundation was strong. Hope Dellon was away on maternity leave after having a baby girl, but her replacement, Lisa Leventer, replied to Anne directly:

> I've now had a chance to read CARDINGTON CRESCENT several times, and I'm happy to say that I agree with Meg Davis — I think in many respects it's your best yet. Having a murder 'in the family' makes the book all the more compelling … we care on a personal level because Emily and Charlotte, with whom we sympathize deeply by now, are affected.[38]

Anne came back to Meg with her revisions for *Cardington Crescent*, and through 1986 Meg sent out 'Thou With Clean Hands' and a manuscript she described as a 'fantasy novel' called 'Sadokhar'. The latter needed substantial cuts, according to Arnold P Goodman of New York literary agents Goodman and Associates.

The book is much too long and rather plodding in pace … Anne Perry has good credentials and it is apparent that she knows her business. But in deciding to write a totally different kind of novel from [what] she has been doing in the past, I think she may have taken a wrong turn.[39]

Meg's endeavours to find an enthusiastic domestic publisher were equally problematic. 'Naturally we're disappointed with Anne's not finding a niche in the UK market the way she has in the States,' she wrote to Goodman. She felt Hale, who had published the first two titles in the Pitt series in the United Kingdom, had been unimpressive in promoting Anne's books. Meg pinpointed what she thought was behind their *laissez-faire* attitude: 'I think the style and approach of the Charlotte series has a peculiarly American flavour: the English generally think differently about their own history.'[40]

The real interest in Anne's Pitt novels still came from the Anglophile North American market, in which St Martin's was a leading publisher. Victorian England was a territory already extensively explored by British readers, and Anne's perspective was not fresh enough to convince commissioning editors that it set her work apart. For the English, Victorian England was about as exotic as Great-aunt Gladys's back room, with its disintegrating family albums and scrapbooks, chipped china, and musty-smelling trunk full of old shoes and dank best-suits. It was too familiar and genetically close to provide the comfortable escapism it gave North American readers.

And Anne's writing had a disquieting optimism that was not quite *bleak* enough to be British. Terrible things happen in Anne's novels, but they always end with a sense of optimism. There is a prevailing justice and a belief that, in the archetypal struggle between good and evil, good will win. This New World positivism was based on an expectation of opportunity, enterprise and social mobility. Anne's books did not communicate the nihilism, the pessimism, the blackness of an Old World controlled by class and convention. For as long as she could remember, Anne had admired America. She had grown up in the Cold War era of superpower envy, when the United States was a strong influence on youth culture around the world, but perhaps it affected her more than most because of her dislocation. Living with what she had done required optimism, but what drove her was a profound American-style belief in redemption through work, and in the integrity of the values implicit in what she wrote.

However, if she wanted to convince British book publishers, she would have to dig into a darker, more psychologically complex place for her material. In response to Meg's inquiries about what St Martin's was doing to get Anne a British publisher, Valari Barocas wrote: 'As you know, in September 1985, we submitted the last two books (BLUEGATE FIELDS and DEATH IN THE DEVIL'S ACRE) to 20 British publishers, but, unfortunately, there were no takers.'[41]

Since 1984, Anne's agents had been trying to sell the Pitt series to film and television studios. Diana Tyler sent one of Anne's books to Frances Heasman at Thorn EMI.

> Firstly, I thoroughly enjoyed the Anne Perry ... but have to say this is the stuff of television and not feature films. I see this as one in a series that Anne Perry has written and is perfect stuff for a television series. Have you thought of approaching Granada who did the period Cribb series?[42]

Christine Park had also sent books to Gerald Hagan and others in the film and television industry, with messages along the same lines: 'it has been suggested to me that you might be interested in a television series based on Anne Perry's celebrated Victorian crime series'.[43] But there was no immediate interest. Despite positive responses about Anne's work, nobody felt it incontrovertibly suited them. Meg took up the cause with a new zeal, making approaches with books she believed were better than ever before.

Negotiating the arrangements with St Martin's for *Cardington Crescent* presented its usual problems. It emerged that the planned publication date was March 1987, when Anne had worked furiously for a deadline at the end of 1986; she had even sent the proofed manuscript by express post. 'She had obligingly dropped everything' to complete it, Meg told Tara

Hartnett. 'This might have been avoided if St Martin's had not taken 3 months to decide to buy the book.'[44]

The delays at St Martin's worried Anne and rankled with Meg. The stand-down period might have been necessary in the beginning, but now it tended to leave things hanging, allowing for mix-ups and confusion, and, perhaps most significantly of all, leaving Anne 'feeling undervalued'.[45] St Martin's graciously refunded the cost of the express postage, stating in their defence that March 1987 had always been their intended month of publication.

The stand-down seemed even more incongruous when the largely positive reviews for *Cardington Crescent* began to flow in. 'Perry carefully turns back the covers of Victorian society for readers,' wrote the critic for the *Knoxville Sentinel*:

> showing them at the same time much about violent crime that is timeless — not only its gruesomeness but also its effect on the families of the victims. The only drawback in an otherwise excellent book is the obliqueness of the ending. It will be difficult for some readers to understand the motives of the murderer. For the most part, however, Perry writes with both clarity and sensitivity unusual in all but the best mystery writers.[46]

After reading *Silence in Hanover Close*, Meg felt sure Anne was on a new and better track. She returned the manuscript with her notes:

> Enclosed is HANOVER CLOSE, which I must say I enjoyed very much. It's a very good study of what love drives people to. It is, as we agreed, a darker 'Charlotte', but no less interesting or enjoyable. Also it's very good to get a look at the other side — Emily 'downstairs', Pitt in 'the Steel' [prison]. And it does have a cracking ending ... Please remember these are just my thoughts — if you don't agree, ignore them.[47]

The manuscript was submitted, and relief came eventually in the form of a telegram from St Martin's accepting the book with a $4,500 advance.

⚉

Silence in Hanover Close has elements of Foreign Office intrigue and political conspiracy, but what makes it work as a novel is what occurs in the private lives of its characters. There are two prisons in this book: one, the socially constructed confinement of widowhood; the other, the Steel. After George's death, Emily's widowhood has become unbearable. Not only is she incarcerated by the Victorian conventions that surround death, but she is beginning to see the shackling effect of privilege on women of her class. Nothing she does matters. Although she recognizes with some exhilaration that she is free of the power of an opinionated husband, an autocratic father, an ambitious mother and a dictatorial old mother-in-law, the cold reality is that time stretches before her empty and meaningless. She thinks of 'all the bleak January days she might fill with needlework, writing letters, playing the piano to an empty room'. It is as if she has been buried alive in the family crypt along with George.

Aunt Adeline offers an insightful balance to this feminist critique of Victorian society in a conversation with Charlotte.

Of course if we all spoke together we could persuade men, or even force them — but we never do speak together. How often have you seen half a dozen women agree and band together for a cause, let alone half a million? … Men, on the other hand, work fairly well together, imagining themselves the protectors and providers of the nation, obliged to do everything they can to preserve the situation precisely as it is — in their control — on the assumption that they know best what is right for us … And there are only too many women who are happy to assist them, since the status quo suits them very well also.

But Emily's concern is not the plight of womanhood but her own boredom, and she solves this by working undercover as a lady's maid in the household where Robert York was found dead three years earlier. This is a politically sensitive 'cold case' that Pitt has been called in to investigate. In October 1884, York was found beaten around the head after a household burglary. The case was left unsolved, and the few items stolen have never appeared on the black market. There has always been a lurking suspicion that York's death might have had something to do with his highly confidential work at the Foreign Office. Secret papers associated with him have gone missing, and now that his widow, Veronica, is set to marry Julian Danver, another Foreign Office employee doing classified work, the York burglary must be reinvestigated so the wedding can go ahead.

During his pursuit of a woman dressed all in cerise, whose appearance at the Yorks' on the night of the murder is a crucial clue, Pitt is discovered at a sordid London address leaning over a prostitute who has had her throat cut open. Suddenly he is arrested and finds himself locked up in one of England's most notorious prisons, charged with murder.

His name is all over the daily papers, and Charlotte and the children must endure the best and the worst of humanity. There is the awful, shaming public abuse, and acts of pure kindness: the man who brings her a bag of herrings and refuses payment; the bundle of sticks left on the doorstep; and the coal bags that seem just a little fuller. The prison door swings shut behind Pitt with a force that reverberated in Anne's memory. This 'great cold place whose massive walls were like misery set in stone' was part of her own experience. She knew the dripping condensation that makes 'even the inner corridors feel cold and sour. Everywhere was the smell of human sweat and stale air.'

The story Anne tells of the prisoner Raeburn is one of her own memories from Auckland's Mt Eden Prison. In the pitch blackness of his seeping cell, Pitt can hear Raeburn crying. He is a simple-minded, aimless man whose misfortune is to be wrongly accused of taking a jailer's watch. When the jailer will not accept his word, he is placed in solitary confinement. Terrified of being alone, he has no thoughts to fill his head or the void of despair over not being believed. His indignant screams become babble and then silence, as he slips from anger to madness then death in Bedlam, the infamous asylum for the insane.

Raeburn is promiscuous and a thief; his only value in the world is his boast that he will not lie, regardless of the circumstances. Now someone does not believe him. Anne's real-life Raeburn was an ignorant and purposeless woman inmate at Mt Eden. She was accused of stealing and was not believed, and Anne, as a teenager, heard her shouts and felt the agony of her despair. 'The incident marked Pitt deeply. He willed himself to forget it, but Raeburn's cries repeated themselves in his head and his imagination filled in the picture of the man's shallow droop-eyed face, witless with fear, stained with weeping.'

In *Silence in Hanover Close*, Anne unlocks this personal, very raw prison experience to bring immediacy to Pitt's time in prison. From this point on, the books reveal a new degree of sympathy for Pitt and an unprecedented authenticity to his experiences, and to the isolation of Emily at home in her high-class comfort or as she lies on her plank-like maid's bed: 'She rolled over, burying her face in the frozen pillow, and cried herself to sleep.'

⚘

One of the highlights of 1987 for Anne was a trip in May to Guernsey. 'Absolutely beautiful place,' she wrote to Meg Davis on the back of a postcard. 'Woods full of winter flowers can hardly put your feet down for them … Longing to do some writing.'[48] The plotting, characterization or writing of the next book was never far from her mind, and her breaks from writing were not long. She was now receiving regular invitations to talk, not just on her North American sojourns but in Britain as well. After her return from Guernsey, Anne addressed an enthusiastic audience in Oxford. She mentioned the Mormon Church, but it was writing that she discussed at length. Meg wrote to her about it in July:

> Certainly I thought you made excellent sense about writing in general. (And I don't think I've ever told you how flattered and touched I am by your remarks about agents.) You must still be on a high from it all. So well done, on all fronts. Every success has been so dearly bought, you certainly deserve to have a few ships come in soon![49]

Meanwhile, Meg was doing her bit to stir some favourable winds in Anne's direction. Close to the end of 1987 she contacted Ernest Hecht

75

at Souvenir Publishing to see if he would be interested in handling the British paperback rights for the Pitt series.

> The first two books were published ... in 1979 and 1980 and are now long out of print; they are the only ones to have appeared in the UK. The first three books have also been published by Mondadori. Unfortunately, St Martin's Press control the UK rights, so any deal would have to be done with them.[50]

Meg began working on a scheme. Initially she approached Ballantine, Anne's paperback publisher: 'would they like to be Anne's primary publisher?'[51] The company's distribution network was bigger, and it might be able to handle a greater volume of Pitt stories. But Ballantine was buying so many paperback rights from St Martin's that it did not want to rock the boat.

After pondering the problem, Meg went back to Anne with the only solution she could see: they needed to create an entirely new series, specifically for Ballantine. 'And providentially Anne had this thing in a cupboard that was *The Face of a Stranger* — really, really great premise, one of the best premises I have ever read.'[52] Anne had been down this path before, in 1984 with the Digby and Ridgeway series that Hope Dellon had refused to publish. Since then, the concept for Monk, a new series detective who is a recovering amnesiac, had developed as a consequence of conversations with Meg and her own maturing experience as a writer. The big difference to the outcome this time was that editor Leona Nevler and Ballantine were willing to take a risk. In fact, they were very keen indeed.

Meg remembers Anne's original idea had been that, at the end of the first book, Monk discovers that:

> he did in fact commit the murder, and so he has got to go underground, and then as an underground private investigator he can take hopeless cases and sort them out by other means, which is actually a very interesting format premise.[53]

Responses to *Silence in Hanover Close* began to filter through from the middle of 1988. *Publishers Weekly*, reviewing it in June, praised its 'totally surprising yet wonderfully plausible finale'. The *Pasadena Star-News* called it 'her strongest book thus far', while Marilyn Stasio, a newly arrived crime columnist for the *New York Times*, described it as a 'fine-mannered shocker'. She acknowledged the merit of Anne's ethical ideas in a potentially amoral genre:

> Although the period detail in these stories always comes decorously draped around the solid bones of a good, gory crime, both atmosphere and event serve as support for the author's main purpose: to dramatize some social injustice calculated to prick the Pitts' (and the reader's) sense of moral outrage.[54]

That year, too, Anne was the subject of an article published in the *Alfred Hitchcock Magazine*. Mary Cannon praised her capacity for luscious Victorian detailing: 'I guess that there's as much ink given to descriptions of room decorations and ladies' gowns as there is to cataloguing Scotland Yard's methods.'[55]

News about Anne's Mormon novel, evolving as rapidly as Meg could manage it into an adventure odyssey, was not so good. They had already discussed Anne's choice of titles for her historical novels. Her Pitts were pretty safe because they were addresses around London. The historical novels, however, were a minefield of possibility. Meg explained that 'Thou With Clean Hands' might not have the same uplifting connotations for everyone, and she was not at all certain, either, about 'My Eagle Comes'. To the initiated it was 'a quotation from some Promethean poem of GK Chesterton',[56] but it had awkward associations and was about as far from being catchy as you could get.

Meg had sent off editorial notes for 'My Eagle Comes', but Anne's changes seemed barely to resemble the recommendations Meg had made. A colleague found Meg in a pub close to MBA, tearfully taking in what had arrived. She knew that 'a good book comes from a happy author',[57] but she could barely contain her frustration. Anne would have to make the alterations and somehow feel pleased about them. 'Sorry Anne — it has to be tighter!' she wrote in a note when she got back to the office.

> Please, before you go any further, have another look at this. Do ring me if you want to talk it over. But we both know how important this one is, and I think we can save a lot of time and effort on your part if we get the structure right first. With lots of love Meg Davis.[58]

There was so much going on with the Pitt and new Monk series that Anne had no time to feel disappointed or negative about Meg's response. It would be another 18 months before she managed to return the manuscript after taking on board Meg's comments. During 1988 and the beginning of 1989, she worked compulsively to complete *Bethlehem Road*, and wrote *The Face of a Stranger*, the first book in the Monk series.

Bethlehem Road was her tenth Pitt novel, so the characters and her approach were familiar territory, but it was familiar, too, in its resonances with her own life. Pitt is woken by a rapping at his door; it is five past one in the morning. Less than half an hour later he is standing at the south end of Westminster Bridge, where, gaping at him, is the gashed throat of a gentleman tied to a lamppost by his white scarf. Sir Lockwood Hamilton, MP, has been discovered by prostitute Hetty Milner as she touts for business and finds 'her prospective client [is] a corpse'. More wealthy theatre-goers are killed in a similar manner, and their corpses left on Westminster Bridge, before the murderer is revealed. But, as in previous Pitt novels, the murders unfold against a particular social backdrop. This time it is the women's suffrage movement.

Charlotte finds herself at a suffrage meeting:

> It was the first time she had been part of such an assembly ... Most had no thought beyond the wild and previously undreamed of possibility that women might actually vote ... [I]t was their faces that interested Charlotte most, the fleeting expressions chasing across them as they

listened to the ideas that almost all society found revolutionary, unnatural, and either ridiculous or dangerous.

Two people caught up this hideous investigation are Africa Dowell and Florence Ivory. Africa is sheltering Florence in her home, and perhaps in another time and place they might have been a same-sex couple, but here in strait-laced English society, where Queen Victoria has determined that lesbians do not exist, they are almost certainly not. Their friendship, however, is profound, and Africa shares Florence's grief at the loss of her child as if the loss were her own.

When Florence left an unhappy marriage, the lawyer and now Westminster Bridge murder victim Vyvyan Etheridge swore he would help her gain custody of her daughter, Pansy. After a spot of hobnobbing at the club, however, Vyvyan is persuaded by his colleagues not to help. 'He allowed them to take my child and give her to her autocratic and loveless father. I am not even permitted to see her,' the distraught Florence explains to Pitt. She reminds readers that it has been just four years since the legislation was passed that recognized women as independent human beings, not their husbands' chattels.

But the most poignant bad marriage in this book is that of Naomi and Garnet Royce. Pitt discovers letters between Naomi and her friend Lizzie, who is a member of a non-conformist sect, remarkably like that of the Church of Latter-day Saints. Naomi becomes involved with Lizzie's church, and their letters reveal that Garnet is completely opposed to his wife's participation. He tells her she must stay in her room until she relinquishes her blasphemous beliefs. 'I told him I will,' Naomi writes to Lizzie, 'but I shall not eat until he permits me to choose for myself, by the light of my own conscience, what faith I will follow.' It becomes a battle of wills, which ends in Naomi starving herself to death. The theme of a woman of integrity standing up against hypocrisy and corrupt authority is one that Anne would return to often.

To cover up his awful crime Garnet has Naomi's maid Elsie Draper, the only witness to his brutality, thrown into Bedlam. He knows no one will believe the word of a madwoman. The spine-chilling dénouement comes when Charlotte goes alone to threaten to expose Garnet by publishing Naomi's correspondence in a book about the church, and he follows her home. At the end of *Bethlehem Road*, things have changed for the Pitts. Emily is remarried. Her handsome new husband, Jack Radley, is one of the guests she met at the house party where George was murdered. As well, Charlotte and Emily's mother, Caroline Ellison, has been widowed. She is now in her mid-fifties, still eligible 'and wearing her widowhood with vigor and a new and rather daring sense of freedom'.

There is also a dawning appreciation in the police force of Pitt's special talents as a detective. His superior, Micah Drummond, promises him a promotion at the end of the case. It means more money and authority, and less legwork, but the high-minded, hands-on Pitt is not sure this is the right combination for him.

⚬

One of the few breaks Anne took from her writing was a trip in September 1988 to Scotland with Meg MacDonald and some American friends. They drove all the way from Suffolk in Anne's car, which, according to Meg, 'went on elastic, chewing gum and glue, and water more than petrol'.[59] They stayed in a cottage at Ardnamurchan Point, the most westerly part of the whole British Isles, a wild, lonely, windy place with stunning views of rugged rocks and turbulent seas.

Anne had promised to take Meg to visit her hometown of Invergordon, on the east coast of Scotland. 'But she had a cold, which gave her a foul temper and she was in a foul mood. She said she couldn't *possibly* take me. So I was pretty angry ... because I was *so* looking forward to it,' Meg recalls. Eventually, though, Meg 'managed to persuade [Anne] and she loved it. We got into the car and it was lovely.'[60]

Leaving their American friends at the cottage, they set off along the treacherously narrow but beautiful single-lane road out of Ardnamurchan. At one of the road's sharpest bends they came across a car with its front wheels over a sheer drop. The stunned driver had cornered too fast and was still sitting in his vehicle. They stopped, got a rope out of the boot, attached it to the back of each car and Anne pulled him off the edge.

The rest of their trip through the majestic Scottish Highlands was long but less eventful. They stayed overnight in Invergordon, and the next day Anne pushed her friend around the town in a wheelchair. Meg suffers from congenital dysplasia of the hip, which had gone undiagnosed when she was young and so was not properly treated. Sometimes she needs a stick to walk, and on occasions a wheelchair.

Invergordon is a port town in the area of Easter Ross. Its deep northern harbour has made it the place of huge petroleum tanks, towering oil rigs, an aluminium smelter, and, from before the Second World War, a base for naval boats and, more recently, cruise ships. But this is in stark contrast to the primal splendour of the landscape and the quaint old town, which seems hewn directly out of grey stone and slate. Meg had been longing to return to Scotland and now felt compelled to come back, so they went to see a real estate agent in the main street. They were told that a woman who might be able to help would be in again in the morning, but when the morning came Meg 'chickened out'. It was Anne who persuaded her, saying: 'No, no, no, we'll go anyway. We'll go. We'll go.'

So [Anne] pushed me in and we talked to the woman. And she said: 'Oh, hang on a sec', and she went through her drawer, and she said: 'Look there's this little cottage. I've never seen this cottage … It's been on the books for a while and I've no idea what it's like. Would you like to see it?'[61]

When they said yes, the real estate agent drove them to Milton, a tiny market centre built around a green with a mercat cross, 6.5 kilometres north-east of Invergordon. Meg fell in love with the little stone cottage, the middle of three in a row, and it was cheap, although £13,000 was still a lot of money for her to find. Meg wanted to buy it there and then, but she needed a deposit. '[So] Anne rang her father up and he wired a thousand-pound deposit straight into the bank.'[62] After signing the forms they returned to Ardnamurchan Point to pick up their American friends, then drove back to Suffolk.

Once home, Meg dropped her bombshell, telling the children she was going back to live in Scotland. 'My daughter, who was seventeen going on eighteen, said: "You can't *do* that, Mum. If you abandon your children, you get put in prison." They were pretty cross about me leaving.' She very nearly changed her mind and 'gave up my dream', but in the end was determined.

> I got a friend of mine, we hired a van, and we stuffed all my goodies into this van and we drove up in the November, in the snow. We got here in the snow. And I had two cats in the back, and a deaf and blind poodle lying on the seat underneath, doped up to the eyeballs because it was a long journey and I didn't know if it was going to make it. And we drove all the way to Scotland.[63]

After Meg had gone, she and Anne were in regular telephone contact, but life was not the same, and Anne was haunted by the memory of vistas of northern seas and Scottish Highlands. Meg had her first snowy Christmas in Scotland, while Anne worked through a wetter festive season in Suffolk.

II

Henry Hulme was one of the people absent from Anne's Christmas table. He had married again in 1955 — 'My wife is about my age with two children (boy 17, girl 12) and has similar interests to me and has been through very difficult times herself'[64] — but new wife Margery did not approve of Anne or want her to be a part of their lives. As a result, Henry and Anne were forced to meet in secret, visiting museums and art galleries away from the Hulmes' house. The only other thing Henry could give Anne was money, and he was as generous as possible to the daughter who began life as Juliet Marion Hulme.

Born on 28 October 1938, in Blackheath, London, Juliet was less than a year old when the Second World War started. During the Blitz, the repeated rap of ack-ack guns, the whining sound of planes, and especially the explosions, woke her up screaming at night and gave her terrible nightmares. Hilda spent many anxious hours alone with her little daughter in air-raid shelters while Henry worked. There were just two brief evacuations from London.

They might have moved to the country for the duration of the war, but for Henry's job. From 1936 to 1938 he had been Chief Assistant at the Royal Observatory in Greenwich; during wartime he was an essential part of Admiralty research, becoming Director of Naval Operational Research in 1945. At the end of the war 'he was one of those detailed to go over and debrief Admiral Dönitz after the surrender'.[65] As it did for many men, the war took him away from his family. Although Juliet had often been ill as a baby, Henry had happy memories of her early years. When she was a toddler she worked with him in the garden of their two-storey semi-detached brick house at 79 Foyle Road in Greenwich. He remembered showing her the weeds to pull out, and although the resulting extractions were not always correct she thought she was 'the cat's pajamas!' When he relaxed at night in his armchair she would sit in his lap, or on the chair-back with her legs draped around his shoulders.

His golden rule was never to talk down to children, and as a father who was an astronomer and a mathematician his pleasure was to share with her his sense of wonder at the mystery of the universe. 'The sun is a star like any other star, and it is about nine minutes away at the speed of light,' he told her. When she was three years old he explained 'that Nazis and Germans were not necessarily the same thing'.[66] While Britain was engaged in an horrific war that made people more xenophobic and anti-Germany by the day, he wanted his daughter to have an open mind and a sense of the liberal, intellectual Germans he had studied with in Leipzig.

At the same time, however, Juliet witnessed the tragic consequences of German militarism at home:

We had German Jewish refugees in the house whom my parents took in, and I can remember one — her name was Van Der Homberg — and she just cried, and cried, and cried. And I was about two and I didn't

83

understand that adults cried because crying was for babies, but I know now why she wept and wept.[67]

Juliet would remember the sirens, and 'going down every night to the air-raid shelter and standing looking at the fighter planes, and the tracer bullets. It was like watching fireworks.'[68] This was a disturbing and disruptive time, especially for the adults around her. Her most memorable experience came at the end of the war:

> One of the things that thrilled me the most was watching the VE Day parade ... My father had offices in Whitehall, so we stood in the window and watched ... If there's one moment in history that captures an overwhelming emotion, that's it.[69]

Juliet was bright, and in spite of her medical complications she could read the newspaper before she went to school. Hilda was responsible for most of this, and she had helped to create an imaginative world for Juliet through the books she read to her and the films she took her to see. There was a broad range of books on their shelves: Arthur Mee's *Children's Encyclopedia*, Lewis Carroll's *Through the Looking Glass* and *Alice in Wonderland*, *Don Quixote* in translation, and the works of Shakespeare. Juliet was taken to see Judy Garland in *The Wizard of Oz*, and somehow on the way home from Lewisham she got lost. After her parents found her, Juliet told them vivid stories of how 'after dark everyone became the Wicked Witch of the West'.

She was a vivacious girl whose fantasy life was as actively lived as her reality. When the other children put away their fairy and witch costumes, she played on, wearing them at the dinner table. It was fun, but also exhausting. Sometimes when they were living in Blackheath, and Hilda fell asleep as she lay on the bed reading a story, Juliet would prise her mother's eyes open. 'Are you still there? What happened next?' Hilda was tired and ill, and after her second child, Jonathan, was born on 21 March 1944, she spent a long time in hospital. Hilda and Henry's blood types were incompatible, and immediately after they arrived home from the maternity hospital she and the baby were readmitted, Hilda in a critical condition.

Hilda's convalescence was long and protracted, and it disrupted all their lives. Juliet took her mother's absence to heart, as young children often do, and blamed everyone, especially Jonathan. But the main difficulty with the siblings' relationship was the six-year gap in their ages, a gulf in life experience that would take years to diminish. The war, the absences of her parents, Jonathan's birth — all these had conspired to make an exceedingly intelligent child determined and sometimes belligerent. Juliet's behaviour could be mature beyond her years and seem free-thinking and creative; at other times, it was just a bad-tempered flouting of authority. She approached almost everything with a disturbing intensity.

From 1945 to 1948 Henry was Scientific Adviser to the Air Ministry, a job which took him on a long trip to the United States when Juliet was six-and-a-half years old. He returned to find her seriously ill with pneumonia. One night the doctor left the child's bedside, telling Hilda: 'There's nothing I can do. I'll be back to sign the death certificate in the morning.'[70] Juliet spent months at home in bed and was frequently hospitalized with respiratory illness. 'When I was in hospital, I wasn't allowed to read. I survived in my imagination. I just shut my eyes and lived in my head. If you can't read, you have to make your own stories — from what you have read.'[71] For two years her schooling was disrupted and it was feared that if she did not move to a warmer climate she might die.

On medical advice, the Hulmes finally approached friends in the Bahamas to have eight-year-old Juliet stay with them for a while. It seemed an expedient and logical solution. Henry had his work in England, and Hilda was coping with two-year-old Jonathan. With Juliet gone, they would have time to consider where they were going to live. In fact, taking Juliet away from her home and her parents' care began a process that would end in disaster.

CHAPTER THREE

I

Anne decided she had had enough of her secluded Suffolk life, and rang Meg MacDonald in April 1989: 'I really loved it there [in Scotland]. I need to come up to visit and to do a manuscript.'[1] So she drove up with her two cats, Poppy and Pansy, and stayed a whole month with Meg. The launch of the Monk series was her big project for the year, her début for Ballantine. She knew it had to be good. If it did not do as well as the Pitts, it had the potential to make things difficult with both Ballantine and St Martin's.

This was the first time Meg MacDonald had helped Anne in any sustained way with a manuscript. They worked solidly. Anne would spend the day toiling over a few handwritten pages, then read them out loud to Meg, who would, in her words, 'pull them to pieces'. '"Why are you starting there?" and poor Anne would prickle defensively: "What do you mean, why am I starting there?"' Meg challenged her about not jumping into the story quickly enough to grab the reader's interest, about repetition, about losing the plot or forgetting details: '"You've just walked through a wall because you haven't opened the door." Or: "You walked in with two kids and you've walked home without them — *where* are they?"' It was tough and ego-bruising, but Anne took it because she wanted the best from her work. She accepted criticism, she pushed her craft to its limits, she brought more of herself to the writing. Meg noticed the difference: 'She went into darker places in a sense to find those stories, because they are a lot darker than the Pitt [novels].'[2]

Writing is a lonely pursuit, and reading it aloud transformed it into an interactive experience. It also brought the text to life. When Anne read her material to Meg she picked up the difficulties and polished them out so that the writing flowed more smoothly. Occasionally, there were a few ruffled feathers and a spot of wounded pride, but almost always the process was revealing and sometimes downright entertaining. She liked knowing Meg was there to chat to, and loved the drives they took in the Scottish countryside.

It was hard to go. She left on a Saturday, and all the way back to Suffolk she pored over the possibilities, not only of her writing, but of where she wanted to live. Returning to an empty house did not help. She no longer felt she belonged in Suffolk any more than she did in Scotland. Where was 'home' for her anyway? For a month she had wistfully watched Meg and could see in her a Highlander come home at last. Anne had no such place. At a pinch, perhaps it was London — but how many people really thought of London as home? The United States might be her spiritual home, but she was no American. Her most defining years had been spent in New Zealand, but that was certainly not home. It occurred to her that perhaps she belonged where she wrote, and now was as good a time as any to move on.

The next day, Sunday, she telephoned Meg: 'Oh, it was so lovely up there! If I'm not encroaching on your territory, do you think I could come and live in Scotland?' Meg responded in her matter-of-fact way: 'I don't see any reason why not.'[3]

Although Meg had a car, she did not have her driver's licence, so a friend took her in his old van to Alness, which is just over 3 kilometres west of Invergordon. As she was going upstairs to see the estate agent, she noticed a photograph on the wall and said to her friend, 'There's Anne's house.' It was a perfect little stone cottage, sitting on its own in a field surrounded by old trees and dry-stone walls. Meg knew Anne would love it. The estate agent took them out to see it that very evening.

'I shouldn't really tell you this,' he said, 'but there are people coming up from London who are really struck on this house. If your friend wants it that much, I advise her to put a bid in *now*.'[4] Anne should make an offer within the week. Exhibiting less scepticism than estate agents possibly deserve, Meg rang Anne, sending her into a panic. She trusted Meg's judgement, but could see no way of selling her place quickly enough to raise the money. In the end, when she listed Fox Cottages the people selling it very kindly said they would lend her the money until her property sold. So on Meg's word, Anne went ahead and bought her cottage in the Scottish Highlands, sight unseen.

❦

The responses to the detailed outline for *The Face of a Stranger* that Anne sent to Meg Davis and Leona Nevler were encouraging. She received their feedback early in the year, and it gave her a sense of where her agent and publisher were expecting the storyline to go. Both were intrigued by the idea of William Monk being a recovering amnesiac who can piece together his old self only from the outside, or from other people's memories and reactions to him — and that as his case proceeds he does not want to solve it, just in case it turns out that he himself is the murderer. But Meg wanted more struggle. 'He is after all repressing the memory of his murder of Grey, working against the terrible fear of facing what he's done and acknowledging himself as a murderer,' read one of her notes to Anne. Leona, on the other hand, was reluctant to make Monk a murderer at all. Finally she put her foot down and vetoed the idea. Meg remembers her rationale.

> [She] felt that Americans wouldn't cope with that kind of darkness, so it had to turn out that he had left the guy for dead but in fact didn't literally kill him, and weirdly for the Americans that lets him off the hook and everything's fine. But it does mean that he can walk away and still be a member of society and solve crimes on a more traditional footing.[5]

Meg thought the book premise was a perfect opportunity for suspense and for the conflicting emotions of a man probing his soul to find the truth about himself bit by bit. It 'ought to build up like a pressure cooker,' she told Anne.[6] Leona thought that the phase of self-discovery should be longer. Anne had imagined that Monk would be fully revealed to himself by the end of the first book, but this seemed a lot to achieve, and perhaps a lost opportunity. Hester Latterly, who becomes Monk's crime-solving partner and later wife, was also put under the spotlight. From the notes Anne circulated, they felt she sounded very like Charlotte. She must be different from Charlotte in the way Monk was different from Pitt. 'What about making her more of a "head nurse" type?' Meg suggested.[7]

Meg and Leona both saw Anne's approach as a clever literary device. Since 1926, when Agatha Christie had smashed convention by making her narrator the murderer in *Who Killed Roger Ackroyd?*, writers of crime detective fiction had been finding innovative ways of tricking the reader and freshening up a well-worn genre. Anne's premise went a step further: the detective was the murderer, and he would carry the consequences of that act through his work and life, and the rest of the series. Crime detective fiction writer and commentator PD James, in her book *Talking About Detective Fiction* (2009), describes the England of the 1920s as:

> a cohesive world, overwhelmingly white and united by a common
> . belief in a religious and moral code based on the Judeo-Christian
> inheritance ... and buttressed by social and political institutions ...
> [that] were accepted as necessary to the well-being of the state: the
> monarchy, the Empire, the Church, the criminal justice system, the
> City, the ancient universities. It was an ordered society in which virtue
> was regarded as normal, crime an aberration, and in which there was
> small sympathy for the criminal.[8]

In the decades between the world wars, Agatha Christie's detective fiction writing reinforced these ideas and institutions, making her an 'arch-purveyor of cosy reassurance'.[9] The world Anne creates, however, is both historical and post-modern. It assumes human existence is an ambiguous complexity of circumstance that means every act — even a moral one — has to be considered in its context. Only in such a framework can Monk be a good man, a sympathetic protagonist *and* a murderer.

This premise also provided a perfect psychological landscape in which Anne could locate her own reflections on the struggle between good and evil and, on the many situations that make this absolute polarization inappropriate, fluid, even accidental. The Pitt series, to date, had been a measured examination of subjects on which Anne took a relatively liberal position: feminism, marriage, the family, poverty, religious hypocrisy, incest, rape, prostitution and homosexuality. But she understood how it *felt* to be Monk. She knew about choice, consequence, and what it was like to see, in other people's eyes, the monster that is the perception of you. If she had been allowed to make Monk a murderer, his life would have been a fictional projection of hers. But Leona and Ballantine were not brave enough to trust that American readers would accept a murderer as a likeable, positive person.

The Face of a Stranger opens on 31 July 1856, in a London hospital where Monk has lain close to death for three weeks. As consciousness dawns, he realizes he can remember nothing. He does not know how he got there or even who he is. 'Panic boiled up inside him again and for a moment he could have screamed. Help me, somebody, who am I? Give me back my life, my self!' He has no past, no identity. He is no one. What he does have is an innate sense of self-preservation, and so he keeps this knowledge to himself. Revealing his amnesia will only make him vulnerable, and somewhere back in the dark recesses of his damaged mind he knows that vulnerability is dangerous. 'Let a little more time pass, a little more identity build, learn to know himself.' On his release from hospital he finds his rooms at 27 Grafton Street, meets his house-keeper, Mrs Worley, and discovers himself for the first time in the mirror. The face he sees looking back is a strong one. He is dark with a 'broad, slightly aquiline nose, wide mouth ... eyes intense luminous gray in the flickering light. It was a powerful face, but not an easy one. If there was humour it would be harsh, of wit rather than laughter.' He estimates that he is anywhere between 35 and 45 years old. But it is in the reaction of others that he begins to see the inner man. Colleagues are frightened of him: they cower at his cruelty and despise his single-minded, selfish ambition. No one cares and no one likes him.

But is this really fair? After all, 'he was hearing only one side to the story — there was no one to defend him, to explain, to give his reasons and say what he knew and perhaps they did not'. His greatest fear, as he returns to work with the Metropolitan Police Force and begins to unravel the deadly bashing of Major Joscelin Grey, is that he is the murderer himself. It would not surprise Runcorn, his superior officer at work. He feels some immense unspoken animosity towards Monk that is not entirely untangled, even at the end of the book. Runcorn, a pompous, petty man, is not entirely appealing himself, but clearly Monk's calculating and callous manner has caused him deep hurt.

Runcorn guesses Monk's identity crisis by spotting gaps in his memory. Towards the end of the book, Monk tells Hester Latterly, a usually independent, sometimes acerbic woman, about his amnesia. Although throughout Monk's murder case they squabble often, she is completely sympathetic about his missing memory:

> How extraordinary — and terrible. I do not always like myself completely — but to lose yourself! I cannot imagine having nothing at all left of all your past — all your experiences, and the reason why you love or hate things.

Hester is the light side to Monk's darkness. If Great-Aunt Vespasia is the older Anne, then tall, slender Hester is her personification of young female goodness. Perhaps in that respect she is rather too ideal, but she does possess a challenging, perceptive quality that Anne admires. With a heartfelt contempt for hypocrisy and incompetence, she will not suffer fools. 'She was highly intelligent, with a gift for logical thought which many people found disturbing — especially men, who did not expect it or like it in a woman.'

Hester is among the first women to join Florence Nightingale at a Scutari troop hospital in Turkey, close to the carnage of the Crimean War. Her fine brain makes her 'invaluable in the administration of the hospitals for the critically injured or desperately ill'. It also makes her a darn good sleuth. She discovers her special snooping talents when her brother Charles, along with Monk, becomes a prime suspect in the murder of Major Joscelin Grey.

Grey is a seemingly righteous Crimean military campaigner who engineers Hester's father's bankruptcy and begins a tragic series of events that culminate in her father's suicide and the subsequent death of her mother from a broken heart. During this investigation, Monk becomes besotted with the desirable Imogen, wife of Charles and sister-in-law of Hester. Like Charlotte Ellison's crush on her brother-in-law Dominic, it will be some time before Monk sees the light. Poor judgement of character and superficial infatuation are themes to which Anne often returns.

For Anne, amnesia is just a convenient means of revealing things retrospectively, a perfect device for the detective fiction writer because it leaves tracts of information obscure and suspenseful. It is not the matter of forgetting that you have murdered someone, either, that ignites her interest: that is short-lived and sensational. What matters to her in *The Face of a Stranger* is Monk's loss of self, the absence of an identity, the lack of a voice to explain — and the horror of seeing himself through others' eyes as brutal and cruel when he *has* to believe that this is only part of the picture.

⚘

In the autumn of 1989, Anne loaded up her car and moved all she owned to the fishing village of Portmahomack in Scotland. The two-bedroom cottage that Meg had chosen for her was on the outskirts of the village, tucked down a narrow road that divides rolling fields. In the hum and buzz of summer, the fields glow golden yellow with hay that is cut and coiled in huge circular bales. The rows made by the harvester stripe the soil and the stubble so rhythmically that it looks like patterned fabric. In winter, the fields sit fallow in frozen stillness. When the snows come, they are a white carpet punctured at the edges by low vegetation, fences, and stark, black trees. Night sometimes falls at three o' clock on a winter afternoon, but in summer the sun never seems to sleep.

The cottages of Portmahomack edge a gentle bay that sweeps around to a rocky peninsula ending with the Tarbat Ness lighthouse, painted red and white like a stick of rock candy. Until the early decades of the twentieth century, the seas around Portmahomack ran with whitefish, and in the harbour the fishing boats were so closely moored it was rumoured that a fisherman could go from one end of the bay to the other without wetting his feet. Romans, Picts and Vikings have visited or settled there, and it was a holy site for the early Christian Church. In excavations below Tarbat Old Church are the remains of a human body that belong to a member of a Pictish monastery, and in the graveyard there are crosses more than 1,000 years old.

Anne found Portmahomack beautiful — the gentle, golden northern light, and the drama of the dawns and sunsets across clear, vaulted skies. But every move has its losses, and in this case it was her cat, Poppy. 'I'm sorry to hear you sounding so down when you phoned,' Meg Davis counselled her in November 1989.

> I wish I could tell you that everything will be fine and that Poppy will reappear, but we both know that as time passes it seems more and more likely that she's having some wild feline adventure somewhere. I wonder if it's not time to let go now. I know perfectly well that she was absolutely the most wonderful cat in the world; but don't forget that the world is full of people who love you, too. And God needs to be trusted.[10]

Anne, who had spent days calling for Poppy, was now staying with friends in the United States, promoting her books and fretting over her lost cat. Meg explained in her letter that the contract had been agreed with Leona at Ballantine and she was expecting it to arrive in the post any day.

Meg had been working so hard she had thought of almost nothing else. One Friday she woke up to the shock realization that she had not been near a hairdresser's for months and could hardly see through her fringe. At the last minute she went locally in Tottenham Court, she explained to Anne:

> The manageress, who was wearing a lurid jumper of some shiny stuff and loads of bangles, started to cut away. 'Certainly needs doing,' she remarked. 'Wot you want round the ears, then?' I tried to explain what

my usual bloke does … She picked at various strands round my ears, and obviously couldn't figure out the way he'd done it. 'Wot he done 'ere, then?' she said, leaning on the back of the chair to guffaw. I escaped with an all right cut; but it certainly takes one down a peg or two to be laughed at by a hairdresser.[11]

One of the things absorbing her attention was a plan to help sell the religious fantasy 'My Eagle Comes', which had undergone a welcome metamorphosis in structure and title in its intervening months with Anne. It was now called 'Tathyr' after its central female protagonist. The manuscript was massively long, but Meg held out new hope for it. She told Anne she liked the way it had opened up to make 'room for various issues, and presented different points of view'.[12] This, she felt, made the whole high-minded venture more human and accessible. Anne's evoking of new countries and their strange 'cultures, customs, and clothes' was also clever. Meg's problem was to sell it. She believed there were readers out there, but that they would only narrowly overlap with Anne's crime fiction audience.

'Tathyr' would have to find a new readership and probably a new publisher, and Meg would need all her guile to move it from manuscript to print. She settled on the idea of acquiring a New York-based sub-agent specifically for that title. Don Maass, a slim, immaculate man of medium build, came with an excellent reputation, which Meg had researched; she had also met him at publishing events. His intelligence and proficient but potentially hard-nosed approach to publishing would suit Anne's needs perfectly.

In November 1989, Meg sent Don a chunk of 'Tathyr', along with a letter setting out the background. She explained that Anne had just delivered *Highgate Rise*, her eleventh Pitt book, to St Martin's, and that they were beginning a new series with Ballantine Fawcett. 'Each book seems to be better than the one before,' she wrote.

Anne is currently no. 6 on Dalton's bestseller list for mysteries … [and] she is starting to see success abroad, with multi-book deals with

Mondadori in Italy and Dumont in Germany. At last, also, we have got her started in England; Souvenir publish her second book in March next year ... And I am now working on an option deal ... for a television series, with a definite eye to the US market. A Prominent Commercial Writer is very keen to adopt them.[13]

She pitched the difficult bit towards the end. Anne wanted to write more 'serious' books, and Meg outlined the progress to date of the history and religious fantasy manuscripts before explaining that:

After several 'dry runs', she has now delivered TATHYR. A large amount of work on both our parts has gone into it. Anne's strengths are, I think, a keen interest in human problems, and a vivid visual imagination, and this is an ambitious, powerful novel. Anne feels strongly that she would like it to be launched in the States.[14]

If Don could find a publisher for 'Tathyr', he could handle the book. Meg knew she was giving him the ugly baby in a rather better-looking family of commercial sellers, but the agent who had been representing Anne in the United States was as reluctant as Leona to tackle the problem of selling it and was relieved when told that Meg was planning to approach Don Maass. So, this suited everyone. The question was, would the manuscript suit him?

Don countered brilliantly. If he was going to take the baby, then he wanted the rest of the family as well. He got back to her at the beginning of January 1990. 'I also love TATHYR,' he wrote.

Now I must ask a blunt question: In representing Anne here, will I gain control of US rights to her detective series? My sources in the retail area tell me that Anne sells extremely well. She is clearly the leading author of the new wave of period mysteries. I like the new Ballantine editions, but I am positive that much more can be done for her on the hardcover side, if not by St. Martin's then by another house. I would love to move her up the ladder, both in advances and in visibility.[15]

As soon as Meg received Don's letter, she rang him in New York. The next day she was still buzzing from their conversation. 'I can't tell you how much it means to me that you're also enthusiastic about Anne's work,' she wrote in a quick follow-up note. 'I'm very fond of the woman, & think she really deserves fortune and popularity.'[16] Don spoke to Anne on the phone and she was equally excited by his ideas. Meg sent Don copies of Anne's previous contracts and royalty statements, and less than a week later she sent a letter formalizing their agreement along with the rest of the 'Tathyr' manuscript: 'I hope you enjoy it as much as the first section.'[17]

One of the major things Meg was discussing with Don was a move from St Martin's Press. Leona had recently made it clear that Ballantine was now happy to become Anne's principal publisher, putting out the Pitts as well as the new Monk series in both hard and soft covers. This was a green light to begin negotiations with Ballantine, but there were three other interested parties as well. In the meantime *Highgate Rise* was awaiting approval from St Martin's. Don explained the strategy to Anne. 'Once the option period is up, or once I have declined an offer, we shall be off and running ... Meanwhile, after several minutes of squinting at the *Times* atlas, I have finally located Portmahomack. It is a pity that you must live in such a congested urban centre.'[18]

The offer Ballantine made was undeniably generous. It was to be a three-book deal for the 'Charlottes' with a royalties advance of $125,000 — that was $35,000 for the first book and $40,000 and $50,000 for the second and third. Ballantine also offered a signing tour in the United States at their own expense. Meg sent the news to Anne with a caution: 'Now, please keep this "officially" under your hat! St Martin's still have some time to run on their option, and Ballantine are sending undated contracts to Don because as you can imagine all hell will break loose if Don is seen to be breaking the option. It'll all be academic by the time we receive the contract here ... CONGRATULATIONS!'[19]

By the time the Ballantine contract arrived in the MBA office the relationship with St Martin's was already over. Their option time was up and they had not responded. 'Thanks again, too, for your mighty support during the [Ballantine] negotiations — you were beyond helpful —

you were magnificent,' Meg wrote to Don.[20] To Anne she exclaimed: 'Hooray — the new Ballantine contracts! ... Of course, if you've got any queries, just ring. Congratulations! Much love Meg.'[21]

The news of Anne's departure hit Hope Dellon at St Martin's like an incendiary device. 'I wanted to let you know how shocked and dismayed I was at the way in which your new US agent, Don Maass, went about ending an association of more than a dozen years,' she wrote to Anne in April 1990.[22] She was affronted by Don's refusal to negotiate, and said that if Anne and her agents were not happy with the arrangement they should have said so and St Martin's would have discussed something better. She mentioned the idea of taking legal action, but knew in the long run that this would only delay rather than stop the deal, so she finished by wishing them well in their new venture.

Responding on Anne's behalf, Meg sent her a long list of the issues that had plagued their relationship over the years: the length between publishing dates; the fact that St Martin's always needed to be chased; the proofs that had to be checked and returned in a 'cripplingly short space of time'; the fact that Anne had financed her own author tours without much publicity support or bookshop liaison; and, finally, the chronic royalty payment history.[23] It was like a troubled marriage that had ended, but, since they shared financial custody of the books they had created together, it was best that they parted amicably — and, more or less, they did.

⁕

In May 1990 Don sent Meg the counter-signed Ballantine contracts along with a cheque for Anne. Meg told him: 'Anne's first act with the money has been to replace her disabled friend's coal-fired heating system, so her friend doesn't have to hump coal any more. This deal is almost turning into a scene from "It's a Wonderful Life"!'[24] Anne's new contractual arrangements with Ballantine meant quite a radical shift in gear. She had nearly always worked on two manuscripts a year, but they had rarely been published within 12 months. The work involved in originating two sustainable plots for two separate books series, writing the manuscripts, and checking and returning the proofs was monumental. Her days now became even more focused on writing, and extended sometimes from early morning to late evening.

The germ of many of her ideas came from either watching television or reading the newspaper. Some aspect of a dramatized programme such as *Babylon Five* or a current event would coalesce with other ideas floating in her head to create something unique that interested her. She loved classical music, especially Liszt, Verdi and Puccini, but television was her main release. She still worked her usual six days a week, and then, in accordance with Mormon practice, spent Sunday at rest, though this included a three-hour church service in Invergordon.

The local Mormon Church had welcomed Anne with enthusiasm. First Meg became a parishioner, then Anne, closely followed by other family members, who began a steady migration north. Initially it was Meg's son Simon and his wife with their baby Jonathan. They stayed in a caravan parked on the grass at Milton village, but as autumn approached Anne suggested they move into Meg's house and Meg stay at her place while she herself was away on her 1990–91 Christmas–New Year tour of the United States. Meg could look after Pansy and the cottage.

Anne's mother, Marion, also moved to Portmahomack, buying a cottage with a glorious view over the bay and a terraced back garden. When Anne returned from the United States, Simon and his wife remained in Meg's place at Milton, while Meg continued living at Portmahomack. In the meantime, Anne stayed a kilometre or so away with her mother at Arn Gate Cottage until she could shift into her new home — a restored barn that had been part of an old piggery on the land next to her cottage. Her purchase of that property had been triggered by the overflow of her septic tank: to make the system work again she had to buy the adjoining field, and the old piggery barn was part of the property. So Meg, who stayed on in Anne's cottage, got a new septic tank, while Anne, with the help of Simon, embarked on an ambitious restoration.

The barn had spectacular views of Dornoch Firth on one side and Moray Firth on the other, and out over the highland of Sutherland. Because the Tarbat Ness Peninsula is long and narrow, the sea is just a few kilometres away on either side of the barn. There had been no horizon for Anne in prison, just snatches of blue or grey glimpsed from a window above her head. At Portmahomack the line between sea and sky seems to stretch to infinity.

It was Henry Hulme's death, on 8 January 1990, that helped Anne pay the £26,000 for the property. Although the money she inherited from her father was helpful, his departure from her life brought a flood of regret. He had not seen her mature into a young woman, nor had he been a substantial part of her life since she was 15 years old.

It was a relationship changed on both sides by catastrophe and guilt. She had helped to bring down the world as they knew it; he felt he had betrayed his daughter at her most vulnerable time. 'I will go down in history as the world's worst father,' he had told media as he left New Zealand in July 1954. But his was a dilemma no father would want to face: a difficult choice between his children. For these reasons Anne's grief was private, tucked away like Henry's photograph in her drawer. It made her sad to see it. She loved him, and his face was a reminder of what was missing and now irretrievable.

Anne never really explained to Meg Davis exactly what the problems were with her father — that he was one of the few people whose public office and profile, not to mention surname, could link her back to New Zealand and the murder. She always carried with her a sense of grief, but no one in her professional life really knew why. 'Dear Meg,' Anne wrote in an undated note, 'I've been keeping this card for something worth saying with it. Thank you for being my friend. Love Anne.'[25]

Things Anne did sometimes seemed quaintly out of step. Unexpected things were significant to her. For instance, a beam of light from a watery grey sky on the sea that she pointed out rapturously to Meg Davis on her visits — now to Scotland rather than Suffolk. Anne might miss the importance of some major 'plotting' discussion she was having with Meg because she was transfixed by something she had seen, and she could be traumatized by events that seemed unimportant to others. She was terrified after getting a traffic infringement notice when she failed to stop on black ice in the snow and ploughed into the back of the car in front.

Her anxiety appeared disproportionate even though a court appearance was involved. Meg tried to calm her down. 'It was just a formality. After all it isn't as if you've killed someone.'[26] But Anne would not be reassured.

⊗

In November 1990, Anne visited Leona Nevler in New York to discuss progress with the Monk series. Meg wrote afterwards: 'Anne is home safely, and very much enjoyed her time with you. Thank you so much for taking such good care of her. I understand from Anne that there are good reviews of FACE OF A STRANGER in *The New York Times*.'[27] Rosemary Herbert, crime fiction commentator for the *New York Times*, had described the book as 'first rate' and a watershed. Anne had published 10 books and was already 'on the map as a mystery novelist':

> But *The Face of a Stranger* represents both a natural progression in Ms Perry's concern with social issues and a significant development away from the formulaic. In fact, the novel is a classic example of the book that turns the author's recognized strengths in an entirely new direction ... [Monk] is literally beside himself; as he doggedly investigates a confounding murder and pursues his own identity ... She understands her amnesiac sleuth so intimately that she knows he can rediscover himself only in moments of inspiration along the trail of his quarry. This, and the fact that Monk has more to learn about himself even as the story concludes, are brilliant touches that effectively blend a contemporary understanding of character with a Victorian sensibility.[28]

Beyond this, there were grumbles about it being 'at times long-winded and repetitive, but richly textured ... solidly absorbing and Perry's best to date'.[29] Almost every reviewer saw it as a mark of Anne's progress as an author and the beginning of even better things. *Publishers Weekly* detected in it the start of 'a pronounced and satisfying psychological dimension ... While Monk's unwillingness to face directly the questions of his past is often a stumbling block, forbearing readers will be amply rewarded by Perry's resolutions of both mysteries.'[30] The book was the Mystery Guild dual main selection, was nominated for an Agatha Award and was on the *Chicago Tribune* bestseller list.

Many of the reviews for Anne's Pitt, *Bethlehem Road*, also published in 1990, were equally affirming. 'A real treat is the beautifully drawn character of a suffragette who has lost her daughter,' wrote the *Publishers Weekly* reviewer. 'Etched with pain and compassion unusual in a detective novel, this characterization makes up for a mildly disappointing turn of plot at the novel's conclusion.'[31] Even the critic for the *New York Times Book Review*, who found that Anne's 'unassailable argument for her feminist cause tends to drag the pace and dull the action', commended her 'finely drawn characters [who] couldn't be more comfortable within the customs and sensibility of their historical period'.[32]

The publication of *The Face of a Stranger* ushered in a new era of opportunity for Anne, and an unprecedented degree of financial security. For the first time in her life she worried about tax — not the prospect of paying back a few hundred scraped-together pounds, but the consequences of huge royalty cheques arriving. There would be problems if they were mishandled: Anne needed help. As Meg wrote to Don in October 1990: 'There is a possibility that the general election will take place in '91 — certainly in '92 — and as you probably know, Labour will undoubtedly raise the taxes drastically.' Tax would become a nightmare that caused Anne to pace the floor and lose sleep.

Not as rewarding, but very exciting, was the television deal Meg was negotiating. An article in *Publishers Weekly* in December 1990 explained that Anne's Pitt series had been optioned in England to producer Hilary Heath and Lynda La Plante: 'The purchase price is pegged at £5000 (close to $10,000) per hour up to 13 episodes. Beyond that the figure per episode rises to £6000 (nearly $12,000). These sums are to be applied against a guaranteed 3% of the producer's net profits.' Also reported was Don Maass's negotiation of the sale of three more Charlotte and Pitt novels 'to Fawcett, which henceforth will publish Perry in both hard- and softcover. Advances for this agreement total $225,000.'[34]

Meg had been working on the television deal for some time, and, she told Don in May, Hilary Heath and murder mystery screenwriter Lynda

La Plante were looking for backers while Lynda wrote the pilot script for their screen adaptation. In between discussions, Meg went tramping in Ireland. It was an idyllic break. 'The footpath took us through pine forests with deer in them, and altogether Ireland gave us an erroneous impression of a place where the sun shines a lot.'[35] By October she could report that 'Lynda is to write the pilot and do the format, with Anne as creative consultant. Other writers would be brought in to do the other episodes.'[36] Hilary Heath and Lynda La Plante were hoping to assign rights to Yorkshire Television. The option payments were not high, but Anne was thrilled.

At the same time as she was discussing television options, Meg was negotiating with Ballantine. 'I had breakfast with Leona Nevler yesterday,' she wrote to Don in September, 'and she says that ... she is ready to do another contract.'[37] But how much ahead did they want to contract the books? Although such an arrangement gave Anne security, it also locked her into a contract that could potentially limit her income. Meg was considering contracting the next four books ahead, and Anne was prepared to go to six. 'How cagey of Leona to propose a new contract now, when Anne still has a total of three books left to deliver,' Don replied.

> We had better look at her motives. First, she knows that Anne — who still vividly remembers the years of struggle — will love this new sign of affirmation. Secondly, she knows that the longer she waits, the more costly Anne's books may become. Thirdly — and here's the important point — she will be sure that Anne will continue to produce a steady stream of the mysteries that have been so successful for Fawcett.[38]

Don was not against the idea of a contract for new books, especially at a potential $50,000 a book, but he was worried that this might tie Anne up for too long, as had happened with St Martin's. He did not want Leona 'feeling complacent', and was concerned that Anne had imitators which meant she needed to keep her innovative edge. This, he thought, could be achieved by writing an historical espionage novel, which he believed no one else had done. 'Nevertheless, the espionage book isn't ready, and I hate to turn away a publisher who is eager to spend money.'[39] So negotiations with Ballantine continued.

⚘

Anne worked prodigiously on her new manuscripts, executing them in remarkably quick succession. *A Dangerous Mourning*, the next in the Monk series, took her imagination back to prison and the finality of hanging. Runcorn calls Monk into his office. Their relationship is still uneasy, and Runcorn reminds Monk of the elevated social status of the grieving family he is about to visit. Sir Basil Moidore has woken to find that his young widowed daughter, Octavia Haslett, has been stabbed. By the time Monk is led into her elegant bedroom in the Moidore mansion on Queen Anne Street, her body is already stiff with rigor mortis. The likely explanation for her unnatural death is that she had interrupted a burglar stealing her jewels.

The pressure begins to mount for the Moidores and their live-in retainers as it becomes clear that Octavia has been killed not by a burglar but by someone inside the house. Percival Garrod, the handsome footman, is implicated when the murder weapon is discovered during a second search of his room. Although Percival is not a nice character, Monk is against his arrest. The socially convenient answer that the murderer is a servant rather than a Moidore is just too easy.

This opinion causes conflict with Runcorn. Monk is ambitious, but prepared to test his grit and integrity by challenging the establishment. He is still exploring the self he does not know, and wants either to discover someone better than he expects or to redefine himself as someone new. Runcorn, on the other hand, although also ambitious, wants 'social acceptability, praise from his superiors, and above all safety'.

But there is no safe place for Monk, not even in the sanctuary of self. Everything must be questioned. No value, no idea, no convention can be trusted. This was a predicament Anne knew. Finding your true self and making peace after the act of murder was a process of rediscovery in the absence of trust.

Although Anne's writing was a creative and financial endeavour independent of her own background, she did draw heavily on conflicts she had observed and felt. Occasionally, her experiences overlap those of her characters. Percival is tried and found guilty of the murder of Octavia Moidore. He is sentenced to hang, and while he awaits execution Monk visits him in prison:

> Too many men who entered here left only to go to the executioner's rope, and the terror and despair of their last days had soaked into the walls till he could feel it skin-crawling like ice as he followed the warder along the stone corridors to the appointed place where he could see Percival for the last time ... At the moment when the trapdoor opened and the noose jerked tight, another crime was being committed.

Anne had heard the sounds of people being executed at Mt Eden prison; while she was there, five men were hanged.

Monk leaves Runcorn and the London Metropolitan Police Force on a point of honour over Percival's wrongful arrest and execution. Thanks to his scrupulous attitude he is now the private investigator that Anne anticipated he would be. Hester Latterly has also left her hospital position. In the case of a young boy close to death she defiantly follows a nursing practice tested in the Crimean War instead of the one stipulated by the hospital doctor. Although she is vindicated by the child's miraculous recovery, she is sacked for insubordination.

It is Hester who introduces Monk to Lady Callandra Daviot, a woman rich enough and liberal enough to want to help support his new career as a private detective. He is now free to investigate cases where 'the police do not realize there has been a crime', where the outcome is to clear someone's name or where the 'victim of injustice' is unable to pay.

Although Monk owes much to Hester's encouragement and contacts, she continues to be a thorn in his side. He finds her unfeminine, aggressive and pushy. 'I should imagine a good many patients have taken up their beds and walked, simply to be free of your ministrations and go where they could suffer in peace.' He is still taken with the gentle Imogen, but on reflection his sidekick colleague on the force, Evan, and Hester Latterly are 'the two people in the world he could trust absolutely'.

Hanging is an obvious subject in this novel, and there are forays into feminism and Victorian attitudes to rape, but behind these lies the elemental matter of the individual's battle to establish and maintain integrity in the face of institutionalized corruption and hypocrisy. Simply put, it is a tale of the cost of having principles, and of a bad man — Monk — taking charge of himself to become good.

Anne's next contracted Monk, *Defend and Betray*, finds its power in the portrayal of an awful human dilemma. Hester's meeting with an old friend, Edith Sorbell, begins a story that turns conventional murder upside down. Edith's brother, war hero General Thaddeus George Randolf Carlyon (who will clearly require an extra-large headstone to accommodate his name), has been found at the bottom of a staircase with the spear from a decorative suit of armour through his chest.

When the murder took place he was on the first-floor landing, hearing the clink of cutlery and crystal and the hum of dinner-party conversation. Initially it looks as though he has fallen over the banister, but what extraordinary bad luck that he should land on such an unsympathetic piece of the interior design. When the police investigate, they discover it is no accident. Everyone at the intimate family dinner comes under suspicion.

General Carlyon's murderer turns out to be his wife, Alexandra. She admits her guilt, but will offer no reason or provocation on which to build a defence. If anyone can defend Alexandra, it is Oliver Rathbone, the handsome barrister friend of Hester and Monk, but he feels desperate because her confession has 'robbed him of every possible weapon he might have used. The only thing still left to him was time.'

Monk is employed to help Rathbone unpick this tangle of family intrigue. The barrister — a serial character who vies with Monk for Hester — demonstrates his brilliance in dramatic court scenes where Alexandra seems already condemned to death. He explains to Hester and Monk why it will be so difficult: 'People do not like their heroes tarnished ... We have a tendency to see people as good or evil; it is so much easier both on the brain and on the emotions ... to place people into one or the other category. Black or white.'

If Alexandra is judged according to black and white absolutes she is guilty, but Monk exposes the diabolical behaviour of her husband and introduces the shades of grey. Alexandra was faced with an awful dilemma: she had to kill her husband to protect her son. But the fact that she has taken a life to save one makes little difference to the remorse she feels.

Don't you think I see his body on that floor every time I lie in the dark? I dream about it — I've redone that deed in my nightmares, and woken up cold as ice, with the sweat standing out on my skin. I'm terrified God will judge me and condemn my soul forever.

Edith's sister Damaris is another tormented soul, who unwittingly gives away her illegitimate baby son to a life of molestation and sodomy. When Hester realizes this, her advice has more of Anne in its message of hope: 'It was a mistake, a sin if you like — but we all sin one way or another. What matters is that you become kinder and wiser because of it, that you become gentler with others, and that you have never repeated it!' In his closing comments, Rathbone reminds the court that Alexandra and her son are victims of a legal system that makes them both chattels. Alexandra's only choice was 'to take the law into her own hands'.

In *Defend and Betray* Anne tackles one of society's greatest taboos — incest — with unflinching honesty. This candour led critics to feel that her writing had substantially more depth. But she also touches on what, for her, is difficult territory. For the first time in one of her novels she mentions New Zealand. As Damaris's husband, Peverell Erskine, takes a cucumber sandwich, he says to his mother-in-law:

'I met a most interesting man who fought in the Maori Wars ten years ago.' He looked at Hester. 'That is in New Zealand, you know? Yes, of course you do. They have the most marvelous birds there. Quite unique, and so beautiful … I love birds, Miss Latterly. Such a variety … right up to an albatross, which flies the oceans of the earth, with a wingspan twice the height of a man.'

⚁

Anne did all her writing in longhand. In Suffolk she used an electric typewriter to type out her finished manuscripts, and in Portmahomack a computer. Without back-up copies or a printer handy, the inevitable happened. 'Something dreadful happened to Anne's computer last night,' Meg wrote to Leona in September 1990, 'and retrieval of [A DANGEROUS MOURNING] from the disk would be difficult. Could you kindly put our minds at rest by confirming when the manuscript arrives — and have a copy made, just for safety's sake.'[40] Fortunately the manuscript reached Ballantine safely, but the scare left an indelible mark. As soon as she could afford to do so, Anne employed Elizabeth Sweeney, a parishioner from the Mormon Church at Invergordon, to type up her handwritten manuscripts. Anne's choice of pen was something of a ritual. She liked a fluid-writing refill pen that would travel swiftly and effortlessly over the paper. But no matter how good the pen, her writing was close to illegible. Don Maass remembers the effort that he and his wife went to each year trying to decipher the few lines of Anne's Christmas card. They spent most of the Christmas period working it out, word by word, like a cryptic puzzle.

Anne's new secretary was made of sterner stuff. There were amusing slip-ups, like the time she had a 'band' rather than a 'bard' playing in the corner of one of Anne's medieval banquet halls, but on the whole she got it right. Maybe she was more acquainted than most with shorthand, which Anne had learnt while in prison. Her handwriting was a hybrid of letters and squiggles that would have well qualified her to be a medical practitioner.

Leona responded to the arrival of the *Dangerous Mourning* script with some direct instructions about where Ballantine now wanted the amnesia storyline to go. 'As I said when we met, I think you should make some more revelations about Monk's past in *Dangerous Mourning*, then finish his self-discovery in Monk III.'[41] They were worried about the device wearing thin with readers, and critics especially, and were anxious for Monk to be a little less dark and angst-ridden.

The amnesia story inevitably involved repetition, which might frustrate regular readers. That was one of the challenges of writing a series. You could never assume your reader had read the preceding book, or any in the series. So each novel had to give newcomers enough information to be getting on with, but not in a way that interrupted the narrative flow or frustrated loyal fans.

Leona was delighted with the third Monk. 'DEFEND AND BETRAY is another wonderful novel,' she wrote to Anne in September 1991.

> Every book you write shows an advance in your development as a serious novelist ... though I was a little bothered at first that Monk comes into the novel so late (page 90; I think), perhaps that is right. It turns out to be more Hester's case than Monk's. And as I told you, I was more attracted to Rathbone than Monk in this book and a little disappointed that Hester seems to be leaning toward Monk — but please don't take this to mean that you should change things![42]

Critical responses to A Dangerous Mourning and Defend and Betray were almost universally positive. The New York Times review of A Dangerous Mourning suggested that Anne's fondness for Victorian melodrama tended to slacken both the suspense and the pace, but thought Monk's amnesia a wonderful device 'rarely employed in detective fiction', and observed that social issues rather than period details were important to Anne because 'the sights, sounds and smells of London in the mid-1880s are second nature to her'. The reviewer also conceded, a little reluctantly, that Hester's actions in the story were a rare gesture of equal opportunity in a male-dominated genre: 'It is fitting that Hester Latterly should succeed where Inspector Monk fails. She is the real hero of the story, making the brilliant male detective seem a bit of a plodder.'[43]

The News, also reviewing A Dangerous Mourning, acknowledged the new and chillingly dark tone in Anne's writing:

> Although the solution to the mystery is logical and satisfactory, it is anything but standard. The far-reaching effects of the crime touch both the guilty and innocent alike, leaving a dark legacy that will change

their lives forever. It will also stay with the reader long after the book is finished.[44]

Although not so convinced by the ending of *Defend and Betray*, which was described as 'a plot device badly overused in current crime fiction', the reviewer for *Publishers Weekly* commended the way 'Perry leads readers gradually through a case involving Carlyon's traumatized son and vengeful daughter, revealing social and moral nuances in the grand tradition of the Victorian novel'.[45]

Anne's Pitt series was also receiving acclaim and commercial success. *Highgate Rise*, the first Pitt published in hardcover and softcover by Ballantine, was released in 1991, and the even more successful *Belgrave Square* in 1992. In *Highgate Rise* the *Publishers Weekly* detected an 'added psychological acuity' to Anne's usually 'well-drawn contrasts of upstairs and downstairs', but, while this novel is a relatively standard case of domestic arson that ends the life of a doctor's wife, *Belgrave Square* is anything but typical. The characters are more desperate and the plot more shadowed by espionage than in any previous Pitt.

'Here is the typescript of [BELGRAVE SQUARE],' Meg wrote when she sent it to Don in February 1991. 'I hope you like this as much as I do. It's a strong book, and shows more confidence than I've ever seen in Anne.'[46] Leona was delighted when it arrived on her desk. When she responded to Anne in July she said: 'Here, at last are my queries on the manuscript of BELGRAVE SQUARE. As you will see they are all about small points. It is a terrific novel and not at all in need of any structural work.'[47]

Belgrave Square begins immediately after the Jack the Ripper killings. London, England and probably the world will never be the same again. In the wake of the Whitechapel terror, Pitt works to find his own killer.

William Weems is discovered in his office with half his head blown off by a blunderbuss full of gold coins from his own coffers. He is a usurer and a petty blackmailer, and it is tempting for Pitt to see this as a fitting end to a despicable life. As one insightful character puts it: 'I think usury, whether local in one man to another, or international in one nation to another, is one of the vilest practices of humanity.' However, Pitt knows it is not his place to judge Weems, and, besides, he and Drummond have been called in to help Lord Sholto Byam, who has a strange link to the dead Weems.

Lord Byam informs Drummond and Pitt that Weems was blackmailing him over a personal tragedy that is now 20 years old. While he had been staying in the country home of his best friend, Lord Frederick Anstiss, Byam had a flirtation with Anstiss's wife Laura that had ended in her throwing herself off the balcony of her bedroom. At the time Lord Anstiss gave the impression that it was an accident, but the generally held belief was that the beautiful Laura had killed herself because Lord Byam refused to take their flirtation further. The latter neglects to explain that Weems has an incriminating letter that could bring down both the Byam and Anstiss dynasties. The reader is kept on tenterhooks until the book's grisly end.

The life of the Pitt family is woven through the story. Charlotte keeps leaving her children, now five and seven, in the care of their young maid Gracie to investigate with Emily, whose fashionable husband Jack is now standing for Parliament. And there are touches in *Belgrave Square* that come directly from Anne's life. The cream and pink Chinese carpet at Lord Byam's home is remarkably similar to the one on her floor at Portmahomack; the rhododendrons might have come straight from the grounds of the Ilam homestead where she lived in Christchurch; there are references to Shakespeare's *Titus Andronicus*, which she admires, and to the Gilbert and Sullivan operas *Ruddigore*, *Princess Ida* and the *Pirates of Penzance*, which she and her father adored. But it is Pansy the cat that gets the cream.

During a discussion about the Victorian fad for wearing decorative stuffed animals in hats and on dresses — 'Don't you remember — it was all the rage a couple of years ago' — young Fanny Hilliard describes what happened when Pansy the mouser saw the stuffed mouse stitched to Aunt Dorabella's gown when she was singing at a soirée.

She swept across the space we had cleared for her, swirling her skirts behind her, raising her hands to illustrate the song — and Pansy, the cat, shot out from under the drapes 'round the piano legs and bolted up Dorabella's skirt after the mouse. Dorabella hit a high note very much higher than she had intended ... Pansy took fright and ran down again ... with the mouse between her teeth, and a sizable piece of the skirt with it.

There were further signs of Anne's rise in popularity. An excited Leona told Meg 'the good news about the book club auction for BELGRAVE SQUARE ($36,000 to the Book-of-the-Month Club) ... That's good news about the film option on THE FACE OF A STRANGER. I don't know that a television film will do much for sales here but it is very nice for Anne.'[48]

Even before it had gone to print, *Belgrave Square* was making them money. The response when it was published, in April 1992, was astonishing. With a letter to Anne, Leona sent 'a wonderful review of BELGRAVE SQUARE in today's *New York Times*. They don't review many mysteries in the daily *Times* so this is impressive indeed. Congratulations.'[49] One comment read: 'The author has the eyes of a hawk for character and nuance and her claws out for the signs of ... criminal injustice.'[50]

Critics and readers alike were detecting a change in Anne's writing, not just for the Monk series, but for the Pitts as well. Certainly the stability of the Ballantine contracts, and their generous terms, contributed to this, as did the pleasure of living in Portmahomack and watching the renovation of the old barn. But there was something more. Behind the new books was a fresh approach. Don and Meg had begun to work with Anne in a more concerted fashion, to tighten the plots, deepen the characters and give them a more political edge. The addition of Don to the team had been something of a turning point, because he was good at plot development. Now, before she began writing a book, Anne's outlines were rigorously discussed, and sometimes rewritten at the trans-Atlantic summit meetings they began to hold annually in January or whenever else the opportunity presented itself. Don liked the idea of introducing intrigue and espionage, while Meg worked on maintaining accuracy and authenticity and making the evolution of the series characters convincing.

'Thanks for the good news regarding the sale of *Belgrave Square* to the BOMC [Book-of-the-Month Club],' Don wrote to Leona at the beginning of 1992. 'Nicely done! Anne's career certainly seems to be on a sharp upward curve. The news reminds me that Kim Hovey of your publicity department has been collecting letters from book stores interested in having Anne sign.'[51]

Don was hoping that a tour could be organized to coincide with the release of *Belgrave Square* in April. As Meg told him, the trip was scheduled from 22 April through to 3 May, and included 'Boston, Minneapolis, and New York, as well as a couple of other cities. Anne says she had a good talk with Kim Hovey, who sounded surprised at the keen reaction she got from the bookshops, but the penny seems to have dropped.'[52]

Anne's spring tour was followed by another whirlwind visit in October with *Defend and Betray*. She visited 17 cities in 23 days, beginning in Toronto, then flying across the United States to the west coast and back again, taking in places such as Seattle, Salt Lake City, Phoenix, Los Angeles, Detroit, Chicago and Houston, and finishing in New York. 'Sunday with your friend, Sunday night, Nov 1, flight back home' finished the itinerary note sent to Anne.[53] The trip was exhausting, but a highlight after months of solid writing. Kim Hovey accompanied Anne to the New York venues, and for other legs of the tour Anne was met and taken to appointments.

One of the important people Anne met between programmed signings was film, television and book agent Ken Sherman. Meg was making progress towards selling the television rights, not only to the Pitt series, but also to *The Face of a Stranger*. To improve her chances of success, especially in the United States, she decided to get an agent to represent Anne in Hollywood. Ken faxed Meg and Diana Tyler at the MBA office:

Just a quick note to let you know it was a treat to meet Anne when she was briefly in LA on her book tour last weekend. We talked a lot and I hope established a good relationship for the future. She's a wonderfully intense and intelligent lady and one can see after meeting her why her books are so successful.[54]

Anne was delighted with the congenial, creative Ken, and at the prospect of her stories being communicated through film.

Linking in with Ken was just one of a number of strategies Meg was employing to help make this happen. She had just gone through an extended period of sending Anne's books and manuscripts to studios and production companies to establish interest. 'Thou With Clean Hands' and Anne's two fantasy novels had gone to Ileen Maisel at Paramount. Ileen's response was positive, but noncommittal. Meg wrote back: 'Anne is delighted at your liking her work, and is forming some ideas about making her books more filmic. She'd be happy to discuss this with you, either by phone — or, her invitation to stay still stands.'[55]

Anne made a concerted effort to become more 'filmic' in her writing, but after Paramount considered the manuscripts, nothing more happened. Meg sent Pitt books and *The Face of a Stranger* to Twentieth Century Fox, Pinewood Studios, and Yorkshire Television, among others. Many of the replies that came back mirrored that of Sarah Horne at Pinewood Studios. 'I thought it an extraordinarily well crafted novel with fascinating characters and an intriguing story ... My concern is that expensive period pieces are very difficult to get off the ground in the current climate.'[56]

The film and television endeavour that looked most promising was the project with Lynda La Plante, whose first episode of *Prime Suspect* was released on British television in 1991 to considerable acclaim. A script for the pilot Pitt episode arrived with Meg at MBA, accompanied by a note from Lynda: 'Please forward on the script to Anne. I am so nervous. I hope she approves — it is only a 1st draft so any changes she wishes to make can be made.'[57] When Anne felt that the script was not close enough in detail or substance to the original books, it was decided that Lynda would work on a second draft with Anne's input, while she and Hilary Heath continued to look for series backers and renewed their option contract on the books.

⚘

At the beginning of 1992 Anne sent Meg her latest manuscript to read, which Meg then forwarded to Don. 'Herewith FARRIERS' LANE by Anne

Perry, the latest in the "Pitt" series. I have some thoughts on this, but on the whole I feel it's extremely good. Anne has developed some fancy plotting since talking to you about it.'[58] After the recommended changes were made, the manuscript was sent to Leona, who was planning a visit to London in the first two weeks of March. Anne was travelling down from Scotland to meet her in London, and Leona wanted to know if Meg would like to join them for dinner, adding: 'I've just read FARRIERS' LANE. It's terrific. I've called Anne and told her how much I liked it.'[59]

Farriers' Lane has a more layered and complex plot than Anne's previous Pitts. There is the nightmare for Charlotte and Emily of their 53-year-old widowed mother, Caroline, chasing a promising young Jewish actor 17 years her junior; the murder of Judge Samuel Stafford and hanging five years earlier of Aaron Godman, also a Jew; and the theme of anti-Semitism and racism running through the book. The story opens with Charlotte and Thomas at the theatre with Caroline, watching a West End production in which Caroline's new beau, Joshua Fielding, is playing the lead.

The drama on stage, however, is nothing compared with the drama in the theatre box nearby. Judge Stafford, who has been staring blindly in front of him, slumps to the floor; his only response to his wife loosening his collar is the 'spasmodic jerking of his limbs'. He has been poisoned with opium.

It seems that the judge was about to reopen the case that had ended in the execution of Aaron Godman for crucifying his friend Kingsley Blaine on a stable door in Farriers' Lane. Godman's sister, actress Tamar Macaulay, vehemently protested her brother's innocence and the case was appealed, but without success. The grounds for Godman's conviction were that Blaine was a married man having an affair with Tamar: Godman was punishing him for cheating on his wife and for fooling Tamar into believing he would marry her. The fact that Godman is a Jew and Blaine was crucified fuels the continuing public condemnation. Has the justice system made a terrible mistake? To what lengths will it go to keep an error hidden?

Anti-Semitism, the legal system, the history of pharmacology and the sale of opium in England are all scrutinized in the novel, but the most personal writing is contained in a visit to Vespasia and the story of Caroline. Vespasia's dog is Anne's Daisy, who, after living with Meg MacDonald across the lane, decided to move in. Anne adored her. She was so clever that when Anne forgot her bath towel Daisy would get it, without instruction. A fictional Daisy sits on Vespasia's floor when Charlotte visits:

> A close-haired black-and-white dog lay on the floor in a patch of sun. She appeared to be something like a lurcher, a cross between whippet and general collie, with perhaps a touch of spaniel in the face. She was highly intelligent, but lean, built for running, and irregularly marked.

Vespasia reacquaints herself with an old flame, Thelonius Quade, a much younger man who fell in love with her some 20 years before when she was married. 'He was one of the few men who was more than her intellectual equal ... If only they had met when — but she never indulged in fruitless regret', and nor did Anne, but this was very much the story of her romantic life with men. Anne had had a relationship in England before she left to live in the United States, several while she was there and one after she returned home. 'In each case I really hoped and prayed that it would go somewhere — and I'm even more grateful that it didn't. It was probably romance and hormonal, up to about 40 [years old] ... Did I have affairs? Yes, I did. Did I sleep with them? You bet I bloody did. Did it go anywhere? No.'[60]

Often the men who most attracted Anne were unavailable because they were married. Nonetheless there were red-hot affairs and infatuations, and one ended soon after she told him about the murder. It was always a quandary whether to tell partners. Her past played on her mind and placed a strain on her relationships, but was there any hope unless she was honest from the beginning? Like Vespasia, she tried not to entertain regrets, but they were there in her lack of physical intimacy and the loneliness she sometimes felt.

Caroline is exactly Anne's age and doing what she would have liked to do herself. She is finding a husband and a soul mate long after other people thought it possible. Her children are mortified by the conduct of their wayward mother. Pitt remonstrates with his wife:

'Charlotte, there's not time for self-indulgence! People don't stop falling in love because they are fifty — or sixty — or any other age! ... Why shouldn't your mother fall in love? When you are fifty Jemima will think you as old and fixed as the framework of the world, because that is what you are to her — the framework of all she knows and that gives her safety and identity. But you will be the same woman inside as you are now, and just as capable of passions.'

Anne has experienced this situation from both positions. The child of a broken marriage whose framework of safety and identity seemed to have disintegrated overnight, she understands and communicates Charlotte's turmoil with conviction. '[Caroline] was Charlotte's mother! The very thought of it made Charlotte feel upset and curiously lonely.' But Anne also knows what it is to live in isolation, like Caroline, who sits at the dinner table with her horrible mother-in-law. 'It was now set merely for the two of them, and they were marooned at either end of it, staring down the long oaken expanse at one another.'

Farriers' Lane came out in spring, and *A Sudden, Fearful Death* in the fall of 1993. Both books were well received, especially by *Publishers Weekly*, which described *A Sudden, Fearful Death* as 'this surpassingly excellent historical and psychologically intricate mystery' in which Anne made 'deft use of history to cast additional light on modern-day issues'. The concerns poignantly communicated in this fourth Monk are the problems of being a woman in Victorian society, which also have an uncomfortable contemporary resonance.

Aspects of women's sexuality bind the plot of *A Sudden, Fearful Death*. There is rape and incest, and their tragic consequences — unwanted pregnancies adding to the astronomical infant mortality rates or abortions that maim or kill both mother and foetus. All this is considered in relation to the sad story of Prudence Barrymore, a woman whose deepest wish is to go to medical school and become a doctor — an ambition that proves 'as astonishing as the pearl in the head of the toad'.[61] She has nursed with Florence Nightingale and Hester on the battlefields of the Crimean War and wants to bring about reforms, but all this is cut short when her strangled body tumbles out of a laundry-chute, along with the linen, in the Royal Free Hospital, where she had been working. Monk is called in by his benefactress, Lady Callandra Daviot, who is a member of the hospital's board of governors. Hester wishes to avenge her friend's death; Callandra wants to protect married surgeon Dr Kristian Beck, whom she secretly loves and who is a suspect in the case. It is a sad story of frustration and self-loathing brought about by endemic discrimination: 'She used to be so angry she was a woman. She wished she could have been a man so she could do all these things,' Prudence's sister Faith explains to Hester. At times it seems only Hester is capable of imagining something as irrational as a woman doctor. Even the admirable Oliver Rathbone cannot comprehend it.

'But medical school? A woman! Can she really have imagined it was possible?'
'Why not?' Hester said furiously.

But the underlying message of A Sudden, Fearful Death is not one of despair. Prudence Barrymore never wasted time on pointless regrets, and nor does Monk as the memory of his ugly past continues to reconstruct itself in his mind. As he advises his client, Julia Penrose, 'we all try to forget what hurts us. It is sometimes the only way we can continue … You have a fearful situation to deal with. Don't look back — look forward, only forward.'

⊗

In October 1992 Don Maass finalized a US$1 million contract with Ballantine 'for 3 each of the "Pitt" and "Monk" series, plus one fantasy novel and one historical novel. This will take Anne up to the end of the decade (Millennium!). It's very nice to have this level of commitment from the publisher,' Meg wrote to Ken Sherman.[62] It was a gratifying result after months of negotiations. The bargaining between Don and Leona had got so intense that Leona ended up calling him a 'jerk' behind his back, which secretly thrilled Meg because she knew that meant Don had taken Leona to the wire. The new million-dollar contract prompted a heightened level of engagement from Ballantine.

Anne toured the United States twice in 1993. '**WELCOME HOME, STAR!!**' Meg Davis's letter began after her April trip. 'It'll be lovely to speak to you on this side of the water again — but not till you've caught up on your sleep! You've certainly earned it, after all that hard work.'[63] The September–October tour was equally successful. 'Anne rang me yesterday and says the tour is going very well indeed ... I've just come back from my brother's Buddhist wedding in Toronto, which certainly woke up the dustier members of the family. And so into the maelstrom of Frankfurt [Book Fair]', Meg wrote to Leona.[64] Ballantine's decision to develop Anne's reputation meant her name was becoming increasingly well established. They invested in publicity so that the queues at book signings got longer and longer.

The dynamic Kim Hovey — who after numerous tours had become a personal friend as well as Anne's publicist — went with Anne to the New York bookstores. She remembers a very elderly woman in 'the village' (Greenwich) who would greet Anne each time with a bunch of flowers and sit in exactly the same chair, then have her books signed at the end of the session. When, suddenly, she did not appear, they guessed that she had died or become too frail to come. Kim remembers people saying often at Anne's talks: 'your book got me through a difficult time when my mother died' or 'it was your books that kept me going when my son was ill'.[65]

While Anne was in Los Angeles she met Ken Sherman to talk about the recently concluded Lynda La Plante deal and the option terms the BBC were trying to negotiate. 'Anne was very pleased to see you last month, by the way,' Meg wrote to Ken in November 1993.

The tour was highly successful, she was absolutely lionized and a lot of copies were sold. She and I go to Paris for a couple of days next week to research her espionage novel about the French Revolution. (I'm going as interpreter, although having been brought up in Montréal; my French puts me on a par with Algerian riff-raff in Parisian eyes.)[66]

Anne's biggest foreign-language market after Germany was France. She was published there by Dix/Dix-huit (10/18) and was a close friend of its commissioning editor, the flamboyant but scrupulous Emmanuelle Heurtebise. It made sense to publish a book set in France, and this was the long-overdue tightening of 'Thou With Clean Hands'.

After returning from Paris, Meg told Don that she had become something of a 'bore on the subject of the Revolution'. She had a sneaking suspicion that Anne's book on the subject, now being rewritten, was 'deviating from the plot as hammered out among the three of us'. Nonetheless she was optimistic, because Anne expected to take longer over editing the book than she did with her detective novels. To Meg's chagrin, Anne 'seemed to waste a lot of time in Paris', particularly in fabric stores and knitting shops. Her eyes lit up when she saw one, and it was impossible to drag her past.

She skipped over all the interesting relics from everyday life in the museum — like masses of really crappy dinner plates with Revolutionary motifs, which everyone must have bought fast in order to be Politically Correct. Neither would she actually stroll through the section where all the Revolutionaries lived, much of which (unlike the rest of the city) is still intact ... We only spent 5 minutes in Notre Dame! ... sometimes she's still a mystery to me.[67]

Meg was reading *Traitor's Gate*, Anne's next Pitt. 'It's well up to standard, and has some great background on how Europe was carving up Africa at the time.'[68] This topped off a good year and an astonishing period of success since the publication of *The Face of a Stranger*. Anne had begun to make bestseller lists all over the world. In New York she had been guest of honour at the annual Malice Domestic Convention and had been presented with the Romantic Times Career Achievement Award.

Her million-dollar contract with Ballantine was followed by a six-book deal in England with Headline. Meg had negotiated, or was negotiating, contracts for the translation of *The Face of a Stranger* into Japanese, Italian, German, Greek, Spanish, Portuguese, Czechoslovakian, Russian, Dutch and Polish, and sales for some of Anne's titles were now in the hundreds of thousands.

As well as this, she had a new principal British publisher, HarperCollins. To begin the relationship, Meg and Anne met managing editor Nick Sayers and other HarperCollins staff in June. 'We've had a tip-off that the whole of New Zealand seems to be celebrating their anniversary of women's suffrage. As this is the main burden of BETHLEHEM ROAD, you may wish to give an extra push to your exports there,' Meg wrote to Nick in July.[69] By August they had reached an agreement over *Farriers' Lane* and Anne's next title, and in December Meg sent Nick the contracts. Her plan was that they meet him and editor Imogen Taylor, who was a keen advocate for Anne's titles, in the New Year. 'Anne and I are very pleased you've taken her on, and look forward to a splendid Future together.'[70]

II

The tip-off from Meg Davis to Nick Sayers probably came from Anne. She knew New Zealand was inordinately proud of its suffrage history, being the first country in the world to give women the vote. It was in New Zealand as the young Juliet that she received her first formal schooling after 14 months of barefoot truancy in the Bahamas and the Bay of Islands. It is doubtful that this was intended when Hilda and Henry bade their eight-year-old daughter a tearful goodbye at the airport in 1946.

Juliet travelled alone to Nassau, on New Providence Island in the Bahamas, to stay with expatriate friends, the Browne family. It was a long, frightening flight with multiple stopovers, and it ended with an emergency landing after two of the engines failed. Although the light, hot, tropical paradise of the Bahamas offered emancipation from the leaden deprivations of post-war London, her time there also meant disorientation and disturbance for Juliet.

Life in the Bahamas was completely alien, and Juliet felt abandoned. She felt she had been exiled, sent thousands of kilometres away from the people to whom she was most closely connected. There was no end to it either. No quick trip home for the holidays. Not even an easy telephone call. She was completely separated from all that she knew.

The addition to the Browne family of a sickly English girl, still fragile from a life of ration books and air-raid shelters, created its own tensions. Most of the time she was boating and playing with the two boys, but she could be cocky and determined, and her mere presence made things stressful between the parents. For Mr Browne she could do no wrong, 'because I was the little girl he didn't have', and nothing right for his wife, who instinctively disliked her and the effect she had on the family.[71]

William was younger and Julian older than Juliet. 'The younger one I got along with well, and the older one hated my guts and beat the crap out of me.'[72] Mrs Browne's favourite was Julian, who was barely tolerated at times by his father, a harsh disciplinarian who preferred William and now Juliet. The situation was volatile but not especially unhappy. When Anne shuts her eyes and thinks of a perfect place, it is the shimmering white sand, aquamarine seas and brilliant skies of the Bahamas that she sees.

After eight months, Juliet — a little taller and stronger, with thick, wavy blondish hair — travelled with the Brownes to New Zealand's Bay of Islands, where she stayed for a further seven months on their private island. It was 'real Swiss Family Robinson stuff', a wild, outdoor existence, free from the routine but also the reassurance of school and family life.[73] Juliet longed to see her parents again, so when she heard that her father had been made rector of Canterbury University College in Christchurch, she was ecstatic.

CHAPTER FOUR

I

The restoration of Anne's stone barn was well under way at the beginning of 1994, although the project would take nearly six years in all to complete. She had chosen an Italianate theme that inspired a large feature fountain in a paved central courtyard, and warm Tuscan shades of yellow, pink, green and blue throughout the house. The dramatic exceptions, showing a Georgian influence, were a rich dark-red dining room, a strong green sitting room, and a vivid yellow drawing room. The grand entrance hall was light-filled and spacious, with double-height ceilings and two glorious chandeliers suspended over an expansive travertine marble floor. The outlook from the entrance hall was onto the courtyard, and a glass conservatory full of exotic plants. Off the hall on the lower floor were the drawing and sitting rooms, a guest room, the dining room, a large country kitchen, an office and a panelled library stocked from floor to ceiling with books.

Two small staircases in the entrance hall led upstairs to a vast master bedroom, with adjoining writing room — an intimate space with a section of antique carved wooden panels. On the level above that was a suite of offices for her typist, and storage cupboards for books and manuscripts. The views from Anne's writing room were inspirational. She could lean back in her chair and see on one side the solitary magnificence of the Moray Firth and on the other Dornoch Firth, and, above, the wide ever-changing skies of northern Scotland.

When project manager Simon MacDonald and his contractors had started removing the old piggery, they found, underneath the jungle of brambles and nettles, that the land was polluted with refuse and asbestos. The site had been a dumping ground for agricultural waste, discarded concrete, engine bits, old baths, oil drums and rotting tyres. Nonetheless they cleared the land around the ruined barn to construct the house and courtyard, and laid out an extensive area of garden, with rose and flower beds edging a large lawn connected to a labyrinth of interlocking bowers, surrounding brick-paved areas and secluded seats. Anne loved roses, and during the long summer days trellised bowers hung heavy with myriad blooms. The renovation was manorial in scale. Having bought the property for £26,000, she invested an 'estimated £500,000' to realize her vision.[1] To help establish and maintain it, she needed staff. So Alex, the husband of her typist Elizabeth Sweeney, became her gardener, she employed a housekeeper, and Simon was her driver and property manager.

Meg MacDonald still lived in Anne's cottage across the lane, and helped to look after the property when Anne went on book tours. In true animal fashion, Meg's and Anne's cats and dogs often seemed to live between the two houses, taking advantage of the best on offer at each place. In her breaks from writing, Anne would often accompany Meg on walks with the dogs. The field adjoining Anne's property was a large area of uncultivated set-aside land that had been left in clover. Set-aside land was an initiative introduced in 1988 by the European Union to reduce cultivated acreage, and with it the agricultural surpluses known colloquially as 'the grain mountain'. While it was unfarmed, 'the skylarks had come back, and there were owls, and the deer had come into the field … hawks were in, buzzards, there was all sorts of things that were coming into the field'.[2] Meg was upset when she learned that the set-aside period had come to an end and the farmer could plough the land again. The fate of the skylarks particularly concerned her, because they were an endangered species.

Once she found out what was happening, Anne promptly went down to the bank, found that she had enough money to buy the field, and did so. She accelerated the regeneration and restocking that had already begun, by planting trees and digging and channelling a natural spring water supply. Ultimately, she had the land put in trust as a wilderness area for public use in perpetuity.

In spite of the people she employed for building, landscaping and planting, Anne was a relatively inconspicuous figure in the village. She often attended market days and village festivals, but as an observer on the edge, standing back. She was generous, contributing surreptitiously to charities and deserving cases by quietly seeking out those involved and making a donation. She had her local friends and associates, but she was a discreet, almost shadowy figure in Portmahomack.[3]

The only time people got an inkling that this tall, middle-aged, auburn-haired woman in her sensible classic clothes was a bestselling author was when she helped the local primary school football team get a new strip of land to play on. 'She went to the trouble of contacting her publishers in the USA who sent 100 books. Anne did a signing session in the local Oystercatcher café and helped raise £300.'[4]

When Meg Davis received a letter inquiring about Anne's life from a 15-year-old honours student writing a paper on a contemporary author for his English class at Canton High School in Connecticut, she answered him by describing the Tarbat Ness Peninsula, the sea views, the house and its lovely setting on the outskirts of Portmahomack.

> Often it's so beautiful she phones me to describe the scene to me in my office in the city. She has three dogs and two cats, and always has neighbours dropping in. This is probably just as well, since she works terribly hard. For relaxation she watches television, listens to opera, and knits sweaters of her own design.[5]

⚘

Life for Meg in the tough London book trade was less idyllic. She and Anne had their meeting with Nick Sayers and Imogen Taylor from HarperCollins at the beginning of the year, and things went well. 'It was nice to see you again last week, and I thought Anne a terrific and unusual lady,' Imogen wrote afterwards.[6] Meg's real worry was the 'Tathyr' manuscript, which they had sent to Ballantine and had heard nothing back on. 'I phoned Leona regarding TATHYR,' Don wrote to Meg on 31 January 1994.

She has no definite plans for the novel yet (pub. date, imprint, etc.) as she has not sat down and read the whole thing right through. She will now do that ... I do think we should be grateful for any prayers anyone sends heavenward for the success of the book. In fact, I expect I'll say a few myself.[7]

Leona's response to 'Tathyr' arrived in March, and she seemed to dislike it intensely. The reader's report from Deborah Hogan, which she included with her covering note, made equally gloomy reading. Leona had inordinate difficulties pronouncing the title, which came out of her mouth awkwardly hyphenated. 'She insisted on calling her "Tat-teer" as if it were some childhood obscenity. She really did make it sound like "pee-pee",' recalls Meg.[8] It appeared from Leona's response and the reader's report that the novel would never sell to Ballantine. A big part of the problem was that it did not fit the conventional form of the fantasy novel.

As Deborah Hogan outlined it, fantasy writing generally depicted a world to which readers wanted to escape. There were strong main characters, 'maybe a reluctant hero, or a person larger than life or with a tragic flaw', but whichever it was, it was someone readers identified with and wanted to be. The essential ingredient was *magic*; and the supernatural elements and the plot, which should build to a nail-biting climax, must be believable.

Anne's 'Tathyr' seemed to belong to an older tradition of eighteenth-century books like Samuel Johnson's *Rasselas* — a spiritual odyssey, a 'journey of the soul's search for truth'. It was beautifully written, with some rich insights and poignant introspection, but it felt contrived and distanced from reality, and the main character, Tathyr, felt artificial and too perfect to be real. It was more like a piece of theology than a spellbinding journey into the imagination. 'Tathyr' must be more convincing. Anne needed to 'make the people feel real, with flaws and strengths — and maybe not kill so many off haphazardly for convenience. It makes them seem even more unreal to be so expendable. There should be more action, more danger, more passion, more moving towards an actual goal ... more tangible magic.'[9]

This was almost the response Meg expected, although not one she wanted to hear. It was disappointing after all the effort they had put into the manuscript, and she worried that Anne might be bitterly disappointed at having to tackle a fairly comprehensive rewrite. Anne, however, remained philosophical. She was not an enthusiastic letter-writer and normally rang the office, so when a card arrived for Meg it made an impression. 'Just a card to say how much I appreciate your time, your friendship & your brains! Thank you!'[10]

Meg was still waiting for the new, improved Lynda La Plante script to arrive. 'Hope Lynda La Plante's writing talent lives up to her reputation,' wrote Ken to Meg in April. 'Ex-President Nixon is being buried today which is good.'[11] Negotiations continued over options on Anne's books with the BBC, playwright Robert Sugarman was eager to produce a stage adaptation of *Farriers' Lane*, and an independent film producer wanted to use Anne in a number of roles, including as presenter for a CD-ROM project on *Macbeth*. Meg agreed to an initial screen test. The other project he suggested, as Meg told Don Maass, was an interactive CD-ROM series entitled:

> *In the Steps of Anne Perry: Anne Perry's London* ... using her detective novels ... If Anne likes him, & he seems on the level, I'd like to pass him over to you ... (Anne Perry's London tickles the hell out of me. Yes, she was born in Blackheath, but it's in danger of being *In the Steps of Anne Perry: Great Wool & Fabric Shops of Our Time*.)[12]

The popularity of Anne's books continued to soar. 'I'm faxing herewith a page from yesterday's *USA Today*, which has FARRIERS' LANE at No. 32 in the top 50 of all books throughout the States,' wrote Meg to Imogen Taylor in February.[13] In March the reviews for Anne's latest Pitt novel, *The Hyde Park Headsman*, began to come through. The slightly bizarre premise for the book — that a serial killer had begun a rampage of apparently random beheadings in Hyde Park — did not seem to dampen the ardour of critics, who were carried along by her convincing portrayals of character and brilliant evocation of place. The *San Diego Union Tribune* was full of praise. 'Anne Perry is not the only mystery writer to choose Victorian England for her canvas; she is simply the best. This well-researched and cleverly plotted thriller should convince any remaining doubters.'[14] The *Toronto Sun* wrote:

> This could be an unimposing little yarn in the hands of many writers, but Perry's immense talents make *The Hyde Park Headsman* one of the best mysteries of the season and confirms her as the finest writer of historical mysteries around today. Fans who remember Perry's early works will find *The Hyde Park Headsman* extremely entertaining reading.[15]

The novel opens with two young lovers discovering Captain Oakley Winthrop's decapitated body in a pleasure boat on the Serpentine in Hyde Park. As more headless corpses are found and the case drags on, there is a public outcry, and fear and consternation reverberate through the halls of power and authority — the House of Commons, the Home Secretary, even 'Her Majesty has expressed her concern'. The person heading the inquiry is the newly promoted Superintendent Thomas Pitt.

On the strength of his elevated status, Pitt has had a new business card printed and bought a substantially bigger home in Bloomsbury, which Charlotte is renovating. She and Emily are still watching with disapproval as their mother misbehaves with her young man. 'It's — it's worse than romantic — it's lush. Yes, that's the word, lush,' exclaims Emily. Anne offers some interesting commentary on the romantic life of a middle-aged woman. Emily thinks her mother is mad, and is risking social condemnation and ostracism. Charlotte, on the other hand, is becoming reconciled. 'I think I would rather have a brief time of real happiness, and take the chance, than an age of gray respectability.' Charlotte's renovations also have a particular resonance for Anne.

> Every day it seemed to be some new disaster had been discovered or some major decision must be made. The builder wore a permanent expression of anxiety and shook his head in doubt, biting his lip, before she had even finished framing her questions to him.

The one thing analogous to Anne's experience that almost no one would have guessed when reading *The Hyde Park Headsman* was the method of murder. There was no blood in the boat and no apparent signs of struggle; Oakley Winthrop's head had been severed with one blow. How could this happen? It is Pitt who comes up with a possible solution: could it be that the victim and his murderer were in the pleasure boat together? Perhaps the murderer dropped something into the water, pointed it out to Winthrop and waited for him to lean over the side of the boat to investigate. It is Charlotte who explains the finer details to Emily: 'Well it's not very difficult to hit someone on the head, if they trust you and are not expecting anything of the sort.' *The Hyde Park Headsman* was dedicated to 'Leona Nevler, with thanks'.

Anne toured with *The Hyde Park Headsman* in the spring of 1994. As the local paper in Birmingham, Alabama, reported on 27 March, she was 'on a grueling, month-long tour of the United States that has taken her from coast to coast and in between. After her last stop in Atlanta on Monday, Perry will have been in 21 cities in 25 days promoting her latest book.'[16] The article went on to explain that she toured at least two months every year, and in between wrote a minimum of two books in longhand on a fine-line legal pad with a card file index for her notes. A positive *USA Today* review of *The Hyde Park Headsman* echoed many others: 'Corpses pile up, secrets are uncovered, scandals averted or met head-on — it's all very satisfying, a lovely way to spend a rainy spring weekend.'[17]

Oakley Winthrop's demise in *The Hyde Park Headsman* has eerie similarities to the murder of Honorah Parker, but almost no one would have been any the wiser had it not been for a new wave of publicity generated by the launch of *Heavenly Creatures*, the 1994 Peter Jackson film based on the Parker–Hulme murder case. Jackson's choice of subject was understandable. The case, a sobering, seminal event in New Zealand's criminal history, led to instant and ongoing international interest and media coverage. Jackson's previous sci-fi splatter movies — *Bad Taste* (1987), *Meet the Feebles* (1989) and *Brain Dead* (1992) — had a cult following but were an acquired taste, as indicated by the *Daily Mail*'s

Anne's maternal grandmother, Marion Reavley. COLLECTION OF ANNE PERRY

Anne's maternal grandfather, Reverend Joseph Reavley (above and right), a Presbyterian minister who served as chaplain in the trenches during the Great War; he gives his name to Joseph Reavley, a central character in her quintet of First World War novels.
COLLECTION OF ANNE PERRY

Photograph of Juliet at one year old, printed as a postcard to send to family and friends, 1939. COLLECTION OF ANNE PERRY

Juliet on the beach at three-and-a-half years old. COLLECTION OF ANNE PERRY

Juliet in winter coat and hat at about three years old. COLLECTION OF ANNE PERRY

Juliet in broad-brimmed summer hat at about seven years old.

Juliet in red tartan trousers standing in front of a flowering hibiscus bush at about eight years old.

Fourteen-year-old Juliet Hulme photographed in the garden of Ilam, the Canterbury University College rectory in Upper Riccarton. First published in the *Christchurch Star-Sun*. New Zealand Herald

The rectory, Ilam House, Upper Riccarton, Christchurch.
The stylish two-storey brick-and-stucco house, with its dozen rooms, servants' quarters and attached flat, is set in 16 hectares of park-like grounds at the end of a long shingle drive lined with enormous trees. PHOTOGRAPH: SUZANNE VINCENT MARSHALL

The beautiful Ilam Stream meanders through the rectory property, surrounded by carefully manicured lawns, luxurious flowerbeds and vast areas of azalea and rhododendron gardens.
PHOTOGRAPH: SUZANNE VINCENT MARSHALL

Henry and Hilda Hulme with Jonathan and Juliet on their arrival in Christchurch in 1948. First published in the *New Zealand Woman's Weekly*.
NEW ZEALAND HERALD

Henry Hulme, photograph taken in 1960. COLLECTION OF ANNE PERRY

Jonathan Hulme went to St John's College, Oxford, where he studied medicine, philosophy and psychology. At Oxford he was a member of the university rifle team.
COLLECTION OF ANNE PERRY

This glamorous cut-down photograph of Hilda Hulme and Bill Perry was found by the author hidden behind another picture in a photograph frame. COLLECTION OF ANNE PERRY

Double portrait photograph of Marion and Bill Perry taken around 1960.
COLLECTION OF ANNE PERRY

Port Levy, where the Hulme family had a holiday home, and where Pauline and Juliet first discovered the '4th World'. PHOTOGRAPH: JOANNE DRAYTON

Christchurch Girls' High School, Cranmer Square, Christchurch; now fallen victim to the 2010 and 2011 earthquakes. PHOTOGRAPH: SUZANNE VINCENT MARSHALL

Christchurch Girls' High School, Cranmer Square, Christchurch. This, the second school structure erected to accommodate CGHS, was opened in September 1881. William Armson's building was altered and more classrooms and buildings added to the site by Collins and Harman. This is where Juliet Hulme and Pauline Parker attended high school.

PHOTOGRAPH: SUZANNE VINCENT MARSHALL

Crowds of sightseers grouped around the entrance to the public gallery on Armagh Street, which was 'packed mainly with fashionably dressed women who scrambled and jostled one another for seats the moment the doors were opened'. First published in the *Christchurch Star-Sun*.

FAIRFAX MEDIA

Pauline Parker and Juliet Hulme leaving the Magistrates' Court after being committed for trial in July 1954. First published in the *Christchurch Star-Sun*. NEW ZEALAND HERALD

ALLEGED SUICIDE THREAT OF TEENAGE MURDERESSES

THE "Schoolgirl Murderers," as the case of Pauline Yvonne Parker and Juliet Marion Hulme is likely to be known in the anthologies of sensational and unusual crimes, have presented New Zealand's prison authorities with an unparalleled problem. Even in larger countries the number of persons under the age of 18 years serving sentences for homicide or murder is extremely small so that there are few precedents for their treatment, but added to this is the abnormal association between the two girls revealed during the trial.

TWO other facts of which the authorities must take some notice—both are reported to have threatened suicide if they are parted and both, according to standard tests, are of an exceptionally high intelligence level.

Unparalleled Problem

PARKER is above that of the average university student and Hulme's, which is quite exceptional, is inside the maximum mark Set for genius. This does not mean that Parker could be a better-than-average University student or that Hulme is a genius but that, by accepted standards of intelligence measure-

CHANGE OF NAME

MRS. HILDA MARION HULME—both of one of the convicted girls, Juliet Hulme, on Friday changed her name by deed poll to Perry. In a statement to "Truth" during the weekend, Mrs. Hulme did not disclose this change, but confirmed the fact that she proposes leaving New Zealand in a few days' time.

"I am distressed to leave Juliet here but I feel that Jonathan has a greater claim on me," she said. Jonathan is her 10-year-old son. He left New Zealand prior to the trial with his father, Dr. Hulme, and when last reported was stated to have left the ship at Marseilles with his father.

Mr. Walter Andrew Bowman Perry, an industrial consultant, who occupied a flat in the Hulme household at Ilam Road, Christchurch, and who gave evidence at the trial, was with Mrs. Hulme when "Truth" spoke to her by telephone. Asked whether he was also leaving New Zealand, Mr. Perry said he was.

It costs approximately ten guineas to change a name by deed poll, including solicitor's charges for the preparation of the deed. It is not compulsory to advertise the change, though it is usually done.

ment, they have the intellectual capacity to be these things.

Those who have the responsibility for their future custody, considering that the girls' intelligences have already been misdirected, will have difficulty in assessing the effect upon them of an indeterminate prison sentence under close security conditions and with the absolute condition that they are to be permanently parted and are not even to correspond with each other.

The separation has already taken place. Hulme was moved on Friday from Paparua Prison, Christchurch, to the women's section of Mt. Eden Gaol, Auckland. Parker will remain at Paparua possibly for another two weeks until the new security section now being prepared at Arohata

compelled to observe, will be the same. The work given to women in both institutions consists of sewing and making garments for the prisons; service and mental hospitals service and laundry work. There are no labour-saving appliances in prison laundries other than hand-turned mangles.

Women's prison working clothing consists of a coarse set of jeans and woollen cardigan with plain underclothing. They are issued with a print frock to wear out of working hours.

They are allowed to see visitors once a week—on Sundays—and can converse with them freely except that they remain under the eye of wardresses. They are allowed to write and receive a limited number of letters, but in the case of Parker and Hulme they will not be allowed to correspond with each other. They can borrow books from the prison libraries.

Both of them will be virtually segregated from the other inmates of the two institutions for the first three months of their imprisonment.

BEHAVIOUR

What will happen to them after the first three months—intended as a "settling-in" period—will probably depend to a considerable degree upon their behaviour during that period. Eventually they must simply become just two more long-term women prisoners. But they will not remain indefinitely in the same prison. Periodically and presumably for equivalent periods, Parker will be transferred to Mt. Eden and Hulme will take her place at Arohata.

Though both will be confined under what the prison authorities call "full security conditions"—in other words, under lock and key and behind barred or grilled windows—there is no comparison between the environment at Arohata and that of the women's section of Mt. Eden.

Mt. Eden is a grim old gaol of the traditional type and its women's section conforms to that pattern. Hulme will live in a stone-walled cell, about feet long by six feet wide, with walls 14 feet high and only a small barred window at the top, out of eye range. Its furniture consists of an iron bedstead, a straw mattress and six blankets with a pillow, a stool and a small cabinet. The floor is of concrete and the only covering is a small mat. There are no heating facilities.

Parker will live at Arohata in a modern, bungalow roof room, about eight feet by 10, its normal-sized window covered by strong meshed wire, its ceiling a grating to cover the light bulb. Its only furniture will be a wooden bedstead and a table and stool fixed to the wall. Bedding alone will be the same as in Mt. Eden. But Arohata is a modern building, not unlike the majority of hospitals—pos-

sibly better than many of them. Its corridors are covered by well-polished linoleum and are shut off by side swinging doors.

The security wing, where Parker will be confined, is closed off from the remainder of the building, with its own exercise yard completely screened from observation. The yard opens one side and one end of the building and is now being surrounded with heavy hurricane netting. It will be roofed in the same way. Afterwards a wooden or tin fence will be built round it.

It is not being prepared simply for Parker's accommodation. A start had been made upon its preparation before the Parker murder occurred. It is intended to deal with recalcitrant or difficult inmates who are considered to be better confined away from the other prisoners.

The workroom in the security wing is a cheerful enough room and its

SEPARATED: Pauline Parker (above), to be sent to Arohata Borstal Institution; Juliet Hulme (left), being held in Mt. Eden, and (lower left) Dr. H. R. Hulme, Juliet's father.

brother. The boy has not been told the details of the case but has been informed that his father is also in hospital.

Mrs. Hulme told the court, during the trial, that Juliet did not like her brother. This was one of the very few occasions when the accused girl showed any emotion. She stared hard at her mother and rose from her seat in the dock, then abruptly subsided.

Dr. Hulme said farewell to his daughter in Paparua prison just before he left New Zealand. The interview lasted only a few moments.

When the two girls are finally allowed to mingle with other inmates of Arohata and Mt. Eden, they will again find the difference between the two institutions. Mt. Eden accommodates long-term women prisoners and short-term women prisoners from the Auckland area. Arohata receives Borstal trainees and the emphasis in dealing with them is mainly upon reformation.

There are at present about 30 women in each institution.

father." He would not say why he had left New Zealand before his daughter's fate was decided "as it would involve too many people."

Those who knew Dr Hulme do not consider him an "unnatural father," but consider that his departure is linked with circumstances disclosed during the case, and with his desire to protect the girls' 16-year-old

windows look out across green fields. Everything at Mt. Eden is behind stone walls, strong and bleak.

The only near-relatives in a position to visit either of the girls is Parker's father.

Mrs. Hulme, it is understood, intends to leave New Zealand very shortly. Her husband, Dr. H. R. Hulme, former Rector of Canterbury University College, is already in England or on his way there. Dr. Hulme left New Zealand, accompanied by his 10-year-old son, just before the lower court hearing of the case.

He made a statement to an Australian newspaper which asked him why he had left New Zealand before the trial, stating that "the world must just consider him an unnatural

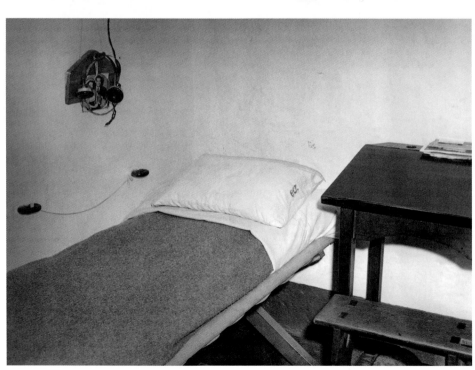

Prison cell, Mt Eden Prison, 1950. *NEW ZEALAND HERALD*

Mt Eden Prison, 1950. *New Zealand Herald*

Early publicity shot of Anne Perry. PHOTOGRAPH: JUDI SCHILLER; COLLECTION OF ANNE PERRY

Meg Davis in her office at MBA Literary Agents Ltd, London, 2010.
PHOTOGRAPH: SUZANNE VINCENT MARSHALL

Anne Perry, author publicity shot.
COLLECTION OF ANNE PERRY

Joanne Drayton, Anne Perry and Meg MacDonald, Portmahomack, Scotland, 2011.
PHOTOGRAPH: SUZANNE VINCENT MARSHALL

Anne Perry, another author publicity shot.

PHOTOGRAPH: MEG MACDONALD; COLLECTION OF ANNE PERRY

Christopher Tookey's description of them as 'three of the most …
revolting films of all time'.[18]

Heavenly Creatures was Peter Jackson's first mainstream movie, and
a film with a mission. His intention was not to unravel a murder, but
to disentangle and understand the fascinating but ultimately dangerous
teenage friendship that had created a sensation in its day. This event had
profoundly influenced the childhoods of young New Zealanders like Fran
Walsh, who originally suggested the idea of the film. 'I first came across it
[the Parker–Hulme case] in the late sixties when I was ten years old. The
Sunday Times devoted two whole pages to the story with an accompanying
illustration of the two girls. I was struck by the description of the dark and
mysterious friendship that existed between them — by the uniqueness of
the world the two girls had created for themselves.'[19]

Peter Jackson and wife and co-producer Fran Walsh intended to take a
more humane approach than that of the tabloid newspapers in the 1950s,
which had branded Pauline Parker and Juliet Hulme 'dirty minded' and
'monstrous'. As Peter Jackson said:

> Innocence. Imagination. Obsession — three words that go a long way
> toward summing up everything that made this film such a fascinating
> story. A murder story about love, a murder story with no villains.[20]

However, the Parker–Hulme story also provided Jackson with a perfect
platform from which to direct his previous 'splatter talents' to a new
audience and to a more sophisticated end. He had the aptitude and
experience to bring to life the childish rapture, the innocent homoerotic
intensity, and the girls' imaginative fairytale worlds of courtly love,
intrigue and violence. The best and worst moments of their teenage years
became his stage. 'You can almost detect relief in the director's voice as
he recalls learning that Juliet used to make plasticine models — thereby
granting him poetic license to recreate her stories with sophisticated
digital animation effects,' wrote a reviewer for *Time Out*.[21]

But it was never Peter Jackson or Fran Walsh's aim to expose the new
identities of either Pauline Parker or Juliet Hulme. In the swirl of public

events around first a play by Michelanne Forster about the pair, called *Daughters of Heaven*, which was staged in Christchurch and Wellington, and then Jackson's film, the inevitable happened. At the party after the première, an old acquaintance of Juliet Hulme's, who was still writing to her, said just a little too much: 'she let something slip — from then on it was a ticking clock'.[22] It had been something of an open secret in New Zealand literary circles that the detective fiction writer Anne Perry might be Juliet Hulme, but that information had never fallen into the hands of anyone motivated to expose it publicly. After picking up the connection in conversation, Lin Ferguson rang Peter Jackson, who spent an hour on the phone trying to persuade her not to run the story. '[Jackson] said, "They're not Nazi war criminals. They don't deserve to be hunted down." I was appalled. It made me feel incredibly guilty,' Ferguson recalled.[23]

There was a profound sensitivity in Christchurch about the Parker–Hulme story, and many people felt uncomfortable about the event being revisited. When Julie Glamuzina and Alison Laurie published *Parker and Hulme: A Lesbian View* in 1991, they experienced a great deal of resistance. In their preface to the book they record a long list of mixed reactions to their proposal. Their book, which looked once more at the event and its impact on New Zealand society, offered an unprecedented examination of 'the social context in which the murder had occurred' and its consequences.[24] The lesbian view announced in the title gave the book a special significance to this community, but many of the points it raised were pertinent to all New Zealanders.

If Julie Glamuzina and Alison Laurie sparked a new interpretation of the Parker–Hulme murder, then Peter Jackson's film made it popular. And he was not the only film director interested in the story — so were English writer Angela Carter, Australian playwright Louis Nowra, film-maker Jane Campion and Dustin Hoffman's production company.[25] Christchurch Girls' High School's decision not to lend Peter Jackson and his production company school uniforms for the filming was a small gesture of defiance in the face of the inevitable. A film on the subject would be made; the only unknowns were when and by whom.

❈

When Lin Ferguson rang Meg Davis in London she was aware of the impact her news would have: 'I knew I was going to blow up this woman's life.'[26] Meg, 'absolutely gob-smacked' by the news,[27] rang Diana Tyler, who was on holiday, and said: 'I hope you're sitting down, because there's something we didn't know about Anne.'[28] While Meg was in Wales, her colleagues at MBA were bombarded with telephone calls and requests to interview and film Anne. During Meg's absence the article on Anne for the *Daily Telegraph* appeared on 5 August 1994. It was a choreographed event. Working under the guidance of publicity agent Lynne Kirwin, MBA, on Anne's behalf, had commissioned their own piece from journalist Sarah Gristwood. The agreement between her and MBA was subject to a number of restrictions.

When Lynne Kirwin faxed the copy for the article to the *Daily Telegraph*'s Veronica Wadley, she explained the arrangement: 'For Anne's protection Sarah has assigned copyright in the piece to Anne herself.' This meant the article was unchangeable and unusable without Anne's permission. She concluded by saying:

> Anne has nothing more she feels she can say, and is adamant that she will not be photographed which she believes looks as though she is exploiting the situation in some way. She is a gentle, good, intensely moral person and her concern is to tell the truth and try to protect the friends and family who have given her such love and support.[29]

To write the article Sarah Gristwood had flown from London to Inverness, and from there was driven to Portmahomack. Her plane was delayed by fog and she arrived very late. As a consequence she spent less than an hour interviewing Anne. Under the circumstances this may have been a good thing, because the woman she met in Portmahomack was in clinical shock. 'Literally half-fainting from distress. A tall, auburn-haired, conservatively dressed woman, slumping sideways in her chair,' Sarah recorded in an article published in the *Guardian* in January 1995. The impact on Sarah was considerable: 'You don't turn sceptical, or size up the ethics of media manipulation. You become, quite simply, partisan.'[30]

That night, Sarah Gristwood flew back to London and wrote her 2,000-word piece which was to be with Lynne Kirwin by early the next morning. Considering the time constraints and the length of the interview, her article gave a remarkably accurate snapshot of events from Anne's perspective. The piece was commissioned and Sarah Gristwood was paid £500 for it, so it was neither free of obligation nor objective, but it was the first time Anne's own interpretation of the case had been communicated publicly, without the previous filters of the medical, legal and penal systems, her parents, tabloid journalists and the media.

Anne said that the disclosure of her identity had been a bombshell. After talking about her childhood and the disorientating effects of illness and separation from her family, and the anguish that created, especially for her mother, she came quickly and inevitably to the murder. Pauline Parker was desperate, even suicidal. 'She felt her mother was the only thing stopping her from leaving a situation she felt was intolerable. I believed at the time her survival depended on her coming with us. Crazy as this sounds I thought it was one life or the other.'[31] She decided to help her friend.

Anne discussed the drugs she took for tuberculosis, which she believed were mind-altering after prolonged use. There was no personal gain for her in killing Honorah Parker, and her judgement had been impaired. But this was not an excuse: she was quite clear about responsibility. 'Once you have admitted that you are at fault, have said "I'm sorry, I'm utterly, totally sorry" without excuse and paid your price then you have to put it behind you. You've got to let go.'[32]

Anne apologized for the murder, but at the same time expressed some of the misery and anger she felt over the way her family had been treated in New Zealand. 'They were just delighted to rip my family down because they were middle class and foreigners. The worst thing was the dirt they put in.' She was especially disturbed by the way her mother had been represented. 'One of the things that hurt me most was the way they painted her.' Not only did Anne carry the guilt of murder; she also felt responsible for the agony it had caused her family. The experience had been profound and life-changing. '[It] makes you try doubly hard all the rest of your life to be as good as you can. It makes you far more careful of mistakes ... because you know the price of doing something that you'll regret ever afterwards.'[33]

When Anne had her interview with Sarah Gristwood she was still waiting for a reaction from the people of Portmahomack. She could not predict what that would be, or how it would affect her mother, who had 'just made herself a decent home in the village and earned love and respect'.[34] But by the time the article came back to MBA for approval before being republished in the *Daily Mirror*, there had been developments. Ruth Needham notified Richard Holledge, executive editor of the *Daily Mirror*, of a change:

> The paragraph that 'she is still waiting for the reaction in her 500-strong Scottish village ...' shall be changed to reflect the fact that all the village know the situation and have stood by her.[35]

The reaction from the village took Anne completely by surprise. There were journalists everywhere, and journalists would make the long journey to the village for months afterwards. In the local Caledonian Hotel bar, David Wilson, solicitor and self-proclaimed 'village worthy', was interviewed about the people's general mood.

> At first there was an overwhelming feeling of astonishment — that someone among us, someone so welcomed, a devout Mormon who gave out hampers to old people at Christmas, could be guilty of matricide. But then almost as quickly folk began saying, 'Och, it was 40 years ago in another hemisphere. The lassie had been in prison and has had to move from place to place. She fits in here. What business is it of ours, what good could be achieved by raking up the past?'[36]

The sensational headlines quickly fell out of pub and local conversation. Most people felt she had 'more than made up for the violent murder of her best pal's mother by her jail sentence and rebuilding her life'.[37] She should be left alone. People rallied around, making quiet gestures of affirmation. There were young people who 'stopped to offer words of comfort' and many messages of support.[38] As Meg Davis recalls, Anne would 'find a little gift of shortbread left on her doorstep from one of the neighbours — very understated, very Scottish ... [But an] absolute vote of confidence in her as a person.'[39]

Among the telephone calls Anne made was one to Kim Hovey, her publicist friend at Ballantine in New York. Kim was sitting at her desk at the end of a long day in the office. She was exhausted. It was around 7pm, everyone had gone home, and she was finishing off a few things before she left. The telephone rang and it was a reporter from New Zealand who wanted to talk about Anne Perry, 'and did I know about her past'. The journalist explained about the murder and the movie, then asked Kim to comment. Caught completely off-guard and in a state of disbelief, Kim said, 'No. There's no way it's the Anne Perry I know. It can't be, you have your facts wrong ... No, there's no way this is Anne.' It was a quick conversation: there was nothing more to say so far as Kim was concerned. Then, about 15 minutes later, the telephone rang again, and it was Anne.

'Kim, I need to talk to you about something.' Then she proceeded to tell her everything. 'I practically fell off my chair, because the Anne Perry who I know and love was nothing like what she was telling me she did in her past.'[40] When the call ended, Kim gathered herself together, then rang her boss, Leona Nevler, to talk about how they would 'address the issues' with media in the United States and with Anne's forthcoming tour promoting Traitor's Gate.

Don Maass was in a Chicago hotel room when he received a message to call Meg Davis. Not realizing she was still in Wales, he spoke to a colleague at MBA, who told him what had happened. 'Oh, come on!' he said. 'You're joking!' But the person at the other end replied, very seriously, 'Unfortunately, I have to tell you that it is true.' As Don recalls, 'I was sitting on the edge of the hotel bed and in an instant it all made sense — so many things fell into place in like ten seconds: William

Monk, Charlotte Pitt, no wonder, no wonder. Oh! My gosh!' He thought about the Anne he had known now for six years, and about the life he now realized she had 'remade', and rang her straight away.

'Anne, I'm so sorry. I'm so sorry for what happened and that this has come forward and that you are going to have to deal with this.'

Anne's voice at the other end was filled with relief.

'Oh, *thank* God! I was worried that I would have lost you, too.'

'Of course not. Of course not,' he said. 'Anne, I know you. I am here to support you and help you through this.'[41] They discussed the fact that *Heavenly Creatures* was going to be released in the United States and that they would have to make a concerted effort to deal with the consequences.

For the first time in 40 years Anne was finding out what people really thought of her. Not just the dependable adult Anne, a notable crime writer of growing fame, but the whole person — the child and the adult. It was both a nightmare experience and a moment of liberation. She used to think: 'Well, this person likes me — but would they if they really knew? When someone has said "I think you're marvelous" or anything, it's always been at the back of my mind.'[42] Now they knew about her past, and judged her according to the quality of the life she had lived since the murder, and not on the basis of a teenage act of insanity. But these were her familiars — friends, neighbours, colleagues and associates. How would the rest of the world handle the outing of Anne Perry as Juliet Hulme?

⁜

An anxious Imogen Taylor from HarperCollins in Hammersmith, London, contacted Ruth Needham at the MBA office for instructions. Already, they were being hounded for an official response to the story. 'Here ... is the fax we received from Jeremy Flint at the *Christchurch Star* this morning. I passed it to Nick Sayers who ... would be most grateful to know as soon as possible what line we should take with the press in general.'[43] In response, Lynne Kirwin sent an official statement.

This event was over forty years ago and since then Anne has slowly rebuilt a life for herself and her family. We can only ask you now not to destroy it. She does not seek to deny what happened, and she never has. But she is deeply grieved at the distress that this will cause to her family and friends, who have given her such unstinting love and support over the years. For their sakes she had hoped that these events could remain in the past.[44]

Lynne Kirwin added that if there was anything HarperCollins felt unable to handle, they were to contact her.

When Meg returned from Wales she was hit by an avalanche of correspondence and messages, among them letters from publishing colleagues. Anne's editor at HarperCollins, Susan Opie, wrote:

I hope that you had a good break, if indeed break is what it turned out to be. You'll have been talking to Nick, I know, about all the news, but I would just like to add that we are keeping our fingers crossed that Anne will be all right. She seems to have come through so much, I'm sure that she can get through this, too.[45]

And Imogen Taylor said:

I just wanted to write and say how sorry I am to see all the press reports on Anne Perry. Very tough for her, and pretty difficult for you too. She's an extraordinary woman of course, with tremendous will and great faith, so I'm sure she'll pull through, but it must be a bitter blow all around.[46]

There were many requests for interviews, among them a letter from David Lomas, producer of the New Zealand current affairs television programme *60 Minutes*, promising a 15-minute segment of the show, which screened in prime time at 7.30pm on Sunday. 'Anne Perry's story is of considerable interest in New Zealand with the release this month of a movie on the Parker–Hulme murder trial. Also in the last two years there has been a stage play and a book about the murder.'[47]

This application was declined, along with requests from Oprah Winfrey, the Gerry Ryan *Tonight Show* in Dublin and the magazines *Who: Weekly* and the Australian *Time and Life*. But Oprah Winfrey was seriously considered by Meg and Kim Hovey, who were working together on the publicity fallout. The long-distance relationship was rocky at times, but they were united in their interest in Oprah Winfrey, who was completely revamping her old-style television talk show to make it more substantial and less sensational. Kim researched the changed programme format after the departure from the show of long-time producer Debra DiMaio. 'I'm not going to be able to spend from now until the year 2000 talking to people about their dysfunction,' Oprah announced to *People* magazine in December 1994. 'Yes, we are dysfunctional. Now, what are we willing to do to change it?'[48] Although Anne was a perfect fit for the new show, and although 'one appearance on *Oprah* could make a book a bestseller',[49] Meg and Kim decided against it because the new format was largely untested. They agreed to interviews for *USA Today* and *People* magazines, and an article appeared in the German magazine *Der Spiegel*. Anne made appearances on NBC television's morning news programme, *The Today Show*, and weekly news magazine *Dateline*, and on the National Public Radio's *Fresh Air* programme, which was syndicated to 450 radio stations across the United States.

As time went on more interviews were added, including one for the ABC's *20/20* programme and an important interview with John Darnton of the *New York Times*. Anne spoke coherently and well in the interviews, but behind the front she was fragile. Meg worried about suicide, and Anne remembers black days when she could hardly function or get herself out of bed. After Lynne Kirwin was released from her role as emergency PR agent, all responsibility for handling publicity fell on MBA and Ballantine.

Each interview was an ordeal, and inevitably Anne was 'forced to pick over the scars', but she was an adept public speaker and this was a matter of survival as an author.[50] And some were a success, such as her *20/20* interview with Barbara Walters, which aired on 19 February 1995. 'I'm so pleased you thought the *20/20* piece went all right,' said Meg to Ken

Sherman. 'I'm waiting to get an English-video copy from the ABC. Anne is good at these things, but I'm glad she didn't show the strain she's been under. I'm also much relieved I didn't look as terrified as I was — although from the sound of it I look at least 10 years younger than I am.'[51] Barbara Walters finished her segment with inimitable style, saying: 'Boy, I never read her before. I sure want to now.'[52]

But negotiating the media and managing Anne's state of mind became a point of friction between Meg and Ballantine. Meg was anxious to protect her client's psychological well-being, while Ballantine was concerned to get her story out to the American people who represented 56 per cent of her readership. Kim announced to Meg that a journalist from the *New York Times* was travelling to interview Anne in Portmahomack. Meg, who wanted to keep Anne calm and was hoping for a more comprehensive article in the *New Yorker*, rang and cancelled the arrangement. Kim and her colleague, who was in charge of publicity for Ballantine on the west coast, 'did their nut with me and un-cancelled him'. As *Heavenly Creatures* opened in London on Friday, 10 February 1995, and was about to go nationwide, 'media interest has got to screaming pitch,' Meg told Don Maass.

> It's a hell of a strain. Anne's bruised and exhausted, & the journalists just want to re-hash it all. But it's so difficult to turn down publicity, when we've been trying so long to build Anne, and on the other hand I'm seriously scared of selling her down the river. The bloody press lie and wheedle.[53]

❈

Most years Anne made two United States tours, one in spring and another in fall, and although three books were published in 1994 — *The Hyde Park Headsman*, *Traitor's Gate* and *The Sins of the Wolf* (the new Monk title) — only the first two were intended to tour. This was a huge relief for Ballantine, because it meant they had more time to plan Anne's spring trip in March 1995.

The Sins of the Wolf, which came out in the midst of the revelations about her identity, was a personal book for Anne. Hester Latterly comes to the fore in this story when she answers an advertisement in a London newspaper. A prominent Edinburgh family is looking for a young woman of good character to accompany elderly Mary Farraline from Edinburgh to London. 'One of Miss Nightingale's ladies would be preferred' because Mrs Farraline's health is precarious. The position is perfect for Hester, who immediately purchases a second-class ticket on an overnight train to Scotland to pick up her charge.

In Edinburgh, 'the Athens of the North', Hester meets the Farralines, who are Scottish publishing magnates and yet another overly privileged, dysfunctional family. But this does not stop Hester accompanying the elderly woman in a first-class carriage on the overnight train to London, or administering her essential medicine. On the journey Mary Farraline reveals herself to be a person of depth and character. 'What an unpredictable faculty memory is. The oddest things will bring back times and places we had long thought lost in the past,' she tells Hester.

When Hester wakes as the train is coming into London she is cold and stiff, but not as cold and stiff as Mary Farraline. Hester calls out, asking if she has slept well. There is no reply. She touches the old lady's shoulder, which is frozen and unyielding. Her face is white, her eyes are shut. Mary Farraline has been dead all night. A sad, shocked Hester must call the stationmaster immediately.

Although the death will make a wretched blot on her curriculum vitae, it is the pearl-encrusted pin belonging to Mary Farraline found in her possession that has Hester thrown into jail for theft, and then murder when the toxicology report shows that Mary has been poisoned. Once again, Anne makes use of her own experience. She knows Hester's cell, 'ten or eleven feet square, with a cot on one side and … a single high, barred window', and the women prisoners belonging to a different social class and none of them guilty.

Anne knows, too, that Monk is right when he contemplates the wardress's attitude to Hester. 'She would hate her also for not having lived up to the privilege with which she was born. To have been given it was bad enough, to have betrayed it was beyond excusing.' In prison Hester finds there is no privacy: 'it was both totally isolated and yet open at any time to intrusion'. On the way to court Hester's prison van is heckled by angry mobs. She can hear the newsboy shouting out the headline about her and the crowd calling for her execution. But the hardest thing is the silence she must assume:

> Connal Murdoch was talking about meeting Hester in the stationmaster's office. It was an extraordinary thing to stand and hear it recounted through someone else's eyes and be unable to speak to correct lies and mistakes.

Oliver Rathbone brings his brilliant legal talent to Hester's defence, and Monk his super sleuthing skills, which take him as far as Mary Farraline's croft in Portmahomack. His journey there is intrepid. He rows across the Moray Firth, hires a horse and puts in a solid ride before he stops in wonder. 'He could see mountains beyond mountains, almost to the heart of Scotland: blue, purple, shimmering white at the peaks against the cobalt sky ... It was vast. He felt as if he could see almost limitlessly.'

Anne dedicated *The Sins of the Wolf* to 'Kimberley Hovey for her help and friendship'. Kim's continued friendship was important to Anne, as were her marketing skills. In spite of all the negative publicity circulating around the murder, Anne's books continued to sell, and Kim was a vital part of the team that achieved it. 'Wonderful to see Anne on the *Publishers Weekly* bestseller list!' Meg wrote to Kim in September. 'I've been waiting for this moment for years — and now can't wait to get to the next rung up! Thank you very much again for your part in making this happen.'[54] And to Don: 'HOORAY FOR US!!! *PUBLISHERS WEEKLY* BESTSELLER LIST!!!'[55] Ballantine's support had been vital. 'I just want to thank you so much for everything you've done for Anne,' she wrote to Leona. 'Besides publishing her superbly ... it's also been great to feel the support of the company as well.'[56]

Leona supported Anne and her crime writing, but 'Tathyr' was another matter. In November Meg told Don that she had broken the news to Anne that 'Leona doesn't like the book and feels the characters could use some more work'. She had reassured Anne that it was more a case of editing than starting from scratch, but there were now implications for the publishing schedule. Perhaps it was time to think about 'selling the book elsewhere'.[57] To Meg's relief, Don rang Anne overnight. 'A BIG thank you for talking with Anne yesterday in such a way that I didn't have a suicidal author on the phone last night! And for promising to look at TATHYR later on and coming up with some ideas.'[58]

Meg also sent Don a pile of fax notes about Anne's French Revolution novel for his comment. 'Please let me know if you can't read them — they were mostly made while we were in the car driving through the countryside! Anne seemed to think better that way. There's piles more notes, plus a plot outline and several drawings to the "shape" of the book, which I don't have copies of.'[59] Anne was under strict instructions from Meg to send her a complete chapter breakdown before she began to write.

Anne still found non-crime books difficult to plot. 'I'm not a good plot constructor. My early historical novels are a shambolic rambling; I used to put in all the research that interested me. With crime novels, you can't waste time.'[60] Although her primary interests in the historical novels were context and characterization, murder tended now to creep in as a stabilizer to structure her storyline, as her French Revolution novel would prove.

Meg was negotiating a deal with Prince Edward's television company, Ardent, for the Monk series. She announced the news to Don in mid-November: 'The Prince had had to be informed, of course, of Anne's past; maybe they even had a natter about it at the Palace! Life just gets stranger.'[61] Edward was generous in his response to Anne's background, reassuring them that he felt she had paid her dues for the crime.

Meg was also helping to organize a 10,000-word piece on Anne for the *New Yorker* by Robert McCrum, editor-in-chief for Faber & Faber, and a novelist and poet. 'We had a very good preliminary chat yesterday … it's a general article and good for her profile. And, happily, Anne meets … Prince Edward next Wednesday. All very exciting!'[62] As she told Ken Sherman, 'I'd never aspired to Anne being discussed in high-brow circles!'[63]

One of the books Anne was working on when her identity was revealed was *Cain His Brother*, published in 1995 and 'dedicated to the people of Portmahomack for their kindness'. Perhaps more than anything else, this novel encapsulated how she felt at the time. It is 1859, and a bitterly cold January, when Genevieve Stonefield visits Monk's offices to enlist his help. Her husband has gone missing and she must find him dead or alive. She has five children to support, and a business she cannot dispose of until Angus Stonefield is found.

The awful possibility is that his twin brother, Caleb, has killed him. For while Angus lives in Mayfair and is a prominent businessman and a 'pillar of respectability and orderly family life', Caleb lives in Blackwall and 'survives by theft, intimidation and violence'. Ultimately, Caleb — who is murderously jealous of his brother's perfect life — is arrested for killing him.

While Hester, Monk's benefactor Callandra and other philanthropic women run a makeshift typhoid hospital in the seedy Limehouse district of London, Monk is engaged in a flirtatious romance with the ravishing Drusilla Wyndham. After meeting by chance on the steps of the Geographic Society in Sackville Street, they see each other a number of times before Drusilla suddenly tears her gown, scratches wildly at her flesh and leaps screaming from their hansom cab. This happens in front of a crowd emerging from a Mayfair party, and Drusilla's performance suggests that Monk is forcing himself on her. Monk is shocked. 'One moment they had been the closest of companions, happy and at ease; the next she had changed as if she had ripped off a mask and exposed something hideous, a creature filled with hatred.'

In his desolation he goes to Hester, who immediately takes his side, working out an amusing scheme to reverse the toxicity of Drusilla's vengeful plan. The effect of Hester's support is subtle but profound. 'Nothing had changed. Yet now he no longer stood alone. That took the despair away, the very worst of the pain.' As Monk investigates, he discovers Drusilla is someone from his past whose life has been ruined by his callous ambition. Oliver Rathbone has the compassion to understand how Monk must feel. He can just imagine 'the bitter horror of living inside a man you did not know. The one thing which in all eternity you could never escape was yourself.'

Monk's efforts to untangle the complex relationship between the good and evil Stonefield twins take him to the Berkshire village of Chilverley, where he meets the vicar, Reverend Nicolson, who has known the Stonefield family for decades. There is a seat and a vast estate. But Angus turns out to be the illegitimate and *only* son of Phineas Ravensbrook — so who is Caleb? Could they be the same person? When the case comes before the court, Reverend Nicolson suggests a solution to the coroner:

> Is it not possible that in his unhappiness, and his feeling of rejection, obligation and loneliness, that the boy created an alternative self ... might it not begin as an escape within the imagination of an unhappy child's hurt and humiliation?

Listening to the proceedings, Monk thinks that 'perhaps no one else in the room could feel so deeply and with such an intimate pity for a man divided against himself, forever in fear of a dark half he did not know'. Anne also knew what it was like to have two identities, good and evil. 'I don't think the world is ever going to forget that I am both of these people ... It's not ever going to go away,' she told Robert McCrum.[64]

⚙

Anne refused to see *Heavenly Creatures*: she regarded it as a 'grotesque and distorted portrait of herself' made by 'idiotic moviemakers'.[65] From reports she had heard about the film, she felt it made two-dimensional caricatures of her family, especially her mother. Anne's life had been turned upside down by a film that had been made, as she pointed out, without her knowledge or support. 'What others see as fair and objective is not [the] way you see yourself,' she explained in interviews.[66] 'There is a good deal of fantasy in the film — which is the film-maker's self expression.'[67]

Her life had been used creatively by Peter Jackson. 'I ask people to bear in mind that it is necessarily fiction in part,' read the draft of her official statement on *Heavenly Creatures*.[68] Here was her 'most painful event' translated into popular art and projected on the big screen. 'Most people in the developed world came to hear about' the film and the revelation of her identity.[69] As she explained, 'it's like having some disfigurement and being stripped naked and set up in the High Street for everyone to walk by and pay their penny and have a look. I would like to put my clothes on and go home, please, be like anybody else.'[70]

Peter Jackson and Fran Walsh, on the other hand, believed they had made a compassionate contribution to a revisionist view of the case. 'These two girls had been demonized in the press and we wanted to know who they were and why they did it, not turn them into monsters,' Fran Walsh told a reporter for the *New York Post*.[71] 'If we had any agenda, it was to show they were human beings and to find out what really happened.' They had used material that was already largely in the public domain to re-examine the vilification of two teenagers. 'It's too bad this has deteriorated to cross fire in the press ... we wanted to tell their story from a humanitarian perspective to New Zealanders who've seen the girls as monsters all this time.'[72] Anne's inflexible attitude and her hurt-filled, ill-informed comments made Peter Jackson and Fran Walsh bridle with indignation. 'In all the interviews we've done for the movie, we've treated her with absolute respect. And while it's clear she has no respect for us.'[73] The version of events Anne was presenting to media appeared to undermine their own work and felt like a conscious act of sabotage.

Miramax's marketing campaign only inflamed a difficult situation. A *New York Daily News* article announced their strategy:

Harvey Weinstein, the Miramax big-wig ... apparently has made so much lucre from his seven films nominated for 22 Academy Awards that he's actually arranged to have an empty seat held at every theatre screening for the award-nominated 'Heavenly Creatures.' He also knows a good publicity stunt when he sees one. The empty seat, he says, is for mystery writer Anne Perry ... Weinstein is hoping the best-selling novelist will finally see the flick while she does a 23-city U.S. tour for her forth coming suspense novel.[74]

The Miramax advertisement for *Heavenly Creatures*, entitled 'Murder, She Wrote!' and published in leading American newspapers, was an open letter to Anne:

> We read that you want to put this all behind you — yet you have very publicly given your opinion on a movie you haven't seen. Our offer to you remains the same: we're holding one seat open at every showing of 'Heavenly Creatures' — just for you. Or we will happily arrange a private screening. We've done everything we can to accommodate you. Please see the movie before you judge it or speak out against it.[75]

The advertisement finished with a challenge: 'There is one piece of the story which still remains a mystery: the whereabouts of Pauline Parker.'[76] When Peter Jackson heard that Miramax was about to use Anne in a cheap advertising stunt, he was horrified. 'At no stage did we want to have Juliet's identity exposed … I especially asked Miramax not to use her in the publicity for the film at all,' he told journalists.[77]

When what Don Maass described as 'the loathsome ad' hit the newspapers, he called Miramax's director of marketing:

> I kept it friendly, asking him whether they intend to continue using that ad (if not, problem over) and to express our hope that in respect of Anne's feelings that they not use her to directly advertise the film. (I said a bit more, actually, though it was understood that the conversation was 'confidential, informational and with no threats made or implied').[78]

Another crisis was ignited by John Darnton's article in the *New York Times* of 14 February 1995. Meg, who 'wish[ed] now he'd stayed cancelled', thought it 'mean-spirited' and harsh.[79] John Darnton took a tough, war correspondent's approach to the story. 'She has participated in a publicity campaign to tell the world "who I am." What began as "damage control" has turned into a single-minded and self-absorbed crusade of revelation, obfuscation, justification and attack.' He outlined the circumstances leading up to the murder, mentioned the issue of lesbianism, gave Anne's rationale for the murder and explained that she now lived in the midst of achievement in 'a Scottish idyll'. His parting comment was churlishly ambiguous:

> The marketing of Miss Perry as someone who has 'courageously faced the world and shared her painful story' raises the usual questions about exploiting the notoriety for gain. Miss Perry insists that her motives are pure.[80]

'What a great idea, to write to *The New York Times*. I have to confess, my thinking lately has been hampered by exhaustion and now also by a bad cold,' Meg wrote to Don on 17 February.[81] Incensed by John Darnton's claims, Don wrote a letter to the editor, which was ultimately published. In it he said the article 'unfairly maligns this author and wilfully ignores the facts'. He was especially appalled at Darnton's assertion that 'expressions of remorse are not volunteered' and listed the television spots, radio interviews and newspaper articles where Anne had 'repeatedly stated how sorry she is'. In response to the 'single-minded and self-absorbed crusade of revelation, obfuscation, justification and attack', he wrote:

> Quite the opposite is true. Ms. Perry's discussion of her life has been open and candid … Far from obscuring the issues, I believe that Anne Perry illuminates for all, both in her books and in her life, the harrowing moral complexities that can attend a murder and its aftermath.[82]

Meg suspected that the tone of John Darnton's piece had been coloured by the fact that he had been abruptly cancelled, then reinstated. Don and Meg discussed the legality of his claims. They both felt a case could be made for libel, but it was a tricky situation and perhaps a public retraction might be more effective. Don felt there would be little sympathy for Anne's case, especially from the media. 'Expressions of worry, weariness, self-pity, being put upon, or of the media being reckless with her, or her mother's, life and privacy are certain to backfire … As wearisome as it is to say "I'm sorry" over and over again forty years after the fact', this was what she must do as the news spread. With the United States book tour just days away, Don had some recommendations:

1) That Anne rest well before the tour. 2) That we reassure her that it's all for the good, and that for the most part her story inspires people. 3) While she is right not to see the film or dwell on the crime, people understandably want to comprehend how such a thing could happen.[83]

Anne was very upset by John Darnton's article. It felt like yet another blow, and one that might have considerable impact because it had been published in one of the world's most influential newspapers. She worried also about the reaction of Ken Sherman, her Hollywood agent; she had grown fond of him and looked forward to their conversations when she visited Los Angeles. But Ken wrote to reassure Meg of his continued commitment. 'I can imagine how frustrated Anne is with all the press and just for the record it has no effect one way or the other in terms of my respect for her and desire to continue working with her.'[84] Meg passed on his kind words, which she told him were 'a big measure of balm … *The New York Times* piece seemed sadly mean-minded, and Anne found it rather bruising.'[85]

By the time Meg received Don's advice for the tour, Anne was already en route to Nottingham for an interview with a religious programme that aired on Sunday, 19 February 1995. She would be out of contact until the next day, but Meg told Don she would pass on his suggestions and fax him Anne's thoughts in return. After Nottingham, Anne had a week's rest before flying to New York. Just before Anne left Portmahomack, Kim Hovey contacted her to add new interviews to the tour list. 'I am going to ring Kim in a moment. I'm angry that she's involved Anne in two more US interviews yesterday,' Meg told Don.

Anne is seriously at the end of her rope, and I'm very concerned for her at the moment. Doing more interviews just frays her worse … I understand Kim's had some flak from Miramax about Anne mouthing off about the film, and the last thing we need is a slanging match.[86]

II

When 10-year-old Juliet met her parents again in 1948, after a 15-month separation, the adjustment was difficult. It was hard to believe that something she had looked forward to for so long could be so awkward. 'I felt very alien.'[87] She found it difficult to know where she belonged, and felt loyal to both the Brownes and her own mother and father. She had learned to survive in another household without the pattern of school but with a rather more rigorous regime of parental discipline, and now she was abruptly returned to the unstructured free-thinking care of the Hulmes.

In Christchurch, Juliet would be a day pupil at St Margaret's College, a private school for girls. 'I hated being a new girl.'[88] She was taunted for being different, a foreigner, but that mattered less because she had the support, briefly before she retired, of the kindly headmistress, Stephanie Young, and she was able to live at home. She clung to her mother and needed constant reassurance, but, because her health was still a concern, after only a year her parents decided to send her back to the warmer climate of the North Island. This time she went to Queenswood School, a privately run Rudolf Steiner school in the Hawke's Bay town of Hastings.

If readjustment to life with her parents had initially been troubled and alienating, the strict boarding school routine and discipline she now encountered was a further shock. She felt completely distanced from both students and staff. Her English accent, her background, her experiences were different from anyone else's. The children teased and bullied her mercilessly, and she hated it. 'Schoolgirls can be terribly cruel, especially if there's anything different about you.'[89] But she was a challenging, even problematic child, and something of a misfit: intelligent, so that she stood out; imaginative, so that she seemed anti-social; unused to playground dynamics and the strictures of formal education, so that she appeared smug and arrogant; obviously physically ill; and bitterly homesick.

Juliet was at boarding school between the ages of 11 and 12, holidaying with her parents three times a year, unable to see them casually or at weekends. 'I used to get so upset. I'd missed three years of school, I was a swot, and swots are not popular. I was unused to school discipline and walked with my head in the air.'[90] When it became obvious that Juliet was intensely unhappy, she was brought back home and enrolled locally at Ilam School.

Since their arrival in Christchurch the Hulmes had lived first in a house on Hackthorne Road in Cashmere, then briefly in Rapaki Road on Murray Aynsley Hill, and finally in the rector's residence, a huge homestead known as Ilam in the affluent suburb of Upper Riccarton. The stylish two-storey brick-and-stucco house, with tennis court, greenhouse and orchard, was set in 16 hectares of park-like grounds at the end of a long shingle drive lined with enormous trees.

The beautiful Ilam Stream meandered through the property, surrounded by carefully manicured lawns, luxurious flowerbeds and vast areas of azalea and rhododendron gardens. In spring these were a mass of dazzling colour — purple, pink, flaming red, orange, creamy lemon, yellow — and the air was saturated with scent. Away from the house — and across the little footbridge that passed a fountain and a waterwheel — was an extensive woodland area where daffodils bloomed in August and September, followed by bluebells in October.

The original old rambling homestead, built by the wealthy John Charles Watts-Russell in 1858, was razed to the ground by fire before the present one was built in 1914 by Edgar Stead, an ornithologist, keen gardener and hybridist, who planted the azalea and rhododendron gardens. When he died in 1949, Ilam was bought by the government as part of the new site for the University of Canterbury, on the condition that the gardens were kept in perpetuity. Canterbury University College, as it was then known, maintained the Ilam gardens, opening them occasionally to the public, and used the homestead as accommodation for its first full-time rector, Henry Hulme, and his family.

Henry was in the job only a few months before he committed a serious tactical error. He was used to a milieu that accommodated dissention and debate, and in this context he was an intellectual prima donna rather than a politician. At Whitehall he had headed teams working on important war projects; in small, faux-Oxbridge Christchurch the biggest issue at that time was where to locate the School of Forestry. Henry might have been decommissioned, but he was not psychologically disengaged from the ethos of war.

Moreover, his appointment was a mismatch. Henry was too con-descendingly British, intellectual and military; Christchurch too isolated, inward-looking and parochial. So he was thinking big rather than small when he voted against his own College Council regarding the site for the proposed school. He failed to understand the significance of scale in what novelist and theatre director Ngaio Marsh called this 'cranky little coda, at the bottom of the world'.[91] His conduct damaged his relationship with his colleagues, and the reverberations continued as more conflicts arose to rattle the Neo-Gothic halls of Canterbury University College.

Those who got to know Henry found him kind and likeable, but he was a difficult man to get to know. Equally, Hilda was admired by some for her social charm and generosity, and disliked by others for being opinionated and aloof. Their social position created an enormous barrier in a city polarized by class into 'haves' and 'have-nots'. Strait-laced, chintzy 1950s Christchurch cultivated a stuffy, pretentious Englishness that was oddly refracted through a colonial lens.

Seen through this lens, the Hulmes were both attractive and repellent. They were a reminder of upper-middle-class Britishness and the lingering romance of croquet played on perfect English lawns. It was love and hate mixed with envy. The Hulmes arrived with privilege and were given the best. They lived in one of the Garden City's most spectacular homes, and the doors of society were thrown open for them.

Hilda was immediately welcomed as a figure of respectability in the community. 'She played a prominent role in the life of the University' and became vice-president of the Christchurch Marriage Guidance Council and its representative on the Canterbury Council of Social Services.[92] She worked as a marriage guidance counsellor, wrote newspaper articles, spoke publicly and organized a lecture series on the subject of the family.

She offered 'good' advice to parents raising children and to married and engaged couples. People listened avidly to her immaculate enunciation on the subject, aired frequently on national radio. In 1951, she was a regular panel member, along with Helen Holmes and Eileen Saunders, of *Candid Comment*, a women's programme broadcast on 3YA. The trio discussed religious education in schools, school uniforms, discipline in the home and child-rearing. Hilda's work at the Marriage Guidance Council meant she moved among the city's social and religious élite, mixing with churchmen such as Anglican Bishop Alwyn Warren as well as prominent lawyers, psychologists and doctors.

Juliet and brother Jonathan, now seven years old, had the run of the Ilam grounds. Jonathan was at Medbury School, and Juliet at the local school and then St Margaret's College again, until her parents decided to move her to Christchurch Girls' High School in May 1952. Juliet had not settled especially well at St Margaret's, and the Hulmes believed she might be more academically extended at the bigger, public school. Before Juliet started, she was given an intelligence test that gave her a score of about 170, when the 'average' score was somewhere between 90 and 110. Juliet's mother was on the Christchurch Girls' High School board, so when she entered 3A, the top academic stream, Juliet was in an enviable position.

3A was bristling with talented young minds. 'It was a strange class because we were led to believe we were a picked bunch,' remembers a fellow classmate. 'We were … pushed every class from day one, and it was quite overbearing.'[93] The girls in 3A were tipped to be the next generation of women leaders and suburban matrons.

But not everyone in 3A came from a privileged background. Among the less advantaged was 14-year-old Pauline Yvonne Rieper. A quiet, more mature girl, she was a little dumpy and frumpy, but extremely bright. Admired as the only one who could get perfect scores in Latin tests, she was regarded as a character by her fellow students: fervid, distant at times, and self-contained because she had spent so much of her childhood sick.

Pauline was born on 26 May 1938, the second daughter of four children to Honorah and Herbert Rieper. Their first child, a son, was a 'blue baby' who died almost immediately; the last, a Down's Syndrome girl, Rosemary, born in March 1949, when Honorah was 41. In between were Pauline and her older sister, Wendy Patricia, just 15 months apart. Their father, Tasmanian-born Herbert Rieper, had lived a colourfully covert life. In 1910, aged 16, he had begun his adventure by coming to New Zealand, then enlisting in the New Zealand Expeditionary Force in 1915 and serving in Cairo, where he met the enchanting Louise McArthur, an Englishwoman born in India and eight years his senior. They married in Cairo and moved to New Zealand, settling in Napier, then shifting to Raetihi. They had two children.

It was at Raetihi, in the office of a firm where they both worked, that Herbert met and fell in love with Honorah Mary Parker, nearly 15 years his junior. He and Honorah ran away together, leaving Louise at Raetihi. By 1936, they were established at 21 Mathesons Road in Phillipstown, an industrial part of Christchurch. Honorah, the daughter of chartered accountant Robert William Parker and his wife Amy, was born on 18 December 1907, in a genteel suburb of Birmingham.

Herbert never got a divorce, so, although he and Honorah lived as man and wife and their children took the surname Rieper, they were never married. There was nothing about the Riepers that suggested their passionate beginning or ruinous secret, but they were always short of money. Herbert slipped the occasional few pounds to his other family, and Pauline's bad health added to the daily struggle of surviving on a working-class wage.

When Pauline was almost five, she was diagnosed with the bone infection osteomyelitis in her left leg. She spent nine months in hospital and nearly lost her life to the debilitating disease, which, even after several operations, left her in severe pain and barely able to walk. For two years after she left hospital, her leg discharged and had to be dressed twice a day.

When Pauline finally returned to primary school, she was so far behind that she had to be given individual tuition. Her rehabilitation became part of the Riepers' way of life. There were dressings and painkillers — aspirin and codeine — which she took until her teenage years, and, because she was immobile for long periods of time, Herbert introduced her to craft-modelling in wood and plasticine. What started as a distraction rapidly became a passion.

The doctors advised her parents not to let her play sport, so she wrote stories, read books, listened to the radio, made models and, once she was properly mobile, went with Wendy to Sunday School at the East

Belt Methodist Church (in Fitzgerald Avenue). The Riepers were not an especially religious family, but Herbert and Honorah made a point of going to church occasionally.

Things seemed to look up a little in 1946 when the family purchased a house in the central city at 31 Gloucester Street. Although now rundown, this had been a salubrious and sought-after area of big homes with elegant pillared porticoes and carriageways. Now many of them were either rental properties or had been divided into multiple flats.

The Riepers' plan for their sprawling, rather shabby house was to take in boarders to supplement Herbert's wage from his job as manager of Dennis Brothers' Fish Shop on Hereford Street. At the back of the Riepers' property was Christchurch Girls' High School. Girls would hang over the corrugated-iron fence and stare into the back yard, making rude comments about 'the house with the rusty roof'.[94] Christchurch Girls' High School had status and history. In 1952 the school celebrated its seventy-fifth anniversary — 'Quite an achievement in a city of only a hundred and one years!' announced the school magazine.

> How little we realize that in 1877, a girls' school was almost unheard of — at all events there were very few, even in England. Many people were against a full education for women ... But the vision of the founders was justified — and through the years, our school has built up a high reputation.[95]

The staff, many of whom had masters degrees, wore black academic gowns. The tone was set by the headmistress, Jean Stewart, a strict, rather unforgiving woman. 'We were young ladies, she thought, and that's the way she liked it. She once told us that she preferred us to say Mundey, Tuesdey, Wednesdey, etc, because that's how the Queen said it.' Miss Stewart was 'short, with attitude and had bunny teeth, not sticking out just large', but it was Miss Milne, deputy headmistress and mathematics teacher for the top streams, who terrified everyone. Girls scattered and the corridors cleared at her approach. Eye contact was universally avoided, because it was like staring at the Medusa. Tall and gaunt, with stooped shoulders, she wore her hair in plaited coils over her ears and pince-nez glasses propped at the end of her nose. 'She had bony ankles,' former pupil Patricia Toon recalls, 'and this with the black gown made me think that she probably parked her broom stick in one of the tall cupboards I once saw in the staff room.'[96]

When Juliet discovered she was going to be taught by Miss Milne, she thought, 'I'm dead, and that's the end to the world — life as we know it has ceased', but Miss Milne turned out to be a 'brilliantly gifted teacher'. Henry had talked to his daughter about the elegance of quadratic equations, but it was Miss Milne who showed her how the magic worked. Her teaching was a revelation. 'It was only a few weeks before I could say: "Yes, I know what you mean when you say that's an elegant solution and that's pedestrian. This one is witty and that one is ordinary" ... That was a moment suddenly when all the lights went on ... I was fumbling around and suddenly everything was clear.' From then on Juliet felt very disappointed if she did not get over 90 per cent for mathematics. This was enormously encouraging after all the schooling she had missed. 'I think Christchurch Girls' High was a pretty damn good school. It was here that [I experienced] that sudden spark of the joy of learning and understanding. It's still with me.'[97]

The school year was under way when Juliet joined 3A, and class friendships were already established. Many of the girls knew each other from club and community groups and primary school. To the rest of the class Juliet 'felt older', although at 13, turning 14 towards the end of the year, she was not much older than most. Her sophistication was more than just a matter of age. 'Juliet was party to a lot of adult conversations of high quality that she would participate in,' remembers a classmate. Well-spoken and elegant, she had 'beautiful posture and always stood very tall ... and was far more confident than a lot of us girls in the class'.[98] This confidence made her seem arrogant, aloof, even haughty. She had the poise and self-assurance to correct their French teacher, the infamous Miss Stevens, whose autocratic manner, nicotine-stained fingers and large frame would long be remembered.

Juliet was the only one in the class daring enough to wear the brims of her summer panama and winter felt hats rakishly turned down, as she had when at St Margaret's. She was given more latitude. 'The teachers were impressed by her. She was the daughter to the rector of the university and, as they'd all been young women who had got to university, that was important,' recalls a classmate.[99]

The friendship between Juliet and Pauline began almost coincidentally. 'When she first started she always used to have lunch with Diane Muirson and Helen Hinton and myself,' remembers Marjorie Webb. 'We used to sit and have lunch, and Juliet would be in our group, and then Pauline came into that group ... mainly because Diane and I had met her ... we did cooking classes together ... and we went to the Methodist camp in the third form and we all tented together.' Pauline, who preferred to be called Paul (though her family called her Yvonne), was 'beautiful, she had this pure white skin ... black curly hair and dark eyes, but she had no sense of it,' Margaret Tyndall remembers.[100] Although she spoke quietly and was extremely reserved, she had a sense of humour and a boyish 'anarchic streak' that made her well liked. Pauline was not an outsider, but she was the deep, brooding type who scowled portentously in the playground and especially in school photographs.

It was a communion of minds and souls when Juliet and Pauline discovered each other in May 1952. 'Shortly after [their] meeting, Juliet remarked "Mummy, I've met someone at last who has a will as strong as my own."'[101] In August that year, when the two girls went for a bicycle ride in the countryside, they shared a growing sense of euphoria. It was exclusive and comforting to have a best friend. After years of dislocating illness and isolation, their solitary lives were suddenly over.

During their ride they stopped by the side of the road and went into a wooded area. There they removed 'their outer clothing and ran amongst the bushes ecstatically. They were so ecstatic that they went home leaving these clothes behind ... there was [now] an indissoluble bond between them. It would seem that two unusual kindred spirits had come together.'[102] From this point on, their relationship grew more intense. Together, they created a richly imaginative fantasy world that found expression in an overwhelming urge to write.

CHAPTER FIVE

I

Anne's tour of the United States, beginning in late February 1995, was more minutely planned than any before. Ballantine held 'high-level meetings' to ensure the best possible outcome, but there was nervousness as Anne began her visits to metropolitan bookstores around the country. Kim Hovey had tried, and largely failed, to moderate journalist John Darnton. 'I would like to talk to you about your trip to Scotland to interview Anne,' she had faxed him on 31 January 1995.

> I know you are anxious to go … early next week but I need to talk to you further regarding the timing of your story in *The New York Times*. I hope that we can come to an agreement on when it will run. It is important that you realize that both Ballantine and Anne's agent, Meg Davis, have been extremely careful about what media interviews Anne has done since the news broke last [July]. Anne did a few select interviews in August and will be doing … more in late February and March when she is on her book tour for TRAITOR'S GATE.[1]

Anne was facing her public for the first time as a murder-mystery writer who had committed murder herself. She was arriving on the back of negative commentary — just days after the publication of John Darnton's article in the *New York Times* — and in the midst of Miramax's publicity campaign for *Heavenly Creatures*. She was tired, and anxious. Would the bookshops reject her because of her past?

But Anne was encouraged by what happened. 'She's had tremendous support from the bookstore community, especially the mystery stores,' announced Kim Hovey in *Bookselling this Week*, 'and I think that her fans are still supportive.'[2] Not one bookstore Kim rang said 'we don't want Anne Perry' and people like Mary Alice Gorman, of the Mystery Lovers Bookshop in Oakmont, Pennsylvania, and Barbara Peters, at The Poisoned Pen in Phoenix, Arizona, declared their support for Anne and her writing. 'We know her personally, and we do care for her as a friend,' said Mary Alice Gorman.[3]

This was important affirmation, but the support of her readers was even more crucial. Her books had always been strongly moralistic. 'I ... expected some people to say *"You hypocrite —* you write stories with this ethical value to them, and look what you really are."'[4] But no one did. 'People were so gracious and understanding,' says Kim, who was present at many of Anne's signings.

> We decided that for the first time she was out doing events that she would answer questions or speak to it. Because there were fans coming to every single signing and they wanted to know what she had to say ... She spoke to her past and what happened — and she went on to show the world that you can have a second chance.[5]

It was especially poignant, as Anne observed, 'for someone who feels there's no hope, to be encouraged; it doesn't have to go on this way. There are more chances in the world than you might think. And compassion, too.'[6] Some regulars doubtless stayed away because they felt what Anne had done was unforgivable, and others came because of the revelations. But her faithful readers were there in the usual numbers, and Anne spoke 'eloquently' and honestly about her youth and what had happened. Ballantine had decided that this tour would be the one and only time she discussed the murder and answered reasonable questions about it; after that they hoped the matter could be dropped.

Nonetheless, the tour was not without its difficulties or distractions. Anne's programme of interviews — strictly vetted by Kim to try to avoid tabloid ambushes — was still dauntingly full, and Miramax's advertising campaign was in high gear. Anne faced a media gauntlet hungry to hear about the murder, and all this in the midst of what must have felt like hysterical praise for Peter Jackson's film. When *Heavenly Creatures* hit the screens it was almost universally acclaimed by critics, who seemed as intoxicated by the teenage crush as the girls themselves.

Richard Corliss of *Time* magazine wrote that the 'obsession, when it takes hold, is not a fragrance but a lethal gas ... [It is] the puppy love, say, that turns rabid as two souls merge in a toxic rapture.' He commended the way Peter Jackson built 'creepy excitement with urgency and great cinematic brio, while neither condescending to the girls nor apologizing for their sin'.[7] Film critic John Griffin said it captured the 'tuning-fork vibrancy of adolescence, its sliding-scale gamut of emotions and its purity'.[8] Christopher Tookey in the *Daily Mail* observed that 'it neither glamorized nor whitewashed the girls, but it makes them immensely sympathetic ... [and while evoking the] stiff, ultra-conventional nature of New Zealand at the time [it] does not take the easy, over-familiar route of blaming society, emotional repression, or bad parents'.[9] The film was praised for its direction, its clever use of special effects made possible by the newly formed Weta Workshop, and for its brilliant casting, especially of the largely unknown Reading-born Kate Winslet. *Heavenly Creatures* featured prominently in international film festivals, winning, among others, the Metro Media Award at the 1994 Toronto International Film Festival and a Silver Lion at the Venice Film Festival the same year, and earning an Academy Award nomination in 1995 for Best Screenplay Written Directly for the Screen. It made the top 10 movies of the year list for *Time*, the *Guardian*, the *Sydney Morning Herald* and the *New Zealand Herald*.

Although the success of the film did not affect Anne directly, she still had to deal with such headlines as 'A Heavenly Trip Toward Hell', 'Obsession amid the gymslips' and 'Natural-born Culler'. There was also the impact of comments like Richard Corliss's: 'the sad creatures who Pauline and Juliet must have been in real life are alchemized [in the film] into figures of horror and beauty'.[10] Although she seemed to have lost no friends, colleagues, bookstore support or readers, Anne was beginning to understand that each media outing of her story brought the expectation of 'a fresh declaration of remorse'.[11]

Anne's people on both sides of the Atlantic waited anxiously to see how the tour would go. Meg Davis was relieved to hear from Ken Sherman in Los Angeles. 'Anne and I are having breakfast this coming Sunday at 8:00 am at her hotel. We had a somewhat rushed chat last week and I gave her my home number in case she cared to vent due to the press which she said has actually been fairly respectful so far.'[12] Sunday dawned warm and sunny, so they ate outside and discussed the progress of Anne's film projects. 'It would be great to be able to read the new Lynda La Plante script though Anne feels La Plante doesn't understand the book/characters. We'll see.'[13]

Lynda La Plante, who optioned the Pitts in 1991, had let the rights go to the BBC when they lapsed in 1992 on the basis that she would be the principal scriptwriter for the series. The BBC, who commissioned the first three episodes from her, was not prepared to make a proper commitment without a workable script and series formula. When the BBC option period ran out in 1994, it was renewed and Lynda La Plante's role as scriptwriter for the series given additional staffing support. 'I was speaking to the producer yesterday. There are now 3 script editors attached to the project, but still no go-ahead from [BBC executive] Alan Yentob till he's seen the first 3 scripts.'[14] When Anne flew home from the States, she and her agents were still waiting to read the final drafts.

⚘

Traitor's Gate was a story about misguided loyalty and betrayal. 'It's impossible to read *Traitor's Gate* without hearing Perry's characters replaying versions of her *own* drama,' said Toronto's *Globe and Mail*.[15] But not all critics saw this as positive or reviewed the book favourably. One described the plot as 'slow-moving and padded with irrelevant scenes and repetitive speeches that are supposed to be conversation. There are so many murder suspects and they are so similar it is hard to keep them straight.'[16]

It is remarkable that, in the face of such enormous stress and disruption, Anne kept producing books. The process of writing was familiar, and her stories offered a comfortable place to escape the anxieties which would roll in now that her identity had been revealed, weathering like high tides, wave by wave. But the continuing crisis had its effect. When Meg sent Don the manuscript for *Pentecost Alley*, the next Pitt, she described it as 'unfortunately, *a mess*'.

> This is a measure, perhaps, of how badly I've spoiled Anne — the book is full of her typist's mistakes and gaps where she couldn't read Anne's writing, so it is now absolutely covered with my scribbles. I've been torn between embarrassment at the unprofessionalism of handing something like this in to Leona, and the awareness of the pressure of time. The latter won out ... I've been a bit concerned at the way Anne has bashed this out, but the book was thoroughly planned beforehand, and I feel it's very much up to form. But of course we'll both have our fingers crossed till we've heard what you think.[17]

In spite of the state of the manuscript, *Pentecost Alley* was 'selected by Book of the Month Club and the guarantee is raised to $30,000', made the bestseller lists of the *San Francisco Chronicle* and the *Wall Street Journal*, and was nominated for a coveted Edgar Award.[18] The story revolves around the discovery of the body of Ada McKinley, a slum prostitute working in Whitechapel. The corpse has injuries that seem disturbingly ritualistic: the fingers and toes have been broken and dislocated, the boots are laced in a strange manner, and water has been poured over the body. Normally Pitt's cases are rarified and political, but this one is sensitive. Items belonging to Finlay FitzJames are found in the room — a badge from a private gentlemen's club and a pair of cufflinks — making it seem as though he is the last person to have seen Ada alive. A witness has also identified a man fitting his description leaving the room.

On the back of the badge, in gold, are the words 'Hellfire Club' and a date: '1881'. Pitt discovers that nine years ago, when Finlay FitzJames was part of a rebellious, hell-raising fraternity of rich young men who frequented the dangerous fringes of Victorian society, another prostitute was killed in exactly the same manner and Finlay was implicated in her death. Pitt is obliged to interview not only Finlay FitzJames, but all the members of the Hellfire Club, most of whom are profoundly embarrassed by the immature antics of their youth.

At the Foreign Office he interviews Finlay FitzJames's boss, Mr Grainger, who assures him that since the club was disbanded FitzJames's private life has never given them cause for concern. 'You understand, Superintendent?' he says to Pitt. 'There are parts of all our lives which fate usually allows us to bury decently. It is only when some other circumstance arises which compels us to face examination that they can be raised again.' Pitt blushes at the thought of his own misdemeanours. 'There was nothing in his past which was shocking — simply clumsy and extremely selfish, things he would far rather Charlotte never knew. They would alter the way she saw him.'

The effect on people of information revealed is one of the themes of this book. It is not entirely new to Anne's writing, but there is a rawness in its communication here that is compelling and personal. Pitt questions Reverend Jago Jones, a Hellfire member who is now preaching and doing missionary work in the slums. He admits to Pitt that when he was young he was indulgent and careless of other people's feelings, just like FitzJames. He believes, though, that redemption is possible.

'One cannot undo the selfishness of youth, but one can leave it behind, learn from its mistakes, and avoid too quick or too cruel a judgment in those who in their turn do likewise.' Pitt did not doubt his sincerity, but he also had the feeling it was a speech he had prepared in his mind for the time he should be asked.

Jago Jones is the model for a type of man Anne will use again in her writing. When Pitt first meets him he sees 'the face of a man who followed his own conscience, whatever the law, whatever the cost'. He rises above his past, his spiritual doubts and the moribund institutions of his religion, and he makes a perfect contrast to the bullying, *nouveau riche* FitzJames family. Tallulah, Finlay FitzJames's sister, breaks with family convention to admire Jago Jones 'working all the hours there are, at giving away his goods to feed the poor … [and] his whole life in service'. Her dilemma is whether she will follow her family's taste for affluent depravity or follow her heart and carry the true cross with Jago Jones.

Pentecost is the feast in the Christian liturgical year that commemorates the descent of the Holy Spirit upon the disciples of Christ after the Resurrection, and there is something decidedly spiritual about the symbolism in this book. But Anne also writes of Emily's smouldering boredom at being a society wife, and of the Pitts' domestic life:

A marmalade-striped kitten came running in from the scullery, then stopped suddenly, its back arched, and took half a dozen steps crabwise, its tail bristling. A coal-black kitten charged in after it and there were squawks and squeals as they tumbled with each other, spitting and scratching harmlessly, to the children's entertainment. Porridge was ignored, and no one argued.

⋈

During the summer of 1995 things began to heat up with regard to the filming of the Pitt and Monk series. After years there was an overwhelming rush of interest — some of it from the biggest players in British television. As Meg explained to Hope Dellon at St Martin's, who still had a financial interest in the first 10 titles of the Pitt series, there were three possibilities: 'Lynda La Plante Productions (she of course has been the champion of the books all along, and has a golden touch for getting drama series commissioned and broadcast); Meridian/Anglia (one of the major ITV companies); and Ardent (the joint managing director is Prince Edward) … I'm happy to discuss it with you at the end of the month, when we meet the three interested producers and look at the whole situation.'[19] 'Good luck,' Hope replied. 'I know the process of seeing books translated to the screen often seems endless, and I hope the results will finally repay all your efforts.'[20]

Although the BBC option on the Pitt series had lapsed, Alan Yentob contacted Meg to request an eight-week extension. At the end of September a new head of series would be appointed and there would be no major decisions on pilots or commissioning until then. But towards the end of August, Meg told Alan Yentob that she and Anne were sick of waiting: '[Anne] is aware of the changes which have taken place within the department during the three years in which the BBC have held the option, but still feels that this has been enough time to decide whether or not to go to a series.'[21] They would be pursuing other possibilities.

The decision to go with Prince Edward's company Ardent was difficult. Not only did it alienate some of the most significant — not to mention persuasive — people in British film and television, but Ardent was a relatively new and untested company. 'The joint managing directors are a top ex-BBC lawyer and Prince Edward, and the other drama personnel are ex-BBC,' Meg explained to the editor at St Martin's. 'The suggested deal here is a one-year option on THE CATER STREET HANGMAN only, but with the first opportunity to option the rest of the series on terms to be agreed.' Their decision was made finally on the basis that Ardent 'seem stylistically closest to Anne's work and have undertaken to consult with her thoroughly from day one: also they happen to be the highest bidder'.[22]

Through this time, the 'typhoon of interest in Anne's personal story' continued.[23] Anne was contacted by Georgina Morley, the editorial director of Macmillan: 'I wanted to write to say how very impressive I thought your appearance on *Midweek* was. It must be very difficult to have the media's attention on you in the aftermath of a fictionalized account of your life and I do sympathize ... I'd love to talk to you about the possibility of publishing your story.'[24] Anne replied that she was not prepared to write an account of her life. Inevitably, it would involve recriminations and excuses, and would touch on other people's lives, which she did not feel at liberty to discuss.

Among the requests that she accepted was one from Alison Parr's National Radio *Sunday Morning* show in New Zealand. Meg was vigilant in her research, contacting Darron Leslie, publicity assistant at HarperCollins in Auckland, to ensure the request was genuine. 'I've been trying to find out something more about the show. I had a nice talk with the (outgoing) producer, who's assured me that they'll be nice to Anne.' She was hoping for further reassurance. 'I may be being over-protective, but Anne's had a rough ride with some of the interviews, and in fact hasn't done any for New Zealand before, so I'm just a bit concerned for her.'[25]

Darron Leslie faxed back directly: 'National Radio as a whole steers way clear of journalism of a tabloid or scandalous nature. [Alison Parr's] show is well researched, well respected and is lively and informative radio. Basically, Meg, no need for concern, things will be fine.'[26] Meg later confirmed an interview with Alison Parr on the basis that 'they won't touch on the "event" or film, which are still a bit sensitive, and which we feel has already been amply covered'.[27]

Anne's interview experiences had been mixed. Some were open and transparent; others, more adversarial and accusatory. These were disturbing, as was some of the mail she received. Much of it was positive, but some was cruel and occasionally sick. One writer, who addressed the outside of the envelope to Anne Perry, began her letter 'Dear Juliet'. She discussed an unhinged business proposition, then issued a challenge:

> I'd like to put this to the test. You could pick me out in a crowd. I have something, I don't know what it is. But I do have something. Leading public figures find me particularly attractive. In fact, anyone who is somebody always makes a beeline for me. Except for Germaine Greer who appears to have no sense of intuition. I walked out on her.[28]

⚭

At the end of 1995, Meg and Don were still waiting for Leona to make a decision on 'Tathyr'. A reworked manuscript had been submitted yet again and Meg dreaded the outcome. 'I can't see our persevering (well, Leona persevering) with non-mysteries if this draft isn't right,' she told Don. She thought the outlook for Anne's fantasy was bleak, and they might have to wait until — as Don had suggested in earlier correspondence — 'any publisher will be grateful for a Perry novel'. Meg was concerned.

> Anne's confidence has taken such a knock with the previous disastrous draft, and it raises the stakes on whether she can write fantasy, but she must, and she'll be sweating to have it published as soon as possible … Oh, mercy, maybe I'm just coming down with a cold.[29]

Anne continued to chalk up successes, while she waited for the reaction to 'Tathyr'. *Weighed in the Balance*, her Monk novel for 1996, was a starred review in the *Publishers Weekly*: 'Careful investigation and astute teamwork produce some astonishing revelations that presage the end of Victorian propriety and an era's pretense of innocence.' The *New York Times Book Review* was full of praise: 'Scenes [are] described in lush, sensuous strokes … Monk, the dark and brooding hero … infuses this luxuriantly detailed series with its romantic soul.'[30]

Weighed in the Balance opens with Sir Oliver Rathbone sitting in his chambers in Vere Street, surveying with satisfaction the achievements of a life perspicaciously spent. 'He was at the pinnacle of his career, and possibly the most highly respected Barrister in England.' His knighthood is recent recognition of his services to criminal justice. But pinnacles can be dangerous. A miscalculation, a disastrous case, the unsteadying draught from opening one's door to a disturbed client, can bring everything crashing down. Rathbone's *bête noir* is Countess Zorah Rostova, who comes to his chambers to enlist his services in a civil case of slander. She is convinced that Friedrich, Crown Prince of the tiny German principality of Felzburg, has been murdered by his wife, Princess Gisela.

Theirs has been one of the great love stories of their time. Twenty years ago, Friedrich was smitten by the gorgeous Gisela, and eloped to live with her in exile, establishing his court in Venice. Now, aged 42, Friedrich suffers a terrible hunting accident that leaves him with broken ribs, a broken collarbone and a leg smashed in three places. Gisela nurses him, but in her care he dies. Countess Zorah, convinced Gisela has poisoned her husband, tells everyone Friedrich has been murdered by his wife, even though she has not a scrap of evidence. Hester cannot believe it when she is told. 'What on earth had possessed Rathbone to take up Zorah's case? His knighthood had gone to his wits. When the Queen touched him on the shoulder with the sword she must have pricked his brain.' It is not only Zorah's reputation at risk here, but Rathbone's too.

In *Weighed in the Balance*, Oliver Rathbone's father, Henry, makes an appearance in his mentoring role when his son comes to him in search of stillness and contemplation. Henry is a mathematician and inventor whose telescope, even in retirement, is trained on the stars. 'He was a tall man, taller than his son, square-shouldered and thin. He had a gentle, aquiline face and farsighted blue eyes. He was obliged to remove his spectacles to study anything closely.' This is Anne's father, Henry Hulme, fictionalized. He admires Oliver's friend Hester, but will not interfere in his son's life to push the relationship. Both Oliver Rathbone and Monk have a 'deep regard for Hester', but it is Monk — the more irked of the two by her independent personality — who begins to see her true worth.

> Even at the very darkest moment, when she must have faced the possibility of his guilt, it had never entered her mind to abandon him. Her loyalty went beyond trust in innocence or in victory, it was the willingness to be there in defeat, even in one which was deserved.

The loyalty Hester extends to Monk is unconditional, an earthly parallel of the absolution offered to sinners by Christ. She is a virtuous presence in his life and her belief in him is redeeming, but she is also a realist made of flesh and blood. Oliver, she decides, 'knew the law, few better, and he had certainly seen crimes of passion and even depravity. But had he really tasted any breadth of ordinary human life, with its frailty, complexity and seeming contradictions?'

After her slanderous remarks, Countess Zorah becomes implicated in the murder of Prince Friedrich herself — and Oliver Rathbone must defend her in what seems a hopeless case. He has to listen to jeering people calling for her execution and watch 'journalists scrambling to escape with their reports' at the end of each day's trial, while 'outside, crowds filled the pavements, jostling and elbowing to see the chief protagonists'. Courtroom and street scenes are brought vividly to life by Anne's own memories, which came more freshly to her mind as a consequence of her interviews with Robert McCrum.

∷

McCrum's long-awaited biographical profile, 'Memories of murder', was published in the *Guardian* on 29 June 1996, but never in the *New Yorker*.

166

When Don Maass asked Meg how the article was progressing, she responded: 'The feeling I get from Robert McCrum [is that] he's letting the facts and quotations speak for themselves, without adding speculation of his own ... he's making an attempt to be evenhanded — praise for Anne but also some critical comments, in the interests of sketching out her character.'[31]

In preparation for McCrum's trip to Scotland, Meg outlined their expectations: 'we recognise that you will need to touch on the murder case, but understand that your intention is to give a profile of Anne as a person and as a writer. Forgive me if I sound over-protective, but some interviews have been savage.'[32]

McCrum's well-researched piece presented a fuller and larger picture of its subject than had been seen before, and it was both critical of and reflective about the woman he met and the myths surrounding her. He interviewed Anne at her home in Portmahomack, where he found the rooms, some still being renovated, 'gloomy, half-furnished, and unlived in'. He recognized in Anne a person who had spent 40 years trying to 'become someone else', and identified this as a time of integration when she was obliged to bring two parts of a life together. 'Now she has been forced to acknowledge that inside or alongside Anne Perry, the successful crime writer, stands the spectral figure of Juliet Hulme.'

But he found the joining incomplete and perhaps impossible. 'I detect in her manner an unassuaged, inner despair. She is both like a child and like an adult, but the two parts seem not to connect', and 'there [is] something damaged about her; she has the wariness that comes from the fear of expressing trust'. His article gave a summarized but thoughtful account of the murder and trial, and set out what he described as 'several, well-rehearsed justifications': the side-effects of prolonged use of isoniazid and streptomycin for tuberculosis; her 'agony' for her father over the marriage break-up; the sense of being 'backed into a corner' by Pauline, who was suffering from an eating disorder and threatening suicide; and her gratitude to Pauline for standing by her when she was in the Christchurch sanatorium balanced against her sense of 'profound debt of obligation' to Pauline for visiting her there.

McCrum weighed up the value of these explanations and discounted

Anne's playing down of the relationship, finding instead 'an adolescent friendship inching towards hysteria'. He made adept biographical links between her life and her books, describing Anne as 'dogmatic' in conversation and asserting that she 'displays an exaggerated belief in the power of positive thinking'. McCrum's observations were clever and astute.

'Strangely, neither [Lin] Ferguson nor any rival reporter has made the same effort to unmask, or even to track down, Pauline Parker,' McCrum observed. Towards the end of his stay in Portmahomack, he asked Anne: 'What is your worst fear?' 'My worst fear about all this,' she replied, 'is that you will find Pauline.'

⊗

'She continues to write, obsessively, perhaps in the hope that she can somehow bury her terrible past in a mountain of fiction'.[33] There is undoubtedly a vein of truth in McCrum's assertion, but the money and the success Anne's writing brought her were probably even more compelling. *Ashworth Hall*, her Pitt for 1997, was very well reviewed. The *Guardian* described it as an 'elegant period novel with a contemporary resonance ... [that] remains utterly convincing', while the *New York Times* perceptively observed: 'this subtle play on sex roles, a constant in this rewarding series, may well be the secret of its profound appeal'.[34] Ashworth Hall — the splendid home of Emily 'sometime Viscountess Ashworth, now Mrs. Jack Radley' — is the setting for personal and political intrigue when powerful groups of Irish Protestants and Catholics are brought to a conference there to tackle the Irish Problem.

Pitt's connection to Emily gives him the perfect cover to be on hand to safeguard proceedings. His boss, Assistant Commissioner Cornwallis, insists that, to keep up the ruse, Pitt must take Charlotte to what will be, for the women, a house party. 'Pitt felt a lightning bolt of alarm at the thought of what danger, or sheer chaos, Charlotte could get herself into. The trouble she might cause with Emily to assist her brought a word of protest to his lips.' While Pitt reels at the thought of his interfering wife accompanying him on a delicate mission, Charlotte concentrates on working out where she can borrow some of the half-dozen dresses a lady might wear in a day, 'not to mention jewelry, shoes, boots, an evening reticule, a shawl, [and] a hat for walking'.

Religious debate, Irish history and upper-class social mores provided Anne with rich material, alongside the tragedy that sits at the heart of this story. For it is not long before the gallant political hero Ainsley Greville, who is trying to broker an agreement between the opposing Catholic and Protestant camps, is found floating, dead, in the tub. It is an ignominious end, Pitt thinks. 'This shell lying half below the bathwater was so familiarly him, and yet not him at all. In a sense it was already no one. The will and intellect were somewhere else.'

But it is Charlotte who operates most effectively in this, her familiar milieu, peeling back the layers of power and ritual to reveal a complex truth. In spite of his laudable façade, it seems that Ainsley Greville was a brutal, corrupt man with more than one enemy. Among them is his future daughter-in-law, Justine Baring, who unsuccessfully attempts to kill him to prevent his exposure of her terrible secret to his son and her fiancé, Piers Greville.

'Can you see the scene … Ainsley laughing at [Piers], telling him his precious betrothed was his father's whore?' says Justine to Charlotte. In the end, Justine must confess to Piers her murderous intentions and youthful prostitution with his father, and beg his forgiveness. He asks for time to think about it, and Charlotte sleeps with Justine to comfort her. 'We bring a lot of our griefs upon ourselves … It doesn't make it hurt any less. Lie down and get warm. Perhaps then you'll sleep a while.'

When Piers offers Justine forgiveness and is prepared to make a new life with her in the United States, she replies:

I shall have to prove to you that I am what I am trying to be. There is no point in saying I am sorry over and over again. I will show it by being there, every hour, every day, every week, until you know it.

Not only does *Ashworth Hall* offer a powerful commentary on forgiveness and redemption through love and endeavour — which almost completely overwhelms the political machinations — but it also has a feminist subtext. Priscilla Walton and Manina Jones, writing about hard-boiled women detectives, argue that the female detective 'actually "normalizes" a certain brand of feminism for readers who would not ordinarily read in this way'.[35] Although Charlotte and Emily are a century and half a world away from being hard-boiled, they do normalize women as powerful figures who define and influence public as well as private outcomes. In spite of his reservations, 'Pitt watched Charlotte with a sudden admiration which was oddly painful. She was so competent, so strong. She did not seem to need support from anyone else. If she was frightened, she hid it.'

Anne's 1997 Monk, *The Silent Cry*, was also well reviewed. The novel begins on a shivering night in January, in a wind-whipped alley in St Giles, as Detective John Evan and PC Shotts stand over the crumpled and barely recognizable bodies of Leighton Duff and his son, Rhys. It is assumed from their horrendous injuries that both men have been beaten to death, but on closer inspection Rhys is discovered to be still alive. What could possibly have brought a respectable solicitor and his son to a London slum full of cheap women, moneylenders, cardsharps, fences and forgers? There is no easy explanation, because, as Rhys regains consciousness, it becomes apparent that he is 'locked in his own world of isolation, hearing and seeing but unable to speak, unable to communicate with anyone the terror and the pain he must feel'. Rhys is still speechless at his trial, after his surprising arrest for the murder of his father.

It is Monk who makes sense of this enigmatic case of patricide, when he is engaged by Vida Hopgood, a factory owner from Seven Dials, to discover who has been raping and beating factory women and part-time prostitutes in the area. In *The Silent Cry* there are thought-provoking reflections on both heterosexual and homosexual rape and, more broadly, on the patriarchal institutions that foster hypocrisy, condone abuse and exclude women. Why, thinks Hester, are women denied 'their use of knowledge and authority ... It was antiquated, blind, rooted in privilege and ignorance. It was worse than unjust, it was dangerous. It was precisely that sort of blinkered idiocy which had kept inadequate men in charge of the battles in the Crimea and cost countless men their lives.'

But this is what it means to be human, according to acknowledged

Christian John Evan. He is a voice for Anne's theology when he explains to Monk that if the world is perfect 'there will be no need for humility or forgiveness … For that matter, neither will there be need for pity or generosity.' An imperfect world tests us all, and malignance, as much as goodness, creates the shades of grey that truly explain the human condition. 'If you think the world is divided into those who are good and those who are bad, you are worse than a fool, you are a moral imbecile, refusing to grow up,' Monk says vehemently to Vida Hopgood.

⁂

At the beginning of 1997, six months after Robert McCrum's article recorded Anne's greatest fear, Pauline Parker was found living in Hoo, close to the historic city of Rochester in Kent, under the name Hilary Nathan. Anne consciously shut out the details of the discovery, but the revelation was still a shock, as was the surname Pauline had chosen. Nathan was the name of the prophet God sent to make King David face up to his betrayal and murder of Uriah the Hittite. As Anne had told Meg MacDonald back in Suffolk, the hypocrisy of seeing David as a virtuous statesman continued to anger her as it had when she and Pauline had discussed it. But of all names, why had Pauline chosen Nathan? Was it just coincidence, or was it deliberate — a constant, penitential reminder of God's judgment?

As Hilary Nathan, Pauline had lived a private, solitary yet constructive existence. At the end of her parole period in 1965, she had left New Zealand to begin a new life in Britain. Initially she worked in a London library, but gave away the profession she trained for in New Zealand to become an instructor at a riding school for disabled children and a teacher at the Abbey Court special-needs school in Strood. By the time she retired in the mid-1990s she was deputy headmistress. When her identity was unmasked, there was a flood of media interest in her story. Her old employers and the residents of Hoo were plied with questions by reporters from the *Daily Mail*, the *Express* and the *New Zealand Woman's Weekly*. Hilary Nathan emerged as a likable, quiet, almost introverted woman who adored horses, riding and the life of the stable.

According to her neighbour, Joyce Hookins, she 'always seemed very nice, and she clearly loved children'.[36] Another villager described her as 'eccentric', a person who 'very much keeps herself to herself. She is ... well spoken and appears very intelligent and well educated. But she is quite childish in a way.'[37] Hilary Nathan collected dolls, which she kept in her living room, and from the street you might just catch a glimpse of a large rocking horse inside the front door. Perhaps in the trappings of childhood she sought to reclaim a youth that had been lost. Only those who have leapt from juvenile to adult in a single act can understand the grief that that entails, and the urge to fill the resulting gulf with innocence. Abbey Court sources remembered her as a 'loner', but one who was 'well liked' and was apt, rather strangely, to turn up 'for class in wellies and battered black sunglasses'.[38]

It was not until Hilary Nathan was in her sixties that she talked to her sister Wendy about the murder of their mother. Hilary was still bemused by events. 'It just got out of hand. Looking back ... it was something that grew and grew out of all proportion.'

> Wendy believes Hilary didn't fully understand the finality of death. 'After it happened she was very sorry about it. It took her about five years to realize what she had done ... [The girls] were ill fated and they went overboard and committed a dreadful crime they have paid for their whole lives.'[39]

After her retirement, Hilary took up an ascetic life of religious contemplation. Hilary does not have television, radio or internet access, and Wendy has become her spokesperson and media interface. 'She is a nun in her way ... she's deeply religious ... she doesn't have any contact with the outside world — she's a reclusive, really. She's a devout Roman Catholic and spends most of her time in prayer.'[40] According to Wendy, Hilary is 'living the life she always dreamed of as a girl' — a genteel country existence with a stable of her own.[41] But it is a solitary life lived in faith and seclusion, and she has taken the name of a prophet synonymous with murder and judgment.

II

Juliet Hulme and Pauline Rieper were both high academic achievers in their first year at high school. They were interested in art and music, and both were excused sport, Juliet for respiratory problems and Pauline because of her osteomyelitis. This threw the two girls together when the rest of the class donned their white blouses and voluminous navy-blue rompers and went to the gymnasium to play netball, or to a grass strip down the side of the school to do field events.

They walked together arm in arm around Cranmer Square and held hands in the playground. Classmates remember that 'they would stay sitting outside the gym, and there was no way they would have a conversation with anyone else'.[42] The exceptions were Margaret Tyndall and Caroline Spencer, who were identified as potential allies.

The girls shared a growing passion for horses. Juliet had her own horse, and they would borrow one for Pauline so they could ride together, sometimes, it seems, illicitly at night. Juliet approached Margaret and Caroline, thinking they might make co-conspirators:

She stalked over: 'We (that is to say Pauline and Juliet) have decided that you (that's Caroline and me) are *wild* enough to join *us* riding horses in the night-time.' I just thought of Caroline's mother and my mother ... my mind raced, I thought it would be cold, then I thought I would have to get on my bike and I am scared of the *dark*.[43]

The plan came to nothing. While none of the others in 3A could imagine being that daringly disobedient, Juliet and Pauline were becoming more adventurous, sometimes escaping at night to pursue their hair-raising schemes. They acted in skits that they wrote and directed. They dressed up in costume, took photographs, listened to the radio, played records, sang, danced and talked endlessly together over cards and board games, read books, went to the theatre and were regular movie-goers.

They spoke on the telephone for hours. Their friendship was intense and euphoric. Now each could share the hormone-driven exhilaration of adolescence with someone of like mind. Pauline filled a huge gap for Juliet. At a time when teenagers naturally rebel and seek the company of their peers, there was an unusual degree of distance and disconnection between Juliet and her parents, caused by her illness, repeated long separations, and Hilda and Henry's high-powered professional and social positions.

Marjorie Webb used to catch the Riccarton tram with Juliet after school. It was just a short walk down Gloucester Street, through Chancery Lane and into the Square. She let Juliet lead the conversation. Although it was:

> a privilege to think she would let me walk with her ... I always used to feel there was a loneliness there when she got home. Somehow or other her father seemed to be her pivot. She never talked much about her mother. She would be going home — and it always seemed to be to her father and her brother.[44]

There was a sense, too, among some of her contemporaries, that behind the flashy intelligence and haughtiness was someone who needed help. Even as a young teenager, Marjorie Webb wondered if much of what they saw was not a façade.

> Young people often put on a front and they appear all in control and quite happy, but you don't really know what they really feel underneath ... and I did wonder [about Juliet] even in those years at school if that was a front and she were protecting [herself] to a degree.[45]

In spite of her privileged way of life, Juliet's essential needs — a reassuring and loving relationship with her parents, balanced by authority — were not being met. Because long separations had not allowed her to bond with her parents, the links she had developed, especially with her mother, tended to be intellectual rather than instinctive.

Pauline was infatuated with Juliet and everything she represented. It was a Cinderella story. Her own sleepy Christchurch childhood of hospital wards and sickness had been one of constraint. There was never enough money, freedom or opportunity. Her father, a dapper little man, was older than most, and her mother more authoritarian. Neither of her parents was highly educated, and education was something she aspired to. Her father's lack of income was embarrassing at school. Writing about children from lower-income families, social scientist Tess Ridge notes:

> Friendships represent secure social assets for children and play a vital role in the development of self and social identity ... All the children in the poverty study saw friendships as having a very protective effect, and the girls in particular viewed their friends as confidantes and supportive alternatives to family ... [but] inadequate housing and lack of resources, including bedroom space and insufficient income to provide extra meals and treats ... [made] it difficult to invite friends to stay.[46]

The Riepers were not desperately poor, but Pauline's mother had to work to the point of exhaustion to keep their boarding house running. A succession of itinerant strangers took up residency for a time, then, when they were familiar figures around the house, moved on. Sometimes Pauline even had to shift rooms to accommodate them. There was no privacy for an intimate joke: every space was public, including the bathroom. The only opportunity for recreation or culture — listening to the radio or a gramophone record, or reading a book — came at the end of a tiring day. It was a 'have-not' working-class life in which Pauline would be trapped, unless she could get away or escape to university.

Juliet was an awakening of hope, the door to another world. She represented money, flamboyance and prospects — and she had chosen Pauline to be her friend, exclusively. It was head-spinning and addictive.

For years Pauline had taken riding lessons. It was a sport she could manage physically, and her English mother still wished a better, more genteel life for her children. Without her parents' knowledge Pauline bought a pacer she named Omar Khayyám and arranged grazing for it at Ilam. When her father found out, months later, he quickly came to see the horse as a positive outlet, and as a distraction from Juliet. In the end, though, even Omar Khayyám came second to the friendship. He was more likely a typical teenage symbol of defiance, of independence.

It was probably Pauline who introduced the idea of plasticine modelling, but Juliet quickly became so involved that an essay she wrote on the subject was published in the school magazine at the end of 1952. In 'My Holiday Hobby' she explained how she made herds of plasticine horses. She began by modelling the stallion, which established the correct scale for the rest. 'This one is a black (taken from "Shetan"), which is Arabic for "the devil". He was a killer and a throwback to the ancient Arab horses.' she wrote. She demonstrates an impressive knowledge of the anatomical structure of horses and of the different breeds. 'I have them all on a green shelf in my bedroom. On the shelf is a hill with an imitation clay bank on one side.' Included with the essay is her competent nocturnal drawing of a racing stallion, and a poem:[47]

SHETAN

His eyes were wild;
    His nostrils flared:
His ears were flat,
    His teeth were bared—
His heaving flanks were flecked
    With blood and foam.

His streaming mane
    Was whipped and caught:
His mighty muscles
    Flexed and taut—
His cruel hooves forever
    Seeking prey.

J.M.H., III A.

Juliet and Pauline became increasingly caught up in writing Arthurian-style fantasies. Initially, they acted out or produced plasticine figures for their main characters and modelled recreations of the scenes they were imagining. At one stage they manufactured a complete masked ball. Eventually, however, the writing dominated everything.

Pauline's 1953 diary, a Christmas present from her father, became an extension of this writing. She began with a New Year's resolution written at the front: 'To be lenient to others'. There was also a key for the 'Saints' Juliet and Pauline had created. This was a list of characters they had made up, based in part on the film actors and singers they idolized and each with an ideal quality or characteristic. Occasionally, they would have a clear-out and introduce new names.

The list of Saints was also a code: HE was Mario Lanza; HIM, James Mason; IT, Harry Lime; THIS, Mel Ferrer; THAT, Jussi Björling; and HIS, Guy Rolfe. The concept was playful, witty and secretive. It reinforced their communion and separateness from the adult world they were beginning to shun. Beyond these recognizable names, the list continued as an exploration of language:

WHOSE+THEY=THEM
THEY+WE=US
WHOSE+WE=WHICH[48]

After the Saints was a summary of the major events of 1952, and, from March on, synopses for stories Pauline was planning to write and a number of poems. Much of the body of the diary consists of matter-of-fact details competently and sometimes evocatively communicated. There are frequent references to the housework Pauline did to help her mother, which she mostly completed willingly. But it was also a place for dreams, thoughts and wild ambitions.

The diary was both a companion and a confessional. It allowed her to express a new, separate, more adult voice, and it was personal and safe. Pauline could record things she knew would be completely unacceptable to her parents, such as the Ceylonese students she sneaked out at night to see, or her sexual liaisons with Nicholas, a law student boarding with the Riepers. She wrote down everything and never hid her diary, so, although her life lacked some of the normal boundaries of privacy, she never feared that her mother or anyone else would read it. It is possible that Juliet kept a similar record, but this was never found.

Pauline's stays with the Hulmes increased in frequency and length. When they were together at the Ilam homestead, the girls disappeared, intent on some planned occupation. There was a personality shift when they were together. Apart, they were vulnerable and morose: together, they were powerful and focused. This initially pleased both the Hulmes and the Riepers, who wanted their daughters to be happy, but it was not long before the attachment seemed too intense. They began spending time together writing that should have been devoted to schoolwork and preparation for examinations. Christchurch Girls' High School contacted Hilda Hulme to express concern that the girls' friendship was 'unhealthy' and having a detrimental effect on their academic progress. Hilda's reaction was predictably liberal: she 'wasn't prepared to interfere in her daughter's friendships'.[49]

Over Easter, the Hulmes took Pauline away with them to their weekend cottage at Port Levy, on Banks Peninsula, 55 kilometres south-east of Christchurch. On the night of Good Friday, 3 April 1953, Pauline wrote ecstatically in her diary:

To-day Juliet and I found the key to the 4th World. We realize now that we have had it in our possession for about six months but we only realized it on the day of the death of Christ. We saw a gateway through the clouds. We sat on the edge of the path and looked down the hill out over the bay. The island looked beautiful. The sea was blue. Everything was full of peace and bliss. We then realized we had the key. We know now that we are not genii as we thought. We have an extra part of our brain which can appreciate the 4th World. Only about 10 people have it. When we die we will go to the 4th World, but meanwhile on two days every year we may use the key and look in to that beautiful world which we have been lucky enough to be allowed to know of, on this Day of Finding the Key to the Way through the Clouds.[50]

Pauline's Port Levy revelation story was a parable of exclusivity and exclusion, bolstered by the arrogance of youth. It separated Pauline and Juliet from the throng of ordinary souls and linked them in eternity to their Saints. It was the poetic, boastful, silly rant of a teenager. The dangerous thing was not the key they discovered to the 4th World, or the megalomania they would later be accused of, but the door that was beginning to shut behind them on ordinariness and adult intervention.

Pauline's Port Levy holiday was a defining and indoctrinating experience. It was here that she began to feel part of the Hulme family. 'The days I spent at Port Levy were the most HEAVENLY ones I have ever experienced. Mrs Hulme did my hair. She calls me her foster daughter.' This was followed on 26 April by: 'Mrs Hulme said she wished I was her daughter.'[51] Hilda was merely attempting to make her daughter's friend feel welcome, but Pauline, understandably, pounced on her light comments as proof of something more. Her own parents seemed insignificant compared with the Hulmes.

Hilda's languid discipline looked liberating and sophisticated beside Honorah's strict regime. Pauline's enchantment with the Hulmes grew in direct proportion to her estrangement at home. She started to separate herself from the family unit, spending more and more time in her room writing, and very significantly she stopped sharing her thoughts and plans with her family. The Riepers, who were being progressively shut out of their daughter's life, felt impotent to do anything about it.

The course of events might have been changed by a plan for Juliet to stay with the Riepers while Hilda and Henry went back to England to attend the Congress of the Universities of the British Commonwealth in London and for a three-and-a-half-month lecture tour. Time together for the girls at the Riepers might have helped normalize things and reinstate a better relationship between Pauline and her parents. But the arrangement was derailed by the shocking revelation that Juliet had tuberculosis in one lung. On the eve of their departure, the Hulmes decided to admit Juliet to the Christchurch Sanatorium and continue with their plans.

Once again, Juliet felt abandoned and betrayed.

The sanatorium, perched on the tussock-covered windswept slopes of the Cashmere Hills overlooking the city, was a frightening place for a young teenager on her own. The low, flat verandah-edged buildings looked more like a collection of prefabricated army huts than a hospital. It was a stark, sterile environment in which people died. No one who visited could escape a pressing awareness of their mortality.

New treatments, however, offered hope for a complete recovery. On his return to Christchurch in 1948, Dr FO Bennett 'was re-appointed as Assistant Physician on the hospital staff and was given charge of the infectious diseases and thus was able to supervise the first treatments of tuberculous meningitis (TB) with streptomycin'.[52] It was a 'miracle' treatment that might in time result in a complete eradication of the disease.

In spite of these positive prospects, Juliet's life at the Christchurch Sanatorium was bleak:

> Each morning I was woken up in this freezing open-air ward, where the water jugs had ice on top, to enormous pills and a needle in my backside. Sometimes they'd catch a nerve and you couldn't walk all day.[53]

In a bed close to Juliet was a classmate from 3A, Joan White, who was admitted almost at the same time. Juliet had visits from schoolmates and acquaintances, but no one who meant as much to her as Pauline. Honorah Rieper brought Pauline to visit three times, but the girls exchanged letters almost daily. Until then their writing had been done in exercise books and was distinct from their everyday experience. Now, in their correspondence, they wrote in role: Juliet became Antoinette and Deborah; Pauline was Gina and Paul. These characters came to life for them with a new poignancy and momentum because of their immediacy. This was not the first time Juliet's mind had transported her from a hospital bed, but now she was not alone. Pauline was with her.

Juliet went into the sanatorium on 21 May and left on 9 September 1953, a week after her parents returned home. Although she was not yet cured of TB, Juliet was released on the promise that Hilda would nurse her at home. In spite of being urged to communicate, in the whole time Juliet was in the sanatorium she wrote only a hurried note and two quick letters to her parents. 'Both were short and appeared to have been written without care,' Hilda recalled.[54]

This lack of communication was followed by Juliet's retreat from family life. She was ill and bed-ridden much of the time, but she stopped reading her books to her mother and involving her parents in her imaginative and psychological landscape. 'When I returned to N.Z.,' Hilda later observed, 'I noticed a marked change in her personality. She seemed very much more withdrawn. I noticed the friendship with Pauline was the only thing that mattered to her.'[55] She also noted a considerable acceleration in the amount of literature her daughter was producing.

Juliet did not return to Christchurch Girls' High School, and without her Pauline's interest in her studies faltered. The excitement and the future lay with Juliet and their writing. In her diary she recorded her mood swings. One day she was ecstatically happy, and the next in despair. In a diary entry made in November 1953, she wrote: 'To-day I felt thoroughly, utterly and completely depressed. I was in one of those moods in which committing suicide sounds heavenly.'[56] These extremes were not incompatible with her stage of life, but there was no parent to mediate them. She had lost faith in the value of Herbert and Honorah's decisions. Her life felt desperately out of control. The only thing she had power over was what she ate.

Researcher in childhood and youth studies Mary Jane Kehily has argued that 'the body is an important site for the exercise of power … [and it] becomes the expression of distress and of the contradictions and paradoxes girls experience around their bodies and sexualities'.[57] Eating disorders such as anorexia and bulimia occur at the highest rates between the ages of 15 and 19, and depression leading to self-harm is not uncommon in this age group. Depressive disorders have 'a constellation of symptoms such as tearfulness, sleep disturbance, loss of appetite and suicidal thoughts', all of which Pauline experienced to varying degrees.[58] She needed help.

She began to lose weight, and the drop was dramatic enough to worry her parents. Hilda noticed it, too. 'Pauline had lost a great deal of weight during my absence and I advised her [Honorah] to seek medical advice.'[59] Pauline had become withdrawn and sullen, and now, although it was not identified as such, she was probably suffering from bulimia. Honorah, concerned about the weight loss and its link to her 'unhealthy' friendship with Juliet, took Pauline in December 1953 to see Dr Bennett, the general physician recommended by the Hulmes. After his examination, he decided she was not in good health and that her weight was of concern. He made a classic diagnosis that the friendship had a homosexual overtone but that both girls were likely to grow out of it.

Honorah had her own techniques for handling Pauline's difficult behaviour. The most effective was the threat that Pauline would not be able to see Juliet. 'The thought is too dreadful,' wrote Pauline in her diary on 20 December. 'Life would be unbearable without Deborah … I rang Deborah and told her the threat. I wish I could die. That is not an idle or temporary impulse, I have decided over the last 2 or 3 weeks that it would be the best thing that could happen altogether, and the thought of death is not fearsome.'[60] Questioned later, Herbert said he did not think Pauline had missed any visits to Juliet.

Pauline began her diary for 1954 with these words: 'My New Year resolution is a far more selfish one than last year, so there is more probability of my keeping it. It is to make my motto "Eat drink and be merry for to-morrow you may be dead".'[61] This would be the year when Honorah decided to encourage Pauline to leave school. Whether it was an idle threat that snowballed into cold reality or a plan in which the antagonistic teenager was complicit, the outcome was disastrous. Without school, Pauline would lose her only possibility of escape from a life she found barren and oppressive. As Tess Ridge writes: 'For these children school holds the potential to provide a new social milieu, the opportunity to encounter other people both similar to and different from themselves, and the chance to be securely embedded in an alternative social universe.'[62]

Pauline's contribution to the fifth-form speech competition right before she left was one her amused classmates never forgot. The instruction was to give a speech on the person students would most like to be. While classmates chose people like Tensing, much favoured after Edmund

Hillary's recent ascent of Everest, Pauline said 'she would have liked to be Nero watching Rome burn'.[63]

Her brilliance and all her high-minded aspirations seemed to have come to nothing now she was enrolled not at snobbish Girls' High but at Digby's Commercial College, where she would learn shorthand and typing.

Classmate Margaret Tyndall remembers her predicament in the family and after she left school: 'Pauline would have been injured: "death by a thousand cuts". Not anything dramatic ... She was human and passionate and blindingly angry.'[64] The only place her ambition and energy had to go was into plans with Juliet for their novels. Their intentions for the future and the storylines they wrote escalated in grandeur and violence.

Initially, their stories were 'quite innocuous' and 'adventurous', not unlike Anthony Hope's *Prisoner of Zenda* in concept, but then the plots became more complex and involved and the characters more violent. 'The first was quite ordinary,' remembered Hilda. 'I did not like the second book nearly so well ... I had long talks with [Juliet] about it. I wished she would not be so extreme in her feelings and that she would write about ordinary people.'[65]

The girls planned to leave New Zealand and travel to New York to find a publisher for their books and subsequently a film company in Hollywood where they would 'choose their actors and supervise the filming of their novels'.[66] The movies would, of course, star the Saints. This was not an untypical teenage dream, but most 1950s adolescents did not have the audacity to believe they could make it come true.

Early in March, Pauline visited shipping companies to enquire about making the journey by sea. As a consequence of this they decided in favour of air travel and began saving money for their tickets. One of the first people they approached to help them raise money was Major Walter Andrew Bowman Perry, who was a tenant at the Hulmes' homestead in Ilam.

Canadian-born Bill Perry, as he was known, was a twice-wounded war hero with Clark Gable good looks (complete with moustache), who had arrived in Christchurch on 22 July 1953. He came as an 'industrial consultant employed by the Associated Industrial Consultants of London' to work on assignment in the city. Henry Hulme met Bill and introduced him to Hilda, who saw him professionally because his marriage had recently broken up. As his friendship with the Hulmes grew, he moved from Church Lane, Merivale, to a self-contained flat with a housekeeper at Ilam.

It was never made clear when the relationship between Hilda and the dashing Bill Perry began. Many marriages were damaged by the war and fell apart in the 1950s. Bill Perry's marriage was already over and the Hulmes' in trouble. Hilda lived life intensely and with passion, and Bill Perry became her intoxication. It was not long before she told Henry about the affair. He seems to have been prepared to accept the situation, at least in the interim.

Bill Perry was an odd person for Juliet to approach about selling her horse to raise money for the trip to Hollywood. Perhaps he seemed more available, more vulnerable to pressure, or maybe he was a surreptitious ally. Undoubtedly she picked up that he had become the focus of her mother's attention. Bill remembered it was March: 'the horse was a thoroughbred and from my inquiries, I knew Juliet would be disappointed. I purchased the horse myself and gave her father £50 ... Juliet approached me one morning and asked me how much the fare [to the United States] would be, I asked her by ship or by air, and she said by air. I told her I thought it would be abt £150. She said, "Oh good, that means we've only got another £50 to get. We've nearly got £100."'[67]

To raise the rest of the money they concocted a number of fanciful schemes that included blackmailing Bill Perry and stealing money from Herbert's place of work. Pauline's nocturnal attempt at burglary ended when she discovered a policeman standing outside the fish shop, and Juliet's extortion was thwarted by an unresponsive Bill Perry. Another idea was prostitution: 'We worked out how much prostitutes would earn and how much we would make in such a profession and "should" gradually changed to "shall",' wrote Pauline in her diary.[68] The one thing they managed to pull off twice was shoplifting, but this was not a fund-raising strategy. They gave away the proceeds to '[delight] the hearts of other people by giving them unexpected presents'.[69] According to Pauline's diary, sister Rosemary was the happy recipient of slippers and socks. The shoplifting was justified as research for their writing: they wanted to experience the adrenaline rush and the criminality. But these were not the only sensations they considered. 'I would like to kill someone sometime because I think it is an experience that is necessary to life,' says one of Pauline's characters.[70] The girls were staying up very late at night, sometimes all night. Often they were only telling stories and giggling, but they were frequently surviving on just a few hours' sleep.

Much of Pauline's and Juliet's thinking and behaviour was disruptive and juvenile, but some of it was also dangerous. Without any firm connection to reality or the adult world of restraint, their skewed adolescent ideas were like pinballs that bounced and deflected until — as any game of chance allows — one bizarre idea scored a tragic hit.

Following his resignation from his position, Henry was returning to England. He made a special effort in April to inform the Riepers that he was going. It came as a huge relief when he told them that Juliet would be accompanying him, and that on the way home he planned to leave her with his sister in South Africa to convalesce. Pauline was desperate to accompany Juliet, but to go she had to have her parents' as well as the Hulmes' permission. Ultimately, no one would give this. Of the four parents, Honorah had been most opposed to the girls' friendship, so the eventual unequivocal and unconditional no was a weight off her shoulders.

Pauline had almost completely rejected both her parents, seeing them as equal obstacles to a happy life. On 13 February 1954, she wrote in her diary:

> There seemed to be no possibility of mother relenting and allowing me to go out to Ilam. This afternoon mother told me I could not go out to Ilam again until I was eight stone and more cheerful. As I am now seven stone there is little hope … she is so unreasonable. Why could mother not die? Dozens of people are dying, thousands are dying every day. So why not mother and father too?[71]

As pressure compounded, her focus shifted so that it was only her mother who seemed to be in the way. Another startling announcement probably contributed to this change, as Pauline recorded in her diary on 24 April. 'Dr and Mrs Hulme are going to divorce. The shock is too great to have penetrated in my mind yet ... Deborah and I spent the day soaring between hell and heaven ... Such a huge amount has happened that we do not know where we are ... But one thing Deborah and I are sticking through everything (We sink or swim together).'[72]

Researcher and educationalist Jane Brown has described the significance of same-sex relationships and the phenomenon of girls sticking together:

> Same sex friendships are fundamental to understanding girls' social worlds, and frequently described by girls 'as the most important thing in their lives' ... The idea that friends should 'stick together', was paramount ... For these particular girls 'being a mate' and 'sticking together' meant presenting a united cohesive front, in the event of threats or attack. As a result, 'standing by your pals' could be key to dealing with intimidation and threats from other young people, or from unwanted attention from adults ... who were perceived to interfere unjustly in girls' lives.[73]

Surrounded by circumstances beyond their control, the girls clung to their friendship as the only constant in their disintegrating lives. Pauline had proven herself a loyal and reliable friend when Juliet's parents went away, and now they were arranging to separate and leave her again. Juliet, on the other hand, stood in the place of Pauline's unsympathetic parents.

Pauline was beginning to see a desperate solution. Her diary entry for 28 April 1954 read:

> Mother went out this afternoon so Deborah and I bathed for some time. However I felt thoroughly depressed afterwards and even quite seriously considered committing suicide. Life seemed so much not worth the living, the death such an easy way out. Anger against Mother boiled up inside me as it is she who is one of the main obstacles in my path. Suddenly a means of ridding myself of this obstacle occurred to me. If she were to die—.[74]

Her ideas quickly began to coalesce. The next day she wrote: 'I did not tell Deborah of my plans for removing Mother. I have made no [illegible word] yet as the last fate I wish to meet is one in a Borstal. I am trying to think of some way. I do not [illegible word] to go to too much trouble but I want it to appear either a natural or accidental death.'[75]

On 30 April she shared her idea with Juliet: 'she is rather worried but does not disagree violently'.[76] The strain on both girls had become unendurable. Their plan to murder Honorah was a release and a comfort, an extreme form of juvenile 'acting out' to relieve tension and anxiety. This often occurs when young people feel let down or betrayed by adults. The adolescent takes a breach of protocol or personal treachery as permission to act in a way that is out of character, rebellious and anti-social. Usually the act is self-abusive, such as disruptive, attention-seeking behaviour, promiscuity, shoplifting, smoking and drug and alcohol abuse, and is often interpreted as a cry for help, but on occasions it can take the form of violence against others.

Because the friendship was ending, both sets of parents were happy for the girls to spend time together. Pauline stayed at Ilam homestead for just over a week starting on Friday, 11 June. It was towards the end of her time there, on 19 June, that she again mentioned the idea of murder. 'Our main [idea] for the day was to moider Mother. This notion is not a new one, but this time it is a definite plan which we intend to carry out. We have worked it out carefully and are both thrilled by the idea. Naturally we feel a trifle nervous, but the pleasure of anticipation is great.'[77]

Herbert picked Pauline up on the afternoon of Sunday, 20 June. They went out to Templeton Farm to see Rosemary, who was now five years old. Pauline, who enjoyed her visits to see and play with her sister, was relaxed and talkative. She seemed to have come to terms with her imminent separation from Juliet.

This, however, was far from the case. On 20 June she wrote in her diary: 'I tidied the room and messed about a little. Afterwards we discussed our plans for moidering Mother and made them a little clearer. Peculiarly enough, I have no (qualms of) conscience (or is it peculiar, we are so mad).'[78] That evening Pauline sat quietly in front of the fire, writing what she told her parents was an opera.

Pauline's mood seemed to lift dramatically, and she applied herself to household chores with new vigour. Honorah told Herbert she was 'pleased ... because Pauline was so bright and had done a lot of work'. At lunchtime on Monday, 21 June, Honorah suggested that she and Pauline 'go out the next day for an afternoon together as [Pauline] was starting work the following Monday'.[79] Pauline convinced her mother to include Juliet in their expedition. That night she recorded in her diary:

Deborah rang and we decided to use a rock in a stocking rather than a sandbag. We discussed the moider fully. I feel very keyed up as though I were planning a Surprise party. Mother has fallen in with everything beautifully and the happy event is to take place tomorrow afternoon. So next time I write in this diary Mother will be dead. How odd yet how pleasing.[80]

It is remarkable how distanced Pauline was from the act of murder, and how abstract it was in her imagination. The girls clinically made plans to take someone's life, yet their concept of death and killing was juvenile and unreal. The use of the hard-boiled, penny-dreadful word 'moider' distanced the act still further. They had no proper notion of what they were about to do or encounter.

Pauline's last diary entry, made before she got out of bed on the morning of 22 June 1954, anticipated a nightmare that would haunt the lives of those involved forever. The event she announced would rob Honorah of her life, and Pauline and her friend Juliet of their childhoods. It would shock sleepy, provincial Christchurch to its core and provide scandalizing copy for newspapers, magazines, radio broadcasts and books worldwide. Under the heading, 'The Day of the Happy Event', she wrote:

I am writing a little of this up on the morning before the death. I felt very excited and 'the night before Christmas-ish' last night. I did not have pleasant dreams though. I am about to rise.[81]

CHAPTER SIX

I

A nne and Meg's meeting at the Ardent offices on Charlotte Street in central London left them awestruck. The production company was located in a towering green and blue building with circular windows that offered vistas of fashionable corporate London. After checking in with security on the ground floor, they took the mirrored lift up to a suite of marble-finished offices where they were served tea in delicate bone-china cups.

At the heart of Ardent was Prince Edward, who brought to the usually ruthless, money-focused and expedient business of film and television production the weight of royal tradition. For Anne and Meg, the ruthless appetite for revenue regardless of cost and the streetwise exercise of expediency, which would ultimately make other private ventures more economically viable, were comfortingly absent from Ardent. It was company lawyer and executive producer Eben Foggitt who had first approached them about televising the Pitt series, and he explained that Ardent came 'with clean hands'. It was a newish company with an unsullied track-record, and things would have to stay pretty much that way because the company's managing director and head of production was a senior member of the Royal Family.

Meg already knew the ascendant producer Phillippa Giles, a force behind the Ardent offer, and a significant player in the group of people charged with kicking off Prince Edward's venture into television drama. The fact that Ardent was prepared to work with freelancer Jane Merrow as principal producer also pleased Anne and Meg. Ardent would produce

The Cater Street Hangman in association with Yorkshire Television, as a pilot for a Pitt series they hoped might run on ITV.

The experienced Trevor R Bowen was chosen as scriptwriter. His most impressive credits included episodes of the Sherlock Holmes series, begun by Granada television in 1984 and starring the inimitable Jeremy Brett, and Ngaio Marsh's *Inspector Alleyn Mysteries* made by the BBC during the early 1990s. June Wyndham-Davies, veteran director of later episodes in the Sherlock Holmes series, was also co-opted as producer. Up-and-coming young actor Keeley Hawes was cast in the role of Charlotte 'pretty early on, but it was hard to find the actor for Pitt'.[1] In the end, Jane Merrow and director Sarah Hellings settled on Eoin McCarthy, an actor who impressed them on stage, and though he had never worked a great deal in television he was the spitting image of Anne's Thomas Pitt.

'The casting director picked them right out of my mind,' Anne would tell Linda Richards of *January Magazine*.[2] The only difficult moment was the inclusion of Kate Winslet's sister, Anna, cast as Dora, because Anne was still very tender about *Heavenly Creatures*. Although she was impressed by Kate Winslet's subsequent career, and ultimately even a little flattered by Jackson's casting of her, Winslet's successes only exacerbated Anne's problems with the film. The more seriously Winslet was taken as an actor — and she was very highly regarded — the more credibility it gave her début starring role as Juliet Hulme. Anne was too mindful of herself and how she was perceived to be overtly annoyed, but the choice of Anna Winslet rankled.

Trevor Bowen worked with her on the screenplay, and although there were departures from the original storyline she was pleased with the outcome. 'The characters are exactly as I wrote them and quite a lot of dialogue is straight from the book.' she observed.[3] As well as her work behind the scenes, Anne 'had her moment of glory when they agreed to let her play a non-speaking role', although, as Meg Davis remembers:

[S]he was a bit miffed to find herself a dowager duchess. The dowager bit took some of the shine off it. But she got all dressed up in a tight corset and really enjoyed herself. They filmed round a stately home near

Liverpool. I was also invited up for a day to watch the filming, which was a real treat, and took the train back to London with Edward. He's a quiet man but a thoughtful and interesting (and very nice) guy.[4]

When they reached the railway station, Meg was not sure how to explain to the prince that she had a ticket for a standard and not a first-class carriage, so she thanked him and said goodbye so she could slip surreptitiously to another part of the train. 'But aren't you returning to London by train, now?' he asked, bemused. When, with embarrassment, she explained the situation, Edward smiled and without hesitation said that he and his bodyguards would accompany her in standard class. It was not long before the train heaved its way out of the station. They chatted for a while about the filming and their inordinately long day on set, and finally, with amorphous shapes whizzing past in blackness outside, things drifted into a drowsy self-contained silence. When Meg nodded herself awake over the manuscript she had on her knee with all good intentions to read, she wondered in horror how long she had slept, and more chillingly what she had looked like while she had done so. The good-natured Prince Edward seemed not to notice, and, if he had, was too magnanimous to say so.

Ardent's made-for-television adaptation of *The Cater Street Hangman*, titled *The Inspector Pitt Mysteries*, screened on ITV one weekday night in December 1998. 'It got an audience of 14.9 [million], an unheard-of size these days, and "won the slot" in that it was the most-watched programme at that time that night.'[5] Reviews were positive, and the company so pleased by the outcome that it threw a big celebrity dinner to mark the success. The signs were good: Ardent's production values were high; the programme was given a prime viewing slot. It seemed only a matter of time before a Pitt series was commissioned by ITV.

※

Also launched in 1998 were another Pitt novel, *Brunswick Gardens*, which offered a powerful and well-received reflection on Darwinism and feminism, and a Monk, *Whited Sepulchres* (released in the United States as *A Breach of Promise*). *Publishers Weekly* described *Whited Sepulchres* as an 'exceptional novel', while *People* selected it as 'A Page-Turner of the Week'. Their critic called it 'captivating ... One of Perry's most engrossing puzzlers ... A period piece in the best sense, the action seamlessly growing out of the social tapestry she weaves.'[6]

The story revolves around brilliant architect Killian Melville, who is in serious need of Oliver Rathbone's help to defend a breach-of-promise case after the daughter of his patron, Barton Lambert, believes he has proposed and is not prepared to proceed with the marriage. It is an odd predicament for a man who is 'probably one of the most original and daring thinkers of his generation'. The season of debutante balls is in full swing and the eligible Rathbone is horrified: 'I was so aware of the matrons parading their daughters, vying with one another for any available unmarried man, I felt like a quarry before the pack myself. I could imagine how one might be cornered, unable to extricate oneself.' Is this what has happened to Killian?

Just months before, Rathbone had almost proposed to Hester, but had been held back by the distinct feeling that she would turn him down. So the elegant barrister is still a free agent, while Monk is being drawn to Hester, in whom he begins to find a soul mate. Her interest in things outside the home and family, her professionalism and reliance on logic make her 'in many ways more like a man, less alien, less mysterious'. Monk is, apparently, one of the few men in Victorian England to find these qualities attractive in a woman.

During Killian's breach-of-promise trial, he is suddenly discovered dead in his flat — poisoned. The trial has been going badly, the prosecution arguing that Killian is having a homosexual relationship with Isaac Wolff. Rathbone is forced to scrutinize his feelings about homosexuality. 'I suppose I imagined that what a man did in his bedroom, providing he injured no one, was his own affair.' But the need to consider this difficult subject becomes redundant when it is revealed that Killian is a *she*, not a *he*.

A male persona gave Killian access to the world of buildings and men. In his final summary address to the court, Rathbone pleads: 'for

God's sake, why can't we allow women to use whatever talents they have without hounding and denying them until they are reduced to pretending to be men in order to be taken at their true value?' The prosecutor, on the other hand, speaks for many when he describes Killian as unnatural in her pursuit of a masculine profession. As soon as she is known to be a woman, the value of her architectural vision is diminished and scorned. The glimpse of hope for a new attitude to women is Monk, who at the end asks Hester to marry him.

> 'Why?' she asked …
>
> 'Because I love you, of course! … And I don't want ever to be without you' …
>
> 'I think that's a good reason,' she said very softly. 'Yes, I will.'

The beginning of 1999 saw Anne's greatest personal coup: the publication of the novel that had been much agonized over, many times restructured and rewritten, and now had a new, improved spelling for its title — *Tathea*. This was her baby, and she swears 'there is not a word in it that I would change'.[7] *Tathea* and its sequel, *Come Armageddon* (released two years later in 2001), are the only books she has written that she rereads often and for pleasure. These books are her theology and her comfort, and the journey of the soul of Tathea, the principal female protagonist, is a metaphor for her own.

Not long after Anne's identity was revealed, Meg Davis 'suggested to Anne she write her autobiography and she kind of grabbed this as a vehicle',[8] using this concept to rework and personalize the manuscript. *Tathea* and *Come Armageddon* are the closest she claims she will ever come to writing an autobiography: the details of her actual life are missing, but the essence of her struggle is there.

Leona Nevler finally decided not to publish any of the incarnations of *Tathea*. As Meg Davis notes, 'MY EAGLE COMES was … cannibalized into TATHEA and COME ARMAGEDDON. I think there was an interim stage, a ms called SADOKHAR. Anne originally saw this as a trilogy.'[9] 'Sadokhar' was to be the first in the series, and 'the one in which Anne tackled the subject of Armageddon', with the other novels looking back at what had gone before. 'We finally swallowed our pride and let Deseret, the Mormon publisher do it. But then were cheered up tremendously when after languishing with Deseret they were about to sell it as a two-book deal to Penguin Putnam in the United States. Leona was a bit put out when a perfectly distinguished publisher picked it up.'[10]

Tathea opens with its namesake, the Queen of Shinabar, narrowly escaping a palace coup, but leaving behind a dead husband and a four-year-old son, both victims of the insurrection. It is a loss for Tathea, but also the beginning of her quest. 'Everyone I loved is gone, everything I thought I knew,' she tells the Sage. 'I want to know if there is any meaning in life. Why do I exist? Who am I?'

She begins her journey by meeting a woman grieving by a desert tomb over a man she hardly knows. When Tathea challenges her to justify this oddly placed emotion, she explains that 'he had life … he had a chance to be brave and to seek the truth, to honour and defend it', yet he wasted it. For Tathea, and for Anne, the ultimate tragedy is not to die but to let life slip through your fingers, but they also share an occasional nagging doubt: 'Was all life … futile, a moment of consciousness between one oblivion and another?'

It is possible to begin by reading *Tathea* as a fantastic spin on a piece of classical mythology, but very soon the Dantesque, perilous nature of the spiritual terrain becomes apparent. This journey is as much mystic as it is fantastical. As Tathea discovers during her nightmare encounters with different peoples and cultures, nothing is as it seems. Duplicity reigns and innocence often masks cruelty and violence. In this precarious universe Tathea is charged with recovering the 'golden Book of the word of God', which is a dialogue between The Man of Holiness and Asmodeus, and taking it safely back to her people.

'There's still a central figure battling to save the world, a magical object, a range of supernatural armies and mortal allies, but [Tathea's] means of saving the world is ultimately by transmitting a religion, not by raising an army and waging war (although she does that too),' writes the critic for *SFX*.[11] It would be convenient to describe this as a battle between good and evil, but the dialogue at the heart of this story is between eroding doubt and spiritual conviction. It is a rhetorical debate that Anne has running on an endless reel inside her head. She polished this conversation for the book, but it was an expression of her internal debate between doubt and religious belief.

The writing of *Come Armageddon* took Anne to a place she struggled to return from and pushed her to the brink of a nervous breakdown. She rang her closest friends in a mood of despair that worried them intensely. When the novel begins, Tathea has spent 500 years in a forest guarding the Book, but the time predicted for the great conflict at the end of the world is drawing near, and when a woman dies giving birth, she knows that the child, Sadokhar, is the leader she has been waiting for. Twenty-eight years later, Sadokhar is the benevolent ruler of an island kingdom at the Edge of the World, where peace and justice reigns. Tyrn Vawr, a beautiful city, has been built, where 'artists and poets, philosophers and dreamers, architects and musicians' live freely. Anne named her home after this mystical, creative place. It is the golden age before the apocalypse.

Eerie expectation of the final war gives way to the terrible realization that Asmodeus, the Enemy, is biding his time. He will live as long as life exists, but his adversaries are mortal. His greatest weapon against his human opponents is Time. The brave Sadokhar decides to provoke the battle — 'We'll make the war happen, I promise!' — and he enters Hell in order to unleash its fury. 'Fool!' screams the hideous Tiyo-Mah, one of Hell's monstrous inhabitants, because no one can leave Hell until the apocalypse. According to his plan, Sadokhar baits her and the forces of evil, until they leave Hell through a portal in a slow, diseased procession to wreak havoc on the world.

Tiyo-Mah, riding a white mule … and behind her came the Lords of Delusion, Corruption, Terror and Despair. After them, on foot, shambled four creatures unlike any … seen before, muscles bulging beneath purple-black skin scarred and pitted, as if from innumerable pustules burst and healed over years.

Hell is brilliantly evoked in some of Anne's most outstanding writing. But even with its high-profile inhabitants gone, Hell is not a nice place to be, especially *forever*. There is no sign of life; not the slightest wind to disturb the white sky. Sadokhar breathes, but there is no air in his lungs, because Hell is not oblivion but endless living death.

> He felt neither hot nor cold, and the only sound was that of his feet on the pebbles, and even they slithered and fell without echo … But when he reached the crest there was nothing ahead of him but more dun-grey dust and rocks and shale to the horizon in every direction, except for the drop behind him … There was still no sense of perspective … He passed an outcrop of rock, and although he walked without turning, he seemed to pass it again. He had no idea whether it was the same one, or any of the countless others that looked alike.

II

Pauline was in a state of suppressed excitement as she helped her mother with the usual round of housework. Before leaving her lavish Ilam home, Juliet went to the garage, where she found half a brick and wrapped it in newspaper. Bill Perry noted that when she left the house 'she was more excited than usually and very gay. She was [wearing] a new dress or skirt which she had purchased only the day before.'[12] Henry drove her to the Riepers', dropping her off in town so she could do some shopping on the way.

Juliet arrived as Honorah was beginning to prepare lunch. After chatting for a while, the girls disappeared upstairs to Pauline's bedroom. There, Juliet handed over the half-brick, which was put inside an old stocking, which in turn was knotted near the ankle and placed in Pauline's shoulder bag. Juliet carried a little pink stone that had come from a brooch. The preparations were complete.

Pauline's father arrived home at noon, earlier than usual, and while he was waiting for lunch he did some work in the back vegetable garden.

At the meal the girls laughed and joked, which pleased Herbert. Just before 1pm, he returned to work and Wendy went back to her job selling lingerie in a department store, leaving Honorah and the girls to clean up and begin their afternoon's adventure.

It was a quick walk from the Gloucester Street house into Cathedral Square, where they caught the bus. The day was crisp and clear. The view from Victoria Park out over the city of Christchurch and across the plains to the Southern Alps would be worth the trip, but Honorah was hoping for more. Thinking back over the past few months, she realized she and Pauline had clashed terribly. There had been the frank chats with the Hulmes about the nature of the girls' relationship, the visits to school, the eating problems they had argued over, and the visit to Dr Bennett — everything had put her at odds with her daughter.

But then had come the miraculous reprieve: Juliet's move to South Africa. Although the imminent separation had cast the girls into an adolescent pit of despondency, Honorah was hoping that this trip would help to sustain the lift in their moods. The outing was one of a number of farewell events she knew Pauline would want before Juliet left, but it was also a bonding opportunity between a mother and a daughter. Sick of being cast as the villain, Honorah was hoping to re-establish communication.

They got off the bus at the terminus and climbed the hill to the kiosk that housed the Victoria Park tearooms. Since this was to be a special treat, Honorah dug deep into her purse to pay for tea for herself, soft drinks for the girls, one orange and one lemon, and a selection of cakes and scones to make it a proper feast. Agnes Ritchie, the proprietor, appreciative of their custom on a quiet winter weekday, chatted amiably with them. 'They all appeared perfectly normal. Quite at ease. They were a quiet group.'[13] She did not see them leave.

Along a ridge was a stone wall that ran almost up to the caretaker's house, kiosk and tearooms. Much of the park is on a large grassed plateau, but on the eastern side of the wall the hillside descends rapidly through a plantation of trees and shrubs into a wide valley. Outside the tearooms Honorah and the girls turned right, and then went through a gap in the old stone wall.

It was just after 3pm when they took the narrow zigzag track, which is steep in places and slippery because it is shaded by bush and overhanging trees. At a secluded spot just past a rustic wooden footbridge about 450 metres down, Juliet placed the small pink stone she had brought with her on the dirt track. A little beyond the bridge, as they turned to go back, Pauline pointed out the stone and Honorah bent down to pick it up …

⚉

Less than 30 minutes after the trio had left the tearooms, Agnes was halfway through serving ice creams to two young women when she glanced up to see Pauline and Juliet running towards the steps of the kiosk. They were 'agitated breathless and gasping'. Both were shouting and it took her a second or two to make out what they were saying: 'Please could somebody help us!' Then from Pauline: 'It's Mummy. She's terribly hurt. She's dead. I think she's dead.' And Juliet: 'It's her mother. She's hurt. She's covered with blood.'[14] Agnes was horrified to see that their clothes were splattered with blood, and that Pauline had splashes of it over her face and in her hair.

They seemed to be in shock. Pauline was extremely pale, and Juliet almost hysterical. It was difficult to work out what had happened even after they settled down. 'Don't make us go down there again. Don't make us go back,' they kept saying.[15] Gradually Agnes managed to get a little bit more out of them: there had been an accident down the path, and Honorah had slipped and hit her head on a rock. Agnes raised the alarm, summoning her husband, caretaker Kenneth Ritchie, who had been burning garden rubbish with his labourer assistant Eric McIlroy at the back of the tearooms, then telephoned for a doctor and an ambulance.

Agnes returned to the girls, offered them water to wash off the blood, and then tried to telephone their fathers. Herbert was away from the shop on business, but she managed to contact Henry, who said he would come immediately. Then she made tea and sat with the girls while they waited. Both remarked to her that it 'seemed like a dream and that they would wake up soon'. When she tried to elicit more information, Juliet said: 'Don't talk about it, don't talk about it.' Pauline was more forthcoming:

198

'She slipped on a plank. We had been down the track and were returning and somehow she slipped on a plank.' She explained that her mother had fallen and hit her head on a brick, and that her 'head kept bumping or banging as she fell'. They had tried to move Honorah, but she was too heavy and they had dropped her. She was worried that this might not have been the right thing to do. Pauline seemed dazed and Juliet anxiety-ridden. 'Will my daddy be long? I wish he would hurry,' she said several times.[16]

While the girls gulped down Agnes's boiling-hot black tea, Kenneth Ritchie and Eric McIlroy followed the track until they found Honorah lying on her back; they knew instantly she was dead. Blood streamed from fatal head wounds, and vomit choked her mouth. They noticed that one of her shoes had been flung some distance from the body, that her possessions (including her dentures) were scattered on the ground, and that not far away lay half a brick and a bloodied lisle stocking. Their stomachs turned as they realized that this was not an accident, but a murder scene. Eric McIlroy stayed with Honorah's body.

The ambulance was just arriving as Kenneth Ritchie returned to the kiosk. As soon as he could, he rang the police. At 4pm Henry arrived, gave his address to the ambulance driver and left a message with Agnes to say he was taking both girls back to Ilam. After consultation with Kenneth Ritchie, Dr Donald Walker, who had arrived in response to Agnes's call, decided to wait for the police: this was clearly a crime scene, and he had no mandate to visit it alone.

A patrol car carrying Sergeant Robert Hope and Constable Donald Molyneaux eventually arrived, after a misdirected trip to Victoria *Lake* in the city. Kenneth Ritchie led the party to where Honorah lay. Dr Walker pronounced her officially dead, and Constable Molyneaux was left to guard the scene while Sergeant Hope returned to the kiosk and then radioed the Central Police Station for reinforcements.

Herbert came as soon as he got the message, driven by a friend. Agnes told him that his wife had been in an accident and that an ambulance had been called, but her lack of clarity about what had happened left Herbert pacing anxiously backwards and forwards outside the kiosk. Initially he was the prime suspect, soon interrogated by Sergeant Hope about his whereabouts that day. 'I was in and out of my shop once or twice during the afternoon and when I returned on one occasion I found the message from Victoria Park and I rang and spoke to Mrs Ritchie.'[17] His errands were all in the city and had taken him nowhere near the park.

When Detectives Gordon Gillies and Archie Tate and Policewoman Audrey Griffiths arrived, they were escorted immediately to the body, where the brick and the bloodied stocking were noted and a decision made to inform senior officers. At this point, Senior Detective Macdonald Brown and Inspector Duncan McKenzie of the CID were brought into the case.

As night was falling, the city coroner, Dr Colin Pearson, pathologist EB Taylor and police photographer William Ramage were also called to the park. With flashlights, they went down the track. The body was still warm when Pearson began examining it. Photographs were taken and a detailed examination of the scene began. Audrey Griffiths accompanied the body to the Christchurch Public Hospital mortuary, where she removed Honorah's 'clothing and effects'. She took an inventory and handed her belongings over to Detective Gillies as evidence.

⚮

In Hilda's words, Juliet and Pauline were 'white and trembling' when they arrived on the Hulmes' doorstep.[18] She saw that their clothes were bloodstained and immediately ran a bath for them. Bill Perry had been out buying a newspaper when he saw Henry's car arrive with the girls. He returned to his flat, not realizing that anything had happened until Hilda came to his door and told him that there had been an accident involving Mrs Rieper. She washed the girls' underclothing and gave Bill their outer garments to take down to Hick's Drapers, a dry-cleaning agency on Fendalton Road.

Juliet and Pauline were given a meal, treated for shock and put to bed in the same room. It was not long after that, that they asked Bill Perry to come up and see them. They had the radio playing. 'Pauline was very, very shocked, I thought, and Juliet was trembling, but a different type of shock from Pauline's. Pauline was almost in a coma.' They needed noise and someone to be there without discussing the incident.

Bill and Hilda, however, knew that the police would soon be interviewing the girls, so they decided to talk to them separately in order to ascertain exactly what had happened. They agreed that Bill should talk to Pauline, and Hilda to her daughter. At this point and later, separately and together, they urged the girls to tell the truth.

Bill recalled that he told Pauline that 'the police were grown up people and that she was only a child and it would be better for me to deal with the police on her behalf'. He urged her to give him a detailed account and explained that they had to have everything 'right as policemen have all sorts of ways of looking at these things'. Pauline repeated the story she had told Agnes Ritchie. When he suggested that perhaps there had been a quarrel during which Honorah had tried to hit Pauline, she said, 'My mother has never struck me.'[19]

Immediately after the tragedy, a traumatized Herbert Rieper gave the police permission to interview his daughter without legal representation. At 8pm Detectives Brown and Tate arrived at Ilam, where they were met by Hilda, Henry and Bill. Hilda took them upstairs to the bedroom where Pauline and Juliet were in bed. Juliet was taken down to the sitting room while they questioned Pauline. She repeated the story that Honorah had fallen.

Halfway through the interview, the police invited Bill into the room and they broached the issue of the half-brick. The interview was then suspended, and downstairs Juliet was questioned with her parents and Bill present. Detective Brown suggested that they were not convinced that she had been there when Honorah died. This seemed to throw Juliet, and Bill asked to be allowed to speak to her in private.

He returned with an announcement that Juliet would like to make a new statement. Juliet said she had given her first version of events so things would be better for Pauline. 'I told that story because I wanted to be loyal to Pauline and did not want to see her in any trouble.'[20] Without legal representation, her new version was taken down in writing. In it she agreed with the police that she had come back to find Honorah already dead. Pauline had explained to her that her mother had fallen and hit her head against a stone.

With this as a lever, Brown went upstairs again to talk to Pauline, with Hilda present. He told her they believed that Juliet had not been involved in Honorah's death, then accused Pauline of murdering her mother. At this point she agreed to answer questions put to her by the police. In answering them she accepted responsibility for her mother's death, and at the same time absolved Juliet. 'My friend does not know anything about it. She was out of sight at the time. She had gone ahead.' She finished by saying, 'As soon as I started to strike my mother I regretted it but could not stop then.'[21]

At the conclusion of the interview, Detective Brown read her back the series of questions and answers, which she accepted as a correct account and signed. Pauline was charged with the murder of her mother, and taken from Ilam homestead to the police station. As the police were leaving they asked Pauline where she got the half-brick, and Hilda, who overheard, was quick to say: 'She did not get it here. She brought it with her.'[22] Pauline's response was immediate: 'No, I took it from home.'

That evening Tate and Brown went to the Riepers' house. Herbert took them up to Pauline's bedroom, where they found two diaries, 14 exercise books and a scrapbook containing actors' photographs. They also removed a pair of lisle stockings identical in colour and style to the one used in the murder. The exercise books were scattered about the room; the diary containing Pauline's last entry was lying on the dressing table close to the bedroom door.

It was the diaries that immediately captured their attention. 'In transcript, the 1953 diary contains 120 pages, with entries completed for nearly every day. The partially completed 1954 diary contains fifty-two pages, again with almost daily entries.'[23] From the diaries they could construct a remarkably clear picture of the months leading up to Honorah's death. Brown took extracts from the diaries and 'Photostat copies of different pages of it'.[24]

At the Ilam homestead, Juliet was close to distraught. She kept the radio on and recited poetry in order to drown out the dreadful events of the day. That night she slept in her mother's arms after Hilda read to her from her favourite poetry. 'Her one repeated sentence was that she didn't wish to talk about it, that she wanted to go to sleep and forget [about] it.'[25]

On Wednesday, 23 June, Detective Gillies picked up from Hick's Drapers the girls' clothes, which had not yet been cleaned, and then took Herbert to identify the body at the Christchurch Hospital Mortuary. 'It is the body of Honorah Mary Parker who has lived with me for 23 years,' he confirmed in his report to the coroner. At 11.10 that morning Brown and Tate went back to Ilam, where Bill was the only adult at home. He escorted the police upstairs to Juliet's bedroom.

'We have reason to believe now that you were present when the fatality occurred. You are suspected of having murdered Mrs Rieper yesterday,' Brown told Juliet, then gave her an official warning.[26] Bill suggested they wait until Juliet's mother returned. While they waited he told her she 'must tell the truth … she broke down, and after a few minutes she told him the story told later to Detective-Sergeant Tate'.[27] She said that they went with some vague hope that they might be able to frighten Honorah into agreeing to Pauline going to South Africa, but what happened instead was a nightmare.

They were well down the track when Honorah had decided it was time to go back. The group turned, and Juliet was walking ahead when she heard noises — there was a quarrel. When she went back, Honorah was on her knees and Pauline was hitting her. Juliet took the stocking and hit her, too. 'I was terrified. I thought that one of them had to die. I wanted to help Pauline. It was terrible.'

Honorah moved convulsively and they both held her down. She could not remember if Honorah said anything or shouted out, because she was too frightened to listen. 'After the first blow was struck I knew it would be necessary to kill her. I was terrified and hysterical.'[28] Her statement was read back to her in the presence of her mother and Bill. She agreed to the contents and wrote: 'The three pages of this statement have been read to me. They are true and correct, signed J.M. Hulme.'[29] She was arrested, taken to the police station and charged with murder.

'After the children returned home, Dr Hulme, Mrs Hulme and I urged them to tell the truth right from the beginning,' Bill explained in a statement given later.[30] Although this advanced the investigation, it left the lawyers with almost no case to defend. The situation was difficult and there were few precedents. Juliet and Pauline, both minors, were questioned by police without legal counsel, yet once they entered the justice system they were tried as adults. The well-meaning recommendation to tell the truth might have been sound parental advice after a misdemeanour, but for murder the proper and appropriate counsel should have come from a lawyer.

There was nothing straight-thinking or normal, however, about the lives of the adults involved in this tragedy. In a single day, the fact that Herbert was not married to Honorah had been publicly revealed, and her surname and that of his children changed to Parker. He had lost his beloved common-law wife, and his daughter had committed matricide. Henry's marriage was ignominiously ending; he had forfeited his position as rector and was leaving New Zealand under a cloud of dissent and disagreement. Hilda was living in a farcical *ménage à trois*, while continuing to work as a marriage guidance counsellor. Bill's role, technically that of adulterer, was undefined and problematic.

There was little wider support in this time of enormous stress. The family and friends of Bill and the Hulmes were in Canada and the United Kingdom, and Herbert was an Australian whose past life he could not easily revisit. Even the Birmingham origins of Honorah's background had disconnected family links and limited the circle of people who could be called on to help.

Then there was the behaviour of Pauline and Juliet in custody, which confounded everyone. The girls did not seem to have properly come to terms with the gravity of the situation. Apart from being repulsed by what had happened, they had shown little sign of remorse.

After Pauline was taken to the station late in the evening of 22 June, she found a piece of paper and continued to describe events as if she were confiding in her diary at home. When she realized that her writing might be incriminating, she attempted to burn it. Margaret Felton, the police matron who confiscated and read the note before it was largely destroyed, recalled Pauline's words. The entry read: 'I find myself in an unexpected place … after having committed my murder. All the H-s have been wonderfully kind and sympathetic. Anyone would think I've been good. I've had a pleasant time with the police talking 19 to the dozen and behaving as though I hadn't a care in the world.' There was a section the policewoman could not remember, then it finished: 'I haven't had a chance to talk to Deborah properly but I am taking the blame for everything.'[31]

On 23 June at 10am, Pauline appeared in court before magistrate Rex Abernethy, charged with her mother's murder. Immediately afterwards, Brown and Tate interviewed her in the latter's office. When they interrogated her about the confiscated note, she told them she would give a true account of everything and sign it if she was allowed to see Juliet. She said Juliet would confirm what she said.

Pauline was left in the office at the police station while Brown and Tate drove out to Ilam, accused Juliet of being involved with Pauline in Honorah's death, and arrested her. On 24 June, she appeared before magistrate Raymond Ferner on a charge of murder; the trial for the girls in the Magistrates' Court was set for 14 July. In the meantime they were remanded to Paparua Prison, just out of Christchurch.

Honorah Parker's funeral service and cremation was held at the Bromley cemetery in Christchurch, on 24 June 1954. It was a quiet, devastating end to a life — laid to rest among old gravestones and pink Summerhill pressed-brick memorial walls and tiny, immaculate rosebush plots. She would be remembered publicly not for her life, but for her death. Newspapers around the world would carry descriptions of her belongings and details of her grizzly end. She would forever be the mother who was murdered, a 45-year-old woman of medium build with greying hair — an ordinary person who became extraordinary in death. However, Pauline's classmate Margaret Tyndall remembers her differently.

She stepped forward like a soldier over the trench out into the guns. She spoke to them and said: 'You can't go.' … At some level that woman has to be credited with the courage to do that. She tried to save her girl and she hadn't much weaponry. It is the most amazing story of gallantry.[32]

⚯

The first headlines about the case were descriptive and restrained, but soon newspapers across New Zealand and abroad were ablaze with the story.

At Christchurch Girls' High School, the pupils of 5A were arriving back from physical education when they were ushered into a special room by Miss Stewart and given strict instructions not to give any school photographs to reporters. 'Miss Burns came in and she said: "There will be no conversation about a *certain event*."' So 5A and the rest of the school 'sat in Cranmer Square eating our lunch and talked of *nothing else* ... You felt like the eyes of the world were upon you ... It was an experience none of us had ever contemplated. Murders don't happen in New Zealand for a start, and *not* in Christchurch.'[33]

In the midst of the public furore, the Hulmes left Ilam homestead. Henry went on 3 July, as he had always planned to do, with their young son Jonathan. He had thought hard about whether to go, but after months of waiting for a position in England he had a job teaching mathematics at Cambridge and working part-time at Aldermaston. The need to begin work, to protect Jonathan from the destructive impact of the trial and to escape a disintegrating marriage and public disgrace bolstered his resolve to go. Henry's virtual absence during the police investigation at Ilam is enigmatic. In his place stood Bill Perry, although it is unclear whether this came about because of paternal neglect, because Bill usurped Henry's role, or perhaps even because of a gentlemen's agreement to exchange places.

Hilda and Bill might have left the country, too, but for the fact that they were subpoenaed by the Crown prosecutor to give evidence. They moved from Ilam, with its dozen rooms, servants' quarters and attached flat, to the weekend cottage at Port Levy. In the weeks before the trial there was a public auction of the Hulmes' 'furniture and house-hold' effects at Ilam. The sense of humiliation and loss must have been intense. As the *NZ*

Truth reported, 'The attendance was far larger than normally seen at such auctions and souvenir hunters paid fabulous prices for mementos from the Hulme home.'[34] With the departure of the Hulmes something indefinable had ended for Christchurch. Gone, in some respects, was the comfortable, century-old fiction of a 'little Britain' at the edge of the Empire.

Before Henry left, legal arrangements were made for Juliet. Terence Arbuthnot Gresson and Brian McClelland, as assistant, were appointed to defend her. Henry Hulme had known Gresson while he was studying at Cambridge University, and they had become reacquainted when Henry moved to Christchurch. Gresson also knew Hilda, after attending a number of social functions at Ilam. Following Henry's departure, Hilda and Bill conducted arrangements for Juliet's defence from Port Levy. When they met the lawyers, they drove nearly 50 kilometres in to Christchurch, much of it on dusty shingle roads.

Pauline was represented by Dr Alec Haslam, with Jim Wicks his assistant. As the family lawyer, Haslam was an obvious choice, but he was also notable for having been a Rhodes scholar, and now, with his own practice in the city, an experienced lawyer.

From the beginning, the counsel for the defence was compromised, as Brian McClelland has recalled. 'When the killing happened they had not called on Terence [Gresson] at all. They let Juliet be interviewed by Detective Archie Tate. She had made a statement admitting that she had taken part in the killing. We couldn't move a yard on the facts.'[35] To compound the difficulties of a full and signed confession, there were the diaries. Although these were accepted as evidence against Pauline only, they were equally damaging to Juliet, a blueprint for shared adolescent treachery.

The two defence teams, who chose to work together, found themselves in an almost impossible position. The facts were irrefutable; the only case they could offer was one of diminished responsibility, which had to be argued in such a way that it could be offered for both girls. Insanity was the strongest and most compelling defence, but 'under section 43 of [New Zealand's] Crimes Act everyone must be presumed to be sane at the time of doing or committing any act until the contrary is proved'.[36]

So the onus was on the counsel for the defence to satisfy the jury that their clients were insane.

In order to investigate the viability of an insanity plea, the defence employed the expert opinion of Dr Reginald Warren Medlicott. At a little over 30 years old, Medlicott was a prodigy in psychiatric health in New Zealand. For seven years he had been the superintendent of Ashburn Hall, a privately owned psychiatric unit near Dunedin. His rising star began with a Rockefeller Fellowship, which gave him a year-long residency at a university hospital in Cleveland, Ohio. After returning to New Zealand he lectured at Otago University's School of Medicine and was a visiting psychiatric physician at Dunedin's Public Hospital. He was a member of the Royal Australasian College of Physicians. His early reputation was impressive, but his experience for the task was limited. He had never given psychiatric evidence at a trial.

While at Paparua, Juliet and Pauline were examined by numerous doctors and psychiatrists. Medlicott saw them separately on 27 and 28 June, and again on 11 and 12 July. These visits lasted between one-and-a-half and two-and-a-half hours. On 14 July, the hearing was held in the Magistrates' Court and the case was referred to the Supreme Court for a trial beginning in late August.

After the hearing, the girls were separated at the request of Gresson, to see if there were any discernible changes in their behaviour. Juliet remained at Paparua Prison and Pauline was sent for a week to Mt Eden Prison in Auckland. Medlicott interviewed both girls again separately on the eve of the Supreme Court trial. 'He also interviewed Herbert Rieper, Hilda Hulme, Dr Francis Bennett, Pauline's sister Wendy and Pauline's grandmother Amy Parker.'[37]

The relationship between Medlicott and the girls was not an easy one. They were, after all, meeting to establish madness. Certainly, both Juliet and Pauline had discussed the naïve idea that a plea of insanity was their best defence and would lead to a swifter release. Juliet admitted to one attending doctor 'that if they were found insane they would probably be out of mental hospital by the time they were 18 or 19 ... They could not see themselves getting out of prison — if they were found sane and convicted — as early as that.'[38] From the beginning, they played up to Medlicott's diagnosis — and he was aware of this: 'When the girls were first interviewed the writer knew that they were trying to prove themselves insane.' Medlicott believed he had rumbled their deceitful plan to act as though they were mad, but this was not entirely the case.

Medlicott read their letters, which formed a 'childishly imaginative' story that spanned 30 or 40 years but was communicated in a few weeks of correspondence between the girls. He also read Pauline's diaries, as well as sections of both girls' novels written in the exercise books. In them he found an abundance of disturbing material. As well as the obvious evidence in their writing, there was the unstable behaviour he had personally observed.

'Both the girls could consciously hallucinate almost at will, hearing music and voices and seeing fleeting scenes,' he would recall in a 1955 article for the *British Journal of Medical Psychology*. Pauline told him: 'You're an infuriating fool, displeasing to look at and have an irritating way of speaking.' After his physical examination of her, she hurled back, 'I hope you break your flaming neck.'[39]

Juliet was more subtle in her superciliousness. 'You do think, don't you?' she sneered. Their arrogance and contempt were, he admitted later, 'so severe I had to restrain myself'.[40] In addition to this, almost everything they wrote challenged his Edwardian sensibilities. As educational behaviourist Colleen McLaughlin has written, 'If girls are to become "nice girls" in the eyes of society then they should be calm, controlled, quiet and not aggressive … aggression in girls is not seen as "normal" and may be seen as an indication of a more deep-seated problem.'[41]

Medlicott read their behaviour, and especially their writings, as proof of a pathological narcissism. He was both astonished and bemused by their reasons for going to the United States.

They would go to Hollywood, choose their actors and supervise the filming of their novels … Ambitious plans are not unusual in adolescents but there was more than usual neglect of reality here. Their books were mostly unfinished and untyped and they were completely uncritical about them. When Juliet started writing she used to read her novel chapter by chapter to her mother but later guarded her writings from everyone and was, like Pauline, completely contemptuous of anyone's opinion ... In actuality their writings, although profuse and imaginative, did not show talent and there was nothing to suggest that they would be published.[42]

They had both been sickly, spoilt children who went into early adolescence already more 'strongly narcissistic' than most, and their meeting had been a confluence of ego and self-centredness. 'Each acted on the other as a resonator increasing the pitch of their narcissism.'[43] In his mind he likened their act of senseless violence and brutality to the activities of the Nazi SS, and saw their combined act of murder as being similar to that perpetrated by Nathan Leopold and Richard Loeb, the sons of Chicago millionaires, whose random crime spree ended in the gratuitous killing of a 14-year-old schoolboy. In Juliet and Pauline's case, it was the threat of separation that turned their narcissism murderous.

Leopold and Loeb's case shared another similarity: their relationship was homosexual. For Medlicott, 'There was no doubt about the fact that the friendship [between the girls] was homosexual' and that this was directly connected to the build-up of pressure and paranoia.

> Repressed homosexuality has a special role in persecutory paranoia, but there is some reason to believe that homosexuality might be prominent in other types of paranoia. The homosexual relationship between Leopold and Loeb has been mentioned, and Burr (1935) states that he cannot recall a case of paranoia in which he really knew the conduct of the patient and did not discover that he was homosexual.[44]

Although the girls flatly denied any homosexual conduct, and Medlicott did not believe their relationship had found physical expression, he was convinced it was a significant factor in their pathology. Their narcissism, paranoia, anxiety and homosexuality caused them to transpose the normal codes. 'Their moral values became reversed and they embraced evil as good.'

In his 1955 article, Medlicott often used the word 'evil'. He wrote of the girls' 'morbid preoccupation with evil', the point where 'they openly embraced evil', and 'the crowning of evil' when Diello became Emperor of Borovina in one of their ceremonies. He was convinced that the girls were lost souls. 'In earlier times one would have said they had become "possessed" by evil spirits.'[45] The problem was that Medlicott's use of the word 'evil' belonged more in a Judeo-Christian theological debate than in a clinical diagnosis or psychological discussion, especially one published in a medical journal. Medlicott's mixing of medical and religious paradigms influenced his analysis of the girls' behaviour and was not helpful to the case.

However, his diagnosis of madness provided perfect ammunition for Gresson and Haslam, who had their work cut out for them. In consultation with Medlicott, they decided to argue a case of *folie à deux*, where delusional beliefs are transmitted from one person to another, resulting in a shared psychosis. They could find no successful precedent for such an approach other than 'just one case in England in which a judge ruled out insanity on the basis that no medical evidence had been called'.[46] Not only was this an extremely difficult case to argue, but the legal definition of insanity barely resembled that of the medical one. The judge at Juliet and Pauline's trial went to great lengths to explain the ramifications of the narrower legal definition.

> The insanity which is to relieve a person from criminal responsibility must be, in the words of the act, such as renders the person in question 'incapable of understanding the nature and quality of the act or omission, or of knowing that such act or omission was wrong'.[47]

The prosecution was led by the newly appointed Crown prosecutor for Christchurch, Alan Brown. Brown was a seasoned criminal lawyer, with three decades of experience as partner in a local law firm, and years under his belt working with the previous prosecutor. This was his first murder trial since his appointment in February of that year, and he was keen to make his mark. Brown was assisted by Peter Thomas Mahon, a promising young Christchurch lawyer who had joined Brown's law firm as a partner in 1941, served in the Second World War, then rejoined the firm to work 'with Brown and the previous Crown Prosecutor'.[48] The prosecution was a honed team, well experienced at working together.

If anyone could be described as a 'hanging judge', then arguably it was the stiff, intractable Francis Boyd Adams. He came from a distinguished legal family in Dunedin, where he was Crown prosecutor for many years, had published books on criminal law and was appointed as a judge of the Supreme Court in 1950. As the Christchurch *Press* later noted, 'There is little doubt that Mr Justice Adams, a staunch religious man, had little sympathy for the girls. "He was," [remembers] Brian McClelland, "an unsympathetic judge to put it mildly" … a clever man but absolutely as hard as nails.'[49]

⌘

The Parker–Hulme trial, as it became known, opened in Christchurch's Supreme Court on Monday, 23 August 1954. The proceedings, which would run for six days, were comprehensively reported in newspapers throughout New Zealand and overseas. A media contingent of 11 reporters followed the case daily. Most of the journalists were New Zealand-based, but there were also reporters from Australia and the United Kingdom.

'Trial Given Prominence in U.K. Papers' said a headline in the Christchurch's *Star-Sun*. 'Not for many years has news from New Zealand received such prominence as the newspapers are giving to the Christchurch murder trial. Each day of the trial most newspapers have published at least half a column, generally on the front page … the two tabloid newspapers, the "Mirror" and the "Daily Sketch", have been given extensive display to the trial on their inside pages.'[50] It was as if a giant Catherine wheel of scandal had been lit and the sparks were flying around the world.

The girls were taken to the Supreme Court early each day to avoid the prying eyes of sightseers crowded around the entrance to the public gallery on Armagh Street. The van backed up flush with the doorway so that the girls could be taken through the court and upstairs to the cells. On the first two days of the trial, bystanders and media gathered outside the courthouse caught glimpses of the pair on the first floor at the barred cell windows, watching photographers aiming camera lenses at them. This ended when court staff taped brown paper over the bottom half of the windows.

Pauline, described by newspapers as 'dark and sullen looking', wore a brown dress and small brown hat for the duration of the trial, while Juliet, described as 'taller, fair, with high cheek bones and a slant to her eyes', was dressed in a green coat and pale green paisley scarf.[51] With the exception of an occasional hour or two, each day of the trial the public gallery filled to capacity with over 100 people. The rear section was 'packed mainly with fashionably dressed women who scrambled and jostled one another for seats the moment the doors were opened ... the same faces were seen day after day'.[52]

It was something of a public freak-show. When the girls entered or left the dock, spectators 'stood and craned their necks for a better view'.[53] Numerous times the court crier had to silence outbursts of laughter from the public gallery. While Juliet and Pauline were in the dock they sat on either side of a police matron. Occasionally they smiled and murmured to each other, sometimes they were visibly upset, but mostly they sat with their heads down; Pauline's sometimes almost touched her knees.

The trial began after the empanelling of an all-male jury. Although women were legally able to sit on juries, they were not automatically called for service and had to make a special application to be included in a panel. In this case, too, the seriousness of the charge would have contributed to an all-male selection. Fourteen jurors were challenged — nine by the defence and five by the prosecution.

The Crown case for the prosecution occupied most of the first two days. In an hour-long opening address, Alan Brown laid out their argument, the gist of which was that the girls had 'conspired' to entice Honorah to a secluded section of Victoria Park with the intention of murdering her. They carried with them the weapon they used to beat her to death.

Their motive was to remove the one obstacle that was preventing Pauline from accompanying Juliet to South Africa. Brown claimed that the prosecution's evidence would prove that this was a murder 'coldly and callously planned, and perpetrated by two highly intelligent, perfectly sane, but precocious and dirty-minded little girls'.[54] The Crown would call 17 witnesses.

The police and medical witnesses described the location and what they found. The shocking account of the state of Honorah's body, already given at the Magistrates' Court hearing, was read out again. Dr Colin Pearson, the pathologist who had examined the body on the evening of the murder and conducted the postmortem the next day, told the court that Honorah had died of 'shock associated with multiple injuries to the head and fractures of the skull'.[55]

He then produced a comprehensive report which listed a total of 45 'discernible injuries', which he detailed, explaining that 'a single blow may produce a number of lacerated wounds'.[56] On the face and scalp he had identified 24 such wounds. There were crushing injuries to the skull and bruising to the neck, which suggested that the head had been held immobile on the ground during the beating. Most of the wounds were serious, Pearson concluded, and it would have taken only a few to render the victim unconscious.

The girls' behaviour before and after the murder was outlined in detail by tearoom manager Agnes Ritchie, and her caretaker husband Kenneth Ritchie described finding the body and his observations of the girls. Brown then called Hilda, Herbert and Bill in turn to give background evidence about the girls' childhoods, the development of their friendship and the events leading up to the murder.

The defence disputed very little of the evidence given in support of the prosecution. The main point Gresson made in his cross-examination of William Ramage, the police photographer, was that the girls had chosen a highly improbable spot to stage a murder intended to look like an accident, as it was flat and well away from any rocks. Ramage reminded him that it was also secluded. Haslam's questioning of Herbert revealed that, although he and Honorah were worried about the girls' friendship,

Pauline had been taken to Dr Bennett 'not so much [for] that as the fact that she had lost a lot of weight'.[57]

Some of the most sensational material of the trial was revealed on 24 August when scrutiny of Pauline's 1954 diary exposed the affair between Bill Perry and Hilda. The description of the awkward moment when Juliet allegedly discovered Hilda and Bill in bed for the first time was read out in court. According to Pauline's account, Juliet had woken up at 2am and gone to look for her mother. When she discovered that Hilda's bedroom was empty, she went on a search that took her to Bill Perry's flat. She climbed the stairs and heard voices, crept to the bedroom door, listened for a while, then threw the door open and turned on the lights to reveal her mother and Bill in bed, sipping tea.

'She was shaking with emotion and shock although she had known what she would find.' Hilda and Bill stared at her in stunned disbelief. 'I suppose you want an explanation,' her mother said as soon as she could collect herself. 'Yes,' Juliet replied, 'I do.' Hilda said that they were in love. 'But I know *that*,' Juliet exclaimed. Hilda 'explained that Dr Hulme knew all about it and that they intended to live as a threesome'.[58]

Hilda vehemently rejected Pauline's version of events. She made the point that there were many inaccuracies in the diaries and that this event was 'recorded in a very distorted and untruthful way'.[59] Hilda's sworn testimony was that she had heard a noise and left her bedroom to make sure nothing was amiss. When she went into Bill's flat she found him in pain, so went downstairs to make tea and brought it up. They were drinking it when she heard the dividing door open.

She called out and there was no reply, until Juliet appeared in her bare feet. 'So you are here,' Juliet said. Hilda went on to say that 'Juliet seemed to be amused at a secret joke of her own, and when I asked her what it was she replied, "Oh, the balloon has gone up." When I asked her to explain, she replied "I was hoping to catch you out." Bill was, in fact, admitted to hospital the next week.'[60]

There were indeed inaccuracies, imaginings and exaggerations in Pauline's diaries, which were given inappropriate weight at times in the trial, but it is clear from both accounts that Juliet was well aware that her mother and Bill were having an affair. This would have been disturbing and stressful, even if she had not caught them in bed or *coitus interruptus*. To find the couple in an ambiguous and apparently illicit liaison brought things to a head for Juliet. As far as she was concerned, the balloon *had* gone up and that felt like permission to act out. Although she may not have blamed them directly, her parents had disappointed her.

This feeling was exacerbated the next morning when Henry announced to Juliet, and Pauline, who had biked over, that he and Hilda were divorcing. This was an enormous shock to both girls. It was also the stuff of scandal in a town that took an ostentatious pride in the purity of its institutions. Hilda was a figure of respectability in the community, and such seemingly promiscuous behaviour by a prominent marriage guidance counsellor made her appear outrageously hypocritical. The impact of her affair with Bill is rumoured to have set back marriage guidance in the country 35 years.[61] There was little public sympathy for her situation. She had betrayed not only her husband and her family, but also the belief invested in her by Christchurch institutions — the university, the church, the education and health systems — that quietly condoned the shallowness of snobbery, breeding and privilege.

In the public imagination Hilda and Henry became neglectful, remote parents. Henry's selfish absence, combined with Hilda's lack of discipline and insufficient support for her daughter, made them figures of contempt. When asked if she had seen Juliet in prison over the two-month remand period, Hilda answered: 'Yes, I have seen her several times.' For many, this did not signal a high degree of commitment. Some of her testimony also seemed to undermine her daughter. She told the court that 'she and Dr Hulme were anxious about defects in Juliet's personality before these events'. When asked by Brown 'Have you called any experts in?' she replied:

Not professionally but privately … These people, who knew Juliet intimately, said that Juliet was highly emotional and would be a responsibility until she developed and acquired a less intense attitude to living … She was always difficult to discipline, and resented discipline.[62]

Hilda was in an unenviable position. Regardless of what she may or may not have done wrong as a parent, whatever she said must have been influenced by the defence counsel's decision to argue a case of *folie à deux*. Defending her daughter amounted to helping prove she was mad.

When asked to name the people whose opinions she had sought privately, she refused. One of these was certainly Dr Bennett, who would take centre-stage along with Medlicott in the next phase of the trial. The case for the defence began late in the afternoon of the second day. Gresson opened with his address:

> Telling the jury that his case would rest on medical evidence ... that would show that the two girls were insane at the time they killed Mrs Parker ... the Crown had seen fit to refer to the accused as ordinary, dirty-minded little girls, but the evidence for the defence would be that they were nothing of the kind, but were mentally sick and were more to be pitied than blamed. Their homosexuality was a symptom of their disease of the mind.[63]

Dr Medlicott, first up for the defence, spent nine long hours in the witness box — the whole of one day, then a lengthy cross-examination by Brown the next. He outlined his programme of interviews with the girls, and explained in more detail his professional diagnosis which formed the cornerstone of the defence case: namely that the girls were suffering from 'paranoia ... in the setting of Folie à deux. Paranoia is a form of systematized delusional insanity.' The most common form of paranoia was persecution; in this case the paranoia was of the 'exalted' type. Medlicott outlined his argument for how the girls came to think of themselves as special. He discussed what he described as their homosexuality, suggesting there was no proof it was a physical relationship and that in the longer term it might have proved to be an 'adolescent pash'. He did, however, relate it directly to their paranoia.

He explored the agency of evil in their psychosis, likening Pauline's diary to an 'evil mirror' reflecting the pair's moral deterioration.

It was obvious that the normal personalities [sic] defences against evil had almost completely gone. It became obvious when I started to discuss borderline religious and philosophic topics with them that they were harbouring weird delusional ideas ... they said they had their own paradise, their own god and religion and their own morality.[64]

He drew special attention to Pauline's diary entry made at Port Levy in April 1954, where she referred to their finding the key to the 4th World and discovering that they had an extra part to their brain. In addition to this, when Brown read a poem titled 'The Ones I Worship' from Pauline's diary, Medlicott said it was symptomatic of their 'terrific exaltation' of themselves:

... The outstanding genius of this pair,
Is understood by few, they are so rare.
Compared with these two every man is a fool
The world is most honoured that they should deign to rule
And above us these Goddesses reign on high.

I worship the power of these lovely two
With that adoring love known to so few
'Tis indeed a miracle, one must feel,
That two such heavenly creatures are real ...[65]

He discussed their shoplifting, attempted burglary, cheating at games with Jonathan, and quoted from a diary entry made in March 1954 that described the Temple of Minerva they had built in the garden at Ilam. They were going to rewrite the Bible, on vellum parchment, and Pauline would illustrate it.

Their fictional writings, he believed, grew more violent the more time they spent together, and Pauline's diary was an increasingly fantastic and fevered account of possession. 'As the diary goes on evil becomes more and more important and one gets the feeling they ultimately become helplessly under its sway.'[66] Medlicott concluded his evidence like this: 'if I were asked today if I considered Parker and Hulme certifiably insane I would answer yes. I myself would have not the slightest hesitation in certifying them.'[67]

Brown's cross-examination of Medlicott was merciless. Brian McClelland remembered it as 'a very rough passage. With the wind behind him from Adams (the judge), he made a mess of Medlicott.'[68] Brown forced the doctor to publicly acknowledge his dearth of experience, especially as an expert witness. He then proceeded to challenge Medlicott's interpretation of the diary entries he used as supporting evidence and almost every one of his contentions, including his conclusion that there was hereditary insanity in the family because the Riepers had had a blue baby and a Down's Syndrome child. This was vigorously challenged:

[Brown]: Do you not consider you were being unjust to the Riepers when you said on Tuesday: 'I consider that background raises a query as to the stock from which she came.'
[Medlicott]: No. I don't think so.
[Brown:] Does it not mean that insanity is hereditary?
[Medlicott:] No, it simply suggests that the stock is defective.[69]

Brown's questioning was intended to highlight the fact that the murder was a consciously pursued, premeditated act both girls knew was wrong. He drew particular attention to Pauline's nocturnal activities with Nicholas, the boarder, to emphasize her heterosexual misconduct — thereby reinforcing his premise that the girls were dirty-minded rather than mad.

The next person called to give evidence for the defence was Dr Bennett, whose connection to the case preceded that of all the other medical witnesses. He was a general practitioner rather than a qualified psychiatrist, and the experience he brought to the case was gained through military service during the Second World War with shell-shock victims. He had seen Pauline in December 1953 and had spoken with Henry about the girls' relationship in May 1954. He had also worked at the Cashmere

Sanatorium, knew Hilda through the Marriage Guidance Council and had socialized with the Hulmes at Ilam.

Bennett's testimony, which would take more than five hours, began with his history of visits. He was one of the first medical practitioners to see the girls after the murder: he saw both of them separately on 24 June and on 6 and 14 August. He agreed unreservedly with Medlicott's diagnosis. He discussed the quality of the girls' fictional writing. They had written a great deal, he explained, but he did 'not consider it of outstanding literary merit'. Intellectually, he found them a little higher than average, 'but they are not intellectual giants'. This was further substantiated during interviews when he challenged Juliet about her concept of the afterlife and death. She said everyone she knew on Earth she would meet in Heaven. 'Even Pauline's mother ... with blood on her face?' he had asked. 'Yes,' Juliet responded. 'Even if we did meet her we would not worry, there is nothing in death.'[70] Bennett saw her concept of Heaven and apparent lack of regret as clear signs of her insanity.

He read extracts from Pauline's diaries and described the girls' deviant behaviour at Ilam, where they endlessly discussed the Saints and the plots of their books, bathed together and slept in the same bed, photographed each other in fancy dress and in the nude, talked until all hours and went out at night, and acted out their plays and fantasies on the lawn.

He was confounded by the little cemetery they had made in the grounds of Ilam that became a temple to Raphael Pan, where they buried a mouse and erected crosses to 'dead ideas'. What stupefied him the most, apart from the murder, was the girls' behaviour when the Queen visited Christchurch in January 1954: in their madness they had neglected to see Her Majesty or the decorations for her visit. Almost as despicably, they cheated at cards and board games with Jonathan. They were deceitful betrayers of trust like 'Judas Iscariot'.

To us sane I hope, it was a murder that was bestial and treacherous and filthy. It is outside all the kindly limits of sanity. It is a thousand miles away from sanity. They are still not sane and in my opinion they never will be sane.[71]

Brown's destruction of Medlicott's testimony had been comprehensive, but his discrediting of Bennett's was so complete that Judge Adams was prompted to ask, before Bennett stepped down, if his argument could be summarized in the words 'that in your opinion they knew the act was contrary to the ordinary moral standards of the community but nevertheless it was not contrary to their own moral standards?' Bennett's response was: 'Yes. You have completely summarized it.'[72] In one sentence this catastrophic admission swept away the defence's argument.

Judge Adams acted swiftly, calling both counsels into his office to discuss his view that the defence had failed to offer a feasible case. His inclination was to dismiss the defence and instruct the jury that 'there was no evidence of insanity at all'. When Peter Mahon said that the prosecution wanted the case decided by the jury, 'Adams said that he did not mind what the Crown wanted. He was telling him that as a matter of law he was going to direct the jury.'[73] That night Peter Mahon and Brian McClelland, assistants for the prosecution and the defence, respectively, combed the law library together, looking for precedents. They found only one, but this — along with Peter Mahon's vehement support for the defence to continue — convinced Adams to resume the trial.

The prosecution's rebuttal began on Friday, 27 August, with Kenneth Stallworthy, the first of three psychiatrists called by the Crown. The senior medical adviser at Avondale Mental Hospital in Auckland, Stallworthy had 15 years' experience in psychiatric hospitals in New Zealand and abroad. He had examined Pauline at Paparua on 26 and 27 July and on 19 August. He had also seen her at Mt Eden on 30 July, and 9 and 11 August. Juliet had been seen at Paparua on 26, 27 and 28 July, and 19 August.

Stallworthy contended that the girls were completely sane. Pauline's diaries were a record of intent. Subsequent to their arrest both girls had given lucid accounts of exactly what happened and repeated these frequently almost verbatim. He refused to accept that their behaviour was paranoid or that there was any reliable medical evidence linking paranoia to homosexuality. In his experience, the only kind of paranoia linked to homosexuality was 'the kind which the individual because of his background and upbringing is unable to accept within himself ... It is repressed homosexuality that is related to paranoia and I think in this case there was nothing repressed about the homosexuality.'[74]

He offered compelling commentary on the diaries. 'I have some experience of adolescents' diaries. I would say that adolescence is commonly a very conceited age and that very often ... [diaries record] the most conceited opinions without the adolescent concerned having any firm and fixed belief in what had been written.' He did not even see the girls' apparent lack of remorse as anything strange. 'It is my experience that it is extremely unusual for criminals to show any regret except at being caught.'[75] This was not beyond the boundaries of normality, and nor were their shoplifting or crazy delinquent escapades.

His experience of the girls was that they were completely rational. 'Hulme, in my interview with her ... displayed a vocabulary, a shrewdness in understanding and answering difficult questions of a highly intelligent and sophisticated person of a much greater age.'[76] She and Pauline never seemed to have any difficulty distinguishing fantasy from reality, and their passion for 'games, bloodshed and violence is exceedingly common in adolescents'.[77] With regard to their religious ideas and ceremonies, Stallworthy said, 'Adolescence is for many people a time of intense questioning of beliefs and I see nothing insane in two highly intelligent adolescents being preoccupied with the hereafter and in even toying with a religion of their own.'[78]

He thought their homosexuality, which he believed had a physical aspect to it, was a common stage for teenagers in their emotional development. 'I feel the homosexuality in this situation had been rather overstressed.' In Stallworthy's mind they were two girls who 'were very, very fond of each other' and the most important thing in their lives was to be together. 'There have been other great loves in the world where one person would stick at nothing to be with the other' — and this was one of them.[79]

The one glitch in Stallworthy's testimony was when Gresson challenged him during cross-examination about the time lapse of more than a month between the murder and his first seeing the girls: Stallworthy admitted that this might have influenced his diagnosis. Gresson also asked him when he had read Pauline's diaries; he had done so after he had written and submitted his report. Stallworthy's evidence was followed by that of James Savill and James Hunter, the medical officer and the superintendent who 'had been attached to the Department of Mental Hygiene for 29 years' at Sunnyside mental hospital in Christchurch.[80] Savill saw Juliet and Pauline separately six times; Hunter saw them three times separately, and interviewed Juliet when Pauline was at Mt Eden. Neither Hunter nor Savill believed they were insane. The medical witnesses were questioned only briefly by the defence counsel.

The next day was Saturday, and the date for a much-anticipated Ranfurly Shield rugby match, but Judge Adams decided that the court would sit in the morning, reconvening at 9.30am. This was the girls' last trip by covered prison van to the Supreme Court. In the dock Pauline appeared more nervous than Juliet, and paler than ever. She scowled as she had throughout the trial, and sometimes when the tension got too much she bit her lip. Juliet, with just the faintest smile on her lips, presented a more self-contained and assured front. At one point in the proceedings, Pauline spoke to Juliet across the policewoman and she smiled.

Counsel for the prosecution and the defence spoke for about 25 minutes each. Brown ended the prosecution's address by saying, 'they are not incurably insane, but incurably bad'. Gresson said that they were 'two unusual girls of unusual personality and their association was ... tragic for them. I think we can all agree on that ... At the time they committed the murder they were ill and not criminally responsible for their actions.'[81] At last, in his summing up, Judge Adams had his opportunity to direct the jury. After a lengthy expiation of the legal concepts of 'knowing' and 'wrong', he said that the jurors 'really' had 'no option but to hold the accused guilty of murder on the ground that the defence of insanity of the required nature and degree had not been proved'.[82]

The jury filed out at 12.10pm to rooms close to the courthouse to consider the previous five days' evidence. At 2.53pm they returned. The atmosphere in the crowded courtroom was tense. Already Brown was showing signs of emotion. Juliet and Pauline glanced up as the 12 men filed in to their seats in the jury box. A flicker of a smile passed across Juliet's face before she regained the largely expressionless demeanour she and Pauline had assumed for much of the trial. 'For long periods both sat with their heads almost down to their knees, apparently engrossed in their own thoughts.'[83] The registrar asked the jury foreman for the jury's verdict. At that moment, Bill, who was sitting with Hilda in seating reserved for witnesses, reached over and put his hand on her arm. 'Guilty' in each case, replied the foreman, without hesitation.

Suddenly, shattering the silence, a young man leapt forward from the back of the upstairs gallery, shouting: 'I protest, I object!' '*Silence!*' boomed the court crier. The offender was quickly bundled away by two policemen who intercepted him from the aisle.

CHAPTER SEVEN

I

Asmodeus, the Enemy, views everything from his vantage point in Erebus, a place of air and shadow that is neither the world nor Hell. He paces back and forth, distraught. Why did Tiyo-Mah pre-empt his instruction and leave Hell with all her hideous fiends? 'A few more years and the warriors Tathea had forged would wither. Age would rack their bones and the waiting would dull their hearts.' It was all going wrong, and it was not his fault.

After all, who could have predicted that Sadokhar would defy all logic and enter Hell? How could anyone have anticipated that kind of 'outrageous sacrifice'? Clutching the keys to the world, he boils in fury. With all this capriciousness how long can he hold on to them? He takes comfort in the knowledge that 'God could raise as many bodies to live for ever as there are stars in the heavens, but He cannot make one soul better than it chooses to be'.

Sadokhar is visited in Hell by a vision of Tathea, who tells him that to escape Hell he must forgive Tornagrain, the man who killed his wife. Forgiveness is Sadokhar's ticket out, but he must become a purer soul than anger and the desire for retribution have made him. It is hard, and initially he fails. In his travels he meets Ozmander, the grotesque Lord of the Undead, an unimaginably ugly creature that towers over him on two enormous legs.

It was almost human … At first it seemed as if the muscles rippled, then before his horrified eyes the flesh broke open and a new limb emerged, skinless and bleeding, only to be consumed again leaving nothing behind except a putrescent scar ... The skin was scaly, bubbling, purple-dark ... the face ... [a] fractured, misshapen torment of legion souls locked together in eternal hatred.

The air around Ozmander reeks with the stench of putrefaction. In the hideous creature Sadokhar glimpses the hatred inside himself, and is struck by a terrible thought: could he be consumed by it forever himself?

In the end Sadokhar destroys Ozmander, the beast outside himself, and then revenge, the beast inside, by forgiving Tornagrain, so they can both escape Hell. With Tornagrain he shares his new wisdom.

You have to become different, so that even if exactly the same things were to happen to you, you would never do that again, but far more than that, you wouldn't want to! ... You must let go of all selfishness and come to know without question that everyone else is as precious, as real and as important as you are, as capable of joy and pain ... Or if they aren't, that's God's judgment to make, not ours.

These are Anne's lessons, and Sadokhar's sojourn in the underworld is her trip to Hell and back with an answer that would help to salve the guilt and despair at the centre of her own life. As the Man of Holiness looks at Sadokhar he sees 'the face of a man who had been redeemed from hell and returned to the earth ... a man who had drunk the fullness of the grace of God'.

But Sadokhar is not the only character whose experiences echo Anne's. Tathea is her over-arching surrogate, and one of the numerous female figures who, Meg Davis believes, are brave enough to 'speak against the status quo and get punished for it'.[1]

Tathea's travels through the Lost Lands carrying the Book can be read as metaphor for the great Mormon migrations. According to anthropologist-historian John Hayward, 'the Mormons have been described as the most systematic, organized, disciplined and successful pioneers in American history'. In 1844 Joseph Smith, leader of the Mormon congregation, was murdered by a mob angry at the Church's unorthodox practices. Brigham Young, its newly elected leader, began an exodus of Mormons west, towards the Rocky Mountains to Utah, where they settled, free from persecution. 'The Mormons saw themselves as Israelites and Brigham Young was their Moses.' Between 1849 and 1852 an estimated 20,000 people were part of the 'Great Migration'.[2]

They carried with them a sacred text, *The Book of Mormon*, which they believed contained the writings of ancient biblical prophets alive in North America from approximately 2600BC, recorded on golden plates and revealed to Joseph Smith in 1830.[3] Like Tathea and her followers, the Mormons were a victimized people convinced of the sacred authenticity of their Book. In *Come Armageddon*, after a series of horrific battles in which the forces of good and evil are lost, the ultimate apocalyptic stand-off is between Asmodeus and Tathea. His strategy is to shatter her faith. With simmering satisfaction he surveys the total destruction, and hisses at her: 'You wanted power and glory and the dominion of God! Well, this is what you have ... desolation! You are Empress of nothing!'

To this gargantuan struggle Tathea brings the weapons of hope and love, and these are themes that flow through the words of the Man of Holiness in the Book, the text of which is included at the end of both *Tathea* and *Come Armageddon*. Although the Man of Holiness is full of wise virtue, there is something deliciously sinister and memorable about his opponent Asmodeus's utterances.

Man is riddled with doubt and ingratitude. In his ignorance and impatience he destroys what he holds. Despair walks beside him and whispers to him in the hallows of the night.

And:

How can an unjust God command respect, far less love? I have heard the prayers, even of the righteous, echo unanswered in the empty caverns of the night.

Asmodeus, or Lucifer, is a class act in literature. In Dante's *The Divine Comedy* he is a tantalizing three-headed beast frozen in the Inferno; in Spenser's *Faerie Queen* a proud female Lucifera; in Milton's *Paradise Lost* the great antagonist Satan; and in Blake's illustrations of *Paradise Lost* a terrifying incarnation of a nightmare figure. The power of Anne's insight in *Tathea* and *Come Armageddon* is to give God's fallen angel, and his voice of scepticism and doubt, as commanding and compelling a presence in the story as that of righteous certainty.

The reviews, first for *Tathea*, then *Come Armageddon*, astonished Meg and Don, who had worked so desperately hard with Anne to see the books in print. Of *Tathea*, Meg said: 'its publication saved me from cutting my own wrists, which I would surely have done if the sod had gone to any more drafts'.[4] The reviewer for *SFX* described *Tathea* as an 'innovative, well-written, intriguing novel, far removed from and far above the norm', while *Publishers Weekly* called it 'ambitious, engrossing ... she has devised here a powerful, inventive meditation on the possibilities that lie in and beyond the origin of religion'.[5] The *Booklist* likened it to *Erewhon*, *Gulliver's Travels* and *Candide*.

Starlog said *Come Armageddon* 'demonstrates a growing authority', and the critic for *SFX* identified it as a 'towering work of philosophy. [Anne Perry] has created a vision of Hell that sticks with you.'[6] Despite good reviews, however, neither of the books sold anywhere near as well as her detective fiction; Meg describes them as 'slow-burners'.

Still left in these books are some of the elements that annoyed Leona Nevler and prompted her refusal to publish. The cast of characters is epic, which makes it hard for the reader to bond with individuals, and sometimes even to remember names. Tathea can be too irritatingly good to be real, and the gratuitous killing of favourite figures can also annoy.

Although Anne's fantasy polarized people as her other writing did not — 'Perry's readers may not follow her here,'[7] said one reviewer — Tathea's exploits did create a new audience that was important to Anne. Not long after the publication of *Come Armageddon*, an email written in German arrived for her at the MBA offices. Staff member Dagmar Wolfinden translated it and sent it on to Anne.

I have read your book, TATHEA, and I am overwhelmed. Only a human being with a deep inner belief could write such a book. I have bought 20 copies and given them to all my friends as presents ... I have discussed your book for hours with friends belonging to our church. I can identify a great deal with what Tathea feels and senses. I have also had answers to some questions regarding my faith ... the conversation between Asmodeus and the servant of the Magnificent, at the end of the book, has touched me very much ... Thank you so much for your testimony.[8]

While Anne anxiously followed the mixed progress of her fantasy novels, her detective fiction continued to fly off bookshop shelves. In 1999 she published *Bedford Square*, her nineteenth Pitt — this was the twentieth anniversary of the series — as well as *The Twisted Root*, her tenth Monk. Although neither had the impact of her millennium publications the following year, *The Twisted Root* was fascinating in terms of the character development of William Monk. In her unpublished paper 'Keeping a Series Interesting', Anne suggests that writing 'a series [today] is a different challenge' from the one faced by Arthur Conan Doyle when he was writing Sherlock Holmes. 'Readers' expectations are higher, and more sophisticated. We are less easily pleased.' Above all, characters must develop in response to the challenges they meet in life: 'No pain, no gain!'

Face it, most of us only learn the hard way, and the hard way makes a better story! Parachuting onto the mountain top is nothing, climbing up to it is everything.[9]

In *The Twisted Root*, Lucius Stourbridge appeals to Monk to help him find his missing fiancée, Miriam Gardiner. Monk, pricked by the poor man's predicament after 'having just returned from an extravagant three-week honeymoon in the Highlands of Scotland', promises to help. Marriage is Monk's mountain, and there is not a parachute in sight. His revelation is that he must stop trying to mould Hester into the 'kind of woman he used to imagine he wanted', and accept her pretty much as is. 'Had he expected her to be a good cook? Surely he knew her better than that? Did he imagine marriage was somehow going to transform her magically into a housekeeper sort of woman? Perhaps he did.' But not for long.

Like Anne's, Hester's interests, when she is not working in tandem with Monk to solve crimes, are professional. She cannot cook, she is not interested in housekeeping. Her ambition is to see the status of nurses raised above that of labourer, and to establish community care units for returning soldiers. 'You are dreaming, my dear,' says her patron and friend Lady Callandra. 'We have not even achieved proper nurses for the poor law infirmaries attached to the workhouses, and you want to have nurses to visit the poor in their homes? You are fifty years before your time. But it's a good dream.' Hester is indeed half a century ahead of her time, both in her professional aspirations and her 'new' marriage, but by giving her unusual ambitions Anne creates opposition and conflict and at the same time draws readers' attention to the universality of these desires for women. While Monk reconfigures his view of gender, there is a happy spin-off: 'something in him had softened'.

In the year 2000, Anne published an astonishing three full-length novels and two short stories, all of which had some special significance. Of all her detective novels, her twentieth Pitt, *Half Moon Street*, is probably the most personally poignant. All her books deal with family dynamics, but when she writes about the Pitts the intensity changes and so does her involvement.

In *Half Moon Street* she originally had Charlotte's grandmother, Mariah, as the murderer. 'That's the only time, I'm pretty sure, that Anne comes close to a first-person account of what it feels like [to murder someone],' recalls Meg. 'Her US publisher at the time insisted that Anne change the story so Grandmama doesn't actually do it.'

In spite of the change, *Half Moon Street* remains a powerful novel. It opens with a spine-chilling discovery. Drifting in a punt is the unidentified body of a man, 'wrists encased in manacles chained to the wooden sides, its ankles apart, chained also'. He is dressed in a long green velvet robe like a dress, his head 'thrown back, mimicking ecstasy', and all around are strewn artificial flowers, in hideous parody of the famous Millais painting *Ophelia*. This is an image that lingers, but then comes the unfolding drama at Caroline and Joshua Fielding's residence.

Caroline's marital bliss with the much younger Joshua is under threat, partly from the amorous attentions of renowned actress Cecily Antrim, but largely because of Caroline's dissolving self-confidence, aggravated by her former mother-in-law, Grandmama Mariah.

> She was seventeen years older than Joshua. It was like poking at an unhealed wound just to say it to herself. Perhaps the old woman, with her vindictive, all-seeing eyes, was right, and she had been a fool to marry a man she was absurdly in love with, who made her laugh and cry, but who in the end would not be able to protect himself from finding her boring.

In order to protect a scandalous secret, Grandmama orchestrates a cunning estrangement of the newly-weds. When she goes to bed that night, expecting a blissful state of satisfaction after her successful meddling, she is surprised at how little pleasure she feels. In fact, 'she drifted in and out of nightmare. She was alone in an icy swamp. She cried out and no one heard her. Blind, inhuman faces peered and did not see. Hate. Everything was drenched and dark with hate. Guilt brought her out in a sweat.' She had hated watching their pleasure in each other's company, but her cruel separation of them has only brought despair. When Caroline discovers Grandmama's duplicity, she is devastated, angry and then pitying, because there is a terrible reason for the old woman's destructive behaviour.

Although Grandmama does not murder anyone, she has unwillingly participated in behaviour for which she cannot forgive herself. 'She has hated herself so long she can find no way back,' Vespasia explains to Caroline. Censorship is hotly debated in this novel. Cecily Antrim believes everything should be open and accessible to everyone, but Vespasia's parting good advice about Grandmama challenges this opinion: 'The most you can do for her is to treat her with some nature of respect, and not allow your new knowledge of her to destroy what little dignity she has left.'

While *Half Moon Street* was well received, it was *Slaves and Obsession*, published in the United States as *Slaves of Obsession*, that made a real impression in 2000. For years Anne's American fans had read Pitts and Monks set in London, the United Kingdom or Europe. Now they were finally rewarded by a book set largely in their country and during their own Civil War. 'American readers loved it. They keep asking when Monk's going to visit America again,' said Don Maass in 2011.[10]

Slaves and Obsession opens at a dinner party at the Alberton mansion in London. Lady Callandra has called Monk in to investigate the blackmail of her friend Daniel Alberton. As the evening proceeds, it becomes apparent that Alberton, an arms dealer, has promised the Confederate South a consignment of 6,000 muskets as they prepare for war. Alberton, hotly challenged by his abolitionist daughter, Merritt, explains his dilemma. He has made a promise, taken a deposit and his word is his honour.

But honour is a dangerous thing in detective fiction. Alberton and his associates are found murdered, and Merritt is suspiciously missing with her Union lover, Lyman Breeland. Merritt's mother appeals to Monk and Hester to follow the eloping couple to the United States and bring them back. On their trans-Atlantic voyage to Washington, Hester observes the departing immigrants:

Many were looking to travel west beyond the war into the open plains, or even to the great Rocky Mountains. There they could find refuge for their religious beliefs, or wide lands where they could hack from the wilderness farms and homesteads they could not aspire to here.

From Washington, the Monks follow the couple's trail to the battlefield of Bull Run. Seeing young soldiers mortally wounded takes Hester back to the carnage of the Crimea. She tends a dying man for whom nursing seems redundant except as a comfort, 'perhaps some kind of dignity, a shred of hope, an acknowledgement that he was still there, and his feelings mattered, urgent, and individual ... the reward was in the doing, and in the hope.' Monk watches, choked with emotion. 'How did Hester keep her head, bear all the pain, the dreadful mutilation of bodies? She had strength beyond his power to imagine.'

Three prevailing themes emerge from this novel. Slavery and racism, the power of obsession, and the revelation of Monk's dark past and its impact.

Anne refuses to take an uncomplicated position, even on the contentious subject of slavery. She challenges people to think beyond the stereotypes and reconfigure their morality. As Don Maass has noted:

Her depiction of America at the time of the Civil War is really amazing, especially as they travel deep [into the country] in the company of [Philo Trace] a Southerner who expresses the Southern point of view in circa 1860 ... and doesn't make a case for slavery exactly but gives Monk and Hester a more nuanced picture of the South ... She projected herself into somebody else and their way of looking at things — and an *unpopular* way of looking at things — and saw how a decent human being from the 1860s would see and accept their society the way it was: and she does that again, and again in her fiction.[11]

Philo Trace explains to Hester and Monk that many holdings in the South are small, with one slave who is treated well because the farmer's livelihood depends on him. Merritt and Lyman Breeland voice the abolitionist position, while Philo Trace enriches our understanding of an abomination that history remembers in more polarized terms.

It is obsession that unites the book's characters. Lyman Breeland is obsessed about civil rights to the extent that he sacrifices everything, including Merritt; Philo Trace is fixated on capturing the fugitive couple; Merritt is consumed by her passion for Lyman. The corrosive power of obsession is summed up by Monk:

Perhaps [Merritt] was one of the world's great lovers, but Breeland was not. He might be one of the world's idealists, or one of its flawed obsessives, not so much a man who supported a cause, as a man who needed a cause to support him, to fulfil a nature otherwise empty.

The dangerous power of obsession is something Anne knew about from her own experience with Pauline Parker. She understood Merritt's motives especially: 'she is passionate and willful and when she gives herself to something, or someone, it is wholeheartedly, and not always wisely'.

As Monk's past comes into clearer focus, he discovers that he worked with unscrupulous businessmen who made their money from the slave trade. He is tormented by the information he has uncovered, and fears that Hester will reject him.

She smiled, but her eyes were filled with sadness. She reached out her hand and touched his cheek. It was a soft gesture. It did not dismiss what he had done, or excuse it, but it set it in the past.

⚘

When Anne's brother, Jonathan, returned to the United Kingdom in 2000, 88-year-old Marion was delighted. As she had got older, she had become less mobile and could not travel to see him. 'I do miss Jonty desperately ... and his two small children are very attractive & delightful,' she had told family friend Nancy Sutherland in June 1995.

Did you know that he married a Chinese nurse, & nearly rocked us off our foundations? ... and now we have these darling [grand]children, [and] it is developing into a strong family with real bonds of affection ... They have a little girl of 10 & boy of 6. She looks like a small exquisite Margot Fonteyn & is a dedicated Ballet Dancer!! He is a sturdy, well built young man, & I'm quite besotted with him.[12]

Now Jonathan and his family were settling in Scotland, not far from Anne and Marion. After years of intermittent contact, long-distance communication and separation, they were finally living close together as a family.

In 1954, aged 10, Jonathan had returned to England with his father. Henry Hulme's job at the Atomic Weapons Research Establishment at Aldermaston, near Reading, meant he was 'in at the Golden Age of the development of the H-bomb, following of course the A-bomb. This was the mid- to late-1950s, and he was basically the chap who designed and sorted out the problems of the British H-bomb.'[13] Jonathan boarded at Bradfield College, which was a 45-minute drive from Reading. At school he was a keen marksman, becoming captain of the shooting team and the first boy from Bradford College to get junior international colours. From there, he went on exhibition (a type of scholarship) to St John's College, Oxford, where he studied medicine and philosophy and psychology. At Oxford he was a member of the university rifle team.

In 1978, after working in hospitals around the south of England, he realized he wanted 'to go somewhere else, so [he] decided to up anchor and went to Rhodesia'. There he was appointed to a position at a black African hospital in Bulawayo, Rhodesia's second largest city. When a colleague was called up for military service over a long weekend and was reluctant to go, Jonathan, who had joined the local gun club, offered to replace him. It was at a referendum time, 'where Ian Smith was saying: "Are we prepared to share power with the blacks? Specifically: Bishop Abel Muzorewa."'

Jonathan travelled with a reserve unit to Matabeleland North and discovered a new vocation. 'I thought: Hang on, I'm enjoying this.' He applied to join the army, becoming a medical officer in the Second Battalion Rhodesian Africa Rifles with his own small military hospital at Fort Victoria in the middle of Schonland, where his battalion was stationed. He took a parachute course and got his wings, and was in the army two or three years when 'after transition to black power, things were getting politically very uncomfortable'. He resigned from the army and lectured in anatomy at a university medical school for another two years before going into private practice.

What pulled Jonathan back to the United Kingdom was the political and economic turbulence in what was now Zimbabwe, and the educational needs of his family. He had met his wife, Sylvia, while on leave in Gloucester. They corresponded for a while, then he returned to England and convinced her to follow him to Rhodesia. 'We got married in a little chapel on the edge of Lake Kyle ... and we had the reception back in the barracks.' They had two children, first Frances, then Henry, four years apart. They needed to go back to the United Kingdom before Frances turned 16, because she had to be in the country two years to be eligible to go to university at the standard fee. They spent a year planning their move to Scotland.

What met them on their arrival was a shock. The climate, the flora and fauna, the landscape, the local school, which dumped the dimmest students in the art class — everything was dramatically different from what they knew. Frances was especially talented at art, and in Zimbabwe art was a privilege for the most able students and a disciplined endeavour. But it was a bonus to be close to Marion and Anne. Since the beginning of his schooling in the United Kingdom, Jonathan's primary parent had been his father, and he had established a close relationship with Henry's second family, especially the son of a similar age, Mike Ducker. For Anne, Marion had been a mainstay, especially since her move to Portmahomack. Until her eyesight failed, Marion read her daughter's manuscripts, and Anne rang her every day and 'often we would talk for ages'.[14] There was piquancy to the relationship, an intensity that came from a mutual feeling of failure.

Anne knew that she had brought the world down upon her mother's head. She had made them both refugees — women without a past — and exposed them to vicious ridicule. But Marion carried her own burden of guilt. She knew that she had not been vigilant, or even aware. She was a clever woman who had miscalculated the situation. Her affair with Bill Perry, the end of her marriage and loss of social position had all been more important to her than her daughter. There had been tragic misjudgments on both sides, but mother and daughter were connected forever by history and a camaraderie forged by blame. They were both fighters, determined not to replicate the dysfunction of their earlier relationship. In her later years, Marion was the mentor to Anne that she failed to be in her youth, and Anne was as receptive and respectful a daughter as any parent could hope for.

> My mother was extremely astute … She was very canny. She had lovely turns of phrase … colourful … very wise, very good judge of a person, very politically aware, few people ever pulled the wool over her eyes, and she did an awful lot of voluntary work helping people. [She said of Prime Minister Tony Blair], when she first saw him, don't trust that young man, he's got the eyes of a horse that would bolt.[15]

Marion lived in her Portmahomack cottage with its stunning sea views for over a decade. The locals fondly referred to her as the Queen Mother, because she was elderly, overdressed and waved benignly while she worked in her English garden. Until the end of her life she served tea, and sherry after 4pm. Marion had an innate understanding of sexual politics. Women deserved equality and power, she believed, but men had it, so the male world attracted her. She was also a woman of her time. When Denis Healey retired from politics, she said: 'he was the last of those who served in the forces and we have now lost the sense of team spirit. Now, it's everyone for themselves. The loyalty that that generation had is gone.'[16]

In 2002, a severe stroke left Marion hospitalized and ultimately bed-ridden in a rest home. Anne rang the hospital for regular updates and visited Marion almost daily. Her mother loved flowers, and in the summer Anne would arrive with new bunches from her garden. The feelings of guilt and anger came back, but there was also relief. 'They can't make my mother suffer now,' Anne told a reporter for the *Glasgow Herald*, in March 2002, 'she's 90 and in hospital after having a massive stroke. But they did make her suffer terribly … I don't run away; I've faced the worst and survived.'[17] It was an emotionally draining time. Anne had always abhorred being left, but this parting would be the worst yet, because it was permanent and it would not be an easy farewell between two untroubled souls.

Anne had the support of Jonathan and his family, who were becoming increasingly significant in her life, and there were also Meg MacDonald and her family. Meg was happy to visit, because she got on well with Marion. When they had first met, Meg did not know what to call her. She thought 'Mrs Perry' was too formal, but she was not one to call an older woman by her first name. 'How would "Mother Perry" suit you?' she suggested, and Marion replied, 'That's perfect!' One day she gave Meg a gold chain. She put it around her neck and said: 'While you're wearing that you'll always be safe.'[18] Meg has never taken it off. She did not go into town without ringing Marion and offering her a ride. 'I'll have my boots on,' Marion would say, and she would be waiting at the door. They would drive around town and chat. One hot summer day they went for a walk to the Tarbat Ness lighthouse.

> It was a beautiful, absolutely beautiful day and there was a little mouse that walked towards us and we both stopped and looked at it cleaning itself ... We went a bit further along and we sat down on this knoll and all of a sudden a little stoat or a weasel came out and started playing round on the grass in front of us ... and we watched this for quite a while and then it scuttled off ... She said: 'All we need now, Meg, is a pod of dolphins.' And I said: 'Mother Perry, if you look over your left shoulder you'll never believe what's in the sea below you.' There was a school of dolphins close enough for her to see because she was getting a bit blind at this stage.[19]

※

When the reviews for *Slaves and Obsession* began appearing, there was a trans-Atlantic whoop of delight from Anne's agents. It was first on the *Booksense* and *Livres Hebdo* bestseller lists, the main selection for the Mystery Guild and number 10 on the *Publishers Weekly* bestseller list. 'This is one of her best,' wrote reviewers for both the *Chicago Tribune* and *Pittsburgh Post-Gazette*. The *New York Times Book Review* agreed, and the critic for *Booklist* wrote: 'The best element in this novel is Perry's depiction of the excitement preceding and the butchery during the Battle of Bull Run, reminiscent of Thackeray's unflinching portrait of Waterloo in *Vanity Fair* ... A remarkable addition to the Perry canon.'[20]

Along with critical accolades came Anne's first major award: an Edgar for her short story 'Heroes', which was reproduced in *The Penguin Book of First World War Stories* in 2000. Named after Edgar Allan Poe, Edgars are coveted awards given out every year by the Mystery Writers of America for mystery writing in fiction, non-fiction, film, television and theatre. Edgars for short stories have been awarded since 1951. What thrilled Anne most about the award was its affirmation of a new possibility for her writing. 'Heroes' introduced First World War chaplain Joseph Reavley, who would reappear in a series of books that she was already thinking about. 'Heroes' was accompanied by another short story, 'A Dish Taken Cold', linked in plot and characterization to the stand-alone novel *The One Thing More*, also published in 2000. The book's title came from Marion. When Anne was asked by a reporter to comment on society's judgment of murderers like the killers of two-year-old James Bulger, she replied, 'My mother always says, "Don't judge yet. If only you knew just one more thing about that person's life ...".'[21] This seemed a fitting title for her novel about the French Revolution, which she had worked on intermittently for years, but with more focus since her trip to France with Meg Davis in November 1993.

France was an avid market for Anne's work. Her agent in Paris was the dynamic, American-born Lora Fountain, who was the partner of Gilbert Shelton, creator of *Fat Freddy's Cat*, and represented artist, illustrator and musician Robert Crumb. Over the years Lora and Anne had developed a close working relationship with Emmanuelle Heurtebise, the commissioning editor for 10/18 (Dix/Dix-huit). The company had published Anne's books in English and in French translation from the early Pitt days, and Emmanuelle had become a staunch supporter and friend. When Anne came to France for research trips, book signings and media interviews, the pair would take time out to shop and have a meal together.

Emmanuelle's fiancé was an Irish-born mathematician, and over dinner he and Anne would become engrossin in conversation. He turned her mathematical universe upside down when he shattered the 'incontrovertible' rule that 'the sum of the interior angles of any triangle has to be 180 degrees'. This had been a fact for Anne until he challenged her. 'You are thinking of Euclidian geometry, aren't you? That's plain geometry on a level; imagine it on a curve.' She was profoundly impressed and liberated by the idea that even mathematical rules could be bent.

It was as if he had suddenly blown the universe apart and reassembled it for me ... Suddenly I thought how much else is there that we assume has to be written in immutable laws that it has to be so, because of something we don't know ... It's so exciting ... all sorts of wonderful things ... Maybe there are all sorts of other things that don't have to be the way we think it's set ... It just broke the idea that certain things have to be.[22]

When the news of Anne's identity broke, Emmanuelle was shocked like everyone else, but it did not change her regard for Anne. She did, however, need a strategy. 'I decided I wouldn't mention anything [to the media] ... as it was not pertinent.'[23] So in France there was silence about Anne's background until one day when Emmanuelle received a telephone call from a prominent French journalist. 'He had just discovered it,' she remembers.

He was angry with me because I never told him ... He was a journalist from the Left Party, supposed to be very, very open-minded ... So [we] had a fight and I was blacklisted by that journal for a long, long time, and he published some very bad words about me ... because of my 'censorship'.[24]

The next time Anne made a major promotional tour of France, the same journalist was quick to ring up the 10/18 offices and make an appointment to see her. When Emmanuelle spotted his name on the media list she told her assistant either to 'cancel him or he has to promise he won't put the subject [of the murder] on the table'. The same day

Emmanuelle was attending an exclusive Parisian cocktail party when she ran into the journalist, who was furious. 'You can't write the questions for me!' he shouted. With equal determination, she shouted back, 'If you take this approach, we will cancel the meeting!' The journalist agreed to cancel the meeting, then stormed off, and Emmanuelle was left surrounded by concerned colleagues, who were supportive of her stand. 'It's not usual for me to be so very angry, I never shout at people, but it was very tense.'[25]

The journalist wrote for an influential magazine, and although it was difficult to say no to the coverage, Emmanuelle knew his approach would be damaging. She was proved correct when his article finally came out, under the headline 'I kill, thus I write'. He had written a cruel exposé of Anne. The piece discussed Pauline Parker without revealing her whereabouts, but told readers that Anne lived in Portmahomack. It also attacked Emmanuelle once more for her censorship.

Lora Fountain rang Emmanuelle immediately. 'Have you *seen* the article?' She had, and was furious. 'You could hear it down the phone,' Lora remembers.[26] She was imagining Emmanuelle's 'face bright red with steam coming out of her ears'. They sat in their respective offices, stunned. Lora called it 'yellow journalism', and Emmanuelle described it as the publishing of 'dirty details'.

10/18 has sold over 3 million copies of Anne's books. The appeal, Emmanuelle believes, is their exoticism. For French readers the Victorian period is foreign and removed from the familiar flavour of their own history. How, then, would this Anglophile French audience react to *The One Thing More*? There was an additional complication. 'In France people don't like foreigners wanting to write about their ... history, so it was tricky with the journalists,' Emmanuelle remembers.

But the readers who loved Pitt and Monk still bought it ... They know she can be trusted with her research about history, so they were comfortable with that ... It's not astonishing that she picked this part of French history. [There were] a lot of echoes [from it] around the world.[27]

The One Thing More opens in 1793, in the crowded public gallery of the National Convention, where the deputies have been debating for three days the sentencing of King Louis XVI, who has been arrested and tried for high treason. They file back, exhausted, and in the flickering candlelight Célie Laurent sees their faces as they make their pronouncements of 'Death'. Since the storming of the Bastille in 1789, Célie's life has changed so that it is barely recognizable. Her husband and infant son are dead, and her genteel way of life has been reduced to one of impoverished servitude as laundress for Monsieur Bernave. She finds herself drawn into a plot that begins as a mission to rescue the king and ends with the revelation of the murderer of Bernave, after the discovery of 'the one thing more' — which is the solution to this complex whodunit.

The backdrop is a fascinating slice of French history that involves a delicious assortment of visionaries and tyrants — including Maximilien Robespierre, Jean-Paul Marat, Louis Antoine de Saint-Just — at a time when Paris is the 'centre of the world'. But the heart of the novel is an intimate tale of personal calamity. In avenging the death of her son, Célie implicates Georges Coigny, an innocent man whose life is now in mortal danger. She 'let her grief destroy her humanity, even her knowledge of what was right'. Now she must save him. Her guilt is more intense because of her crisis of faith. Although Célie hates the Church, 'its hypocrisy, its oppression and its greed', she needs 'its promises of a God who loved'. As Georges explains, the Church offers hope, 'and faith in a justice beyond anything there is here ... which is too often a farce, or worse. If we are all there is ... we haven't got much, have we?'

Célie and her fellow conspirators are, of course, unsuccessful in their plot to save the king and he is guillotined, like so many other aristocrats and commoners whose severed heads fill the wicker baskets of the Place de la Révolution. 'There were stories of heads that moved, eyes, tongues.' This is the justice of the convention, and Célie has no authority to change it. The only power she has is personal, and it takes the form of her own redemption. At the end of the book, as she rushes through the streets to meet Georges Coigny, she realizes that 'the guilt, the contempt for herself was gone'.

II

The frozen stillness in the courtroom had ended. People murmured, moved uneasily in their seats, turned to one another and shook their heads. The registrar, GE Pollock, asked Pauline, then Juliet, if they had anything to say, and 'their Counsel in each case said they had no further submissions to make'. The girls stood impassively in the dock. Justice Adams asked for formal confirmation of their ages, and, while the judge and lawyers conferred, Pauline spoke to Juliet, who smiled back reassuringly. Haslam and Gresson suggested that 'there was proof in the testimony of Mr Rieper and Mrs Hulme respectively — of the age of the accused': Pauline was 16, Juliet 15.[28]

When Brown came to make his submission that the relevant evidence should be read to the jury, he broke down. This was not the first sign during the morning that his emotions were close to the surface. At times he had to clear his throat to continue, his voice trembled and he kept rubbing his hands over his eyes. Having ascertained the girls' ages by means of a jury ruling, Adams stiffly, and to a hushed courtroom, pronounced the sentence:

> You both being held to be under the age of 18, the sentence of the Court
> is detention during Her Majesty's pleasure. That sentence is passed
> upon each of you.[29]

He then ordered the prisoners to be removed from court. Juliet, Pauline and the policewoman filed out, taking the door to the cells upstairs. Pauline looked directly ahead of her. Juliet glanced towards her mother, whose eyes were shut in despair. After the girls had gone, the judge addressed the jury, thanking them for their 'long and careful attention to the case'.[30] Because of the nature of the trial, he suggested they might consider taking a three-year exemption period from jury service, starting that day.

At 3.40pm, the covered prison van that had transported the girls to the Supreme Court each day took them away to Paparua Prison, where they would begin their sentences. The prison superintendent told the newspapers that although the girls were in separate cells, they saw each other at exercise sessions in the morning and again in the afternoon.

Juliet and Pauline were saved from the gallows by a recent law change. Section 5 of the Capital Punishment Act 1950, which reintroduced the death penalty to New Zealand, stated that 'where a person convicted of an offence punishable with death was under 18 the sentence passed should be a sentence of detention during Her Majesty's pleasure instead of a sentence of death'.[31] Their case was the first time section 5 had been applied. The issue of capital punishment was as contentious in New Zealand as it was in the United Kingdom, from where it had come in codified form in 1840 when New Zealand became a British territory.

In Britain the matter was raised controversially when the Marilyn Monroe-like Ruth Ellis was hanged on 13 July 1955 for the murder of her gigolo boyfriend David Blakely. There was a storm of protest from opponents of capital punishment, among them regular columnist 'Cassandra', writing on the front page of the Daily Mail:

> It's a fine day for hay-making ... And if you feel that way — and I mourn to say that millions of you do — it's a fine day for a hanging ... If you read this before nine o'clock this morning, the last dreadful and obscene preparations for hanging Ruth Ellis will be moving up to their fierce and sickening climax ... If you read this after nine o'clock, the murderess, Ruth Ellis, will be gone. The one thing that brings stature and dignity to mankind and raises us above the beasts of the field will have been denied her — pity and the hope of ultimate redemption ... If you read these words of mine at mid-day the grave will have been dug ... and the Chaplain will have read the burial service.[32]

Ruth Ellis was the last woman to be executed in the United Kingdom; however, capital punishment was not properly abolished until after the executions, on 13 August 1964, of Peter Anthony Allen and Gwynne Owen Evans for the killing of John Alan West.

In New Zealand, the first execution took place in 1842. The Labour

Party, which became the government in 1935, was against the death penalty and soon promoted legislative reform. The Crimes Amendment Act, passed in 1941, changed the penalty for murder from death by execution to a life sentence with hard labour. A change of government in 1949 heralded a more conservative era. Almost as soon as the National Party assumed power, it reintroduced capital punishment for murder, which had been a campaign pledge. During National's three terms in power, from 1949 to 1958, 22 people were sentenced to death; eight of these were hanged. Attorney-General and Minister of Justice Clifton Webb was prudent in his use of the death penalty, but his successor Jack Marshall was not. Between 1955, when Marshall assumed office, and 1958, when he left, there were five executions.

Section 5 contained a number of clauses that were about to cause the Minister of Justice a headache in Juliet and Pauline's case. Juvenile prisoners were to be 'detained in such a place and under such condition' as the minister directed, and could 'at any time be discharged' under a licence which, if it was contravened, could be revoked. As the *Truth* reporter pointed out, 'it does not mean that Juliet Hulme or Pauline Parker will necessarily be detained in a prison or a penal institution'.[33] In the case of James Frederick Dodd and Cyril James Pascoe, there were fewer difficulties over the execution of their sentence or where they would be detained. Dodd and Pascoe, aged 15 and 14 respectively, were found guilty of the murder of Raymond Douglas Brinkman at Te Whakarae near Taumarunui on 12 January 1947. Because of the repeal of the capital punishment legislation in 1941, both boys' sentences were automatically commuted to life imprisonment.[34] Mercy was recommended for Pascoe, who was released from prison early in 1954 after serving seven years. Dodd was still in prison when Juliet and Pauline were sentenced, and was the only juvenile in prison in New Zealand for murder at the time. For the boys there was no death penalty pending or section 5 amendment to negotiate, and there was more choice of facilities for incarceration. Because there was only a small number of female serious offenders in New Zealand, and few juvenile prisoners, it was difficult to find the right place for Juliet and Pauline. The choices were: Arohata Borstal, a women's and girls' reformatory situated close to Wellington; Paparua, where there 'is a small prison of the bungalow type to house three or four women on remand or short sentence'; and Auckland or Mt Eden Prison, which had a small unit to accommodate older women and young women considered unsuitable for Arohata. The dilemma for authorities was whether a reformatory institution such Arohata was sufficiently stringent to manage the girls' punishment and detention. 'Borstal,' wrote one commentator, 'is designed as corrective treatment, and is not designed for holding perpetrators of this type of crime, however young.'[35] Whatever was decided would be a compromise, further complicated by the need to separate the girls, which was seen as an imperative. Should they remain at Paparua, they would continue seeing each other twice a day; if they were remanded together to another institution, there would be inevitable contact.

To add to this difficulty, according to newspaper reports both girls were threatening to commit suicide if they were parted, and there was also the problem of their intelligence. Both were deemed to be exceptionally bright — one reporter claimed Juliet was 'inside the maximum mark set for genius'.[36] What obligation did this put on those responsible for their custody, and what extra facilities might be required, if any? And how would an undetermined sentence affect two highly intelligent girls? As a *Star Sun* headline said, 'Detention of Murderesses Is Problem'. To solve this problem it was decided that the Secretary of Justice, Sam Barnett, who was also Controller General of Prisons, would meet and consult with psychiatrists and physicians on 2 September before making his recommendation to Minister Webb. The matter would then be discussed in Cabinet before a final decision was made. The result was that Juliet would be moved from Paparua to the women's section of Mt Eden Prison. Pauline would remain at Paparua until a 'new security section now being prepared at Arohata Women's Borstal institution near Porirua is completed. She is likely to be its first inmate.'[37] It was also decided that the girls should be treated as if they were adult serious offenders, not minors. 'They will wear the ordinary prison clothes, eat ordinary prison food, do the ordinary prison tasks set long-sentence women prisoners and be subject to the ordinary prison discipline.'[38]

The prisons to which the girls were sent were dramatically different. Arohata was a local, low-security modern institution in the process of expansion. Mt Eden was a nineteenth-century fortress-style catchment prison for the country's worst offenders. The reason for the inequality in accommodation arose partly from the contrasting perceptions of the two girls, promulgated especially by the media. Juliet was identified as the more forceful character and the more dazzlingly brilliant of the two. 'Hulme is the more dominant personality and the leader of the two,' the Secretary for Justice was reported in the *Dominion* as saying.[39] The implication was that she had manipulated, even led events, and therefore had greater culpability and the stronger will that would need to be controlled or broken in custody.

Although it was never overtly stated, there was a generally held belief, too, that Juliet was 'snobby' and 'arrogant'. There was a strange twist in public feeling, perhaps intensified by a sense of betrayal. Everything English had a gloss, glamour and authority in New Zealand — until it fell short. And the Hulmes were judged to have fallen terribly short. Juliet undoubtedly symbolized more, but both girls were vilified, occasionally in hysterical fashion. Brown's phrase 'dirty-minded little girls' resounded through the press, as did Medlicott's 'grossly insane'. Such a reaction was promoted by a trial that set out to establish guilt or innocence on the basis of 'badness' *versus* 'madness'. Both sides of this dichotomy would outlive the trial and continue to fan public outrage and contempt in almost equal measure. But the essential, over-arching label was 'evil'. This contained both bad and mad, but was bigger and beyond human redemption. 'Entries in Diary "Like An Evil Mirror",' read a headline in the *New Zealand Herald*, during the trial. 'The barbarity and hopelessly irrational confidence of the accused, their youth, and Parker's diary reflected the deterioration of the two girls "like an evil mirror",' ran the text. And they were callous and unfeeling. 'Girls Hear Murder Verdict Unmoved,' read the heading in the *NZ Truth* after their sentencing.

In court, the girls' juvenile fictional writings had been meticulously interrogated. Adolescent fantasy was listened to with the same grim intensity as aspects of the murder, and given the same weight. Pauline's diary was read largely as a factual account, and, although it was not used in evidence against Juliet, it was seen as a reflection of her thoughts, motives and actions, too. This made brilliant newspaper copy, as did revelations of the intensity of the girls' relationship, and their alleged homosexual conduct, which was viewed publicly, at least, as an 'abomination'. There was no attempt to understand or interpret events from any other perspective: whether mad or bad, the girls were remorseless killers.

As Joann Deak and Teresa Barker write in *Girls Will Be Girls*:

It would be a mistake to say that *most* girls live just this side of anorexia, depression, and suicide … But it is no exaggeration to say that *most* girls are in touch with these grim realities as part of the context of their everyday lives.[40]

The issues Pauline and Juliet faced — such as anorexia, depression and suicide, and the tight pairing of a friendship 'pash' — were commensurate with their age. A fantasy-fuelled coupling of girls in their early to mid-teens was common, as were assignations to run away and stay together regardless and forever.[41]

Although juvenile murder — and matricide especially — are rare, many aspects of the girls' behaviour were not. The teenage years are a time of gradual separation from family. This usually happens in tandem with intensifying and sometimes exclusive same-sex peer relationships. It is part of a natural preparation for adulthood. Ultimately, the sense of urgency in the 'pash' dissipates, or is overwhelmed by life events and hormones that pull in new and incompatible directions. Joann Deak and Teresa Barker call them 'the "smarter-than-thou" years': when teenagers reject their parents as models and mentors, and experiment, take risks, and rebel against convention. According to developmental psychobiology researchers Laurence Steinberg and BJ Casey, this is evolutionary — it is how human nature has evolved, and is therefore universal across time and culture. The ordeal for parents is how to guide adolescents through this turbulent period of re-alignment and initiation. Deak and Barker's advice is:

... you need to be as sure as you can be about the bottom line, the core value or philosophy you have as a parent. After that, you need to *really* understand the problem. The only way to do this is by engaging, connecting, interacting with your daughter.[42]

In a crisis, this connection with a parent or guardian is crucial. 'Friendship and loss are two very clear examples of crucible events in the lives of girls ... most girls have a very high need for a close friend during the ages of about nine to fourteen.'[43] For Juliet and Pauline, the threat of separation became a crucible event. If either set of their parents had been more involved with the girls, they would have realized the significance of the problem. 'Being an effective parent is like being a tightrope walker on the fine line of setting the boundaries and opportunities for a child.'

Honorah Parker's rigidity alienated Pauline, setting her adrift. Hilda Hulme's overly liberal parenting left Juliet rudderless. With little guidance from their parents, the girls were left, in the words of Deak and Barker, to 'negotiate the gray' alone while their parents floundered in the murk of their own personal traumas.

What makes negotiating the gray such a challenge is the fact that most of us are helping our girls negotiating the gray at the same time we are negotiating the gray ourselves, both in our own lives and also in our roles as parents ... Most adults ... are struggling with their own identity, priorities, and values.[44]

Hilda was conducting an affair with Bill, Henry had been forced to resign and was planning to leave the country, and Henry's resignation signalled a shift of roles, positions and countries. Honorah and Herbert faced ongoing challenges, too — a Down's Syndrome daughter in psychiatric care, financial constraints, the burden of a secret wife and family, and the socially treacherous fact that they had never married. All the significant adult lives in this situation were in flux and under stress.

In her seminal book *Cries Unheard: Story of Mary Bell*, Gitta Sereny examines the 1968 murders of two small boys by Mary Bell (aged 11) and

Norma Bell (aged 13). (They were unrelated, even though they shared the same surname.) The pair formed a pact of friendship and, although they were younger and from more deprived backgrounds, there are resonances with Juliet and Pauline.

> The essential contradiction of the trial was that 'killing' had a fantasy connotation for both these children, and neither of them ... understood 'death' in the sense of 'for ever' or of 'loss' ... [They] could not conceive that every action has a consequence ... [and they dissociated themselves from the act itself using a] psychological blocking mechanism which protects the mind from the unbearable ...[45]

People watching Mary Bell in court and when she testified were horrified by her apparent heartlessness, seeing it as proof of something monstrously evil. 'Yes, I remember,' says Mary Bell, 'we laughed — I can't think why and what about, but whenever we looked at each other, we laughed.' Twenty-five years later, at the 1993 trial of Robert Thompson and Jon Venables for the killing of James Bulger, Sereny observed 'the two boys doing exactly the same [thing, laughing] almost every time their eyes met'.[46]

Sereny describes the overwhelming disturbance of the trial for these children, who, in spite of 'careful provision', were still grossly ill-prepared for both the spectacle and the mind-numbing boredom of the courtroom. In the dock, their compelling, sometimes compulsive, childish friendship collided head-on with the solemnity of the situation and the seriousness of their crime. To the public their behaviour seemed unambiguous: they were cruel and dispassionate. Yet they were also immature children 'acting up' on an adult stage. In Sereny's experience, trauma affects children differently: some are 'silent to the point of being catatonic', while others are 'hyperactive' and excitable.[47]

Although Juliet and Pauline were older than either of these sets of children, the similarities are clear, and in the Parker–Hulme case there was the added teenage component. The arrogant rebelliousness so common in adolescence explains some of the girls' conceited, surly behaviour, and self-righteous consternation when things were read out in court as facts that they felt were misconstrued or wrong. Juliet had no voice in court. She was frustrated and angry with her lawyer for not allowing her to rebut what she felt were gross distortions, especially in the prosecution's depiction of her and Pauline as 'dirty-minded little girls'.

As Anne would say much later, 'There was never, ever a sexual element to our friendship … It was the 'fifties, for goodness sake. I was naïve about such things. We were certainly not lovers.'[48] Both Juliet and Pauline were visibly disturbed by this accusation, and by the interpretation of Pauline's diary where she wrote of going to see George at 2am. 'They thought this was a person … In court, I wanted to scream, [it's] the toilet, you fool.'[49] They felt misunderstood and misrepresented, and were visibly annoyed; and, to add yet another layer of complexity to any interpretation of the girls' behaviour in court, because the defence case was that they were insane, this had to have had an impact on how they behaved and how they were perceived.

Mary Bell has spoken about the unreality of the murder and the trial. 'A lot of the time, anyway, I thought all of it had nothing to do with me, [it was] as if I wasn't there, you know, or there but standing outside looking in.'[50] Juliet and Pauline talked of the same sense of 'unreality' and disembodiment, and they had equally ill-formed — and, as it turned out, problematic — ideas about killing, death and consequence. They thought the killing would be immediate, just a single blow to Honorah's head. For them, death was not final, but rather an abstraction uninformed by any personal experience. Their notion of consequence was also vague. They both had an idea that being caught might mean going to jail, but neither knew what that really entailed. In spite of their intelligence, they displayed an astonishing degree of naïveté in these three crucial areas.

Surviving the crucible event together was paramount, and they believed Honorah Parker was the obstacle to achieving that. According to the research of developmental psychologist Laurence Steinberg, 'teens take more risks not because they don't understand the dangers but because they weigh risk versus reward differently … In situations where risk can get them something they want, they value the reward more heavily than adults do.'[51] Juliet and Pauline knew they might be held accountable, but the reward of their companionship and future together seemed greater than the risk. Pauline was desperate to be overseas with Juliet, and Juliet felt a consuming obligation to, and investment in, their relationship. It was the first real, intense friendship either of them had had — and at that point in their life, it was everything.

If Juliet and Pauline broke one of society's greatest taboos by committing matricide, Hilda broke another, by abandoning her daughter. All through the trial she had been the scapegoat parent for scandalized condemnation. While New Zealand formed a special committee to establish 'a long-term project for the investigation of juvenile delinquency in all its aspects', Hilda was vilified in the media as the mother from Hell.[52] She was a perfect target for public fear and vitriol. In the post-war years, a new animal known as 'the teenager' was emerging, along with a social phenomenon referred to as 'the generation gap' — which would soon prove to be less of a gap than a chasm. The morally loose, fickle mother of a 'murderess' must in some way be complicit in this frightening development. The media made sure their readers saw the link. 'Left Without Goodbye Visit to Her Daughter,' read the headline for the NZ Truth as she left the country.[53]

Directly beside an NZ Truth article published on 23 September 1954, and tucked under the headline 'Misconduct Among Children and Adolescents' was a photograph of Hilda and Bill Perry fleeing New Zealand. The caption read: 'JULIET HULME'S MOTHER IN SYDNEY: Mrs. Hilda Marion Perry, formerly Hulme, mother of one of the Christchurch teenage murderesses on arrival in Sydney, accompanied by a witness in the trial, Walter Andrew Bowman Perry. Both appeared shocked by the crowd of photographers.' The article on misconduct, in the adjoining two columns, opened: 'URGENT legislative action to impose control over the importation and sale of morally harmful literature is expected to be taken as a result of recommendations made in the report of the special committee which had been investigating misconduct among children and adolescents.'

There was a growing sense of confusion and panic about the 'baby boomer' generation and its immediate predecessors, whose ideas about themselves and the world were being shaped by a rising wave of global popular culture in the form of books, pamphlets, magazines, comics, records, radio, film, theatre, travel — and the beginnings of television. Authorities on both sides of the Tasman were left gaping. In Australia, Liberal MP KM McCaw urged the legislative assembly of New South Wales to form an expert committee and make their own enquiries into juvenile delinquency:

> Current revelations of widespread juvenile delinquency in New Zealand, following similar experiences in South Australia, must give every parent cause for serious thought. Is this delinquency something new? Is it the particular product of our modern way of life, can it be arrested and how extensive is it?[54]

In preparation for leaving New Zealand, Hilda Hulme changed her surname by deed-poll to Perry. She was under no obligation to publish the fact or to inform anyone, but a journalist made the point that this was usually done. 'In a statement to the "Truth" during this weekend, Mrs Hulme did not disclose this change, but confirmed the fact that she proposes leaving New Zealand in a few days' time.'[55]

She and Bill left New Zealand two weeks after the trial, flying first from Christchurch to Sydney. Even close friends and associates were unaware of the details of their plans, and only four people went to the airport to see them off: defence lawyers Terence Gresson and Brian McClelland and 'two intimate friends, a man associated with the legal profession in Christchurch and his wife'.[56]

The press was unsure how the couple would travel from Australia to the United Kingdom. It was noted that their suitcases were labelled 'Melbourne' and it was believed they were planning to travel by sea, but when passengers on the Christchurch to Sydney flight were quizzed, they said they had been told the Perrys were flying to London via Singapore. The subterfuge seemed to have worked.

But the photograph taken in Sydney clearly shows the stress on their faces, which are grim and drawn — especially Hilda's. Although there is an aspect of glamour in the orchid pinned to her shoulder, the heavy grey winter coat is clearly meant for travel to an approaching English winter.

Speaking on behalf of his de facto partner, Bill Perry said, 'We firmly believe that Juliet is mad. We've evidence of two psychiatrists to say so. Mrs Perry is sorry to leave Juliet but she believes that her son has now greater need of her.'[57] It seemed too clipped and perfunctory to feel sincere, but by this stage there was almost nothing they could say or do that would shed a positive light on their actions.

When Hilda did plead for clemency on the basis 'that it was not right to send her 16-year-old daughter, Juliet Hulme to gaol for murder "because what she most needed was love, care, attention and affection",' the media undermined her.[58]

> Mrs Perry's published concern for her daughter's welfare is difficult to reconcile with the fact that she went to see the girl only occasionally after her arrest and then only, it is understood, after a message had been passed that her daughter wanted to see her ... It is a little incongruous, to say the least, that Mrs Perry having left New Zealand under the circumstances she did should express her concern for her daughter's welfare, her objections to the alleged inhumanity of her sentence and her own intentions of 'going on a trip in search of rest and peace'.[59]

Henry Hulme saw his daughter immediately before he left New Zealand in July, readers were reminded. Little mention was made of the fact that he had been absent from proceedings since the beginning of July.

Even so, it is hard to reconcile Hilda's actions with any concept of unconditional affection. Her visits to see Juliet were intermittent, and she absented herself from further care for her daughter in New Zealand as quickly as she could. Not to consider her actions in context, however, skews the picture. Hilda was a social pariah, as was Bill Perry. If they ever wanted to construct a life together, they had to leave. New Zealand was not her home; she was an expatriate far from her extended family and her son. Her parental obligations were split, and it was probably her own sense of self-preservation that tipped the scales.

Juliet was abandoned by both her parents at the beginning of the most 'horrific' experience of her life. On Friday, 3 September 1954, she was flown by an Air Force plane to Whenuapai airbase, where she was met by Superintendent Horace Hayward and escorted to Mt Eden. It had been a 'chilling moment' standing in the dock listening as court officials clustered around Judge Adams to discuss the sentence, but this was worse. The building was intended to be terrifying. Modelled on the Victorian Dartmoor and Pentridge prisons, it was constructed by prison labour over a period of 35 years, beginning in the latter part of the nineteenth century.

With massive grey stone walls, ugly Colonial Gothic castellations, and menacing watch-towers, it was the perfect expression of a prison designed to punish. Changing views on the incarceration of prisoners meant that some were calling for the prison's closure even before its completion in 1917. Conditions worsened over the years — suppurating walls, a leaking roof, poor ventilation, high humidity and overcrowding. In summer, the prison was like an oven; in winter, the mildew-laden dampness and cold seeped into the bones. Outrage about the state of what the media called a 'brutal Victorian fortress' forced the government, in 1951, to agree to the prison's demolition. This was indefinitely postponed the year before Juliet's imprisonment because of a lack of funds.

The stale smell of cooking, disinfectant and carbolic soap, mixed with body and food waste, came in sickening waves as steel door after steel door banged shut and were bolted behind her. Juliet was formally accepted into the prison, given a shower and handed her prison clothes, which consisted of a coarse pair of denim jeans, a woollen cardigan, plain prison underclothing, and a 'print frock to wear out of working hours'. Prison officials explained that she would be kept in solitary confinement for the first three months: this was referred to as her 'settling-in' period. During that time she would only be able to see approved visitors for half an hour a week, and immediately her workday ended she was shut in her cell until lights-out. The 'special visitors' included Dora Sagar, an official prison visitor, and Felicity Maidment and her husband Professor Kenneth Maidment, who were Auckland friends of the Hulmes.

Juliet's stone cell was 'eight feet long by six feet wide [2.4 by 1.8 metres], with walls 14 feet [4.2 metres] high'.[60] At the top of one wall was a tiny barred window 'out of eye range'. In *The Ballad of Reading Gaol*, Oscar Wilde wrote 'that little tent of blue/Which prisoners call the sky'. Juliet could not even see that. Against one wall was a narrow wooden cot, with a straw mattress, six blankets and a pillow. There was a stool and a small cabinet in which to stow a few personal possessions. There was no heating or air-conditioning, and no running water or proper toilet facilities. The concrete floor was partly covered by a small mat.

While in solitary confinement she rose at 5.45am, 'slopped out' the pan she used as a toilet, then washed in cold water, ate her breakfast of porridge and went to work. 'It was cold, there were rats, canvas sheets and calico underwear. I had to wash out my sanitary towels by hand.'[61] (When she worked in the laundry she had to wash out other women's sanitary towels.) Her working day ran from 8am to a little after 4pm and, according to Felicity Maidment, consisted of 'scrubbing & polishing black corridor floors. Two or three times a week she spends in the sewing room' and she also worked in the prison laundry.[62] Both Juliet and Pauline sewed, making clothes for the prison and mental hospital services, and worked in the laundry. This was part of an initiative in the 1950s to make hard labour productive, and to impart skills and training that would be useful for prisoners when they were released.

'There are no labour saving appliances in prison laundries other than hand-turned mangles' boasted an article in *NZ Truth*.[63] Juliet carried huge, heavy bundles of wet canvas sheets, and propelled the industrial-sized mangles until she collapsed. She was off her medication for tuberculosis, which was determined after medical tests to be inactive, but she was still unwell. The stress, the work, the damp conditions and the remnants of the disease proved too much. After a spell in the prison infirmary, suffering from exhaustion, a heavy chill and respiratory problems, Juliet was shifted to a lighter work regime, mostly in the sewing room, making uniforms under the supervision of Grace Powell. Juliet had few visitors, few letters, and no contact with prisoners other than during work hours, and even this was kept to a minimum.

Anne's Edgar for her short story 'Heroes', reproduced in *The Penguin Book of First World War Stories* in 2000. PHOTOGRAPH: JOANNE DRAYTON

Meg MacDonald, Scotland, 2011.
Photograph: Suzanne Vincent Marshall

Don Maass and Meg Davis, Anne's USA and UK agents, 2005. Photograph: Lisa Rector-Maass

Anne Perry with panelists at the Surrey International Writers' Conference, 2011.
Photograph: Suzanne Vincent Marshall

Anne's home in Portmahomack is called 'Tyrn Vawr', after the mystical creative city that developed in the golden age before the Apocalypse in *Come Armageddon*.
PHOTOGRAPH: MEG MACDONALD
Following pages: Garden at Tyrn Vawr. PHOTOGRAPHS: MEG MACDONALD

Anne in the drawing room at Tyrn Vawr in Portmahomack, Scotland.
PHOTOGRAPH: JOANNE DRAYTON

This page: Interior and courtyard of Tyrn Vawr. Photographs: Joanne Drayton

Walk to the Tarbat Ness lighthouse with Peggy and Abbie, Portmahomack, Scotland, 2010.
PHOTOGRAPH: JOANNE DRAYTON

Portmahomack, Scotland (below and over page). PHOTOGRAPHS: JOANNE DRAYTON

She was ill, isolated and in despair. 'I remember I used to lie on my bed and feel physically sick every night from the smell and the nervous tension. If I fell asleep, I'd have nightmares about what had happened. I felt so alone.' To stay sane, she used to imagine things and recite poetry; sometimes when desperate to go to sleep she would count 'one, two, three, four ... one, two, three, four — over and over again — just to shut things out'.[64] One night, after months in prison, she had a moment of revelation, an epiphany of sorts, when she fully accepted and understood what she had done. 'Don't run away, I told myself. I faced what I had done. I knew it was wrong. There was no evasion. I had done a terrible, vile thing.'[65] She got out of bed, knelt down and prayed: 'I just begged for forgiveness. I said sorry again and again — I really meant it. It was a monumental moment [that] I knew was right.'[66]

CHAPTER EIGHT

I

Although the reviews of *The One Thing More* were not as enthusiastic as Anne might have hoped for, she was delighted by the response to her 2001 Pitt, *The Whitechapel Conspiracy*. She was writing with greater fluidity than ever before, and the territory was familiar. Don Maass's espionage path for the Pitts was also paying off. 'It's a beauty,' said the *New York Times*, 'brilliantly presented, ingeniously developed and packed with political implications that reverberate on every level of British society ... Pitt delivers Perry's most harrowing insights into the secret lives of the elegant Victorians who have long enchanted and repelled her.' *Publishers Weekly* was also impressed, giving the book a starred review: 'Edgar-Award winner Anne Perry pulls out the stops and delivers one of the finest performances of her career ... This is a mesmerizing and suspenseful tale, rich in period detail, rife with articulate and believable characters.'[1]

The Whitechapel Conspiracy opens in a crowded courtroom at the Old Bailey with Superintendent Pitt in the dock being cross-examined by Ardal Juster for the prosecution. It is Pitt's evidence in the witness stand that results in John Adinett, a decorated soldier, being sent to the gallows for killing his friend. When Pitt is inexplicably redeployed in Whitechapel to investigate anarchist groups, the connection between Adinett's trial and secret terrorist plots soon becomes horrifyingly clear. Although the Pitt series was never intended to plumb Anne's psyche and experiences in the way the Monk novels do, his role does evolve. 'Pitt speaks for me a lot, especially in the later books.' Pitt is fairly straightforward — but he joins special branch and has to face ethical dilemmas. 'One is always thinking and you put it into your characters — these are the thoughts that have passed through my mind.'[2]

In *The Whitechapel Conspiracy* Anne not only presents Pitt with a pivotal dilemma, she also gives him the dangerous task of challenging the establishment. Institutional corruption occurs because people are too afraid to interrogate the status quo: 'It frightens people to question things.'[3] She places her detectives in ambiguous situations that test their core principles of courage, nobility and honour, and adds vulnerability and doubt to give them depth. 'Doubt is crippling, but without it, we have no intelligence. You need it in order to get rid of it. You have to test things against doubt.'[4]

At some point, all Anne's major characters are pitted against the powers that be. This external conflict is mirrored by an internal struggle.

[Take] your series main characters and [stand] them at the edge of the abyss, face to face with the ultimate power of evil, the Devil, if you like. Ask them what they really believe. If they tell the truth, then they are free. But if they lie, then they are over the edge into the darkness … So this had better be the truth! What is precious? What matters more than anything else? What is beautiful, everlasting, worth living or dying for?[5]

Her characters do not always live up to this test of self-discovery, because people do not know how they will act until they are challenged. 'We none of us know ourselves. We don't really know other people. It's a big learning curve and it's something really interesting to write about.'[6]

The Whitechapel Conspiracy is marked by the rich, complex and involved style of writing she admires in such contemporary detective fiction doyens as Michael Connelly, Jeffery Deaver and Robert Crais. Her author models are 'mostly American men' who 'show unexpected compassion for their characters — true gentleness is a great strength'.[7]

Connelly's main series character, Los Angeles Police Department Detective Hieronymus (Harry) Bosch, is named after the late-medieval Dutch painter Hieronymus Bosch. On the wall behind his computer

Connelly has a print of 'Hell', from Bosch's surreal, demonic triptych *The Garden of Earthly Delights*. Connelly treats his Harry Bosch, Mickey Haller and Jack McEvoy series like a panoramic canvas across which his people move, interact and collide. The series are open and interconnected, so main characters can move fluidly between them, propelling plots and casting fresh light on familiar figures like Harry Bosch. The layering of this approach appealed to Anne, as did the lateral thinking of Jeffery Deaver, who twists assumptions and turns clichés back on themselves, especially in short-story collections such as *Twisted*. His sophisticated integration of research also impressed her.

> Jeffery Deaver is brilliant at this. Recently Lincoln Rhyme, one of his series characters … investigated electricity supply to a large area of New York State, with great detail about electrical power, its strengths, dangers and vital uses. Do I care about electricity? Not really, not the technical details … Did I care about it in the story? Was it interesting? You bet![8]

In the opening decade of the new millennium, Anne began to see her series as increasingly fluid and layered, like Connelly's. In *Half Moon Street* she had turned the spotlight on Grandmama Mariah, examining her unhappy past. She would continue along these lines with other characters, thinking back into their lives to help explain their actions and who they have become.

Sometimes people need to step outside the everyday to get a perspective on themselves, and to a degree this is what Monk experiences after the obliteration of his memory as he recreates himself through the perceptions of others. He has been slowly piecing his life together. After *A Funeral in Blue*, released in 2001, there is only 'the one thing more', which is revealed in *Death of a Stranger* in 2002.

The underlying themes in *A Funeral in Blue* are redemption through compassion, anti-Semitism and the significance of identity. The redemption in this story is Runcorn's — and Monk's, to a degree, for recognizing it.

Runcorn, Monk's acerbic former boss and longtime opponent, attends the funeral of Sarah Mackeson, a prostitute who had been found murdered in an artist's studio, along with a surgeon's wife. Monk is also at the funeral. As Runcorn stands by the grave, overwhelmed with pity, Monk realizes, 'with a sharp savour of satisfaction', that the other man is 'embarrassed at having been caught in an act of uncharacteristic compassion. After all, Sarah Mackeson was a loose woman, the kind he [usually] despised.' Initially Monk gloats over Runcorn's softening, but betters himself by seeing the integrity in it.

The theme of identity comes through in the storyline of Dr Kristian Beck. It is his wife's body that is found alongside that of Sarah Mackeson, and during the investigation it is revealed that Kristian is not the good Catholic he has always believed himself to be, but a Jew. 'His heritage, his very blood, was different. He was one of the people he had been brought up to think of as outsiders, somehow inferior, and yet a people who had given the Western world the core of its soul, and so much of its culture.' However, it is Kristian's self-discovery that fuels Monk's burning desire to 'know his own roots, the meaning of his identity that hung only in shadows and pieces in his own mind ... What of the truth about himself ... Where was his blood tie to the past?'

Death of a Stranger opens with a prologue in which Monk reflects on the man he now is.

> In the past he would not have shared the core inside him with anyone, nor allowed someone to become important enough to him that her presence could make or mar his life. He was surprised how much he preferred the man he had become.

He thinks also about how radically the revelations of identity have 'overturned' the foundations of Kristian Beck's life:

> If Monk were at last to know himself as most people do automatically — the religious ties, the allegiances, the family loves and hates — might he, too, discover a stranger inside his skin, and one he could not like?

Monk pursues his former self against a curtain of murderous industrial intrigue. Katrina Harcus asks him to investigate her businessman fiancé to ensure he is not a fraud; at the same time, a railway mogul is found dead in a sleazy London brothel. The fraudulent fiancé and murdered magnate are connected, and so is Monk, or at least the old Monk. As his investigations proceed, Monk is confronted by evidence linking him to corruption and the wrongful trial and imprisonment of his old-life friend and mentor, Arrol Dundas. It seems that Monk was Dundas's betrayer.

As he reads more about the trial in newspapers at the library, memories begin to come back. There are flashes of vision, voices inside his head, 'white faces twisted with grief'. He cannot explain the screams, the shouts, the children. 'He was so tired he longed for sleep ... but he was afraid of what horror might return to him the moment he lost control of his thoughts.'

He worries again about how Hester will react. 'It would be best of all if Hester were beside him, understanding everything and holding no criticism or blame, and that would be impossible. To do that she would have to be without moral judgement. And what use would she be then, what real person at all?' He wonders how his terrible past will affect their future together.

Monk is then implicated in the tragic death of Katrina Harcus, and connects together the terrible sequence of events, but at the end of the story he finds himself. Redemption does not come from his actions as a heroic protagonist or from the bringing together of his 'selves'; it comes from the knowledge of how much he has changed. Full knowledge of himself gives him a vantage point from which to survey his recovery of compassion and humanity. Monk's redemption is not celestial, but temporal and seated in the will to be better.

Death of a Stranger took Anne to number 26 on the *New York Times* bestseller list. 'At last,' said the critic for the *New York Times Book Review*:

The secrets of Monk's past are dramatically revealed and the mystery of his identity conclusively resolved. After holding out for so long on this tantalizing puzzle, Perry might have made it the sole focus of her story. Instead she draws out the suspense with a parallel plot ... As ... her descriptions of these miserable streets and their wretched inhabitants still have the power to shock, so do her own unsentimental views on the appalling price of progress during the industrial age. Monk is not alone in his journey to enlightenment.[9]

Ballantine's Leona Nevler had thought that the puzzle of Monk's identity might have lasted for three novels; it had continued through 13 books, sometimes to the frustration of critics who wished he would either find — or get over — himself more quickly. It was a powerful premise that Anne informed with her own experiences. As Hester's brother Charles tells her in *A Funeral in Blue*, 'One can never know another person as well as one thinks ... Perhaps one cannot even know oneself.'

⚌

The idea of a series set during the First World War appealed to both Anne and her agents. Anne was looking for a challenge, and Don and Meg were seeking a fresh market. 'I want these books to have a strong moral dimension,' Anne told Don Maass during their annual story summit. But the war had been well traversed by some of the twentieth century's greatest writers. What fresh approach was there? Anne planned to use the character of Joseph Reavley from her short story 'Heroes'.

Don challenged her to think about the transformation of her character in this searing experience of death and destruction: 'What is the thing that Joseph needs to learn? What is the practical application of searching his faith ... What would be the sermon he would preach at the end of the war? What he would say: this is what I've learnt; this is how I've changed; and this is what faith means *now*?'

Anne finally responded:

You know, when it's that bad, and when you're in Joseph's position, and all you can do is comfort the dying, and there's nothing you can say that will ... help their shattered faith at that moment. The only thing you can do … is what Jesus did, and say: 'I will watch with you. I will be there for you.'[10]

In 2001, Meg Davis and Anne made plans for an expedition to the medieval town of Ypres, in Belgium, to do some research in the fields and trenches where soldiers had fought and died. Since his return to the United Kingdom in 2000, Jonathan had become increasingly involved in the research for his sister's books. Initially, he had considered going back into private practice as a general practitioner, but because he had been in Zimbabwe for so long he would have been obliged to sit extensive medical examinations, which he decided not to tackle. His interest in history made the role of research assistant to Anne very appealing, and he could see a value in it: 'I regard it as investing in the family business.'[11] Jonathan's name was automatically added to the expedition list, and he was put in charge of the travel arrangements and the programme of events.

Meg Davis decided that Meg MacDonald should also come: 'I felt she had always made a big contribution to Anne's writing'. She was aware, however, that the inclusion could well add stress to the situation, as Meg MacDonald and Jonathan did not always get along. In fact, Jonathan's arrival in Scotland with his young family had created a degree of tension and realignment in Anne's life. Meg, and her son Simon and his family, especially, had staked their claim both in Portmahomack and with Anne, as friends and family retainers. Jonathan and his family seemed like interlopers. On the other hand, Jonathan had felt compelled to leave Zimbabwe, and he had rejoined his mother and sister.

It was a chilly day in November 2003 when Anne, the two Megs and Jonathan caught the EuroStar from Waterloo Station to Lille in northern France. 'I fell out with Jonathan big-time,' Meg Davis remembers. 'It was a classic case of my training as an agent to organize every last thing in detail coming up against Jonathan's much more relaxed but equally effective style. Fortunately, by the end of the trip we were good friends again.'

On the train she asked him what size car he had hired. 'And we get to Lille and sure enough, it's *tiny* and the car-hire people don't speak English and Jonathan doesn't speak French.' There was no chance of fitting themselves and four enormous suitcases into the little vehicle, and they did not want to take the massive and expensive Mercedes that seemed to be the only alternative. After much gesturing, and some rusty French from Meg Davis, they left Lille with elevated blood pressures and a suitable vehicle.

'We finally have a car with all the suitcases in it,' recalls Meg. '"So, Jonathan, where are you going to drive us to so we can look at famous battle grounds?" He has *no* map of Belgium! He's got *no* maps; he's got *no* guidebook. We are driving towards [Ypres] ... and we don't actually know how to find it. "So where the hell is this hotel?"' He had no address for that either, but he did remember the name, which he felt sure would stand out immediately they arrived.

They followed the road signs and their hotel was in the centre of town, and easily found. Nevertheless, the meticulously organized Meg — who had been reading books about the First World War for months — was still fuming over Jonathan's relaxed approach. 'I [swore and] slammed the ... door in his face and stomped off to buy some maps and embarrassed myself by stomping into the bank instead of the information centre.'[12]

It was cold at Ypres. When they arrived at the battlefields the next morning, the grass was blanched by heavy frost. There were no fences, no hedgerows; just a huge, seemingly endless expanse stretching as far as the eye could see. The old trenches are:

> all overgrown with grass now, but you can see some of the bunkers where they lived ... you can kick around and find bits of shells. Jeepers, these were flying round in the air ninety years ago.[13]

They stopped at the Menin Gate, a moving monument to 54,896 British and Commonwealth soldiers whose bodies were never recovered from the mire and the carnage in Ypres Salient, which was the site of some of the most appalling and costly battles of the war.

The gate was originally an eastern entrance through the town ramparts and across the moat. Ypres, the last Belgian town outside German control, was a communication hub, crucial to keeping Allied supply lines to the Channel open. It was also the place where the troops began their journey to the front lines.

Anne was deeply affected by the trip to Ypres and seeing the Menin Gate. The terrible loss of life, the sheer scale of that loss of life, would stay with her while she wrote and help her to re-construct the world of 'one of the most noble people I have ever written about', Joseph Reavley.[14]

Although *No Graves As Yet*, published in 2003, was 'dedicated to MY GRANDFATHER Capt. Joseph Reavley, who served as chaplain in the trenches during the Great War', and the character bears his name, the book is not based on the man's personal experiences. But the character of Joseph Reavley does have a special presence, and a sense of flesh and blood that is compellingly evoked.

The novel begins at a Cambridge cricket match in late June 1914. It is one of those hot, cloudless, dazzling summer days. Joseph Reavley, lecturer in Biblical languages at St John's College, is standing watching his students play when he realizes someone is behind him, and he turns to see his Secret Intelligence Service brother, Matthew. The news Matthew brings will change Joseph's life: their parents have been killed in a terrible car crash, but there is a sinister subtext.

The night before his death, their father John Reavley, a retired MP, had telephoned Matthew to tell him that 'someone had given him a document outlining a plot so hideous it would change the world we know, ruin England, and everything we stand for, for ever ... He said it reaches as high as the royal family.' The authorities decide that the cause of their parents' car accident is human error, and when Matthew and Joseph search the family home for the document there is no sign of it. Was John Reavley wrong? Is this a fabrication?

Joseph, who has in his study a 'bust of Dante ... that genius of poetry, imagination, the art of story, and above all, the understanding of the nature of good and evil', is a man who has known personal tragedy. He has swapped parish ministry for academic life because of a crisis of faith. 'Joseph knew better than others how one can temporarily forget a cataclysm in one's life, then remember it again with surprise and the renewal of pain.' His wife and unborn child had died suddenly, and teaching has taken him away from the questions he found impossible to answer.

Don Maass believes that Anne's First World War series contains her 'most brilliant antagonist' — the Peacemaker, a twisted powerbroker high in the British machinery of state. His ambitions are good, but his means to achieve them are utterly despicable. He wants to divide the world according to two superpowers. The document the Reavley brothers so desperately seek is an unsigned treaty between Kaiser Wilhelm II of Germany and King George V of England, 'the terms of which were shatteringly simple. Britain would stand aside and allow Germany to invade and conquer Belgium, France … Luxembourg, saving the hundreds of thousands of lives … In return a new Anglo-German Empire would be formed with unassailable power on land and sea.'

Most of Europe would come under German control, and the British Empire would be bolstered by the alliance. The remaining continents and riches of the world would be divided between Germany and the United Kingdom. The man commissioned to pen the treaty and its duplicate is so appalled that he steals both copies and sends one to John Reavley, thereby sealing his and his wife's fate. Although the murderer of the Reavley parents is revealed, at the end of the book the mastermind Peacemaker is still at large: 'whoever it is, he's brilliant, ruthless, and he's still out there'.

But war is the flipside of the Peacemaker's 'dishonourable peace', and in *Shoulder the Sky*, the next novel in the quintet, the story resumes in the trenches at Ypres. It is like a scene from hell: the filthy food, the stench of decay, the sound of bombs and the 'grotesque ruin of no man's land, the mud, the ice-rimmed craters with the limbs of dead men poking up as if in some last, desperate hold on life'. But Anne's brilliant twist — and the irony of the series — is that all this killing and human despair can have more dignity and hope than peace itself. It is a premise that challenges readers to think differently — to see goodness and truth as fluid, fragile and sometimes contradictory.

Joseph is now chaplain to the young men he knew in his Cambridgeshire village of St Giles, and he must minister to them as they are slaughtered in the killing fields of Ypres, while knowing that the Peacemaker has another solution. But there are other tests for Joseph. This is Anne's favourite book in the series, perhaps because of the complexity of the trials Joseph must face.

Eldon Prentice, a grasping, insensitive war correspondent, is found dead on the battlefield. It quickly becomes apparent that he is not a casualty of war but a murder victim. Prentice was so dangerous a person that Joseph might almost have killed him himself, and when he tracks down the killer, he finds it is someone he both loves and admires. Joseph's calibre as a man and as a priest are equally tested when he travels by troopship across the Aegean Sea to Anzac Cove on the Gallipoli Peninsula. He is on Secret Service business for his brother, but on the beach he cares for Australian and New Zealand soldiers:

> He helped medical orderlies, most of whom had little training. One was a veterinary surgeon from somewhere in New Zealand. He was skilled and worked with frantic dedication and an air of confidence. It was very reassuring to those who did not see his moments of panic as he reached for medicines and equipment he did not have, and fumbled now and then in human anatomy.

When Joseph's mission is completed, he escapes Anzac Cove and is on board a cargo ship when it is seized and scuttled by a German U-boat, and he and a war correspondent named Richard Mason are set adrift in a lifeboat. Mason is in league with the Peacemaker and plans to publish an article that will expose the shocking strategic miscalculation of Gallipoli and its unimaginable loss of life. 'You preach your gospel, I'll preach mine,' he announces to Joseph. 'You want to protect people from the truth, for what you think is the greater good. I think they have the right to know what they're signing up for, what the battle will cost them.'

Joseph believes it is imperative for morale, and for the war effort, that he prevents Mason from publishing. They are alone at sea. The power to stop Mason is in Joseph's hands. Should he let him live and publish his article, or kill him? These are the kinds of dilemmas that Anne loves to put before her main protagonists. The greater the internal crisis generated, the more interesting she finds it.

Flanders is a test for more than just one Reavley. Judith, Joseph's sister, is also there. Young, aimless and impetuous in civilian life, she now works for the Voluntary Aid Detachment as an ambulance driver. Judith is another of Anne's Nightingale women — strong, saintly and self-sacrificial — who find meaning in a life helping others. Judith's older sister, Hannah, notices the change. 'She's so competent lately, so ... full of purpose. She's just as emotional as ever, but now it all has direction. It seems almost wicked to say it, but the war has given her something. She's ... found herself.'

Hannah is a wife and mother, so the conflict has a very different impact on her life. Her husband, Archie, is a naval commander, so war means waiting, and watching her man and her world change almost beyond recognition.

I don't want women bank managers, women police, women taxi drivers, and I don't want to be able to vote for Members of Parliament. I want to do what women have always done ... I hate uncertainty, anger, fighting, destroying everything we used to value.

In *Angels in the Gloom*, Anne's third First World War novel, published in 2005, a seriously injured Joseph is invalided back to his home village of St Giles in Cambridgeshire. He arrives there just in time for the murder of Theo Blaine, a young scientist working on top-secret torpedo development. As he recovers his health, Joseph finds himself called on to minister to Blaine's widow and other grieving members of the village who have lost sons and husbands. The current minister, Hallam Kerr, is 'the kind of man who falls into the Church as an occupation because he really isn't adequate to make a respectable living at any other profession'. Kerr is driven by a need for security and social standing rather than vocation, and the demands of war reveal his faith to be as shallow as his mercenary motives.

'Look me in the face, Captain Reavley, and tell me you believe in
God! ... Do you still think there's a God in control of all this, then?' ...
Joseph looked at the anguish in [Kerr's] eyes, the fury and despair, the
knowledge that he was falling into an abyss that had no bottom, and
he was helpless to stop it.

Joseph knows that abyss well, but has eluded it so far because at some
profound level he still believes.

A parallel plot to Joseph's St Giles convalescence is Matthew's ongoing
search for the Peacemaker and his agents. Among the possibilities are
Irish-born double agents Patrick Hannassey and his daughter Detta.
The two meet covertly, as Anne and her father had done.

They would have sat together, probably on a bench in Regent's
Park, watching the ducks, and talked about whatever the problem
was. They might have walked around an art gallery, seeing what
was for sale, looking for bargains, old watercolours that needed
cleaning and restoring, the foxing taken off, and refreshed to show
their beauty.

Patrick Hannassey collects and restores watercolours, just as Henry
Hulme had done. The ones he gave Anne are on the walls of her home
in Portmahomack. But Hannassey is also a spy whom Matthew follows
to sea on his brother-in-law's ship, the *Cormorant*, which becomes
spectacularly involved in the biggest naval engagement of the war.

Anne found the transition from the Victorian era to a new period
challenging and difficult, and she wondered at times whether she would
succeed. Don advised her on the over-arching theme and its relationship
to the individual book plots; Meg Davis investigated the period with
special reference to characterization, scene authenticity and the overall
outline; and Jonathan researched the First World War, mapping a
framework of battles, locations, personnel, policy and propaganda. He
shared his army insights, knowledge of firearms and medicine, and added
what he thought was an important ingredient.

At times I'll say: 'I don't think you've got enough testosterone there. I like that bit but we need to hype it up. These aren't dons at the high table of the senior common room smacking each other with handbags. These are men fighting a war.'[15]

Meg MacDonald continued in her role as critic and commentator, listening to Anne reading sections of the books, and suggesting developments and alterations. It was a shared effort, and they all waited anxiously for a response to the new venture.

The critical reaction to the launch of Anne's First World War series was enthusiastic, and warmed as each of the first three books was released. *No Graves As Yet* was given a starred review in *Publishers Weekly*: 'This absorbing mystery/spy thriller, set in tranquil Cambridge just before the onset of the Great War, marks a powerful start to bestseller Perry's much anticipated new series.' 'Perry's melancholy evocation of the "eternal afternoon" that would soon turn to night all over England is lovely,' said the *New York Times*, while the *Chronicle* described it as a 'dazzling story' of 'sheer brilliance'.

Shoulder the Sky and *Angels in the Gloom* both made the extended *New York Times* bestseller list, in October 2004 and September 2005, respectively. Of the former, the *Book Report* reviewer wrote: 'Perry's descriptions of warfare are accurate, and accordingly are horrific, though not gratuitously so ... Perry's writing has never been better than it is in *Shoulder the Sky* ... Read one and you'll be hooked for good. Highly recommended.'[16] Critics liked the fast and exciting narrative pace of the novels, but also remarked on their thought-provoking qualities and their 'study of the ethics of politics and morality in war-time'.[17] The series viewed the First World War from a moral perspective, and not just at an individual level, but in terms of institutions and states. The books also covered the cataclysmic changes brought by the war: social reform and mobility, the enfranchisement of women in the United Kingdom, the erosion of old class hierarchies and values, and a generation of men damaged or lost, their women widowed or unmarried.

Even more than detective fiction, the British owned this material as part of its history, yet the most avid followers of the series continued to be North Americans. This was partly a result of Anne's reluctance to face the British media. Journalists could be considerate, but to sell newspapers or magazines they often covered the Parker–Hulme murder rather than Anne's novels. As Jonathan explained to Meg Davis when *No Graves As Yet* was released, 'each time Anne talks to the Press about the past, they present it as they want and it always backfires. She gets depressed and sulks and we all get the backwash!'[18] Although it had been nearly 10 years since Anne's identity had been revealed, Meg had learned to accept and live with the negative press coverage. 'There will never be an interview here — at least for the foreseeable future — without reference to the past; all we can do is keep it down to the minimum.'[19]

Anne was contractually obliged to participate in the promotion of her books, and more than once Meg had to mollify her incensed publishers when interviews in the United Kingdom were cancelled after Anne lost her nerve. For example, Anne's British publisher, Headline, was justifiably annoyed when Meg called off an interview with Jackie McGlone from the *Scotsman*. Headline's Lucy Ramsey wanted an assurance that it would not happen again: 'If we have to cancel Anne's interviews this time we won't feel able to set any up in the future as journalists would be wary ...'[20]

Meg was in a difficult position. Her instinct was to protect Anne, but she needed to build Anne's profile. In 2002 the *Telegraph* had published a disparaging article that Meg described to Jonathan as 'a horrible shock — a respected broadsheet who previously had been very fair to Anne'. However, she also pointed out that 'Anne's books are lagging behind in this country through lack of publicity, and we can't afford to let this go any longer'.[21] In the midst of this email discussion between Meg and Jonathan, Anne was on a seven-week author tour of the United States, where she felt more at ease with the media. Don sent Meg an update: 'Kim Hovey reports that in its third week No Graves has lifted from 24 to 19 on the *Times* extended bestseller list. Anne's tour is going well, Kim reports, and its effects are showing.'[22] On one side of the Atlantic Anne was reported to be reclusive and recalcitrant; on the other she was understood to be open and accessible. The challenge for Meg was to bring the British media perception into closer alignment with that of the United States.

In March 2004 she wrote to Jane Morpeth at Headline with a challenge:

Anne's done a few [interviews] recently — and yes, I recognize that this wasn't entirely plain sailing, but I do feel that was about her nerves on stepping into the UK limelight properly for the first time, and I've found that her confidence is growing ... She ought to be so much bigger in the UK than she is at the moment, and we've always recognized that this is because she's wanted us to hold back on the promotion. But now's the moment for a good push, don't you think?[23]

⊗

Anne worked consistently on her contracted schedule of Pitts and Monks while she researched and wrote the First World War series. *Southampton Row*, her twenty-second Pitt, was released to acclaim in 2002. This was the first book written and published after Leona Nevler left Ballantine in late July 2001. Technically she had been made redundant, but it was an odd decision that left Meg Davis shocked. 'I sent her flowers and took her to dinner when I was in New York a couple of months later. We met once or twice after that when she was at Penguin which she enjoyed hugely — it was back to her roots of up-market women's fiction.' Anne needed a champion at Ballantine to speak up for her work, especially at commissioning meetings, and Meg Davis was anxious to know whether the new editor would appreciate what he had inherited 'or neglect them — or even dump them!' She and Don Maass decided to meet Leona's successor, Joe Blades, as soon as possible:

I bought a particularly severe suit, as Don and I decided to play it as 'good cop and bad cop' ... The UK agent descending from on high was designed to impress on Joe how valuable a writer Anne is ... [but] Joe turned out to be a lovely man, and an able champion of Anne ... He had a cat he was so devoted to that he'd had a watch face made with a picture of it; years after the death of the cat, he was still wearing it.

After their appointment with Joe Blades, Don and Meg had lunch with Kim Hovey and then carried on to a meeting with a theatre company. As they went into the theatre a group of young 'actors were coming out, and teased us for looking like Mulder and Scully' — so Meg felt they had got the suit look for Joe Blades exactly right.[24]

The success of *Southampton Row*, which followed on from *The Whitechapel Conspiracy*, was the perfect beginning to a new working relationship. This novel is as much about conspiracy and Victorian politics as it is about murder. Pitt's allegiance to his job with Secret Intelligence is sorely tested when, on the eve of his departure for a well-earned family holiday on the edge of Dartmoor, he is ordered to remain in London. His nemesis, Charles Voisey, is seeking election to Parliament in a few days, to promote his ghastly plans and unscrupulous secret society. He is standing against long-serving Liberal candidate Aubrey Serracold, whose eccentric wife's toying with the occult threatens to discredit him.

Charlotte, the children and maid Gracie leave for the country while Pitt tries to head off his electioneering arch-rival. Certainly if the family stays in London they will be at risk of deadly reprisal, either from Voisey or his society. Late-night séances, a clairvoyant found cruelly murdered in her Southampton Row apartment, and a family in terrible jeopardy are the ingredients that make this story both a compelling read and a clever snapshot of the times.

Southampton Row rocketed to number five on the *New York Times* bestseller list, and was number seven on the bestseller lists for both the *Washington Post* and the *Publishing News*, and the reviews were highly complimentary. Everyone had been a little apprehensive about the degree of interconnectedness between *Southampton Row* and its predecessor, but this seemed to have no impact on either its critical reception or its sales. Anne was delighted with the book's success. Increasingly she was seeing her writing not as separate novels or in series, but as a broad picture in which characters could be linked and stories could move through time. It was enormously liberating and exciting.

It was disappointing, then, to discover that her number-five book was not in the row of the *New York Times* bestseller books lined up on the shelf and numbered from one to 50, when she entered an airport bookshop in the United States. All the other titles were there: just number five was missing. When she asked a staff member to explain the book's absence, he said: 'It's set in the Victorian period and no one reads those sorts of books these days, anyway.' His logic was so flawed she felt certain the absence was personal. At once, she had the thrill of the achievement and the sting of exclusion, as was often the reality for Anne.[25]

Anne's next Pitt, *Seven Dials*, was published at the beginning of 2003. 'A positive SEVEN DIALS review in PW [*Publishers Weekly*] greets our return from the holidays,' said Joe Blades's ebullient email to Anne and her agents:

> A hard copy is in the mail to you, but here's an excerpt ... 'The trail leads Charlotte into the dark and dangerous alleys of London's Seven Dials district, and eventually she and Thomas discover that the two cases intersect in a horrifying way. Perry once again delivers a complex and satisfying tale that fans of the series will devour.' Congratulations!!! A wonderful way to begin the new year.[26]

Joe Blades delighted in giving Anne regular and encouraging updates on the book's progress. 'For the week March 2, SEVEN DIALS clocks in at Number 27. That's definitely news for celebration here at the midpoint of the present week!!!' he wrote, and 'The *New York Times* bestsellers for March 9 have been announced, and SEVEN DIALS is still on the 'extended'/'expanded' list — at Number 30. We say hooray all over again!'[27]

Anne's books were beginning to make Ballantine, and everyone else involved, real money. 'Anne's sub-agents are just now reaping the rewards of many years' hard work — equally her foreign publishers,' Don Maass wrote to Meg in September 2003. She was so prolific and successful that her industry was becoming an empire. But her income was diverse, and fractured again by foreign rights and sales, so that it was difficult even for her agents to keep track. Regarding the acceleration of short-story contracts, Don wrote to Meg: 'I do not mind that Anne agrees to write so many; that's fine, it makes her feel good and serves many purposes. What I do not like is being uninformed and out of the loop.'[28]

Their annual story summits were an important part of keeping in touch and helping Anne maintain continuity across her various projects, especially the Pitt series, which now spanned nearly 25 years. They tried to make the sessions enjoyable social occasions, too. In February 2003, Meg emailed Don with some suggestions for their 'Annual summit':

Anne & I have looked at our diaries and the optimum weekend for us would be 23/24 August ... Before that I'm in Canada seeing my mum, and after that Anne's booked up ... Ideally it needs to be timed with Anne being ready to start on the next Pitt. Anne's quite keen on 'something decadent near Oxford' — I think she's after a luxury hotel where she can get a facial etc — and while this sounds just what the doctor ordered for you and me too, heaven knows what the price will be like ... With business the way it is, I don't know how we'll explain this in our accounts ... In old age I know I'm going to be Margaret Rutherford, prodding people with my stick when they don't do what I say. I'm in training for this right now. Consequently I'm reading the penultimate draft of the new Monk very quickly, just to catch any problems — Anne forgetting three major plot points last time gave me the heebie jeebies ... It's beginning to feel like all I ever read is various things by Anne.[29]

Although most of these collaborative occasions were positive, there were times when Anne felt 'hounded' and overpowered. When Don communicated Anne's feelings to Meg, she was quick to find ways of making the editorial process less painful. As she wrote to Don, the 'new email method will give us plenty of forum, and more thinking time too — we won't have to cram 1000 good ideas into 3 days, but see how much more we can do over a space of months.'[30] Anne did not use email herself, but her agents and publishers could send messages to Jonathan or to Elizabeth Sweeney, and they could print them out. Then it was just a matter of a telephone call to settle an approach or clarify an issue.

Towards the end of 2003, another idea Anne had been considering for some time came to fruition: a 40,000-word Christmas novella that explored the back-story of one of her characters. This releasing of her characters from their serial existence was an outcome of her new fluid, free-form approach to writing. At about the same time Anne had sent Joe Blades a gift. In his email response, he wrote: 'in a way, in return, I have a gift for you — terrific news: there's a spectacular review of A CHRISTMAS JOURNEY in today's *Wall Street Journal*':

> 'Anne Perry's A *Christmas Journey* is that rarest of seasonal thrillers: one that exemplifies the message and the spirit of the holiday ... This brief work has an almost Jamesian subtlety, and with its powerful message of responsibility and redemption — "We need both to forgive and to be forgiven" — it conveys a moral force in keeping with the season.' Exactly what we wanted to see in print, Anne. So beautiful and so richly deserved! Congratulations! What a fine way to begin ... the holiday season.[31]

II

Although prison life improved after Juliet left solitary confinement, conditions at Mt Eden for a lifer were bleak.

> [There were] between thirty-five and forty cells for the women ... and we had two five-minute showers a week and two toilets, one had a half-door and the other one was out in the open. We had sanitary towels that you folded up and used and washed, and sometimes your legs would chafe until they bled ... And there were rats. They didn't actually come into the cells. The cells were black stone floor and whitewashed walls [and there were] canvas sheets.[32]

Breakfast consisted of lumpy porridge. Food for the evening meals was a rotation of three dishes, which included 'corned beef hash, and meatballs ... and brown bread ... tapioca pudding made with water'. There were few vegetables, only two eggs a year, and fruit was severely rationed. 'You could have fruit once a fortnight — a small bag ... which would be a day's ration today ... if you were a lifer [this privilege came] only after you'd served your first year [in prison].'

Even after she shifted to a cell in the main part of the women's section, Juliet 'used to feel nauseated *every* night for a long, long time: years ... just tension I should think, just stress ... I used to sit up half the night thinking I was going to throw up ... But they put the light out so you have no light on the inside and you just sit there in the dark.' To cope with the black hole of night, and 'stay sane', she would recite poems to herself — 'to say it over and over — it's the music of it' — memorized from the 17 poetry books she had with her. It was 'the stuff I've grown up with': Byron, Shelley, Keats, Swinburne, Chesterton, Brooke, Flecker, and Edward FitzGerald's translation of *The Rubáiyát of Omar Khayyám*.[33]

At times, feelings of loneliness and isolation almost overwhelmed Juliet. She felt abandoned, and shut away from everything familiar, with no parent or close companion to help her. Every day was a battle, as she told her mother's close friend, Nancy Sutherland: 'I'm afraid three quarters of my energy is used in organizing my mental army to fight against misery. The other quarter is dispersed in all sorts of ways. And any talents I might possess I use as ammunition. This isn't as desperate as it may sound at all but a truth for all that.'[34] Rather than give in to self-pity, though, there was a dawning determination to make the most of a terrible situation.

The difference between surviving and not surviving is accepting that this is something that you've brought upon yourself, you're not being unjustly treated. I don't think I ever met anybody else that was guilty — everyone else was innocent — it was always someone else's fault ... But [on the other hand] if you beat yourself up [it's no good] ... I never felt that I was wicked, but I accepted that no one else was doing it to me.

What she told herself then was what she would say to an inmate if she was visiting now: 'Okay, you are going to make something of this. Now stop whingeing and get on with it.'[35] She took responsibility for her actions and came to terms with her sentence, even the fact that it had no definite end, but she never accepted the evil or insane labels. She knew how she was perceived: 'they had obviously got me tagged as a complete raving monster: I was fifteen and *sick*'.

Juliet wanted to find her own way, reach her own conclusions and make a new start. After almost a year at Mt Eden she could write:

I will never look back but I find it very hard because there seem to be so many people unremittingly trying to bind me down & say 'you must do this or that or the other' all of which tightens a net around me & makes me feel panicky. I will make a new character & a good one. I've learnt my lesson & I'm sorry & I'll never lose my head again. I'll rehabilitate myself, grow into a new person and live — but I must do it myself without being watched over & dictated to. I must do it myself, no one can do it for me or help me. You can't learn to swim in a bath.

Sorry to get so worked up about it. It's something that has been worrying me for a while … if you can see any way of cutting that net or loosening it, tell me. I must leave the past completely behind & remake myself without its surroundings — can you understand that sort of black panic that I'll always be shut in … It's like a vast grey parachute that is open behind & above me. If I cut off all the strings I shall really make something of myself, because I've learnt the hard way & I know what not to do better than most other people. But 1 string will bring the whole lot along. 1 string alone is enough.[36]

Juliet was allowed weekly visitors, who were approved by the prison officials and strictly supervised by wardresses. 'Any visitors she has will be officials, doctors who take an interest in the case, or official prison visitors,' the *NZ Truth* told its readers.[37] To a degree this was true: there were few visits of a purely personal nature for Juliet — no family, no contemporary friends, and just few acquaintances of significance came to see her. She cherished visits from family friends. Felicity Maidment visited weekly for a time, Dora Sagar was a regular — and 'Vivien Dixon came to see me the other day. I was really delighted to see her. She was so nice.'[38] Henry had made a point of asking his special friend, Vivien, to visit Juliet. As a matter of procedure, the Anglican Church Army allocated her a prison visitor, named Captain Stanley Banyard.

In 1975, when historian Russell Stone interviewed the elderly Captain Banyard for his history of Selwyn Village, *In the Time of Age*, Juliet was the only person Banyard mentioned from his years of prison visiting.

> As soon as he visited her, he was immediately struck by how formidable was the intelligence of this girl. She would have left him standing — he was a well-intentioned, ordinary, humble sort of a person … [Juliet] was dispirited … and immediately he said … 'there must be a continuation of her education'.

So Captain Banyard arranged to have School Certificate material made available, and some of these were the books of poetry that Juliet memorized. He was stunned by how effortlessly she passed her examinations.

> [Juliet's] plight … her sex, I suppose, and her youth, and the isolation that she had to go through, seemed to make such an impression upon [Banyard] that he regarded it as one of the most memorable achievements he had as a prison visitor. He wasn't prepared to let her languish there. He could see that she was very intelligent and there was going to be a life after imprisonment.[39]

The educational opportunities for Juliet at Mt Eden prison were limited, and although she did some study she has no recollection of it: 'They didn't have a prison library and there was no education. But I do have gaps in my memory.' As well as Captain Banyard, there were others anxious to see her education continued. In December 1954, Juliet wrote to Nancy Sutherland outlining her proposed course of study:

You said in your Xmas card (thank you for it) that you thought it would be a good idea if I did some lessons. You will be pleased to hear that I am. And under proper supervision as well. English, Maths, History, Latin, Italian and Greek. The first five are for school certificate ... I have been writing a few essays which they seem to be very pleased with and other things in general (writing that is) so I now have heart again where that is concerned.[40]

She had specially assigned tutors for some subjects and took correspondence lessons, apparently passing both School Certificate and University Entrance. However, what Juliet learnt scholastically was clearly less significant to her than the plays and poetry she read and repeated to herself to give her nights music.

Juliet was allowed to write 'only once a week and once a fortnight to friends and two pages'.[41] Her early prison letters were frenetic with detail, but they settled, and she deeply appreciated people's responses and contributions. 'Thank you very much indeed for the cake you sent me and the letter. It was very kind of you indeed and I am more grateful than I can say,' she wrote to Nancy Sutherland on 6 November 1954. The cake was a sixteenth birthday present that she would not be allowed to eat until Christmas, when food restrictions were relaxed.

Although her parents wrote to her only intermittently, and restrictions and censorship meant there was little scope for intimate exchange, the letters were an important connection for Juliet to the outside world, as was her correspondence with her old headmistress from St Margaret's College. Juliet had been at the school for only a term before Stephanie Young retired in 1949, but once she went to prison, a correspondence began.

She wrote to me even after I came back to Britain. All the years in New Zealand, she wrote to me. She was headmistress when I was a new girl ... Why did she do that to one lost child? She's a remarkable woman ... she wrote to me until she died.[42]

Stephanie Young's biographer Ruth Fry describes her as 'a gifted teacher and an educationalist concerned with increasing women's opportunities'.[43] Born in Gloucestershire, England, in 1890, she was one of numerous 'women graduates of Oxford University who made careers in education'. Her father was an Anglican clergyman and her brother, Guy, a chaplain to the New Zealand forces who was killed at Passchendaele.

After marrying her brother's best friend, Charles Le Fanu Young, Stephanie emigrated to New Zealand in 1918. Charles Young took a position at Christ's College and Stephanie was matron there until her husband died at the age of 26 of complications from being gassed in the First World War. Stephanie, left with a 14-month-old son named Guy, began a 10-year stint teaching history at Christchurch Girls' High School, then became headmistress of St Margaret's College in 1931. She would have known the Hulmes through serving on the Canterbury University College Council from 1936 to 1952, and this may have prompted her to write to Juliet, but her motives would have come more from the fact that she was a liberal thinker, a compassionate woman and a devout Christian. And she understood suffering: her much-loved son died of tuberculosis in 1957 while she was still writing to Juliet in prison.

But all the visits in the world, all the opportunities for study, all the letters, could not take the place of her family. When Nancy Sutherland wrote and asked about her plans for the future, Juliet replied: 'I should like to go to Italy & most of the Mediterranean and back to England of course because of father & mother & Jonty. I miss them very much indeed of course, particularly father.'[44] It was Henry whom she longed to see, so when the news arrived of his remarriage, it was a blow. For a time afterwards Juliet talked of Pauline again and began knitting her a jersey.

Henry had communicated the news by letter in such a forthright, matter-of-fact kind of way that the prison authorities had sent his first attempt back, explaining that he needed to communicate the news in 'different', gentler terms. His second, considerably belated, attempt still shocked her and caused a desperate reaching out for reassurance. But, once again, she composed herself. 'I hear from mother & father regularly & they both write wonderful letters,' she told Nancy Sutherland.

I have also heard from Margery [her father's new wife] now. She wrote a beautiful letter too. You need never fear I shall be upset or resentful about the marriage. I was shocked of course but I think it is a marvelous thing — in fact the only thing.[45]

Although Henry's actions were deemed to be callous, his intentions were far from that. He explained himself to Nancy Sutherland. 'I think they felt I have not been sufficiently reassuring to Juliet that [my marriage] would make no difference to my feelings for her! Actually I didn't wish to make a great to-do about it because I didn't want to upset her! However there's no pleasing everyone!'[46] In fact, he cared a great deal about Juliet and he wrote regularly to those visiting her and followed her progress.

In despairing correspondence with Vivien Dixon, he wrote that Juliet seemed from her letters to be 'completely removed' and preoccupied with herself and her 'grandiose ideas' about poetry and writing. 'I'm desperately sorry for her but it would be bad for her to sympathise in any way with her present state … Medlicott feels strongly that to encourage this would reduce the slight chances of her recovery.'[47] Henry accepted Medlicott's diagnosis, yet he had not seen or talked to his daughter since before his departure on 3 July 1954. Undoubtedly, his judgment was influenced by Medlicott's expert opinion and the prevailing pessimism of the doctor's diagnosis. So when things seemed to be improving, Henry was greatly relieved. In July 1955, he wrote optimistically to Nancy: 'Juliet is showing considerable signs of improvement — I dare not build up hopes — at least I try to keep myself prepared for all eventualities.'[48]

And he was fiercely proud of, and grateful to, Jonathan for his emotional resilience. The boy had settled well in school and adapted to his parents' separation and subsequent marriages with remarkable balance. 'One thing only had worried him! — he asked Hilda if we were being divorced — on being told "yes" — he said he was relieved because he has been worried that Hilda might be "living in bigamy".'[49]

There was no contest or conflict between the Hulmes. Hilda agreed that Henry would have custody of Jonathan, 'though naturally she will want to see a lot of him, and I would not wish otherwise'. Henry saw Hilda (now called Marion) and Bill regularly, especially in the early months after their return, and felt deeply for 'the terrific strain' both of them had been through.[50] 'She has had a hell of a time & feels Juliet's loss terribly.'[51]

⚭

Juliet made friends and allies among her fellow prisoners. 'You take your friends where you can find them. You have to learn how to survive.'

> I was bullied quite a lot to begin with, but I very quickly learned if I succumbed to it someone else would step in bigger and stronger than I was to defend me ... There was one big Maori girl who used to swear at me up and down, and one day I finally lost my temper and I turned round and gave her a real mouthful back, and we became quite good friends after that ... There is hardly ever anyone else to look out for you except the friends you make.[52]

Although Juliet was occasionally propositioned by lesbians and women prisoners seeking domination, comfort or affection, she was not deeply disturbed. 'I was bothered a few times in prison ... nobody ever did anything to me. Somebody grabbed me and kissed me once ... [but] I was never injured and I was never assaulted ... not [like] the sort of thing you see in fiction going on in prison [today].'[53]

What she felt hardest to cope with was the intellectual isolation, the lack of the intelligent companionship she had got in abundance from Pauline. She missed having a talented friend to talk to, to plan with and to create — a kind of cerebral soul mate. Mt Eden was an endless grey hell of ignorance and sameness. There was no one her age, no one with her background or intelligence and no end in sight.

> That was the hardest thing. You can't tick the days off to anything, because you have no idea ... The tension of waiting and hoping ... The loneliness of no intellectual companionship ... a lot of years without it ... Fifteen until twenty-one with none ... the intellectual loneliness of being in a place like that was hard.[54]

284

The three other women serving life sentences for murder at Mt Eden Prison at the time were Phyllis Freeman, Pansy Louise Frances Haskell, and Edna May Wilson, all decades older than Juliet. Phyllis Freeman, aged 38, was a domestic worker convicted of murdering Joyce Morrison at Enfield. The killing had taken place in 1942, but the trial did not occur until six years later, in 1948, when the body of Joyce Morrison was exhumed and experts determined the cause of death as strychnine poisoning. Pansy Haskell, 55 years old, was found guilty of murdering her lover's wife, Gladys Rusden. It seems the provocation for Rusden's violent end was that she refused to divorce her husband. Her battered body was found at the couple's One Tree Hill home in Auckland on 5 June 1947. Haskell was charged and convicted after a retrial lasting nine days.

But the strangest and perhaps most touching tale belonged to Edna Wilson, a 46-year-old laundress. She was sentenced to death for the murder in Napier of Harriet Sarah Player, aged 81, and Sarah Eliza Armitage, aged 72, on 8 September 1953. The motive for the murders was theft. Some years before, Edna Wilson had started the Hawke's Bay Tailwaggers Club, a society for the care and protection of unwanted and injured animals. Hard times had meant a shortfall of club funds, which she intended to replace with the money she stole from her elderly victims. When the Tailwaggers books were scrutinized by the court, it was revealed that 'most of the club's money and her own wages were spent on caring for animals'.[55] Wilson's death sentence was commuted to life imprisonment.

Generally, women in prison at this time had little secondary education, occupied unskilled jobs, and came from lower socio-economic backgrounds, and many were Maori.

Among the prisoners who made a special impression on Juliet was a woman she came to realize was 'very sub-normal'. It was the worst thing she experienced in prison. The sense of desperation and injustice, and her powerlessness to help, had an enormous impact.

There was a young woman there ... I can still remember her face ... You'll see she crops up in my books every now and again. She was a very weak personality, she did all sorts of [negative] things, but she had one core of self-respect and pride in her — *she never lied*. She took things that didn't belong to her … and she slept around, but she didn't lie. It was her *raison d'être*. And they accused her of stealing something and she said 'No', and they didn't believe her. She refused to admit it, because as far as she was concerned she hadn't. And I believed her. They finally got her to the point where she got hysterical, and then they put her down in solitary confinement … She was force-fed eventually, and it killed her … I can still remember hearing, that … They killed her because they didn't believe her … I've never, forgotten … What they did to her was brutal … psychologically they tortured her to death.[56]

The other terrible occurrences that rocked the numbing repetition of Juliet's prison life were the hangings. The first man condemned, after the death penalty was restored in 1950, was Malcolm McSherry. He was quickly reprieved, but there was a growing intolerance of clemency and a belief that if hanging were to operate as a proper deterrent, then examples must be made. All the eight hangings that occurred between 1951 and 1957 took place at Mt Eden.

The first person hanged during this time was Urewera mill-worker William Fiori, who was convicted in February 1952 of killing his boss and boss's wife, in order to steal money. He was officially described as 'borderline-feeble-minded'. Prison authorities conducted a clever ruse. 'On Thursday 13 March 1952, a notice on the walls inside the prison advertised that Kerridge Odeon was to sponsor a movie showing in the prison that evening. Most prisoners attended the rare event.'[57]

While the prisoners watched their film, Fiori was moved from the isolation cells in the west wing to the opposite end of the prison's east block, where the metal scaffolding of the gallows was erected. He was held briefly in cells there, until he was stripped of his prison clothes and dressed in canvas overalls and slippers. His arms and thighs were immobilized with heavy straps and he hobbled up the 17 steps to the gallows platform. Once he was positioned there, his ankles were tied, a white hood was put over his head and the noose was positioned around his neck.

Prior to this he had been given the option of taking religious counsel before going to the gallows, and now he was given the opportunity to say a last word. At 8.03pm, the sheriff lowered his hand with the warrant of execution in it, as a signal to the hangman to pull the lever to the trap door.

The next hangings began after Juliet had been in the prison for 11 months. Frederick Foster, aged 26, was hanged on 7 July 1955 for the shooting of his teenage ex-girlfriend in Auckland; Edward Te Whiu, aged 20, was executed on 18 August for killing of an elderly woman in Whangarei while burgling her house; Harvey Attwood, aged 34, was executed on 13 October for killing a friend after a drunken altercation in Te Anau; and Albert Black, aged 20, was hanged on 5 December for stabbing a romantic rival in the neck in Auckland.

The stress on many members of the prison staff was immense. Prison Superintendent Horace Haywood is reputed to have burst into tears when the news came through that young Edward Te Whiu was to be hung. According to prison psychologist Don McKenzie, the execution of Te Whiu was a 'terrible drain on Haywood' and every compassionate person within earshot.

The whole [Te Whiu] family [were] crying and shouting in the courtyard ... I can particularly remember Te Whiu's father with his big hat on. And his mother and all the carry-on, crying.[58]

A depressed mood, an air of general despondency, preceded executions at Mt Eden prison. Before hangings, trial-runs were conducted with the gallows mechanism that included a sandbag attached to the rope. The sandbag, estimated to be the same weight as the prisoner, was dropped through the trapdoor in ghoulish preparation for the real thing. This happened every 24 hours for 14 days after the death sentence was confirmed. Initially, the steel trapdoor created a loud echoing crash through the prison. Efforts to muffle it were not entirely successful.

On the evenings of the hangings 'an expectant hush fell over the whole institution as the hour of seven approached'.[59] The prison went into lock-down, and all prisoners other than those on special duties were secured in their cells. In advance of the hanging, prisoner peepholes were closed and an immense length of seagrass matting was rolled out the full east–west length of the prison to deaden the footsteps of prisoner and hanging party along the resounding stone corridors. After the appointed hour there was some banging on the doors from prisoners, but otherwise routine was restored until the next awful execution.

Like the rest of the prisoners, Juliet felt, heard and waited for these events. 'There were some pretty bad things that happened,' she remembers.

> An experience you don't ever want to have again is to be in a prison the night before they hang somebody ... And they did, that's something else again ... the atmosphere in a place like that when you know they are going to hang someone ... That's pretty bad.[60]

'No psychiatric treatment has been given to Juliet Hulme, the 15-year-old [sic] now in the Auckland Gaol serving a life sentence,' the *New Zealand Herald* announced in December 1954, and that was how it remained.[61] Juliet received almost no counselling while she was in prison. Mt Eden's psychologist Don McKenzie was directed to make an assessment of Juliet soon after she arrived, and continued to visit:

> for quite a while, I don't know how long, to see if I was insane or sane. I used to enjoy talking to him. Nice man. But I remember eventually him saying: 'Look you know really I can't keep this up any longer. You're the sanest person, I've ever met.' I did enjoy speaking to him, but it didn't last.[62]

McKenzie's task was to assess Juliet's mental state, and his conclusion seems to have been exactly that of the expert medical witness for the prosecution, Kenneth Stallworthy. Once her state of mind was deemed satisfactory, McKenzie's task was completed and the interviews ceased.

Juliet's mainstay among the wardresses of the prison was Grace Powell, whose sewing room was a sanctuary. 'We are making prisoners' shirts,' she wrote to Nancy Sutherland:

It is pleasant work. By the time I leave here I'll be able to make all Father's shirts, Mother's dresses, my own and some underwear. Maybe! I've made 4 pairs of brassieres since I've been here ... Out of unbleached calico for us not satin but on the same sort of principle.[63]

Grace Powell grew fond of Juliet and took an interest in her well-being. Many years later, when interviewed by Robert McCrum, she would say, 'Juliet was quality. You couldn't help but like her. I treated her like a daughter.'[64] When Anne's identity was revealed, Grace Powell sent her a book on roses and they corresponded until she died.

Juliet hated being continually 'grubby', and was repulsed by the lice-infested hair of other prisoners. There was a dearth of regular showers, and medical and dental treatment was also scant. Juliet remembers when her wisdom teeth became impacted and abscessed. 'It was a week before they got around to doing something about it. I couldn't eat, I couldn't drink — I could hear the crack [when the abscess popped]. It was not a place where your [health was a priority].'[65]

There were few distractions other than work. There were no games, exercise was brief and only on weekends, and there were no radios until an inmate had been there for a number of years. Juliet, however, found her *métier* in knitting, which she was allowed to do. 'I am still knitting hard so I also understand about counting pennies,' she wrote to Nancy. 'I knit 3 times as fast as I earn. But I manage & I enjoy it.'[66] Juliet worked with a book propped on her knee. She sent Nancy a picture of a red jersey she was knitting. 'I've done four more since, nearly finished a fifth, started well on a sixth and got a seventh planned. I knit and read at the same time.'[67]

CHAPTER NINE

I

In 2004, an email from Meg Davis arrived in Joe Blades's office at Ballantine in New York. 'Anne just rang me,' she explained, 'she's seen the bound galleys and the dedication [for *Long Spoon Lane*] is missing ... It should read: In memory of Mother H Marion Perry with gratitude 30th January, 1912 – 19th January, 2004.'[1] These words marked the end of an arduous and heartbreaking time for Anne. After Marion's stroke, Anne visited her in the nursing home in Invergordon four times a week.

> I used to go Tuesdays, Thursdays, Saturdays and Sundays, and I only failed if I was away on business ... I always took her the nicest flowers, or the raspberries or the grapes or something, and I would sit and talk to her and she could understand but she couldn't respond. I hated that ... I hated even the smell of the place.[2]

Marion's face would light up when Anne arrived, but towards the end she was often asleep through the entire visit 'and didn't know I'd been, but I knew I'd been'. It was a one-and-a-half hour round trip, which Anne did, in spite of her daunting schedule, for nearly two years. Elizabeth, her secretary, visited, occasionally Meg MacDonald, and Jonathan too, although not as often as his sister. As Anne says, 'Your daughter's a daughter for all of your life.'[3]

She became Marion's mainstay, and when her mother died, something important to Anne died with her. 'I miss her badly. I still find the best rose in the garden and then think, with a pang, that I can't take [it] to her.'[4] In a life marred by turbulence and tragedy, Anne and Marion had found peace. They accepted one another's limitations and renounced any thought of blame. The closest Anne has ever come to recrimination was a general comment she made in a conversation on parenting. She was talking about leniency and punishment.

At what point does forgiveness turn into enablement and complicity with the person in doing [the wrong thing] ... what you have said in words is 'this is wrong and you must stop', but what you have said in action is 'there isn't any price to it' ... It takes an event of some sort to make you realize 'this is not what I want to do'. Then I think you do have the right to turn to the person who could have stopped it and say: 'You let me go on doing that; you watched me walk off the brink of destruction; you watched me go right over the edge and you never said *anything*. You didn't care enough, you wanted your peace and comfort and no difficulties, and you let me do that.'[5]

No one will know whether Anne ever had this conversation with Marion, or whether her visits were something deeper — an expiation of guilt or an expression of repentance. Certainly Anne had come to understand the value to a daughter of a mother's life, and the cost of taking it.

⚭

The Shifting Tide, released in 2004, was the first Monk book Jonathan worked on with Anne. He was becoming more a part of her everyday life, helping her with research, then often cooking them both a midday meal. His office at Anne's became a repository for books about Victorian England — Henry Mayhew's *London Labour & the London Poor*, Lynn McDonald's *Collected Works of Florence Nightingale* and her letters from the Crimean War, Peter Ackroyd's *London: The Biography*, Benita Cullingford's *British Chimney Sweeps: Five Centuries of Chimney Sweeps*, the *London Encyclopedia*. He and Anne decided that Monk needed a change of scene and a new revenue source after his patroness, Lady Callandra Daviot, had fallen in love with Dr Kristian Beck and was planning to marry and move to Vienna.

'Why don't we put him looking after the longest street in London, which is the Thames,' Jonathan suggested to Anne. 'In fact, the first police force formed in England was the River Police and they pre-date Robert Peel's Bobbies, or the Peelers, by about twenty or thirty years.'[6] In *The Shifting Tide* Monk moves from the streets of London to the tidal Thames, where the *Maude Idris*, loaded with 'ebony, spices, and fourteen first-grade tusks of ivory', has just arrived from Zanzibar.

When the precious tusks are found to be missing and the sailor guarding them dead with his head bashed in, Monk is charged with recovering the prized cargo and apprehending the murderer. The back-story to this brackish tale of intrigue is the progress of the paupers' hospital that Hester has established for women who are destitute and, as so often in Victorian England, prostitutes. It runs on charitable donations and the philanthropic labour of well-placed women looking for a mission in life, like Margaret Ballinger and Claudine Burroughs. Hester works relentlessly, 'her face exhausted with days and nights of snatched sleep'.

While Hester is washing down the murdered body of Ruth Clark, she finds the horrifying signs of bubonic plague. This unhappy woman is the harbinger of catastrophic Black Death. Where could the disease have come from other than Africa — and what link does it have to the *Maude Idris*? The hospital is immediately quarantined. 'No one can leave … at any time or for any reason,' Hester explains to the patients and staff. 'Whatever happens, we cannot allow the disease to spread. In the fourteenth century it killed nearly half of Europe.' So no one can escape, and the clinic is patrolled by men with pit-bull terriers. Powerless, Hester must wait and watch as people succumb to the disease and die an agonizing death.

In a novel released at last from plotting the unmasking of Monk's identity, suspense is brilliantly maintained. The apocalyptic threat of the Black Death tests values and pushes the main characters to the brink. When a whole continent is threatened with extinction, what is the value of saving one life from the gallows, thinks Rathbone. 'Then he knew that in its own way, it was the shred of sanity they had to cling to. It was one thing that perhaps was within his power, and in that they could hold onto reason, and hope.'

Rathbone decides that it is Margaret Ballinger rather than Hester whom he loves. Hester finally emerges triumphant from the hospital quarantine, but not without witnessing the sad end of Mercy, a woman torn between family ties and the need to save the world.

Slowly, Hester ... bent to her knees. She had prayed often for the dead ... but before now it had been for the comfort of those remaining. This time it was for Mercy, and it was directed to no listener except that divine power who judges and forgives the souls of men.

The reviews were rapturous, especially about the evocation of setting. 'The images of Victorian London which she creates are so rich and thick you could almost grab them by the handful and squeeze out the drops. Perry keeps the reader guessing and puzzling right from the start,' wrote the critic for the *Yorkshire Evening Post*. As always, said *Publishers Weekly*, 'Perry uses her characters and story to comment on ethical issues that remain as relevant today as they were in Victorian times. Expect another bestseller.' The *New York Times* wrote: 'she doesn't paint quaint pictures of a distant time; she projects herself into a living moment in the past, opens her eyes and describes what she sees ... As the sailor says, "River's full o' tales", and Perry knows how to bring them to life.'[7]

From the response it seemed that Monk had made a successful transition to a new territory in London. In the next Monk, *Dark Assassin*, his role becomes professional as he takes over the role of head of the River Police from the inspiring Inspector Durban, who has been burnt to death in a shipboard fire. Anne's cat — a namesake and identical down to a whisker — makes a guest appearance at Monk's new headquarters.

Humphrey, the station cat, a large white animal with a ginger tail, was provided with a basket by the stove and as much milk as he could drink.

Mice were his affair to catch for himself, which he did whenever he could be bothered, or nobody had fed him with other titbits.

At dusk, while Monk is out in a boat on the river with his men, they look up at a distant bridge. In the half-light they see a young man and woman plunge into the water struggling — or was it struggling? Was one trying to stop the other falling or jumping, or was this a murder that accidentally took both victim and perpetrator into the inky waters of the Thames?

Dark Assassin is a tale of sinister big-business intrigue around the construction of London's sewers. There are no labour laws to protect navvy workers from the cruel conditions or from the terrible digging machines that bite and scour massive tunnels under the city, threatening fatal flooding from underground streams, gas explosions, and massive cave-ins.

Monk must find his place in a constabulary that loved its dead boss. He must earn trust and respect while identifying and defeating his opponents. To solve this corporate crime he enlists the assistance of Scuff, a river urchin who knows the Thames's ugly undercurrents, and his old opponent, Runcorn. When Scuff is shot by a professional assassin, a devastated Monk opens up to a man transformed — Runcorn. 'There was a sudden gentleness in Runcorn's face. Monk was beginning to realize how much he had changed in the last two years.' The dénouement involves a thrilling multi-character chase through the sewer tunnels.

Dark Assassin made the *New York Times*, *Wall Street Journal* and *Booksense* bestseller lists and was nominated for a prestigious Macavity Award in 2007. The fine reviews included one from Jeffery Deaver, who wrote: '*Dark Assassin* is brilliant: that rare blend of novel that's a page-turning thriller yet literary ... [it] continues Anne Perry's peerless tradition of blending compelling plotting with superbly realized human emotion and exquisite period detail.' Such praise was enormously rewarding, as were the increasing number of references, in reviews, to the literary quality of her writing. The near-miss on the Macavity Award, though disappointing, also testified to this. But still she longed to write historical novels that were not part of a crime series. Recognizing this, Meg did some research and discovered that little fiction had been written about the Byzantine

Empire. 'I thought that sensually, and with the intrigue, it was right up Anne's street.'[8]

Meg began making preparations for a trip. 'I've been talking to Anne about our meeting at the end of the year,' she wrote to Don Maass in August 2004.

As for the venue, how would you feel about Constantinople? This is kind of tough on you because it's a long way, but I think if we're seriously going to sit down and develop a series set there, we should really see the place. I'm presuming you haven't been. I haven't. Anne has and says it's marvelous … Also, I gather Anne's planning to bring Jonathan.'[9]

By September her plans were advancing. She got back to Don with some reasonable prices for hotels and extremely cheap flights, because nobody else seemed to want to go there. Earlier, she had had some qualms. 'It's not far from a couple of war zones and it's a very long journey for you, so maybe this is really a bad idea. And I don't speak much Turkish.'[10] The other option was Venice — also one of the theatres of the Byzantine Empire for the story they were hatching — but it was deathly cold at that time of year. The trip finally took place towards the end of 2004, and Jonathan recalls a 'marvellous few days' exploring the Greek Orthodox sectors of an ancient city that was once the centre of the Christian world. The magnificent Hagia Sophia, with its glowing mosaics, was breathtaking as were, in a quieter way, the tiny churches off the tourist track, with their richly painted, intimate icons that have been the focus of devotion for hundreds of years.

From one of the ruined palaces they visited, they could look out towards the Bosphorus and, remembers Jonathan, 'go down into a little town and have fresh cooked fish … [and] when you look at the bridges going across there must be a thousand people there with fishing rods'.[11]

The year 2004 also saw the launch of the Anne Perry website. 'Great to see it running,' Meg wrote to Jonathan, whom she was hoping would take on a support role for the web-master. 'I've had an email this morning tearing me off a strip for allowing bad grammar on the site of a respectable author and I feel very embarrassed. Also, there are a lot of very bad factual errors which will be leading readers in entirely wrong directions.'[12] There was room for improvement, but it was a necessary evolution.

As well as the future, there was the past. This year was the fiftieth anniversary of the Parker–Hulme case and predictably an email arrived: Chris Cooke at Television New Zealand was advising them of plans to produce a programme on the murder and asking for Anne's participation. Meg declined on Anne's behalf, but the memories were rekindled. The agency also received a letter from a member of the extended Parker family. It was a reasonable request to communicate with Anne: 'I'm very keen to write to you about something that has been on my mind for many years. But, I imagine you have been pestered so much that you would rather not hear from me.'[13] For Anne it was a painful look back when, after half a century, she just wanted to move forward.

In 2004 Anne wrote three short stories and the introduction to Penguin's *The Sherlock Holmes Mysteries*. Towards the end of the year Don heard from Meg that Joe Blades at Ballantine had offered the same deal as the previous year for the 'Xmas novella, A CHRISTMAS GUEST. That's [a good amount], since that is pretty much exactly what the books seem to be earning, I suggest we accept. Okay with you?'[14]

Still ticking along, and with more potential for excitement and financial return, were Anne's film and television ventures. There were rollover option contracts on the Pitts and the Monks, and concrete interest in the First World War series. Daria Jovicic, producer and co-founder of Wild Bear Films in New York, and producer of the film *Girl with a Pearl Earring*, was interested in the Monk series, especially *The Face of a Stranger*. Ken Sherman was in regular contact with Jane Merrow about the venture. 'Daria Jovicic is still deeply dedicated to this project and has now attached Jonathan Kaplan as Director, which we are very pleased about,' she told him.[15] Julian Fellowes — actor, screenwriter for the film *Gosford Park* and later writer of the acclaimed television series *Downton Abbey* — had written a 'very good first draft' of a script that was now several years old and was also waiting to see what would happen.[16]

With Anne's permission, Meg made moves in 2005 towards establishing a more public profile for her author. In July she emailed Jane Morpeth and Lucy Ramsay at Headline to begin the process.

You've deferred to Anne's sensitivities about her past, which has held back what you might otherwise have done for publicity and marketing. As you also know, Anne has said in the last few years that she wants to 'take the brakes' off now. Her nephew and niece are now grown up enough that she feels they can withstand any adverse publicity. Accordingly, you've been more active in promoting her, which we've noticed and appreciated. Now that Anne's had a couple of years to get used to this idea ... [she would] now like to do everything possible to maximize her profile in this country. As a complement to Headline's efforts, we wondered how you would feel if Anne engaged [British PR company] Colman Getty?[17]

Headline had no reservations, so Anne and Meg interviewed a number of public relations people and decided on energetic and positive solo operator Diane Hinds. Her impact was immediate. Within a short time she generated £3 million of advertising value. There were radio interviews, extensive articles in leading newspapers and multiple television events. After working with Anne for only two weeks, Diane was especially excited to get her on ITV's very popular *This Morning* show. She thought the programme would handle Anne's past sensitively; this was a coup.

On the day, Diane escorted Anne to the interview and was sitting in the green room watching the monitor as the live broadcast began. 'I thought "I've lost my job", because the male presenter was laying into her. It was awful. He put her on trial again. It was horrendous. And I was thinking, "I've got to go in there and stop it."' But she had no idea where, in the rabbit warren of corridors, the studio was located, or how to get there. 'They broke for an advert and came back to her and it was still aggressive, but it soon ended. I walked out of there with Anne and kept saying, "I'm sorry, I'm really sorry, I'm so, so, sorry." ... I thought that was it.'

The publicity generated was huge, and more television opportunities materialized as a result, but Diane kept asking herself if it was worth it. She was also wondering how she could have got it so wrong. The producer rang Diane, apologized profusely for the way things had been handled, and sent a big bouquet of flowers for Anne to Diane's home address.

Anne was traumatized by the incident. For a long time she was silent and her hands shook. Later she would remember it as one of the worst experiences she has ever had. 'It was absolutely appalling ... in public ... no taking any of that back.' When Meg Davis saw the programme, she was horrified and rang Diane. In the end they decided they would just let it lie. Bringing in lawyers would only draw more of the wrong sort of publicity, and the last thing they wanted was a media stand-off.

When Anne had finally collected herself in the car afterwards, she reassured Diane: 'Look, you don't have any control over this, you're doing your job.' Diane was astounded by how 'gracious and understanding she was, because I thought that's it — at the end of this week, I'm history ... Artists on the whole can be quite egotistical, and they will take it out on the nearest person, normally the PR ... I learnt that I've got the most amazing client.'[18]

After their ordeal they became firm friends, and Diane continued to promote Anne's profile in the United Kingdom. She organized book and speaking tours, workshops, public events, and interviews in Portmahomack. The results were mixed. There were headlines like 'I'm the *Heavenly Creatures* murderer' for a September 2005 article in the *Daily Mail* and 'Murder She Wrote' for *Real Magazine*, but there were also the more positive 'My Home, Anne Perry: Author of her own destiny' for the *Independent* and 'Rising from the Ashes' in *At Your Leisure*, both published in 2006.

⚭

There was something intensely personal to Anne about the storylines of the last two novels in the First World War series. In the rawness of these final wintry narratives, both the author and her characters are revealed. In *At Some Disputed Barricade*, published in August 2006 and set in the last years of the war, Joseph Reavley surveys the carnage. What is the value of life and what the price of taking it? 'It was a pretense that in the seas of blood each death was somehow important. The whole of the Western Front was strewn with broken bodies; many of them would never be found.'

His mission is to track down the murderer of Major Howard Northrup, a hopelessly incompetent, tyrannical commander who sends men to their deaths just to satisfy his insatiable ego. When he is found shot through the head after a kangaroo court-martial by his own men, one or all must pay.

Joseph has already sent his friend Sam Wetherall, guilty of another justified war killing, over the trenches into no man's land with a new identity. He could not dob Sam in, nor could he live with the knowledge that his friend is a murderer, so he helped him to stage his own death and wept over the grave, knowing his friend's body was not there. Sam has missed the firing squad, but is now sentenced to a life as a fugitive.

> Joseph could barely even guess at the pain losing his identity must have caused [Sam], hollowing out places of loneliness, character, and grief he could not imagine … the enormity of [the] situation began to sink in: the endless state of not belonging; the loneliness for anything deeper than [a] passing acquaintance; the knowledge that you were forever a stranger.

But Joseph is smarter now and more conscious of the 'complexity behind an apparently simple act', and he will not make the same mistake again. This time he is 'prepared to lie, evade, whatever was necessary, and live with his conscience'. The value of truth without context is tested in this incident, and Joseph discovers that truth is much more circumstantial and mutable than he had imagined. 'To do the right thing was necessary, to need to be seen to do it was a luxury, even a self-indulgence, and completely irrelevant.'

Anne's characters pick their way through a minefield of ethical issues. Their journeys are treacherous, and sometimes 'Quixotic … [and] absurd', but they are also singular and courageous. It is the questions they ask that are important. 'I am halfway through the 4th book in the series,' wrote one of Anne's readers in April 2007, 'and I must admit to being more morally challenged than I have been in a very long time. You compellingly present diametrically opposite sides of an argument with equal thought and reason. I cannot say how much reading these books has made me think and analyze my own views of right and wrong.'[19]

In August 2006 Anne heard from Vicki Mellor at Headline about the final First World War novel, due to be published a year later, in August 2007.

> I just wanted to write and say that I have just finished the manuscript for WE SHALL NOT SLEEP and I loved it. I have to admit that I shed a tear at the end; both at the fact that from your writing you could feel what it meant to the troops when peace was eventually secured in the First World War, but also at the thought that I wouldn't be able to read about the Reavleys anymore. As with all great books though, I am sure that the characters will live on in my mind.[20]

We Shall Not Sleep is set in the last few months before armistice is declared on 11 November 1918. The world has altered. Thirty-five million people are 'missing, dead or injured; a continent spread with ruin', but the ultimate price is not the fallen or the lost, but the living who remain and are changed forever. It is not whether there will be a peace, but what kind it will be, and whether it can be maintained. The Peacemaker, talking to his double agent Richard Mason, states, 'Do I have to explain to you what happens to a nation if we rob it of its identity, its means of regeneration, its faith in its own worth and destiny? ... Nothing good is built upon hatred.' Like so many of the Peacemaker's pronouncements, this is a telling observation.

This, however, is also the man who had the Reavley parents killed, and who perpetrates vile deeds as a sacrifice to greater good. 'Much that the Peacemaker wanted is right, and perhaps to begin with he was the most far-sighted, the sanest of us all, but he usurped power to which he had no right. He is a man fatally flawed by the weakness to abuse it.' The Peacemaker is proof that all behaviour must be scrutinized and audited, and that no one can sit superciliously behind good intentions while their actions are corrupt.

There is a memorable episode towards the end of the book. Joseph is crossing Flanders in an ambulance, from the trenches at Ypres, when he comes across a village whose inhabitants have stoned to death a young woman named Monique, mistakenly believing her to have been a traitor. When they realize their terrible mistake, they are overwhelmed by remorse. What kind of penitence is there for murder? When Joseph finds it almost impossible to forgive them their crime, his brother Matthew remonstrates with him: 'there's always a way back, Joe, from anywhere … You told me that. If you can't help them, what hope is there for any of us?' His romantic interest, Lizzie, equally sure he should intercede, adds: 'You don't have to lie to them. Tell them how hard it will be, just don't say it's impossible.' In the end Joseph sees his error and apologizes for standing in judgement. He tells the villagers: 'I have no right to [judge]. That is something you will have to do for yourself. You know what you did, and why, and what drove you. And you know she didn't deserve it.'

The last two novels in Anne's First World War series were well reviewed, both for their vivid descriptions of war and for their moral dimension. The *Publishers Weekly* reviewer noted that at the end of *We Shall Not Sleep* Anne 'neatly and satisfactorily ties up all the loose ends from the preceding novels'.[21] Left unresolved, however, is the fate of Monique's murderers and whether they will ever find a way to forgive themselves.

❧

'I just had lunch with Meg and we talked about your recent trip to Naples,' Vicki Mellor wrote to Anne in December 2007, 'it sounds wonderful. I would love to visit the caverns under the city — they sound fascinating.' Anne was enchanted with Italy, especially the hidden history and craggy southern coast around the Isle of Capri, and the ominous smoking cone of Mount Vesuvius. This trip for her was one of the special rewards of writing. She was invited to lecture to students of English literature at the University of Naples by 'the most absolutely delightful person',

Annamaria Palombi, who had a villa on the Isle of Capri with exquisite vistas over rocks to an aquamarine sea.

Although Annamaria Palombi's husband, Elio, did not speak much English, they were able to communicate well enough to enjoy each other's company. 'He's a most remarkable man,' Anne remembers. 'He was a judge, then he went back to being an advocate ... for people who weren't represented properly, for cases that have gone skew-whiff ... What a beautiful man ... That's something money can't buy, the opportunity to meet people who are truly remarkable ... That's the sort of thing [writing does]: you meet wonderful people and they treat you as if they know you ... because they've have read what you've written.'[22]

Although Italy was not as big a market for Anne's books as Germany, France or Spain, from her early days at St Martin's her Italian publisher Mondadori had enthusiastically represented her Pitt and Monk books. The experiences from her trip to Naples and Capri began to take shape as an idea for a novel set in Italy between the wars.

On her return to Portmahomack, Anne had to adjust to the idea of a new but strategic incursion into her private life. At a film festival in Edinburgh, Meg had met young director Dana Linkiewicz and they had talked about the idea of making a television documentary about Anne. They agreed between them that this would happen towards the end of 2007. Dana Linkiewicz's plan was to shadow Anne with a sound and camera crew for three weeks, 'recording her day-to-day activities'.[23] Writing to confirm the arrangement, Meg set out their expectations: 'We understand that the events of 1954–60 may need to be touched upon, but you undertake to do this with the utmost sensitivity and that this will occupy the least possible amount of the portrait.'[24]

Footage was shot on location at Anne's home, in the village and the surrounding district and, at the end of filming, Dana and her crew returned to her base in Stahnsdorf, Germany. She edited through the early months of 2008, then came back to Portmahomack to show a preview. There were some anxious moments for Dana: 'as I traveled to Scotland, I was excited and did not know what everyone would think of the film'.[25] Anne was on a book tour in Spain when Meg responded formally with feedback. There were reservations. 'I know Anne felt a bit bruised by how she seemed to come across in the film, and it sounds different from the professional persona that's been very carefully constructed over the years by her and her publishers and agents.'[26] However, the documentary was accepted on the basis that Dana made some minor changes. 'I was very glad that Anne approved of the film — it showed a grandeur towards something that will never be easy for her.'[27]

While Meg and Dana negotiated over the documentary, there was an incident in Spain. Anne appreciated the freedom of no longer having to be secretive about her identity, and she enjoyed travelling and meeting people, but there was always an anxiety, a 'numbness that never goes from some places — and you're always waiting for the moment'. It happened during a public presentation:

> A woman came in [to the auditorium] with a placard saying I should have been drowned at birth and screaming at me, she had to be removed … it was very embarrassing and then I had to give a speech … People pick on a public figure and attach all their demons, and the fact that they know nothing about you has nothing to do with it.

Always, there was that lingering chance of public humiliation or worse for Anne. 'There are lots of things [that are] positive … it's just that the negative is so numbing.'[28]

Since A Christmas Journey, which explored an episode in the young life of Lady Vespasia, was published in 2003, the Christmas novellas had been a successful addition to Anne's list. After Vespasia, Henry Rathbone, Grandmama Ellison, Charlotte's brother-in-law Duncan Corde and Monk's ex-boss Runcorn had been featured, but it was not until A Christmas Grace, published in 2008, that one of the books made the New York Times extended bestseller list. This novella focused on the spirited exploits of Charlotte's sister, Emily Radley. Anne's publisher at Headline, Vicki Mellor, knew it was a winner when she read it. 'I also wanted to let you know that I have just finished A CHRISTMAS GRACE and thought it was beautiful. It is very emotive and powerful, and your descriptions of Ireland, and particularly the storm, are so vivid that I felt like I was there.'[29]

This success added frisson to discussions about the next novella. Meg emailed Vicki an update. 'I sent Anne back to do a revision and cut some repetition, so needed to give this a further look before sending it. She's also taken the point that A CHRISTMAS CASKET is not the most cheerful of seasonal titles, however much "casket" is defined as "jewel box". It's now (at least provisionally) A CHRISTMAS PROMISE.'[30] With any hint of morbidity removed from its title, A *Christmas Promise*, featuring the Pitts' maid Gracie, was published in 2009.

It tells the story of how the diminutive Gracie is found alone and weeping in the squalid streets of London after the murder of her father. 'The pathetic voices of the children in Charles Dickens' bleak accounts of the miseries of life in the slums of Victorian London find an echo in this poignant little vignette of a Christmas book,' wrote the *Washington Times* reviewer, and the *Wall Street Journal* noted that Anne had 'made good, with style, on her Christmas promise', while the *Yorkshire Evening Post* amusingly exclaimed, 'if you don't have a lump in your throat by the time you finish the final few pages, you shouldn't have had all that sherry'.

After the First World War series came to an end in 2007, discussions about their filming moved from speculation to hard copy. Although the books were highly cinematic, representing a quintet was challenging. Under the title 'The Peacemaker', John Sealey had written the first draft of a screenplay. Meg sent the manuscript to Ken Sherman, who felt it was too ambitious in the amount of material it contained, and too derivative — 'lacking a personal style or spin of his own'.[31] The problems of staging a First World War series for film or television were immense in terms of both scale and budget. The solution, Meg suggested to Sealey, was 're-inventing this as one film which encapsulates the series'.[32]

While they were still awaiting an answer from Wild Bear about *The Face of a Stranger*, another approach was discussed. Meg outlined the situation to Ken. 'From my conversation with Alchemy yesterday, they'd be keen to do anything with Anne; they just prefer the Monk series because it's darker and richer. If things get really tricky with Wild Bear, maybe (with a bit of luck) we could persuade Alchemy to take the Pitt series (which is getting darker anyway as the series goes on, and could be developed to be darker).'[33] If Alchemy were to take over from Wild Bear, they were not interested in using the Julian Fellowes script. On the other hand, Jane Merrow explained to Ken, 'in case Alchemy goes pear shaped, which I really hope it does not, Gary Kurtz of *Star Wars* fame is interested in the script provided Julian's attached'.[34]

In August 2008 Alchemy took out an option on the Monk series with a view to moving them out of their Victorian frame and giving them a contemporary American setting. Anne was delighted with the idea of the United States and saw a real advantage, because the death penalty would give them added dramatic tension. Ken outlined the process to Meg. 'The idea would be for Anne … to come over here to pitch the contemporized "Monk", or whatever it will be called at that point, to network or cable companies, and possibly bring in a show runner i.e. someone already network-acceptable as a writer to work with Anne and … to co-author the script.' One of the people being considered was 'Dawn DeNoon who's on *Law and Order* which Anne loves if I remember correctly.'[35]

⚯

On 28 October 2008, Anne celebrated her seventieth birthday. Her most meaningful present, which came from Jonathan and her stepbrother, Mike Ducker, was an astonishing find in a second-hand store. 'It's the plays of Shaw and it must have been nearly eighty years afterwards … [from when it was presented to] my father … He got the Smith Prize which is the highest prize [at Cambridge] for Mathematics … and this is the book, the actual book he was given.'[36]

Her film and television options were taking her down a route that would involve her directly in the business of scriptwriting. This was something she felt more compelled to do than ever before. She was keen to write with other people and believed a television series could achieve this. There was no speedy way to make this happen, however. All the major decisions concerning the Alchemy project were being made in California, and were dependent on big-budget backing and alliances.

Anne was beginning to find the isolation of the Highlands oppressive, and wanted to spend more time with creative people in cosmopolitan Los Angeles. Waiting for a resolution and for filming to begin was tedious. 'There are aspects to getting older, when you don't have the blazing hope you have when you were younger. I am beginning to feel that there are one or two things that I would like to have in life — and *get on with it, already* ...'.

She was concerned about money, and dogged by the sense that time was running out. 'I find I worry more ... I think: "Get on with it, don't tell me it will happen in x years' time, I haven't got x years to wait." ... A lot of my friends are packing it in now ... you have to have a faith to keep going, because sometimes it doesn't look like it's going to be possible.'[37]Her dream was still to work in Hollywood on the adaptation of her books to film, and her greatest anxiety was that by the time it finally happened she would be too old or infirm to participate. Her creative imagination was her comfort, a place to escape to and a sign of her redemption. The strategy to handle the tension was by now a reflex: keep writing.

The title that seized her imagination in 2008 was *The Sheen on the Silk*, the fruition of her trip to Istanbul three years earlier. With the help of Meg and Don, she had developed a 100-page outline of the book to work from, and, as she wrote, memories of her trip came to life in the settings and scenes she created. A journey by car with a guide was especially vivid. 'The extraordinary thing was going across the water and driving up the Asiatic side, and standing there in the grey stone ruins of a castle and seeing the blue, blue sea, which was the Black Sea, and looking at the vegetation. It was exactly identical to what you find here if you went to the west coast — bracken, pine trees, brambles ... I could have gone out to the headland here and seen the same stuff, but the light, you can't recreate the light.'[38]

As she wrote *The Sheen on the Silk*, reviews began to appear for her latest Pitt, *Buckingham Palace Gardens*, published in February. It is darker than her previous Pitts, as Meg had promised Ken Sherman, but perhaps its greatest achievement is to set a murder story in Queen Victoria's Royal Household, with her son the Prince of Wales as a prime suspect, and make it completely convincing. From *The Whitechapel Conspiracy* onwards, Anne had built up the role of Victor Narraway, 'a lean man with a shock of dark hair, threaded with gray, and a face in which the intelligence was dangerously obvious', until he plays a pivotal role as Britain's principal spook.

When the cruelly carved-up body of a prostitute is discovered in a linen cupboard in Buckingham Palace in the early hours of the morning, it is Narraway from Special Branch who is called in, and he passes the interrogation part of the investigation over to Pitt. Together they stand in front of the cupboard doors, sickened by the sight of the poor woman, 'who lay on her back, and was obscenely naked, breasts exposed, thighs apart. Her throat had been cut from one side to the other and her lower abdomen slashed open, leaving her entrails bulging pale where they protruded from the dark blood.' There was blood splattered up the walls, soaking into the piles of sheets and collecting in a large scarlet puddle on the floor. It would have been a shocking discovery in Whitechapel, but in the elegant confines of Buckingham Palace it is an abomination.

Pitt's angry reaction to the killing proves to be almost an exception in the Royal Household, where most simply want a speedy, discreet conclusion before the queen, who is away, is back in residence. As Pitt pieces together the events of the evening, he finds that the Prince of Wales and his house guests enjoyed more than just cigars and port after their wives retired. A small group of prostitutes had covertly entered the palace to give the prince's party the type of illicit pleasure that is alien to most marriage beds.

After investigating palace security and checking the whereabouts of domestic staff, it becomes clear that the murderer is either the Prince of Wales or one of his entrepreneur guests, invited to invest in a scheme to build a trans-African railway from Cairo to Cape Town. With the assistance of maid Gracie, who is deputized as a palace plant, this privileged crowd becomes the focus of Pitt's enquiries. It is a collision of class, a situation where meritocracy and ruling élite are pitted against each other.

Anne's writing in *Buckingham Palace Gardens* has a fluidity that is one of the key achievements of her late novels, and exposition builds seamlessly through dialogue and scene change. All the elements that made her earlier books appealing are here, but less self-consciously so. In April 2008 the novel reached number 12 on the *New York Times* bestseller list, and was nominated in 2008 for the Romantic Times Best Novel and for an Agatha Award for Best Novel in 2009.[39]

Buckingham Palace Gardens was dedicated 'to my friends Meg MacDonald and Meg Davis, for their unfailing help and encouragement', and was a fitting tribute to two pivotal people in Anne's life. Meg Davis had now been working with Anne for 25 years. 'Yes, here we still are,' Meg wrote to a colleague in Canada. 'As you say, agents seem to go on forever — although I cheer myself up by realizing that even though I feel like The Ancient Mariner when advising our young agents here, there are still plenty of scarily active and successful agents around to whom I'm still a promising young whippersnapper.'[40]

Not only did Meg feel there was more she could achieve with Anne's writing, but she was keen to pick up the pace. Anne's prodigious output was creating a backlog of books waiting to be released. She decided to approach Susanna Porter, Anne's new editor at Ballantine, with the suggestion that the rate of production be increased.

> As you'll remember, [the slower rate of publication] was pretty much imposed on us … at the same time as you were taking over as Anne's US publisher … Now, a couple of years later, I'd like to address with you whether this is having the desired effect of increasing sales. I'm under a great deal of concerted pressure from all of Anne's other publishers, all of whom report that this is in fact slowing momentum dangerously.[41]

Susanna Porter was less keen to pick up the pace. For her there was still virtue in not flooding the market with Anne Perry titles that competed directly with each other.

When the manuscript for *The Sheen on the Silk* was finally submitted, it was 260,000 words long, and Vicki Mellor at Headline had doubts. 'I am very aware that Anne has put a lot of hard work and thought into this novel,' she told Susanna Porter, 'and that she fully intends for it to be an epic, and in some ways a signature novel, and that we both want to help her achieve this.'[42] The problem was its size. Vicki Mellor was not even sure they could bind it for printing at that length.

Ballantine wanted clarification of aspects of the complex plot and, because it was so long, some substantial cuts. Anne easily elucidated the plot tangles, but the cuts were a sticking point. Meg communicated to her Anne's sense that too much had been sacrificed. 'In particular, it's the religious and philosophical nuances where she felt the cuts had been too deep. And, as you know, Dante is very special to her as a poet and as someone whose writing her grandfather loved. She was thrilled when the dates were found to overlap, so perhaps we might indulge her.'[43] The resulting compromise brought *The Sheen on the Silk* to print.

Like Anne's French Revolution novel, *The Sheen on the Silk* is set at a crucial time when decisions made by pivotal people have the potential to change the world. The book opens with the arrival of Anna Zarides in Constantinople, in 1273. It is a city on fire with riches, religion, culture and political intrigue, but its blaze is in imminent danger of being extinguished. For surrounding Constantinople are the rising powers of Europe and the Middle East. To the north and south are Barbarians and Infidels, to the east ferocious Ottomans, and to the west the brutish Venetian Empire that had mounted a crusade nearly 70 years before and sacked the city — and to top this off, a warring pope.

To garner the support of the west, Constantinople must placate the Church of Rome, but there is a fundamental schism in belief. Orthodox Constantinople does not believe in the existence of the Holy Spirit, and the Church of Rome does. Will Emperor Michael Palaeologus convince Orthodox Christians in Constantinople to give up their souls to save their skins? The city is on the verge of civil war.

Against a backdrop of religious slaughter and assassination, Anna Zarides attempts to find out whether her twin brother is innocent or guilty of a murder for which he has been banished to the desert. Even a noblewoman in this world is confined and never privy to the conversations that count. Anna's solution is to disguise herself as a eunuch doctor named Anastasius. She finds mobility in the role of medic, and freedom in the persona of a eunuch who can oscillate between masculine and feminine. In disguise, Anna meets Giuliano Dandolo, a sea captain who finds himself inexplicably drawn to this ambiguous and beautiful human being. A love story and a quest weave their ways between the cities of Venice, Rome and Constantinople, getting darker and more terrifying as they proceed.

Dedicated to Jonathan, and released in 2010, *The Sheen on the Silk* rapidly found a place on the *New York Times* extended bestseller list. As critics and readers understood, it brought what could have been dry church history to life. 'Readers whose tastes tend toward epic-sized mysteries set in a far-flung past will jump right in, captivated by the intriguing story and the author's seemingly effortless grasp of her historical setting. This could open up a whole new readership for the versatile Perry,' commented the reviewer for *Booklist*.[44]

The Sheen on the Silk was translated into French, German, Spanish and Serbian. Anne toured France, promoting the novel with her 10/18 publisher, Emmanuelle Heurtebise. In one bookstore two young men caught their attention, hanging back and appearing shy. They were holding the English version and they were looking at it. 'We would like to read it in English,' they said, 'we've never done that before. We are not sure our English is as good as it deserves, but we would like to try.' Emmanuelle thought it was strange that they would want to try with 'a big, big, big book like that' and Anne asked if they might prefer the French version. They were adamant, however. 'But we have a question for you. There is a word we can't understand on the back cover.' Emmanuelle offered to help. '*Eunuch!*' they said. '*Oh là là!*' said Emmanuelle. 'Okay, over to you, Anne. *Good luck!*'[45] Anne explained without missing a beat. This was the kind of encounter that made all the hours of writing worthwhile.

Although delighted with the response to *The Sheen on the Silk*, Anne knew that her crime novels were her bread and butter, and this was important during a global recession in publishing. *Execution Dock*, her Monk published in March 2009, was the first title to show the impact of the financial crisis. Although it was well received critically, and gained a starred review in the *Publishers Weekly* and the *Library Journal*, there were fewer rights sales to international publishers, who were beginning to feel the pinch.

The book opens with Monk chasing Jericho Phillips, a man who is wanted for the murder of a 13-year-old boy named Fig. The boy's body has been found on the river near Greenwich with his throat cut so violently that he has almost been decapitated. Phillips is a pimp who deals in child pornography. He has a boat on the river where men with money and power go to buy pornography and sexual favours from children. Phillips is hard to convict, because he is protected by his wealthy patrons and customers.

When Monk captures Phillips, he is charged with the murder and Rathbone is asked by his father-in-law, Arthur Ballinger, to defend the case. At first Rathbone sees only the positives. 'It would please him to assist Margaret's father in a matter that was important to him. It would make Margaret herself happy, and it would draw him closer into the family.' He uses every skill he has to see Phillips freed, even stooping to using personal information against both Hester and Monk when they are giving evidence.

He draws attention to everything that he knows will undermine Hester's credibility, that 'she was feminine; he had harped on about her womanliness. She was vulnerable; he had subtly reminded them that she was childless.' His manipulation is so artful that Phillips is set free.

Rathbone then begins to realize what he has done and tries to justify it: 'I did what I had to do, to uphold the law.' Hester responds, 'So now do what you can to uphold justice.' Rathbone must face not only his terrible mistake, but also the fact that he does not really know his wife or her family. He tells his wife, Margaret: 'It takes courage ... I think those who have never made any grand mistakes do not realize how much that costs.' This is telling commentary from Anne, as are Monk's words to Hester: 'I didn't want to talk about my past, and I didn't care about [Durban's]. For any of us, it's who you are today that matters.' Hester's epiphany is to ignore Monk's request that she leave her philanthropic work at the hospital in Portpool Lane. It is central to everything she values and 'she could not allow him to simply remove it because he thought he could'.

The fearless street urchin Scuff, who finds a home with the Monks in the later books, provided a model for a character Anne developed to appear in a series of six short historical novels she was commissioned by publisher Barrington Stoke to write for reading-impaired children, especially boys. These were to be published in 2011. 'A young teenage boy (who has difficulty in reading himself) dreams he's at each historical event.'[46] By the beginning of 2009 Anne had delivered the manuscripts for the conquest of the Spanish Armada in 1588, the story of Thomas Becket's murder in Canterbury Cathedral in 1170 and the execution of Edith Cavell in 1915. Each was a short, vivid immersion in history.

Through 2009 and 2010 Anne worked on these stories, her latest Pitt (*Betrayal at Lisson Grove*), a new Monk (*Acceptable Loss*) and on television scripts for her Monk series. 'Looks like the contemporary series that Anne's been discussing … is our big hope,' Ken Sherman wrote to Meg in February 2009.[47] In April 2009, Meg, Diane Hinds and Anne travelled to Washington to collect a Lifetime Achievement Award in honour of her contribution to crime fiction writing.

Towards the end of 2009, Dana Linkiewicz's documentary, *Anne Perry: Interiors*, was released with a minor change requested by Meg Davis. 'Anne, as you know, is very aware of how her life impacts on her family, and we need to be careful of their sensibilities. We've given you a lot of freedom and openness, and it's really just this small detail that we need to insist on … If you could confirm that you've made the cut, I'll send you an agreement signed by Anne.'[48] Linkiewicz's 70-minute film sensitively evokes Anne's place and the people to whom she feels most connected. Her house, the farmland it sits on, the countryside and dramatic seascapes of Portmahomack are hauntingly portrayed. The murder is never represented, but subtly remains like a trace of loss and tragedy.

The documentary opens with Anne talking at the Surrey International Writers' Festival in Vancouver, which is an annual event for her, then moves back home to Portmahomack, where it follows the routines of a writer's life. It captures the tensions, especially between Anne, Meg

MacDonald and Jonathan, and leaves an uncanny sense of *déjà vu* in the relationship between Anne and Meg, in which there is an unavoidable resonance with the friendship of Juliet and Pauline. The film's release in New Zealand provoked an inevitable renewal of interest in the murder yet again. Chris Cooke from Television New Zealand emailed Anne in March 2010, requesting an interview and 'an honest and frank discussion' about what had happened. This was the perfect opportunity, he felt, for her to 'step out of her comfort zone'. He suggested they visit Christchurch together, and Ilam, because the homestead was still there. Pauline's sister, Wendy, had taken exception to Anne's assertion that she believed Pauline would have committed suicide if she had not helped to kill Honorah. Cook suggested that 'if you were of a mind to apologize to Wendy I'm sure this can be arranged. So happens I am a trained restorative justice facilitator so can assist in such a process.'[49]

They also had an approach from me, in October 2009, proposing to write a biography of Anne. Meg sent an email to Vicki Mellor, Susanna Porter and Don Maass. 'I don't think this particular author is the right person. She's based in New Zealand, which will put Anne's hackles up. She's published a biography of Ngaio Marsh ... But it seems a good moment to review the issue of whether a biography of Anne would be a good thing now.'[50] In the end they decided that the timing was not right, and that a biography might well 'scare up a lot of discussion that we've all spent years trying to bury'.[51]

I received an email from Meg: 'Dear Joanne Drayton, I'm sorry to say that even Anne's publishers don't feel it's the right time for a biography, so we're putting this whole issue on the back-burner for the foreseeable future.'[52]

I tried again on 28 April 2010: 'You may feel this is a case of what part of "no" don't you understand, but I am approaching you again to let you know I now have a confirmed contract with HarperCollins NZ to write a literary biography of Anne Perry. Once again I am writing to solicit your/her participation with this project.' The next day Meg replied with a short email requesting more information: 'Was there a proposal you sent to HarperCollins, perhaps?'[53] A day later my proposal arrived in her office at MBA. The concluding paragraph stated:

> It is amazing to have discovered a voice for Juliet Hulme in the writing
> of Anne Perry, and New Zealand needs to listen. It is time to move out
> of the 1950s, the details of which have been frozen in time and ground
> over long enough. In today's context this is punitive and embarrassing.
> Anne Perry's life story needs to grow, to leave behind the terrible mistake
> of a young teenager and mature to acknowledge the remarkable adult
> contribution and achievements of one of the world's most well-known
> crime doyennes.

'Thanks, Joanne — this is very useful. I'll talk to Anne and get back to
you as soon as possible,' Meg wrote when the proposal arrived. Then,
21 minutes later: 'Discussions have moved on more quickly than I
anticipated. Can Anne and I meet you when you're here [in London] in
the summer?'[54] ...

II

'There is no comparison between the environment at Arohata and that
of the women's section of Mt Eden,' wrote NZ Truth in September 1954.
Pauline's prison life was considerably less severe than Juliet's. Her cell
was 'a wooden, sound proof room about eight feet by 10', which had a:

> normal-sized window covered by strong meshed wire, its ceiling a grating
> to cover the light bulb. Its only furniture ... a wooden bedstead and a
> table and stool fixed to the wall ... Arohata is a modern building, not
> unlike the majority of hospitals, possibly better. Its corridors are covered
> by well-polished linoleum and are shut off by wide swinging doors.[55]

The original intention had been that Juliet and Pauline would spend
time at both prisons, 'presumably for equivalent periods', but this never
happened. Juliet survived four years in Mt Eden before she was moved

to the less stringent Arohata. After her epiphany she relinquished any obvious desire to see Pauline, although for months after the murder memories of the friendship were a touchstone in times of distress. But accepting the blame for what she did and renouncing the friendship became intrinsic to the lessons she felt she had learnt.

> There is one thing about doing something for which you pay very, very heavily and which you profoundly regret. You are a great deal more careful about ever doing anything you are going to regret. It certainly affects your understanding of stepping out of line ... You are far more careful of not doing it again than would have been otherwise ... I've been burned and you never go near the fire again. You don't even go in the same room as the fire.[56]

Juliet said she participated in the murder out of a sense of 'misplaced loyalty', and although this does not fully acknowledge the obsessive intensity of the attachment, it does explain why it was easier for her to give up the friendship and move on. Pauline yearned for much longer to see and hear news of Juliet. It was only after converting to Catholicism, towards the end of her stay in prison, that Pauline began to see their relationship as what in other circumstances it might have been — a teenage pash that could quickly have burnt itself out.

During her stay at Arohata, Pauline 'enrolled for correspondence courses in English, French, Latin, Mathematics, Drawing and Design, and later Maori'.[57] She passed School Certificate and University Entrance, and after matriculating took papers towards a Bachelor of Arts degree. To keep the young women separate, when Juliet was moved to Arohata, Pauline was transferred to Paparua Prison near Christchurch. Once there, she was visited and instructed by various academics from the University of Canterbury. Professor of English John Garrett's standard joke became: 'If you're an ordinary student, you get an ordinary tutor. Kill someone, and you get the professor.'[58]

While Pauline was at Arohata, her father was the only family member she saw, but after she had been there for a year he found it too difficult to continue. The grief he felt over the loss of his wife was exacerbated by the legal costs he was forced to pay for years after the trial. It was only when the courts realized the financial burden he was under that the money was waived. At Paparua, Pauline was able to re-establish some contact with her family.

☒

In August 1958, Juliet was moved to the secure block at Arohata. It was closed off and separate from the rest of the prison, and had its own screened and completely private exercise yard rimmed with razor-wire that ran along one side of the building and at the end. 'The workroom in the security wing is a cheerful enough room and its windows look out across green fields,' *NZ Truth* told its readers.[59] Juliet had her first proper glimpse of the outside world after four years behind the grim stone walls of Mt Eden. She drank in the views and the less punitive physical environment and routine, and impressed authorities with her ability to adjust and comply. Both she and Pauline were regarded as model prisoners.

Although politicians and newspapers announced that Juliet and Pauline would be treated like any other lifers, their age, gender, class and the high-profile nature of the case made this impossible. Their time in prison was far more assiduously managed than that of most inmates.

In fact, according to Alison Laurie and Julie Glamuzina, Sam Barnett 'took a direct and personal interest in them' and regular reports on their progress were sent directly to him.[60] Barnett was a friend of Henry Hulme, which undoubtedly had an influence. His overseeing of their progress reports was unusual, as was the degree to which their mail and visitor lists were scrutinized. Hate mail from cranks and problematic correspondence had to be separated from legitimate letters. Magazines and visits from evangelizing fundamentalist groups such as the Moral Re-Armament Organization were also intercepted.

Both girls had some behind-the-scenes protection from elements in the prison that might pose a danger to them. At Mt Eden, Grace Powell took a special interest, and, according to Don McKenzie, Superintendent

Haywood and his wife took Juliet into their home on the occasional weekend.

Any titbits of official or anecdotal information from prison were immediately reported in the press, and there were also letters to the editor. On the day Juliet was taken to Mt Eden, Eric T Price wrote to the *New Zealand Herald*:

> From the report of the decision of the Cabinet with reference to the two girls convicted of murder, it would seem that the purpose is to inflict the greatest punishment possible. It may be desirable to separate them for other reasons, but one would like to think that the purpose was reformative, not punitive. Some day these girls will be released. The kind of people they will then be will depend to a large extent on how they are treated during the long years of imprisonment.[61]

Their release was as thorny a problem as their initial imprisonment. The media were trigger-happy. London's *Sunday Express* announced to readers that Juliet 'would be released before her [twenty-first] birthday'. This was contradicted by a *New Zealand Herald* article on 17 February 1959, which quoted Minister of Justice Rex Mason's comment that 'the release from prison of Juliet Hulme ... has not been considered yet'. The next day another article appeared in the *New Zealand Herald*, correcting the *Sydney Sunday*, which had quoted a parole board member as 'saying Parker and Hulme would be released soon'. The *Herald* announced the government's official line: 'the question of Hulme's release comes up before the Executive Council on March 31 [1959]'.[62]

This frenzy of speculation fuelled an already hot topic. Accompanying the conjecture were commentaries expounding the girls' achievements in prison and speculating on their future rehabilitation. The *New Zealand Herald* told readers: '[An ex-inmate] has said Hulme had developed into an expert dressmaker and had ideas of setting up a dress shop in England ... Hulme has said she never wants to see Parker again.'[63]

When the liberation finally happened, however, everyone was caught out. By the time the girls' release hit the newspapers, Juliet was already long gone, 'her destination unknown to all except a few senior officers of the Justice Department'.[64] Juliet and Pauline were released two weeks apart, so there would be no possibility of their meeting. Juliet left the country in mid-November, and the official announcement was delayed until 4 December 1959. In total each girl had served a little over five years in prison. Barnett told the newspapers: 'we realized that eventually and inevitably their release would become known but we wanted to give them as fair a start as possible'.[65]

'I didn't really know it was going to happen until just about when it did, just a day or two before,' Anne recalls. A small deputation brought her the news and she was given the opportunity to select her own first name. 'They told me, something very ordinary. It had to be Jane, Mary, Margaret, Elizabeth, Anne, one of those sorts of things ... nothing unusual, nothing different, nothing to draw any attention, whatsoever ... All the interesting names I could have had, they said: "Oh no, you can't have anything like that." '[66] So reluctantly she chose 'Anne' and then was instructed to take the surname 'Stewart', which was her maternal grandmother's maiden name.

After her new identity was established, she was issued with a passport. 'I had to give up my past — the hardest thing imaginable — and begin a life in a new identity ... knowing even a tiny slip could unravel everything.'[67]

> They took me out [of prison]. It was like someone walking out of a dark cave into the light. They put me on a plane ... We changed planes at Sydney, and there was a few hours in between until the next flight. I remember getting out in Darwin and it was like walking into a hot, wet blanket. Very hot. We hit an electric storm, I remember that — a very, very frightening electric storm going from Darwin along to Bangkok, Karachi, and my father and his wife met me in Rome. And then we drove from Rome, through Italy and across to Britain, and then up to Northumberland.[68]

Marion was waiting for Anne when she arrived in the village of Hexham in Northumberland.

I was so shell-shocked and totally stunned. It was the first time in five-and-a-half years that I could choose whether I ate or what I ate, or didn't, or get up or go to bed if I wanted to, or walk outside when I wanted to. Or see a sunset. I hadn't seen a sunset in all that time, or listened to any decent music or seen the horizon — and I still get a kick out of that one. It doesn't wear off.[69]

In Hexham, Anne was unable to talk about her experiences. Her family, desperate to forget the whole affair, could not bring themselves to discuss it. 'Mother never talked to me about my crime,' she told Amanda Cable of the *Daily Mail* in 2005.

She felt we should leave it behind. I think, in many ways, she didn't want to feel guilty. Maybe she thought that if she'd been there for me more as a teenager, this may not have happened. But I didn't want her to think that I blamed her. If I ever talked about how I felt, it would distress her. So we chose not to.[70]

Anne was completely ill prepared for life at the dawn of the 1960s. Since her referral to the Christchurch Sanatorium in 1953, she had been 'shut away, out of circulation'. She had never worn make-up, mixed with other adolescents, been out on dates:

It took me a long time to learn to fit into society again. I remember feeling so awkward and detached ... I had to learn to do a job and behave like other people. In many ways I was a 12-year-old, and yet I had seen things that I hope most people will never see ... and most of the people I know have absolutely no idea of what that is like. They know something happened and what the newspapers have said, but they don't know what it's actually like.

The most desirable practical skill she left prison with was shorthand typing, so she did secretarial work while she adjusted to life in the outside world.

Anne lived with Marion and Bill for nearly two years before taking a flat in Newcastle-upon-Tyne with three other women. 'I — of all things — I did the cooking. We were all very hard-up, and I knew I had to cook quite a few things that would feed a number of people on nothing very much ... I was the oldest person there and over twenty-one, and the others were young, and so I was kind of responsible in a fashion, legally because I was of age.'[71] Christine Lynch, one of the girls in her flat, became a close, lifelong friend. Anne returned to Hexham to see Marion and Bill for visits and the occasional weekend stay.

Anne worked at the local John Lewis department store in Newcastle-upon-Tyne, and started dating. But all the time there was a lingering consciousness that she was concealing a secret life. When people asked her about her past 'I never lied, but I evaded. I would say I'd been ill and I'd been abroad.'[72] The fabrication was easy with mere acquaintances, but more difficult with people she wanted to know better. 'I was always dreading the day I'd have to tell somebody what I had done. But in the end I only felt close enough to one boyfriend to tell him.' She thought quite a bit about having a family in her twenties, and the idea of a conventional life appealed, but none of her romances ever proceeded to marriage; nor was her maternal instinct strong enough to need to have a child.

For years she battled feelings of social awkwardness and periods of depression, but gradually these became less frequent. She moved into a bed-sit with a 'shared toilet and bath' and became a stewardess for a local airline, 'but not a particularly good one'. It would later rate as her worst job ever. 'We were waitresses in the sky.' She lacked patience and hated being patronized and ordered around. It would rankle 'when men snapped their fingers and asked me to bring them something' and privately she felt like throwing it in their lap.[73] Her job as an assistant purser on the Hull–Gothenburg ferry was a better fit.

During this period, Anne decided to change her surname by deed-poll from Stewart to Perry. Bill had married Marion, and it made more sense and drew less attention to have just the two surnames in the family — Hulme and Perry. It felt right, too. 'Bill adopted me ... he was happy to own me. He always treated me as his own.'[74]

Changing her surname may have helped Anne avoid potentially risky and revealing questions, but it also linked her directly to the Parker–Hulme murder. The case bubbled away in people's subconsciousness, occasionally erupting with the publication of a book, an anthology or a dictionary entry, or a feature newspaper or magazine article. While Juliet and Pauline were in prison, the case had already been included in Rupert Furneaux's *Famous Criminal Cases* (1955) and in Tom Gurr and HH Cox's *Famous Australasian Crimes* (1957). (In 1958, Gurr and Cox fictionalized the case in a bestselling novel called *Obsession*.) Furneaux's preface states, 'In New Zealand we have a case which may well become world famous as the most terrible crime of the century.' His chapter on the murder concludes:

Complete egoists, they were insane only in the sense that their ideas were those of animals rather than of human beings. Their law was the law of the jungle and like wild animals they must be caged until they have shown themselves capable of living together with other human beings.[75]

Gurr and Cox's *Famous Australasian Crimes* was inaccurate in detail, but perhaps not in vision. With remarkable foresight, they wrote 'Juliet Hulme will be the one who will serve a short sentence; and it is possible that, under another name, the world in time will recognize a writer of talent.'[76] Of the crime they concluded: 'the normal mind shrinks from the implications of this tragic story. In many other crimes, lessons of some sort or other are to be found. Here there is little but horror, sadness, and bafflement.'

The books continued after Juliet and Pauline were released. In 1965 the case was included in Charles Franklin's *The World's Worst Murderers*, and in 1973 in both Leonard Gribble's *The Hallmark of Horror* and Gerald Sparrow's *Queens of Crime*, which refers to the girls as 'Satan's children'.

Media coverage was extensive at the time of the murder, and it continued into the 1960s. In December 1954, *Time* magazine ran an article entitled 'Rebels or Psychopaths?' that tried to fashion a link between the girls and delinquency, and to fathom the ominous rise of the younger generation. 'The youth of the world today is touched with madness, literally sick with an aberrant condition of mind formerly confined to a few distressed souls but now epidemic over the earth.'[77] In 1964 the London Evening Standard fanned the story into life again for British readers with an account of the murder and an examination of its frightening undercurrent of 'homosexual intensity'. In New Zealand the story was revived for holiday readers as part of a summer series for the Dominion Sunday Times in 1969. The editorial commentary never evolved or changed much. Once the tale had become a socio-cultural touchstone, why change it?

There was also other, less public commentary. Detective Sergeant Archie Tate wrote about the case for the Australian Police Journal in 1955. The same year Dr Reginald Medlicott published 'Paranoia of the Exalted Type in a Setting of Folie à Deux: A Study of Two Adolescent Homicides' in the British Journal of Medical Psychology, and, in 1970, 'An examination of the necessity for a concept of evil: Some aspects of evil as a form of perversion', for the British Journal of Medical Psychology. In the first article, Medlicott compared the Parker–Hulme murder 'to cases like that of Albert Fish, who mutilated and murdered children, and to Ian Brady and Myra Hindley, the Manchester Moors killers'.[78]

⚔

Nothing Anne had done in Newcastle-upon-Tyne stretched her intellectually or satisfied her imagination, so she decided to pursue the dream she and Pauline had shared of going to the United States. 'I was drawn to America compulsively. I would have to be, or I wouldn't have taken the five years breaking my heart to get there.' The authorities told her: 'Look, you can go anywhere else in the world, but that one you cannot have. You can't, and that's it.' But Anne persevered. 'If you look at the pattern of my life: if I didn't have hope against sense I wouldn't have survived it. If I didn't believe in miracles and that impossible things can be done.' She employed a lawyer to represent and argue her case, and believes it was reviewed at the highest governmental level. Eventually an immigration visa was granted and she left.

I got in telling the absolute truth. They know more about me than I know about me ... America has always treated me very, very well ... I owe America a great deal and I hope I never ever, ever forget that, because they accepted me and acceptance always means a lot, but especially to somebody in my situation ... and very often that's the making of somebody. It's a great gift to think the best of someone.[79]

For Anne, California was a place alive with possibility. She had always felt like a 'very peculiarly shaped peg' in a round hole. 'That's why I felt I belonged in California, because there are lots of funny shaped pegs.' One day she joined thousands of people on a Los Angeles boulevard to watch a Halloween parade, with bands, cheerleaders and floats.

The most memorable thing I saw was 'The Three Graces' in silver lamé full-length dresses and they were all *blokes*, and they were all *black*, and they were all about *six foot five* ... and I thought: 'Yeah! This is Hollywood! Do your thing, fellow'! Do your thing! If you're a six-foot-five black American bloke and you want to dress up in a silver lamé full-length dress — *go for it!* [80]

The United States authorities knew they were taking a risk by letting Anne Perry into the country, but their acceptance helped her to rejoin the human race.

POSTSCRIPT

'I think we had 6th July in the diary. Would 2.30 suit you?'[1] Meg Davis had written. The day dawned at last and it was unbelievably *hot* in London, which completely blew apart my packing, done in New Zealand. That morning had been a frantic rush around shops to buy a lighter summer jacket so I would not steam like a melting snowman during the interview. Meg Davis's words — 'if Anne feels comfortable with you' — kept rolling around in my head. Of course she had to feel comfortable with me, I thought — that was only logical — but how could anyone feel comfortable with me when I felt so hot and sticky myself?

I arrived early and, as I waited nervously on the red sofa seat in MBA's reception, I recalled Meg's preparatory advice: 'Anne's been asked extensively — even obsessively — about the murder, and it really upsets her to talk about it, and she feels she's said every last thing she has to say.'[2] If I was going to dredge it all up again, she would probably leave the room.

When Meg Davis arrived and introduced herself, she was warmer and less formal than I had imagined. She ushered me up the narrow staircase to her office, where floor-to-ceiling bookshelves were stacked with Anne Perry books.

The woman waiting for me there was tall and immaculately made-up, and dressed in a form-fitting black jacket with a crisp white blazer-like trim. She had vivid, chestnut-coloured hair, a commanding voice and riveting eyes.

The moment had arrived and it was intensely disconcerting to hear the prattle that came out of my mouth. Then we stumbled onto the topic of family origins. 'My ancient ancestors were Scandinavian,' I blurted out. 'How do you know?' she enquired.

I explained that I had Dupuytren's contracture — the 'curse of the Vikings' — in the palms of my hands. It is an inherited syndrome that can eventually claw your fingers, but that day it proved a happy affliction. 'Oh. Well, do I have Dupuytren's?' Anne asked, offering me the palm of her hand. I felt around for the sinewy ridges and telltale nodules, then took the other hand and examined it. 'Completely untouched by any

Vikings,' I announced with unwarranted authority.

Perhaps it was the human contact, but after that we settled down to a fascinating afternoon, some of which I tape-recorded. We talked about Anne's life, her books, her family, until Meg Davis, shifting awkwardly in her seat, interrupted and said: 'Look, it's 6.30 and I have to be getting home, so if you two want to continue this conversation in a pub somewhere, please do. But I've got to go.'

And so we did, though not in a pub and not that night. I was planning to see an exhibition at the Edinburgh Museum, so Anne invited me to come to Portmahomack and talk more there.

◈

Summer in Portmahomack can have blistering days that become balmy, light-filled evenings. My partner and I took a room in the Castle Hotel by the waterfront, where the sea crashes and rushes back across a grey pebble beach just metres from the front door. After my first day interviewing Anne, I arrived back at the hotel full of nervous energy. Spotting this, and an opportunity to have his two black Labradors exercised, Sandy, the proprietor, said, 'Why don't you and your friend take Peggy and Abbie for a walk down to Tarbat Ness lighthouse?' And that's exactly what we did.

Once we left the village there was no one about. The sky was an intense blue, with delicate swirls of white fluffy clouds; the slender country lane snaked its way through rolling countryside heavy with summer smells; the dogs ambled, unmoved by herds of Highland cattle or by hares that dashed across their path. When we reached the rock-candy lighthouse I had to remind myself that this must be an exceptional day, even here.

In a noisy bar-room conversation back at the hotel that evening, one of the locals told me, in a raised voice, that old Mrs Perry's ashes had been scattered at the lighthouse.

I spent a total of three days with Anne on that visit. We would start about 9am and finish at 4pm or 5pm. Each day, Jonathan Hulme, who is a good cook, would make lunch for us all. Anne introduced me to the people who work with her, and to Humphrey the cat. She showed me around her lovely garden and her fields of set-aside land that are now in trust. At the end of my stay, we agreed to meet again in the New Year.

⚔

I arrived in Portmahomack on 2 January 2011 to a very different land-scape. In London, where I had been conducting interviews and working on the Anne Perry files at MBA, it was the coldest winter for decades. In Scotland, there was so much snow and ice we took the train to Edinburgh, then hired a car, because we could not trust that Inverness Airport would stay open.

Our second meeting followed a similar pattern to the summer sessions, but this time lasted the whole week, Monday to Sunday, when I visited Anne's Mormon church in Invergordon. This series of interviews went deeper. I asked her about her life and her books — never the murder — but when she felt relaxed she told me things. I began to realize that I was probably the first properly informed person to whom she had spoken about the murder since the 1950s.

It was a remarkable experience. We talked about philosophy, writing, books, poetry, music, places, pets and people — the good, the bad and the hypocritical — and sometimes we switched off the recorder and went for a walk or watched a favourite television programme or a recorded opera, or she read a piece of poetry to me. Each night I looked forward to our session the next day, but for Anne it was a much more raw and demanding process.

> This has been a very difficult week. Very emotional, because ... I realize how much I miss my parents — as friends. It is difficult going through all these things ... I have lived with being demonized for so long that it is part of what I expect to be found ... Most of the time to people I am having to try to explain myself and it doesn't come across ... Many of us are alone like that, but to my parents I wouldn't have had to. I guess I'm still looking for somebody to whom I don't have to explain myself, because they've got it.[3]

Anne Perry explains herself in her writing, in the stories of flawed protagonists who fail the world and themselves but can transcend their past to find forgiveness. They battle their history, the corrupting influences of the world and their own fallibility and self-doubt. It is a familiar literary conceit that, for Anne, has become a default position. Its suspense and resolution are perfectly suited to crime fiction. She writes prodigiously, and with imagination and penetrating intelligence. And until the world finally 'gets it', and she can forgive herself, it is a story she will tell over and over again.

ENDNOTES

Unless otherwise indicated, all interviews are with the author.

Abbreviations

NAMES

AP	Anne Perry	KS	Ken Sherman
CP	Christine Park	LK	Lynne Kirwin
DL	Dana Linkiewicz	LN	Leona Nevler
DM	Don Maass	MD	Meg Davis
DT	Diana Tyler	MM	Meg MacDonald
EH	Emmanuelle Heurtebise	MP	Marion Perry
HD	Hope Dellon	NC	Nancy Colbert
IT	Imogen Taylor	NS	Nancy Sutherland
JB	Joe Blades	RN	Ruth Needham
JD	Joanne Drayton	SP	Susanna Porter
JF	Janet Freer	TM	Thomas McCormack
JH	Jonathan Hulme	VM	Vicki Mellor
KH	Kim Hovey		

PUBLICATIONS AND INSTITUTIONS

ANZ	Archives New Zealand	NYTBR	*New York Times Book Review*
DT	*Daily Times*	NZH	*New Zealand Herald*
MBA	Author file, MBA Literary Agents, London	NZT	*NZ Truth*
		PW	*Publishers Weekly*
NW	*Nursery World*	SST	*Sunday Star Times*
NYT	*New York Times*	TGM	*Globe and Mail* (Toronto)

Prelude

1. MD int, London, 14 Dec 2010.
2. Ibid.
3. SST, 1 Dec 2002.
4. Robert McCrum, 'Anne Perry: The crime writer who killed: memories of murder', *Guardian*, 29 Jun 1996, p 12.
5. Newspaper article, no publishing details, dated 12 Nov 2002, and AP int by Angela Neustatter [probably for *Guardian*], MBA.
6. MD int, London, 14 Dec 2010.

Chapter One

1. AP int, Portmahomack, 5 Jan 2011.
2. AP int, Portmahomack, 7 Jan 2011.
3. AP int, Portmahomack, 5 Jan 2011.
4. AP quoted in McCrum, 'Anne Perry', p 19.
5. AP int, Portmahomack, 5 Jan 2011.
6. AP quoted in McCrum, 'Anne Perry', p 19.
7. *Magazine*, 25 Feb 2006, MBA.
8. AP int, Portmahomack, 3 Jan 2011.
9. Ibid.
10. Ron Larter, *A Brief History of Elder Thomas Price Smith,1806–1896: Father and Founder of the LDS Church in East Anglia*, Ron Larter (publisher), 2008, pp 3, 10, 14.
11. Letter AP to DT, 27 Jan 1977, MBA.
12. Letter JF to AP, c Jan 1977, MBA.
13. Letter AP to DT, 1 Jun 1977, MBA.
14. Letter AP to JF, 16 Jun 1977, MBA.
15. AP int, London, 6 Jul 2010.
16. Letter TM to JF, 7 Oct 1977, MBA.
17. Letter TM to JF, c Oct 1977, MBA.
18. Letter JF to TM, 24 Nov 1977, MBA.

19. AP int, Portmahomack, 3 Jan 2011.
20. Ibid.
21. Letter JF to TM, 19 Oct 1977, MBA.
22. MM int, Portmahomack, 5 Jan 2011.
23. Ibid.
24. Ibid.
25. Ibid.
26. Letter AP to JF, 20 May 1978, MBA.
27. Ibid.
28. Letter AP to JF, 1 Feb 1979, MBA.
29. Letter HD to JF, 10 Aug 1979, MBA.
30. Ibid.
31. Letter AP to JF, 14 Feb 1979, MBA.
32. Ibid.
33. Joseph Fielding Smith, 'The Relief Society Organized by Revelation', *Relief Society Magazine* 52 (Jan 1965), p 4.
34. Newspaper reviews, MBA.
35. Newspaper review, 15 Jan 1981, [no more details], MBA.
36. Letter Nan Talese, 6 Dec 1979, MBA.
37. Letter HD to Charles Neighbors, 28 May 1980, MBA.
38. Ibid.
39. Letter JF to NC, 2 Oct 1981, MBA.
40. Letter JF to NC, 21 Oct 1981, MBA.
41. Letter NC to AP, 22 Apr 1981, MBA.
42. Letter JF to NC, 31 Mar 1981, MBA.
43. *San Diego Union*, 19 Apr 1981, MBA.
44. Letter JF to NC, 8 Sep 1981, MBA.
45. Letter JF to St Martin's Press, 23 Jun 1981, MBA.
46. Letter HD to Charles Neighbors, c 1981, MBA.
47. Letter JF to NC, 31 Mar 1981, MBA.
48. Letter JF to NC, 9 Mar 1982, MBA.
49. Letter AP to DT, 5 May 1982, MBA.
50. Letter AP to CP, 7 Oct 1982, MBA.
51. Letter HD to AP, 19 Nov 1982, MBA.
52. McCrum, 'Anne Perry', p 12.
53. Faxed article, 14 Nov 1994, [no more details], MBA.

Chapter Two

1. Letter HD to NC, 21 Jan 1983, MBA.
2. Letter AP to NC, 9 Mar 1983, MBA.
3. Letter CP to St Martin's Press, 4 Sep 1983, MBA.
4. Letter CP to HD, 21 Sep 1983, MBA.
5. Letter CP to HD, 15 Dec 1983, MBA.
6. Letter HD to CP, 23 Jan 1984, MBA.
7. Letter CP to HD, 12 Jan 1984, MBA.
8. Letter AP to CP, 25 Jan 1984, MBA.
9. Letter CP to Maureen Waller, 13 Jun 1984, MBA.
10. AP int, Portmahomack, 6 Jan 2011.
11. Note DT to CP, [no date], MBA.
12. Letter CP to Margaret Elliot, 4 Jul 1984, MBA.
13. Letter DT to AP, 11 Sep 1984, MBA.
14. Letter CP to AP, 17 Oct 1984, MBA.
15. Letter AP to CP, 23 Oct 1984, MBA.
16. Letter CP to HD, 29 Oct 1984, MBA.
17. Letter CP to AP, 10 Dec 1984, MBA.
18. AP int, Portmahomack, 5 Jan 2011.
19. *Philadelphia Inquirer*, 20 Jan 1985, MBA.
20. *Sun*, 2 Nov 19[85], MBA.
21. MM int, Portmahomack, 5 Jan 2011.
22. Card AP to JF, [undated], MBA.
23. Letter CP to AP, 28 Jan 1985, MBA.
24. MD int, London, 15 Dec 2010.
25. Letter MD to HD, 25 Feb 1985, MBA.
26. Letter MD to AP, 12 Feb 1985, MBA.
27. MD int, London, 14 Dec 2010.
28. Ibid.
29. Email MD to JD, 26 Jan 2012.
30. MD int, London, 15 Dec 2010.
31. Letter MD to AP, 15 Aug 1985, MBA.
32. MD int, London, 14 Dec 2010.
33. Letter AP to MD, 31 Jul 1985, MBA.
34. Letter AP to MD, 5 Dec 1985, MBA.
35. MM int, Portmahomack, 5 Jan 2011.
36. Letter AP to MD, 11 Nov 1985, MBA.
37. Letter MD to AP, 20 Feb 1986, MBA.
38. Letter Lisa Leventer to AP, [undated], MBA.
39. Letter Arnold Goodman to MD, 7 May 1986, MBA.
40. Letter MD to Arnold Goodman, 6 Feb 1986, MBA.
41. Letter Valari Barocas to MD, 23 Sep 1986, MBA.
42. Letter Frances Heasman to DT, 6 Nov 1984, MBA.
43. Letter CP to Gerald Hagan, 28 Nov 1984, MBA.
44. Letter MD to Tara Hartnett, 17 Sep 1986, MBA.

45. Meg Davis int, London, 14 Dec 2010.
46. *Knoxville Sentinel*, 19 Apr 1987, MBA.
47. Letter from MD to AP, 18 May 1987, MBA.
48. Postcard AP to MD, 26 May 1987, MBA.
49. Letter MD to AP, 9 Jul 1987, MBA.
50. Letter MD to Ernest Hecht, 10 Dec 1987, MBA.
51. MD int, London, 14 Dec 2010.
52. Ibid.
53. Ibid.
54. Review Marilyn Stasio, *NYT*, [no pub details], MBA.
55. Article Mary Cannon on AP, *Alfred Hitchcock Magazine*, Feb 1988, MBA.
56. Email MD to JD, 26 Jul 2011.
57. MD int, London, 15 Dec 2010.
58. Letter MD to AP, 11 Jan 1988, MBA.
59. MM int, Portmahomack, 5 Jan 2011.
60. Ibid.
61. Ibid.
62. Ibid.
63. Ibid.
64. Letter Henry Hulme to NS, 2 Jul 1955, NS's Parker–Hulme papers, Accession 1996, Macmillan Brown Archives, University of Canterbury, Christchurch.
65. AP int, Portmahomack, 4 Jan 2011.
66. *At Your Leisure*, 12 Oct 2006, np, MBA.
67. AP int, Portmahomack, 4 Jan 2011.
68. Ibid.
69. Ibid.
70. AP int, Portmahomack, 3 Jan 2011.
71. *PW*, 27 Mar 1995, MBA.

Chapter Three

1. MM int, Portmahomack, 5 Jan 2011.
2. Ibid.
3. Ibid.
4. Ibid.
5. MD int, London, 14 Dec 2010.
6. Letter MD to AP, 4 Jan 1989, MBA.
7. Ibid.
8. PD James, *Talking About Detective Fiction*, London, Bodleian Library and Faber & Faber, 2009, p 70.
9. Ibid.
10. Letter MD to AP, 29 Nov 1989, MBA.
11. Ibid.
12. Letter MD to AP, 8 Sep 1989, MBA.
13. Letter MD to DM, 28 Nov 1989, MBA.
14. Ibid.
15. Letter DM to MD, 2 Jan 1990, MBA.
16. Letter MD to DM, 11 Jan 1990, MBA.
17. Letter MD to DM, 15 Jan 1990, MBA.
18. Letter DM to AP, 14 Feb 1990, MBA.
19. Letter MD to AP, 26 Feb 1990, MBA.
20. Letter MD to DM, c Feb 1990, MBA.
21. Letter MD to AP, c Feb 1990, MBA.
22. Letter HD to AP, 5 Apr 1990, MBA.
23. Letter MD to HD, 17 Apr 1990, MBA.
24. Letter MD to DM, 16 May 1990, MBA.
25. Picture card from AP, [undated, c 1990], MBA.
26. MD int, London, 14 Dec 2010.
27. Letter MD to LN, 21 Nov 1990, MBA.
28. *NYT*, [?] Nov 1990, MBA.
29. *Kirkus Reviews*, 15 Aug 1990, MBA.
30. *PW*, 14 Sep 1990, p 113, MBA.
31. *PW*, 22 Jun 1990, MBA.
32. *NYTBR*, 5 Aug 1990, MBA.
33. Letter MD to DM, 1 Oct 1990, MBA.
34. Article Paul Nathan, *PW*, 4 Dec 1990, MBA.
35. Letter MD to DM, 4 May 1990, MBA.
36. Letter MD to DM, 15 Oct 1990, MBA.
37. Letter MD to DM, 26 Sep 1990, MBA.
38. Letter DM to MD, 28 Sep 1990, MBA.
39. Ibid.
40. Letter MD to LN, 6 Sep [1990], MBA.
41. Letter LN to AP, 28 Oct 1990, MBA.
42. Letter LN to AP, 25 Sep 1991, MBA.
43. *NYTBR*, 20 Oct 1991, MBA.
44. *News*, 5 Oct 1991, MBA.
45. *PW*, 27 Jul 1992, MBA.
46. Letter MD to DM, 11 Feb 1991, MBA.
47. Letter LN to AP, 12 Jul 1991, MBA.
48. Letter LN to MD, 16 Dec 1991, MBA.
49. Letter LN to AP, 12 Jun 1992, MBA.
50. *NYTBR*, [no pub details], MBA.
51. Letter DM to LN, 9 Jan 1992, MBA.
52. Letter MD to DM, 20 Jan 1992, MBA.
53. AP's itinerary for trip for *Defend and Betray*, 9 Sep 1992, MBA.
54. Fax KS to MD and DT, 22 Oct 1992, MBA.
55. Letter MD to Ileen Maisel, 15 Jul 1991, MBA.
56. Letter Sarah Horne to MD, 2 Apr 1991, MBA.

57. Letter Lynda La Plante to MD, [undated], MBA.
58. Letter MD to DM, 20 Jan 1992, MBA.
59. Letter LN to MD, 10 Feb 1992, MBA.
60. AP int, Portmahomack, 6 Jan 2011.
61. Germaine Greer, *The Obstacle Race*, London, Book Club Associates, 1980, p 4.
62. Letter MD to KS, 12 Nov 1992, MBA.
63. Letter MD to AP, 29 Apr 1993, MBA.
64. Letter MD to LN, 28 Sep 1993, MBA.
65. KH int, New York, 19 Jan 2011.
66. Letter MD to KS, 18 Nov 1993, MBA.
67. Letter MD to DM, 7 Dec 1993, MBA.
68. Ibid.
69. Letter MD to Nick Sayers, 28 Jul 1993, MBA.
70. Letter MD to Nick Sayers, 20 Dec 1993, MBA.
71. AP int, Portmahomack, 3 Jan 2011.
72. Ibid.
73. *NW*, 23 Feb [1995?], p 11, MBA.

Chapter Four

1. *Sunday Times*, 13 Nov 2005, MBA.
2. MM int, Portmahomack, 5 Jan 2011.
3. Conversations with David Wilson and Robert Corbet, Portmahomack, Jul 2010, Jan 2011.
4. Copy faxed by David Love, *Daily Mirror Scottish* to RN, 5 Aug 1994, MBA.
5. Letter MD to Brian Barlow, 23 Mar 1994, MBA.
6. Letter IT to MD, 15 Feb 1994, MBA.
7. Letter DM to MD, 31 Jan 1994, MBA.
8. Email MD to JD, 1 Aug 2011.
9. Reader report Deborah Hogan, sent by LN to MD, 18 Mar 1994, MBA.
10. Card AP to MD, c Mar 1994, MBA.
11. Letter KS to MD, 27 Apr 1994, MBA.
12. Letter MD to DM, 26 Apr 1994, MBA.
13. Letter MD to IT, 18 Feb 1994, MBA.
14. *San Diego Union Tribune*, 20 Mar 1994, MBA.
15. *Toronto Sun*, 20 Mar 1994, MBA.
16. *Birmingham, AL News*, 27 Mar 1994, MBA.
17. *USA Today*, 4 Jul 1994, MBA.
18. *Daily Mail*, 10 Feb 1995, MBA.
19. Screening notes for *Heavenly Creatures* from Miramax, MBA.
20. Ibid.
21. *Time Out*, 25 Jan – 1 Feb 1993, MBA.
22. *You*, 15 Jan [1995?], MBA.
23. *You*, 15 Jan [1995?], (Report by Sarah Gristwood), MBA.
24. Julie Glamuzina and Alison Laurie, *Parker and Hulme: A Lesbian View*, Auckland, New Women's Press, 1991, p 12.
25. *You*, 15 Jan [1995?], MBA.
26. McCrum, 'Anne Perry', p 19.
27. *Sydney Morning Herald*, 22 Jan 1995, MBA.
28. MD int, London, 14 Dec 2010.
29. Accompanying letter/fax to Sarah Gristwood's int from LK to Veronica Wadley, *DT*, 2 Aug 1994, MBA.
30. *Guardian*, 30 Jan 1995, MBA.
31. Sarah Gristwood's article faxed to LK for pub *DT*, 5 Aug 1994, MBA.
32. Ibid.
33. Ibid.
34. Ibid.
35. Letter RN to Richard Holledge, 5 Aug 1994, MBA.
36. *Independent*, 10 Feb 1995.
37. Copy faxed by David Love, *Daily Mirror Scottish* to RN, 5 Aug 1994, MBA.
38. Ibid.
39. MD int, London, 14 Dec 2010.
40. KH int, New York, 19 Jan 2011.
41. DM int, New York, 18 Jan 2011.
42. 'Blood Memory: Writer Anne Perry once took part in a murder', [no pub details, c 1994], MBA.
43. Fax IT to RN, 2 Aug 1994, MBA.
44. Fax RN to Jennifer Parr and Nick Sayers, 2 Aug 1994, MBA.
45. Letter Susan Opie to MD, 10 Aug 1994, MBA.
46. Letter IT to MD, [c Aug 1994], MBA.
47. Letter David Lomas to RN, 5 Aug 1994, MBA.
48. *People*, 9 Dec 1994, p 88, MBA.
49. *September*, 9 Dec 1994, p 24, MBA.
50. *Newsday*, 20 Feb 1995, MBA.
51. Faxed letter MD to KS, 15 Feb 1995, MBA.
52. *SST*, 1 Dec 2002, MBA.
53. Letter MD to DM, 15 Feb 1995, MBA.
54. Letter MD to KH, 27 Sep 1994, MBA.
55. Letter MD to DM, 27 Sep 1994, MBA.
56. Letter MD to LN, 27 Sep 1994, MBA.
57. Letter MD to DM, 29 Nov 1994, MBA.

58. Letter MD to DM, 30 Nov 1994, MBA.
59. Letter MD to DM, 18 Nov 1994, MBA.
60. *TGM*, 11 Mar 1995, MBA.
61. Letter MD to DM, 15 Nov 1994, MBA.
62. Letter MD to DM, 9 Dec 1994, MBA.
63. Letter MD to KS, 8 Nov 1994, MBA.
64. McCrum, 'Anne Perry', p 19.
65. *Daily Mail*, 16 Feb 1995; *Newsday*, 20 [Feb] 1995; letter MD to DM, 17 Feb 1995, MBA.
66. *Newsday*, 20 [Feb] 1995, MBA.
67. Philip Marchand, 'Author tries to avoid past as a teenage murderess', [no more details], MBA.
68. Letter MD to AP, 18 Oct 1994, draft statement of official reaction to *Heavenly Creatures*, MBA.
69. *Irish Sunday Independent*, 4 Dec 2005, MBA.
70. *NYT*, 14 Feb 1995, MBA.
71. *New York Post*, 20 Feb 1995, MBA.
72. *Newsday*, 20 [Feb] 1995, MBA.
73. Ibid.
74. *New York Daily News*, 17 Feb 1995, MBA.
75. Miramax ad entitled 'Murder, She Wrote!', faxed [10 Mar 1995], MBA.
76. Ibid.
77. Fax article, 14 Nov 1994, [no more details], MBA.
78. Letter DM to MD, 7 Mar 1995, MBA.
79. Letter MD to DM, 15 Feb 1995, MBA.
80. *NYT*, 14 Feb 1995, MBA.
81. Letter MD to DM, 17 Feb 1995, MBA.
82. Letter DM to editor *NYT*, 15 Feb 1995, MBA.
83. Fax DM to MD, 17 Feb 1995, MBA.
84. Letter KS to MD, 16 Feb 1995, MBA.
85. Fax MD to KS, 16 Feb 1995, MBA.
86. Letter MD to DM, 17 Feb 1995, MBA.
87. McCrum, 'Anne Perry', p 12.
88. AP int, Portmahomack, 4 Jan 2011.
89. *Real Magazine*, 20 Jan 2006, MBA.
90. *NW*, 23 Feb [1995?], MBA.
91. Ngaio Marsh (with RM Burdon), *New Zealand*, London, Collins, 1942, p 34.
92. Glamuzina and Laurie, *Parker and Hulme*, p 41.
93. CGHS 3A classmates int, Christchurch, 10 Sep 2010.
94. Ibid.
95. *Christchurch Girls' High School Magazine: Seventy-fifth Anniversary Number 1877–1952*, No 110, December, 1952, p 2.
96. Email Patricia Drayton to JD, 29 Aug 2011.
97. AP int, Portmahomack, 4 Jan 2011.
98. CGHS 3A classmates int, Christchurch, 10 Sep 2010.
99. Ibid.
100. Ibid.
101. RW Medlicott, 'Paranoia of the Exalted Type in a Setting of *Folie à Deux*: A Study of Two Adolescent Homicides', *British Journal of Medical Psychology*, 28(4), 1955, p 207.
102. Ibid.

Chapter Five

1. Fax KH to John Darnton, 31 Jan 1995, MBA.
2. *Bookselling this Week*, 12 Dec 1994, MBA.
3. Ibid.
4. Sarah Gristwood's faxed article for *DT*, 5 Aug 1994, MBA.
5. KH int, New York, 19 Jan 2011.
6. *You*, 15 Jan [1995?], MBA.
7. Richard Corliss, *Time*, 21 Nov 1994, MBA.
8. John Griffin, 'Murder and make-believe', [no more details], MBA.
9. Article by Christopher Tookey, *Daily Mail*, 10 February 1995, p 42, MBA.
10. Corliss, *Time*, MBA.
11. *TGM*, 11 Mar 1995, MBA.
12. Letter KS to MD, 20 Mar 1995, MBA.
13. Faxed letter KS to MD, 26 Mar 1995, MBA.
14. Letter MD to KS, 28 Apr 1994, MBA.
15. *TGM*, 11 Mar 1995, MBA.
16. *Brantford Expositor*, 20 May 1995, MBA.
17. Letter MD to DM, 16 Jun 1995, MBA.
18. MBA.
19. Letter MD to HD, 4 Aug 1995, MBA.
20. Letter HD to MD, [undated], MBA.
21. Letter MD to Alan Yentob, 23 Aug 1995, MBA.
22. Letter MD to Valari Barocas, 5 Sep 1995, MBA.
23. Letter MD to KS, 15 Aug 1994, MBA.
24. Letter Georgina Morley to AP, 21 Feb 1995, MBA.
25. Letter MD to Darron Leslie, 1 Nov 1995, MBA.

26. Letter Darron Leslie to MD, 2 Nov 1995, MBA.
27. Letter MD to Darron Leslie, [c Nov] 1995, MBA.
28. Letter [details confidential] to 'Juliet' with business plan, 26 Oct 1995, MBA.
29. Letter MD to DM, 20 Nov 1995, MBA.
30. *NYTBR*, [no more details], MBA.
31. Letter MD to DM, 8 Mar 1995, MBA.
32. Letter MD to Robert McCrum, 27 Oct 1994, MBA.
33. McCrum, 'Anne Perry', p 19.
34. *Guardian* and *NYT*, [no more details], MBA.
35. In Alexander Howe and Christine Jackson (eds), *Marcia Muller and the Female Private Eye*, North Carolina, McFarland, 2008, p 6.
36. *Express*, 6 Jan 1997, MBA.
37. *Daily Mail*, 6 Jan 1997, MBA.
38. Ibid.
39. *NZ Woman's Weekly*, 6 Jan 1997, MBA.
40. Ibid.
41. *Express*, 6 Jan 1997, MBA.
42. CGHS 3A classmates int, Christchurch, 10 Sep 2010.
43. Ibid.
44. Ibid.
45. Ibid.
46. In Gwynedd Lloyd (ed), *'Problem' Girls: Understanding and supporting troubled and troublesome girls and young women*, London and New York, RoutledgeFalmer, 2005, pp 26–7.
47. *Christchurch Girls' High School Magazine: Seventy-fifth Anniversary Number 1877–1952*, pp 40–1.
48. Medlicott, 'Paranoia ...', p 208.
49. Glamuzina and Laurie, *Parker and Hulme*, p 72.
50. Quoted in Medlicott, 'Paranoia ...', pp 208–9.
51. Quoted in Glamuzina and Laurie, *Parker and Hulme*, p 67.
52. FO Bennett, *A Canterbury Tale: The Autobiography of Dr Francis Bennett*, Wellington, Oxford University Press, 1980, p 238.
53. *NW*, 23 Feb [1995?], MBA.
54. Hilda Hulme, Coroner's Report, Item: J 46 Acc 1954/1048 Box 427, ANZ, Wellington.
55. Ibid.
56. Quoted in Medlicott, 'Paranoia ...', p 211.
57. In Lloyd, *'Problem' Girls*, p 55.
58. Ibid, p 52.
59. Hilda Hulme, Coroner's Report.
60. Quoted in Medlicott, 'Paranoia ...', p 211.
61. Ibid.
62. In Lloyd, *'Problem' Girls*, p 28.
63. CGHS 3A classmates int, Christchurch, 10 Sep 2010.
64. Ibid.
65. *NZH*, 24 Aug 1954, p 10.
66. Quoted in Medlicott, 'Paranoia ...', p 211.
67. Walter Andrew Bowman Perry, Coroner's Report, Item: J 46 Acc 1954/1048 Box 427, ANZ, Wellington.
68. Quoted in Medlicott, 'Paranoia ...', p 211.
69. *Press*, 28 Aug 1954, p 8.
70. Quoted in Medlicott, 'Paranoia ...', p 210.
71. *Press*, 17 Jun 1989, p 23.
72. Quoted in Glamuzina and Laurie, *Parker and Hulme*, p 73.
73. In Lloyd, *'Problem' Girls*, pp 68–9, 70.
74. Quoted in Medlicott, 'Paranoia ...', p 212.
75. Quoted in Glamuzina and Laurie, *Parker and Hulme*, 1991, p 74.
76. Quoted in Medlicott, 'Paranoia ...', p 212.
77. Quoted in Medlicott, 'Paranoia ...', p 214.
78. Ibid.
79. Herbert Rieper, Coroner's Report, Item: J 46 Acc 1954/1048 Box 427, ANZ, Wellington.
80. Quoted in Medlicott, 'Paranoia ...', p 214.
81. Quoted in Glamuzina and Laurie, *Parker and Hulme*, p 20.

Chapter Six

1. Email MD to JD, 6 Oct 2011.
2. *January Magazine*, januarymagazine.com/profiles/perry.html.
3. Ibid.
4. Email MD to JD, 6 Oct 2011.
5. Ibid.
6. *PW*, [no more details], MBA.
7. AP int, Portmahomack, 4 Jan 2011.
8. Email MD to JD, 27 Jul 2011.
9. Email MD to JD, 1 Aug 2011.
10. Email MD to JD, 6 Oct 2011.
11. *SFX*, [no more details], MBA.

12. Walter Andrew Bowman Perry, Coroner's Report, Item: J 46 Acc 1954/1048 Box 427, ANZ, Wellington.
13. Agnes Ritchie, Coroner's Report, Item: J 46 Acc 1954/1048 Box 427, ANZ, Wellington.
14. Ibid.
15. Ibid.
16. Ibid.
17. Herbert Rieper, Coroner's Report, Item: J 46 Acc 1954/1048 Box 427, ANZ, Wellington.
18. Hilda Hulme, Coroner's Report, Item: J 46 Acc 1954/1048 Box 427, ANZ, Wellington.
19. Perry, Coroner's Report.
20. NZH, 24 Aug 1954, p 10.
21. Press, 17 Jun 1989, p 23.
22. Star-Sun, 24 Aug 1954, p 3.
23. Glamuzina and Laurie, Parker and Hulme, p 76.
24. McDonald Brown, Coroner's Report, Item: J 46 Acc 1954/1048 Box 427, ANZ, Wellington.
25. Hilda Hulme, Coroner's Report.
26. Brown, Coroner's Report.
27. Star-Sun, 24 Aug 1954, p 3.
28. Press, 17 Jun 1989, p 23.
29. Archie Brian Tate, Coroner's Report, Item: J 46 Acc 1954/1048 Box 427, ANZ, Wellington.
30. Perry, Coroner's Report.
31. Quoted in Glamuzina and Laurie, Parker and Hulme, p 25 and Medlicott, 'Paranoia …', p 215.
32. CGHS 3A classmates int, Christchurch, 10 Sep 2010.
33. Ibid.
34. NZT, 15 Sep 1954, p 5.
35. Press, 5 Oct 1991, p 5.
36. Press, 30 Aug 1954, p 12.
37. Glamuzina and Laurie, Parker and Hulme, p 88.
38. NZH, 28 Aug 1954, p 12.
39. Quoted in Medlicott, 'Paranoia …', p 215.
40. Press, 17 Jun 1989, p 23.
41. In Lloyd, 'Problem' Girls, p 54.
42. Quoted in Medlicott, 'Paranoia …', pp 211–12.
43. Ibid, p 219.
44. Ibid, p 222.
45. Ibid, p 217.
46. Press, 5 Oct 1991, p 5.
47. Press, 30 Aug 1954, p 12.
48. Glamuzina and Laurie, Parker and Hulme, p 82.
49. Press, 5 Oct 1991, p 5.
50. Star-Sun, 28 Aug 1954, p 1.
51. NZH, 30 Aug 1954, p 10.
52. NZT, 1 Sep 1954, p 20.
53. Ibid.
54. Press, 30 Aug 1954, p 12.
55. Star-Sun, 23 Aug 1954, p 1.
56. Colin Thomas Bushby Pearson, Coroner's Report, Item: J 46 Acc 1954/1048 Box 427, ANZ, Wellington.
57. NZH, 24 Aug 1954, p 10.
58. Star-Sun, 24 Aug 1954, p 3.
59. Ibid.
60. Ibid.
61. Glamuzina and Laurie, Parker and Hulme, p 57.
62. Star-Sun, 24 Aug 1954, p 3.
63. Press, 25 Aug 1954.
64. Quoted in Glamuzina and Laurie, Parker and Hulme, p 90.
65. Quoted in Medlicott, 'Paranoia …', p 209.
66. Press, 25 Aug 1954.
67. Ibid.
68. Press, 5 Oct 1991, p 5.
69. NZH, 26 Aug 1954, p 12.
70. NZH, 30 Aug 1954.
71. Quoted in Glamuzina and Laurie, Parker and Hulme, p 93.
72. Quoted in Glamuzina and Laurie, Parker and Hulme, p 94.
73. Press, 5 Oct 1991, p 5.
74. Quoted in Glamuzina and Laurie, Parker and Hulme, p 95.
75. Press, 28 Aug 1954, p 8.
76. NZH, 28 Aug 1954, p 12.
77. Ibid.
78. Press, 28 Aug 1954, p 8.
79. Ibid.
80. Ibid.
81. Press, 30 August 1954.
82. Quoted in Glamuzina and Laurie, Parker and Hulme, p 97.
83. NZH, 30 Aug 1954, p 10.

Chapter Seven

1. Email MD to JD, 1 Aug 2011.

2. John Haywood, *The Great Migrations: From the Earliest Humans to the Age of Globalization*, Quercus (www.quercusbooks. co.uk), p 224.
3. *Book of Mormon Student Manual*, Salt Lake City, Utah: The Church of Jesus Christ of Latter-day Saints, 1996, (ch 6, 1 Nephi 19).
4. Email MD to JD, 6 Oct 2011.
5. *SFX* and *Booklist*, [no more details], MBA.
6. *Starlog* and *SFX*, [no more details], MBA.
7. *Booklist*, [no more details], MBA.
8. Email Heidi Jahnke to AP, c Feb 2003, MBA.
9. 'Keeping a Series Interesting', unpublished paper by AP.
10. DM int, New York, 18 Jan 2011.
11. Ibid.
12. Letter MP to NS, 27 Jun 1995, NS's Parker–Hulme papers.
13. And following quotes, Jonathan Hulme int, Portmahomack, 6 Jan 2011.
14. AP int, Portmahomack, 7 Jan 2011.
15. AP int, Portmahomack, 4 Jan 2011.
16. Ibid.
17. *Glasgow Herald*, 16 Mar 2002.
18. MM int, Portmahomack, 5 Jan 2011.
19. Ibid.
20. *Chicago Tribune, Pittsburgh Post-Gazette, NYTBR* and the *Booklist*, [no more details], MBA.
21. *TGM*, 11 March 1995, MBA.
22. AP int, Portmahomack, 8 Jan 2011.
23. EH int, Paris, 13 Jan 2011.
24. Ibid.
25. Ibid.
26. Lora Fountain int, Paris, 13 Jan 2011.
27. EH int, Paris, 13 Jan 2011.
28. *NZH*, 30 Aug 1954.
29. Ibid.
30. Ibid.
31. *Star-Sun*, 30 Aug 1954, p 4.
32. Quoted in *True Crime: Crimes of Passion*, London, Time Life, [undated, c 2010], p 130.
33. *NZT*, 1 Sep 1954, p 22.
34. Ibid.
35. *Star-Sun*, 31 Aug 1954, p 11.
36. *NZT*, 8 Sep 1954, p 21.
37. Ibid.
38. Ibid.
39. Quoted in Glamuzina and Laurie, *Parker and Hulme*, p 101.
40. Joann Deak and Teresa Barker, *Girls Will Be Girls: Raising Confident and Courageous Daughters*, New York, Hyperion, 2002, p 12.
41. Alison Horspool int, Auckland, 3 Jul 2011.
42. Deak and Barker, *Girls Will Be Girls*, p 28.
43. Ibid, p 51.
44. Ibid, p 27.
45. Gitta Sereny, *Cries Unheard: Story of Mary Bell*, London, Macmillan, 1998, p 102.
46. Ibid, p 34.
47. Ibid, pp 104–5.
48. *SST*, 1 Dec 2002, MBA.
49. *NW*, 23 Feb [1995?], MBA.
50. Sereny, *Cries Unheard*, p 45.
51. Quoted in David Dobbs, 'The New Science of the Teenage Brain', *National Geographic*, 220(4), p 54.
52. *NZT*, 6 Oct 1954.
53. *NZT*, 29 Sep 1954, p 5.
54. *NZT*, 6 Oct 1954, p 44.
55. *NZT*, 8 Oct 1954, p 21.
56. *NZT*, 15 Sep 1954, p 5.
57. Ibid.
58. *NZT*, 29 Sep 1954, p 5.
59. Ibid.
60. *NZT*, 15 Sep 1954, p 5.
61. Article with int by Angela Neustatter, 12 Nov 2002 [no more details], MBA.
62. Letter Felicity Maidment to NS, 25 Oct 1954, NS's Parker–Hulme papers.
63. *NZT*, 15 Sep 1954, p 5.
64. AP int, Portmahomack, 3 Jan 2011.
65. *SST*, 1 Dec 2002, MBA.
66. *Real Magazine*, 20 Jan 2006, MBA.

Chapter Eight

1. *NYT* and *PW*, [no more details], MBA.
2. AP int, Portmahomack, 11 Jul 2010.
3. AP int, London, 6 Jul 2010.
4. AP int, Portmahomack, 12 Jul 2010.
5. 'Keeping a Series Interesting', unpublished paper by AP.
6. AP int, London, 6 Jul 2010.
7. Ibid.
8. 'Keeping a Series Interesting'.
9. *NYTBR* [no more details], MBA.
10. DM int, New York, 18 Jan 2011.
11. JH int, Portmahomack, 6 Jan 2011.

12. MD int, London, 14 Dec 2010.
13. JH int, Portmahomack, 6 Jan 2011.
14. AP int, London, 6 Jul 2010.
15. JH int, Portmahomack, 6 Jan 2011.
16. *PW, NYT, Chronicle* and *Book Report*, [no more details], MBA.
17. *Lady Magazine*, [no more details], MBA.
18. Email JH to MD, 7 Oct 2003, MBA.
19. Email MD to JH, 14 Oct 2003, MBA.
20. Email Lucy Ramsey to MD, 14 Oct 2003, MBA.
21. Email MD to JH, 14 Oct 2003, MBA.
22. Email DM to MD [no more details], MBA.
23. Emails MD to Jane Morpeth, 3, 8 Mar 2004, MBA.
24. Email MD to JD, 19 Nov 2011.
25. AP int London, 6 Jul 2010.
26. Email JB to AP and MD, 6 Jan 2003, MBA.
27. Email JB to AP and MD, 26 Feb 2003, MBA.
28. Email DM to MD, 14 Feb 2003, MBA.
29. Email MD to DM, 6 Feb 2003, MBA.
30. Email MD to DM, 30 Jul 2003, MBA.
31. Email JB to AP, 12 Dec 2003, MBA.
32. AP int, Portmahomack, 3 Jan 2011.
33. Ibid.
34. Letter Juliet Hulme to NS, 26 Feb [1955], NS's Parker–Hulme papers.
35. AP int, Portmahomack, 4 Jan 2011.
36. Letter Juliet Hulme to NS, 25 Aug [1955], NS's Parker–Hulme papers.
37. *NZT*, 29 Sep 1954, p 5.
38. Letter Juliet Hulme to NS, 26 Feb [1955], NS's Parker–Hulme papers.
39. Russell Stone int, Auckland, 20 Nov 2011.
40. Letter Juliet Hulme to NS, 26 Dec [1954], NS's Parker–Hulme papers.
41. Letter Juliet Hulme to NS, 6 Nov [1954], NS's Parker–Hulme papers.
42. AP int, Portmahomack, 3 Jan 2011.
43. Ruth Fry, 'Stephanie Grace Young (1890–1983): Headmistress, educationalist', www.teara.govt.nz/en/biographies/4y2.
44. Letter Juliet Hulme to NS, 6 Nov [1954], NS's Parker–Hulme papers.
45. Letter Juliet Hulme to NS, 25 Aug [1955], NS's Parker–Hulme papers.
46. Letter Henry Hulme to NS, 2 Jul 1955, NS's Parker–Hulme papers.
47. Letter Henry Hulme to Vivien Dixon, 16 Nov 1954, NS's Parker–Hulme papers.
48. Letter Henry Hulme to NS, 2 Jul 1955, NS's Parker–Hulme papers.
49. Letter Henry Hulme to NS, 11 Jan 1955, NS's Parker–Hulme papers.
50. Letter Henry Hulme to NS, 14 Nov 1954, NS's Parker–Hulme papers.
51. Letter Henry Hulme to NS, 16 Dec 1954, NS's Parker–Hulme papers.
52. AP int, Portmahomack, 4 Jan 2011.
53. Ibid.
54. Ibid.
55. *NZT*, 8 Sep 1954.
56. AP int, Portmahomack, 4 Jan 2011.
57. Greg Newbold, *The Problem of Prisons: Corrections Reform in New Zealand Since 1840*, Wellington, Dunmore, 2007, p 244.
58. Ibid, p 250.
59. Ibid, p 247.
60. AP int, Portmahomack, 4 Jan 2011.
61. *NZH*, 13 Dec 1954, p 8.
62. AP int, Portmahomack, 3 Jan 2011.
63. Letter Juliet Hulme to NS, 26 Feb [1955], NS's Parker–Hulme papers.
64. McCrum, 'Anne Perry, p 16.
65. AP int, Portmahomack, 4 Jan 2011.
66. Letter Juliet Hulme to NS, 25 Aug [1955], NS's Parker–Hulme papers.
67. Letter Juliet Hulme to NS, 26 Feb [1955], NS's Parker–Hulme papers.

Chapter Nine

1. Email MD to JB, [no more details], MBA.
2. AP int, Portmahomack, 6 Jan 2011.
3. Ibid.
4. *Daily Mail*, 28 Sep 2005 (int by Amanda Cable), MBA.
5. AP int, Portmahomack, 8 Jan 2011.
6. JH int, Portmahomack, 6 Jan 2011.
7. *Yorkshire Evening Post, PW* and *NYT*, [no more details], MBA.
8. Email MD to JD, 22 Jan 2012.
9. Email MD to DM, 12 Aug 2004, MBA.
10. Email MD to DM, 9 Jun 2004, MBA.
11. JH int, Portmahomack, 6 Jan 2011.
12. Letter MD to JH, 17 May 2004, MBA.
13. Details confidential, MBA.
14. Email MD to DM, 26 Oct 2004, MBA.

15. Email Jane Merrow to KS, 12 Oct 2007, MBA.
16. Email from MD to Andrea Asimow, 28 Mar 2008, MBA.
17. Email MD to Jane Morpeth and Lucy Ramsey, 22 Jul 2005, MBA.
18. Diana Hinds int, London, 31 Dec 2010.
19. Details confidential, 29 Apr 2007, MBA.
20. Email VM to AP, 9 Aug 2006, MBA.
21. *PW* [no more details], MBA.
22. AP int, Portmahomack, 3 Jan 2011.
23. Letter MD to DL, 2 Jul 2007, MBA.
24. Ibid.
25. Email DL to MD, 21 Jul 2008, MBA.
26. Email MD to DL, 15 Jul 2008, MBA.
27. Email DL to MD, 21 Jul 2008, MBA.
28. AP int, Portmahomack, 3 Jan 2011.
29. Email VM to AP, 10 Dec 2007, MBA.
30. Email MD to VM, 10 Jul 2008, MBA.
31. Email KS to MD, 1 Jan 2008, MBA.
32. Email MD to John Sealey, [no more details], MBA.
33. Email MD to KS, 17 Apr 2008, MBA.
34. Email Jane Merrow to KS, 27 Jun 2008, MBA.
35. Email KS to MD, 2 Dec 2008, MBA.
36. AP int, Portmahomack, 3 Jan 2011.
37. AP int, Portmahomack, 4 Jan 2011.
38. AP int, Portmahomack, 3 Jan 2011.
39. *Good Book Guide* and *Baltimore Sun*, [no more details], MBA.
40. Email MD to Linda McKnight, 14 Aug 2008, MBA.
41. Email MD to SP, 15 Feb 2008, MBA.
42. Email VM to SP, 26 Jan 2009, MBA.
43. Email MD to SP, 14 Apr 2009, MBA.
44. *Booklist*, [no more details], MBA.
45. EH int, Paris, 13 Jan 2011.
46. Email MD to Kent Educational TV, 28 Jan 2009, MBA.
47. Email KS to MD, 26 Feb 2009, MBA.
48. Email MD to DL, 8 Jan 2009, MBA.
49. Email Chris Cooke to MD and AP, 24 Mar 2010, MBA.
50. Email MD to VM, SP and DM, 16 Oct 2009, MBA.
51. Email SP to MD, VM and DM, [c Oct 2009], MBA.
52. Email MD to JD, 3 Nov 2009.
53. Email MD to JD, 29 Apr 2010.
54. Email MD to JD, 1 May 2010.
55. *NZT*, 8 Sep 1954, p 21.
56. AP int, Portmahomack, 4 Jan 2011.
57. Glamuzina and Laurie, *Parker and Hulme*, p 105.
58. Kerry Greenwood (ed), *On Murder 2: True Crime Writing in Australia*, Melbourne, Black Inc, 2002, pp 247–66.
59. *NZT*, 8 Sep 1954, p 21.
60. Glamuzina and Laurie, *Parker and Hulme*, p 104.
61. *NZH*, 3 Sep 1954, p 10.
62. *NZH*, 16 Feb 1959, p 10.
63. Ibid.
64. *NZH*, 4 Dec 1959, p 12.
65. Ibid.
66. AP int, Portmahomack, 7 Jan 2011.
67. Article with int by Angela Neustatter, 12 Nov 2002 [no more details], MBA.
68. AP int, Portmahomack, 7 Jan 2011.
69. Ibid.
70. Int by Amanda Cable, *Daily Mail*, 28 Sep 2005, MBA.
71. AP int, Portmahomack, 7 Jan 2011.
72. McCrum, 'Anne Perry', p 16.
73. AP int, Portmahomack, 7 Jan 2011.
74. Ibid.
75. Rupert Furneaux, *Famous Criminal Cases*, London, Wingate, 1955, p 47.
76. Tom Gurr and HH Cox, *Famous Australasian Crimes*, London, Muller, c 1957, p 167.
77. *Time*, 6 Dec 1954, p 26.
78. Glamuzina and Laurie, *Parker and Hulme*, 1991, p 110.
79. AP int, Portmahomack, 4 Jan 2011.
80. AP int, London, 6 Jul 2010.

Postscript

1. Email MD to JD, 8 Jun 2010.
2. Email MD to JD, 13 May 2010.
3. AP int, Portmahomack, 7 Jan 2011.

SELECT BIBLIOGRAPHY

ANNE PERRY

Thomas and Charlotte Pitt series

The Cater Street Hangman, 1979
US: St Martin's Press/Fawcett; UK: HarperCollins; Italy: Mondadori Omnibus Giallo; Germany: Dumont; France: 10/18; Spain: Plaza y Janés; Serbia: Media 11

Callander Square, 1980
US: St Martin's Press/Fawcett; Italy: Mondadori (Classici del Giallo); Germany: Dumont; Spain: Plaza y Janés; Serbia: Media 11; France: 10/18; Portugal: Gótica

Paragon Walk, 1981
US: St Martin's Press/Fawcett; Italy: Mondadori Omnibus Giallo; Germany: Dumont; France: 10/18; Spain: Plaza y Janés

Resurrection Row, 1981
US: St Martin's Press/Fawcett; Italy: Mondadori Omnibus Giallo; Germany: Heyne; France: 10/18; Spain: Plaza y Janés

Rutland Place, 1983
US: St Martin's Press/Fawcett; Italy: Mondadori; Germany: Heyne; Spain: Plaza y Janés; France: 10/18; Portugal: Gótica

Bluegate Fields, 1984
US: St Martin's Press/Fawcett; UK: Souvenir/HarperCollins; Italy: Mondadori; Germany: Heyne; Spain: Plaza y Janés; Japan: Shueisha; France: 10/18

Death in the Devil's Acre, 1985
US: St Martin's Press/Fawcett; UK: Souvenir/HarperCollins; Italy: Mondadori; Spain: Plaza y Janés, Germany: Heyne, France: 10/18

Cardington Crescent, 1987
US: St Martin's Press/Fawcett; UK: Souvenir/HarperCollins; Italy: Mondadori; Germany: Heyne; Spain: Plaza y Janés; France: 10/18

Silence in Hanover Close, 1988
US: St Martin's Press/Fawcett; UK: Souvenir/HarperCollins; Italy: Mondadori; Germany: Heyne; Spain: Plaza y Janés; France: 10/18

Bethlehem Road, 1990
US: St Martin's Press/Fawcett; UK: Souvenir/HarperCollins; Italy: Mondadori; Germany: Heyne; Spain: Plaza y Janés; France: 10/18

Highgate Rise, 1991
US: Ballantine/Fawcett; UK: Souvenir/HarperCollins; Italy: Mondadori; Germany: Heyne; Spain: Plaza y Janés; France: 10/18

Belgrave Square, 1992
US: Ballantine/Fawcett; UK: Souvenir/HarperCollins; Germany: Heyne; Italy: Mondadori; Portugal: Circulo de Leitores; Spain: Plaza y Janés; France: 10/18

Farriers' Lane, 1993
US: Ballantine/Fawcett; UK: HarperCollins; Italy: Mondadori; Germany: Heyne; Spain: Plaza y Janés; France: 10/18

The Hyde Park Headsman, 1994
US: Ballantine/Fawcett; UK: HarperCollins; Germany: Heyne; Italy: Mondadori; Spain: Plaza y Janés

Traitor's Gate, 1995
US: Ballantine/Fawcett; UK: HarperCollins; Germany: Heyne; Italy: Mondadori; Spain: Plaza y Janés; France: 10/18; Poland: Zysk

Pentecost Alley, 1996
US: Ballantine/Fawcett; UK: HarperCollins; Germany: Heyne; Italy: Mondadori; Spain: Plaza y Janés; Greece: Kanaki; Japan: Shueisha; Poland: Zysk; Portugal: Livros do Brasil; France: 10/18

Ashworth Hall, 1997
US: Ballantine/Fawcett; UK: HarperCollins; Germany: Heyne; Italy: Mondadori; Spain: Plaza y Janés; Portugal: Livros do Brasil; France: 10/18

Brunswick Gardens, 1998
US: Ballantine/Fawcett; UK: HarperCollins; Germany: Heyne; Spain: Plaza y Janés; France: 10/18

Bedford Square, 1999
US: Ballantine/Fawcett; UK: Headline; Germany: Heyne; Italy: Mondadori; France: 10/18; Spain: Plaza y Janés

Half Moon Street, 2000
US: Ballantine/Fawcett; UK: Headline; Germany: Heyne; Italy: Mondadori; France: 10/18; Spain: Mondadori/El Pais

The Whitechapel Conspiracy, 2001
US: Ballantine/Fawcett; UK: Headline; Germany: Heyne; Italy: Mondadori; Spain: Plaza y Janés

Southampton Row, 2002
US: Ballantine; UK: Headline; Germany:
Heyne; Italy: Mondadori; Spain: Plaza y Janés;
France: 10/18

Seven Dials, 2003
US: Ballantine; UK: Headline; Spain: Plaza
y Janés; Italy: Mondadori; France: 10/18;
Germany: Heyne

Long Spoon Lane, 2005
US: Ballantine; UK: Headline; Germany:
Heyne; France: 10/18; Italy: Fanucci Editore;
Spain: Plaza y Janés

Buckingham Palace Gardens, 2008
US: Ballantine; UK: Headline; Germany:
Heyne; France: 10/18; Spain: Random House
Mondadori

Betrayal at Lisson Grove, 2011
US: Ballantine; UK: Headline; Germany:
Heyne

William Monk series

The Face of a Stranger, 1990
US: Ballantine/Fawcett; UK: Headline; Japan:
Tokyo Sogen Sha; Italy: Mondadori; Germany:
Wilhelm Goldmann; Greece: Kanaki; Spain:
Ediciones B; Portugal: Editoria Gótica; Czech
Rep: Moba; Russia: Arabesque; Netherlands:
ZNU; Poland: Zysk

A Dangerous Mourning, 1991
US: Ballantine/Fawcett; UK: Headline; Italy:
Mondadori; Japan: Tokyo Sogen Sha; Russia:
Arabesque; France: 10/18; Netherlands:
ZNU; Germany: Wilhelm Goldmann; Spain:
Ediciones B; Portugal: Editoria Gótica; Czech
Rep: Moba

Defend and Betray, 1992
US: Ballantine/Fawcett; UK: Headline;
Germany: Goldmann; Italy: Mondadori;
Portugal: Gótica; Japan: Tokyo Sogen Sha;
Greece: Kanaki; Spain: Ediciones B

A Sudden, Fearful Death, 1993
US: Ballantine/Fawcett; UK: Headline;
Germany: Goldmann; Italy: Mondadori;
Greece: Kanaki; Spain: Ediciones B; France:
10/18; Portugal: Gótica

The Sins of the Wolf, 1994
US: Ballantine/Fawcett; UK: Headline;
Germany: Goldmann; Italy: Mondadori;
France: 10/18; Spain: Ediciones B; Portugal:
Gótica

Cain His Brother, 1995
US: Ballantine/Fawcett; UK: Headline;
Germany: Goldmann; Italy: Mondadori;
Greece: Kanaki; France: 10/18; Spain:
Ediciones B; Portugal: Editoria Gótica

Weighed in the Balance, 1996
US: Ballantine/Fawcett; UK: Headline;
Germany: Goldmann; Italy: Mondadori; Spain:
Ediciones B; France: 10/18

The Silent Cry, 1997
US: Ballantine/Fawcett; UK: Headline;
Germany: Goldmann; Italy: Mondadori; Spain:
Ediciones B; France: 10/18

Whited Sepulchres/A Breach of Promise (USA
title), 1998
US: Ballantine/Fawcett; UK: Headline;
Germany: Goldmann; Spain: Ediciones B;
France: 10/18; Italy: Mondadori

The Twisted Root, 1999
US: Ballantine/Fawcett; UK: Headline;
Germany: Goldmann; Italy: Mondadori; Spain:
Ediciones B; France: 10/18

Slaves and Obsession/Slaves of Obsession (USA
title), 2000
US: Ballantine/Fawcett; UK: Headline;
Germany: Goldmann; Italy: Mondadori;
France: 10/18; Spain: Plaza y Janés

A Funeral In Blue, 2001
US: Ballantine/Fawcett; UK: Headline;
Germany: Goldmann; France: 10/18; Poland:
Zysk; Czech Rep: Moba; Italy: Mondadori

Death of a Stranger, 2002
US: Ballantine/Fawcett; UK: Headline; Italy:
Mondadori; France: 10/18; Spain: Ediciones B;
Germany: Bertelsmann

The Shifting Tide, 2004
US: Ballantine; UK: Headline; Spain:
Ediciones B; Germany: Bertelsmann; Italy:
Mondadori; France: 10/18

Dark Assassin, 2006
US: Ballantine; UK: Headline; Spain:
Ediciones B

Execution Dock, 2009
US: Ballantine; UK: Headline; France: 10/18

Acceptable Loss, 2011
US: Ballantine; UK: Headline

A Sunless Sea, 2012
US: Ballantine; UK: Headline

First World War Quintet, featuring Joseph and Matthew Reavley

No Graves As Yet, 2003
US: Ballantine; UK: Headline; Netherlands: ZNU; Spain: Ediciones B; Germany: Bast; France: 10/18; Italy: Fanucci

Shoulder the Sky, 2004
UK: Headline; Germany: Bastei Lübbe; Spain: Ediciones B; France: 10/18; Italy: Fanucci Editore

Angels in the Gloom, 2005
UK: Headline; France: 10/18; Spain: Ediciones B SA; Germany: Bastei Lübbe

At Some Disputed Barricade, 2006
UK: Headline; Germany: Bastei Lübbe; Spain: Ediciones B SA; France: 10/18; Italy: Hobby E Work Publishing

We Shall Not Sleep, 2007
UK: Headline; Germany: Bastei Lübbe; Spain: Ediciones B SA; France: 10/18

'Heroes', *The Penguin Book of First World War Stories*, Penguin, 2000

Fantasy novels

Tathea, 1999
US: Deseret Books/Penguin Putnam; UK: Headline; Germany: Heyne

Come Armageddon, 2001
US: Penguin Putnam; UK: Headline

French Revolution Period

The One Thing More, 2000
US: Ballantine/Fawcett; UK: Headline; Germany: Heyne; Italy: Mondadori; France: 10/18; Spain: Ediciones Robinbook

Books for those with reading difficulties

US, UK: Barrington Stoke (published 2011–2012)

Blood Red Rose

Rose of No Man's Land

Tudor Rose

Other books

The Sheen on the Silk, 2010
US: Random House; UK: Headline; France: 10/18; Germany: Heyne; Spain: Ediciones B SA; Serbia: Media II

Christmas novellas

A Christmas Journey, 2003
US: Ballantine; UK: Headline; Germany: Heyne; France: 10/18; Spain: Bolsillo; Poland: Zysk

A Christmas Visitor, 2004
US: Ballantine; UK: Headline; Germany: Heyne; France: 10/18; Spain: Ediciones B SA

A Christmas Guest, 2005
US: Ballantine; UK: Headline; France: 10/18; Spain: De Bolsillo

A Christmas Secret, 2006
US: Ballantine; UK: Headline; France: 10/18; Spain: De Bolsillo

A Christmas Beginning, 2007
US: Ballantine; UK: Headline; France: 10/18; Spain: Ediciones B SA; Germany: Heyne

A Christmas Grace, 2008
US: Ballantine; UK: Headline; Germany: Heyne

A Christmas Promise, 2009
US: Ballantine; UK: Headline; Germany: Heyne

A Christmas Odyssey, 2010
US: Ballantine; UK: Headline

A Christmas Homecoming, 2011
US: Ballantine; UK: Headline

OTHER PUBLISHED SOURCES

Books and Articles

Betz, Phyllis M, *Lesbian Detective Fiction: Woman as Author, Subject and Reader*, North Carolina, McFarland, 2006.

Bennett, FO, *A Canterbury Tale: The Autobiography of Dr Francis Bennett*, Wellington, Oxford University Press, 1980.

Bennett, FO, *The Tenth Home*, Auckland, Blackwood & Janet Paul, 1966.

Beaglehole, Ernest, *Mental Health in New Zealand*, Wellington, New Zealand University Press, 1950.

Brabazon, James, *Dorothy L. Sayers*, New York, Charles Scribner's Sons, 1981.

Bunkle, Phillida and Beryl Hughes (eds), *Women in New Zealand Society*, Auckland, Allen & Unwin, 1980.

Capote, Truman, *In Cold Blood*, New York, Penguin, first published 1966, 2006.

Constable, Linda, 'Controversy in the air', *Landfall*, 1956, pp 242–5.

Curran, John, *Agatha Christie's Secret Notebooks*, London, HarperCollins, 2009.

Davis, Carol Anne, *Children Who Kill: Profiles of Pre-Teen and Teenage Killers*, London, Allison & Busby, 2003.

Deak, Joann and Teresa Barker, *Girls Will Be Girls: Raising Confident and Courageous Daughters*, New York, Hyperion, 2002.

Dobbs, David, 'The New Science of the Teenage Brain', *National Geographic*, 220(4), pp 36–59.

Eldred-Grigg, Stevan, *A New History of Canterbury*, Dunedin, McIndoe, 1982.

Emrys, AB, *Wilkie Collins, Vera Caspary and the Evolution of the Casebook Novel*, North Carolina, McFarland, 2011.

Faderman, Lillian, *Surpassing the Love of Men: Romantic Friendship and Love between Women from the Renaissance to the Present*, New York, William Morrow, 1981.

Fido, Martin, *The Chronicle of Crime: The Infamous Felons of Modern History and the Hideous Crimes*, London, Carlton, 1993.

Franklin, Charles, *The World's Worst Murders: Exciting and Authentic Accounts of the Great Classics of Murder*, London, Odhams Books, 1965.

Fry, Ruth, 'Stephanie Grace Young (1890–1983): Headmistress, educationalist', www.teara.govt.nz/en/biographies/4y2.

Furneaux, Rupert, *Famous Criminal Cases*, London, Wingate, 1955.

Gardiner, Muriel, *The Deadly Innocents: Portraits of Children Who Kill*, London, Hogarth Press, 1977.

Gaute, JHH and Robin Odell, *The Murderer's Who's Who*, London, Harrap, 1979.

Glamuzina, Julie and Alison Laurie, *Parker and Hulme: A Lesbian View*, Auckland, New Women's Press, 1991.

Graham, Peter, *So Brilliantly Clever: Parker, Hulme and the Murder that Shocked the World*, Wellington, Awa Press, 2011.

Greenwood, Kerry (ed), *On Murder 2: True Crime Writing in Australia*, Melbourne, Black Inc., 2002.

Gribble, Leonard, *The Hallmark of Horror*, London, Long, 1973.

Gurr, Tom and HH Cox, *Famous Australian Crimes*, London, Muller, 1957.

Gurr, Tom and HH Cox, *Obsession*, London, Muller, 1958.

Haycraft, Howard, *Murder for Pleasure: The Life and Times of the Detective Story*, London, Peter Davis, 1942.

Haycraft, Howard, *The Art of the Mystery Story: A Collection of Critical Essays*, New York, Biblo & Tannen, 1976 (first published 1946).

Haywood, John, *The Great Migrations: From the Earliest Humans to the Age of Globalization*, Quercus (www.quercusbooks.co.uk).

Herbert, Rosemary (ed), *The Oxford Companion to Crime & Mystery Writing*, New York and Oxford, Oxford University Press, 1999.

Hills, Stuart L, *Demystifying Social Deviance*, New York, McGraw-Hill, 1980.

Howe, Alexander N and Christine A Jackson (eds), *Marcia Muller and the Female Private Eye: Essays on the Novels that Defined a Subgenre*, North Carolina, McFarland, 2008.

Hyde, Margaret O and Elizabeth Held Forsyth, *The Violent Mind*, New York, Franklin Watts, 1991.

James, PD, 'A Life of Crime', *Independent Magazine*, 56 (September 1989), pp 50–3.

James, PD, 'From Puzzle to Novel', in Reginald Hill and HRF Keating (eds), *Crime Writers: reflections on crime fiction*, BBC, London, 1978.

James, PD, *Talking About Detective Fiction*, London, Bodleian Library and Faber & Faber, 2009.

Jones, RG, *Killer Couples: Terrifying True Stories of the World's Deadliest Duos*, London, WH Allen, 1989.

Larter, Ron, *A Brief History of Elder Thomas Price Smith, 1806–1896: Father and Founder of the LDS Church in East Anglia*, Ron Larter (publisher), 2008.

Lloyd, Gwynedd, 'Problem' Girls: Understanding and Supporting Troubled and Troublesome Girls and Young Women, London and New York, RoutledgeFalmer, 2005.

Maass, Don, The Fire in Fiction: Passion, Purpose, and Techniques to Make Your Novel Great, Cincinnati, Writer's Digest Books, 2009.

Maass, Don, Writing the Breakout Novel, with foreword by Anne Perry, Cincinnati, Writer's Digest Books, 2009.

Mann, Jessica, Deadlier Than the Male: An Investigation into Feminine Crime Writing, Newton Abbott, David & Charles, 1981.

McCrum, Robert, 'Anne Perry: The crime writer who killed: memories of murder', Guardian, 29 June 1996, pp 12–19.

Medlicott, RW, 'An examination of the necessity for a concept of evil: Some aspects of evil as a form of perversion', British Journal of Medical Psychology, 43(3), pp 271–80, 1970.

Medlicott, RW, 'Paranoia of the Exalted Type in a Setting of Folie à Deux: A Study of Two Adolescent Homicides', British Journal of Medical Psychology, 28(4), 1955, p 207.

Medlicott, RW, 'Sociopathic Personality Disturbance', in PJ Lawrence (ed), Mental Health and the Community, Canterbury Mental Council, Christchurch, 1963.

Medlicott, RW, 'Some Reflections on the Parker–Hulme, Leopold–Loeb Cases with Special Reference to the Concept of Omnipotence', New Zealand Law Journal, 37(22), 1961.

Medlicott, RW, 'The Place of Electronarcosis in Psychiatric Treatment: A Clinical Assessment based on the Treatment of Four Hundred Patients', New Zealand Medical Journal, LIII, 1954.

Moffat, Mary Jane and Charlotte Painter, Revelations: Diaries of Women, New York, Vintage Press, 1975.

Mohr, JW and CK McKnight, 'Violence as a Function of Age and Relationship with Special Reference to Matricide', Canadian Psychiatric Association Journal, 16, 1971.

Morris, Greggory W, The Kids Next Door: Sons and Daughters Who Kill Their Parents, New York, William Morrow, 1985.

Newbold, Greg, The Problem of Prisons: Corrections Reform in New Zealand Since 1840, Wellington, Dunmore, 2007.

Nicholas, M, The World's Wickedest Women, London, Octopus Books, 1984.

Orwell, George, Decline of the English Murder: and Other Essays, London, Penguin, 1965 (first published 1946).

Sayers, Dorothy, Creed of Chaos? London, Hodder & Stoughton, 1940.

Sayers, Dorothy, The Greatest Drama Ever Staged, London, Hodder & Stoughton, 1938.

Sereny, Gitta, Cries Unheard: Story of Mary Bell, London, Macmillan, 1998

Smith, Frank, Crimes and Victims, London, Abbeydale Press, 2007.

Smith, Joseph Fielding, 'The Relief Society Organized by Revelation', Relief Society Magazine, 52, January 1965.

Sparrow, Gerald, Queens of Crime, London, Arthur Baker, 1973.

Sparrow, Gerald, Women Who Murder, London, Arthur Baker, 1970.

Sprague, Rosamond (ed), A Matter of Eternity: Selections From the Writings of Dorothy L. Sayers, London, Oxford, AR Mowbray, 1973.

Symons, Julian, Bloody Murder: From the Detective Story to the Crime Novel: A Story, London, Faber & Faber, 1972.

Tate, AB, 'The Parker–Hulme Murder', Australian Police Journal, July 1955.

True Crime: Crimes of Passion, London, Time Life, [undated, c 2010].

Wagstaff, Vanessa and Stephen Poole, Agatha Christie: A Reader's Companion, London, Aurum Press, 2006.

Wilson, Colin and Patricia Pitman, Encyclopedia of Murder, London and Sydney, Pan Books, 1984.

Wilson, Patrick, Murderess: A Study of the Women Executed in Britain since 1843, London, Michael Joseph, 1971.

Winn, Dilys, Murderess Ink: The Better Half of the Mystery, New York, Bell Publishing, 1979.

UNPUBLISHED SOURCES

Alexander Turnbull Library, Wellington

Archives New Zealand, Wellington

Auckland Libraries, Special Collections

Christchurch City Libraries, Special Collections

Macmillan Brown Library, University of
Canterbury, Christchurch

MBA Literary Agents author file, London

NEWSPAPERS

New Zealand Newspapers

Christchurch Star-Sun, 1954

Dominion, 1950–59

Dominion Sunday Times, 1969, 1987

Evening Post, 1950–59

New Zealand Herald, 1950–59

NZ Listener, 1950–59, 1991, 2010

NZ Truth, 1950–59

NZ Woman's Weekly, 1954, 1994, 2002, 2011

People's Voice, 1950–54

Press, 1950–54, 1958–59

Australian Newspapers

Sydney Morning Herald, 1954

Sun, 1954

British Newspapers

Daily Express, 1954, 1955, 1957, 1959, 1967

Daily Mail, 1954

Daily Mirror, 1954

Daily Sketch, 1954

Daily Telegraph, 1954

Evening News, 1954

London Evening Standard, 1964

Time Magazine, 1954

Times London, 1954

INTERVIEWS

Christchurch Girls' High School 3A classmates
Margaret Luisetti, Brenda Blake, Margaret
Dacre, Carline Maze, Marjorie Smart and
Jan Spang, interview with biographer,
Christchurch, 10 September 2010.

Davis, Meg, interview, London,
13–21 December 2010.

Drayton, Patricia, in conversation, 2010–11.

Fountain, Lora and Emmanuelle Heurtebise,
interview, Paris, 12 January 2011.

Hinds, Diana, interview, London, 31 December
2010.

Horspool, Alison, interview, Auckland, 3 July
2011.

Hovey, Kim, interview, New York, 19 January
2011.

Hulme, Jonathan, interview, Portmahomack,
6 January 2011.

Maass, Don, interview, New York, 18 January
2011.

MacDonald, Meg, interview, Portmahomack,
5 January 2011.

Mornin, Sonya, in conversation, Auckland,
October 2011.

Opie, Susan, in conversation, London, 7 July
2010.

Perry, Anne, interview, London, 6 July 2010.

Perry, Anne, interviews, Portmahomack,
11–13 July 2010.

Perry, Anne, interviews, Portmahomack,
2–9 January 2011.

Perry, Anne, in conversation, Vancouver,
20–22 October 2011.

Porter, Susanna, interview, New York,
19 January 2011.

Sherman, Ken, interview, New York, 20 January
2011.

Stone, Russell, interview, Auckland,
20 November 2011.

Webster, Beth, interview, Auckland, c March
2011.

INDEX

ABC's *20/20* programme   137–8

Adams, Judge Francis Boyd   212, 219, 221, 223, 243, 255

adolescence   158, 168, 174, 210, 222, 247, 250

adultery   38, 58

affairs   67, 114–15, 184, 215–16, 236, 249

agents, *see* publishing agents

Alchemy Productions   304–5

Allingham, Margery   31, 48

Ardent Productions   141, 162–3, 189, 191

Arn Gate Cottage   14, 98

Arohata Borstal (Wellington)   245–7, 314–16

Atomic Weapons Research Establishment (Aldermaston)   19, 206, 235

Bahamas   85

Ballantine Publishers   51, 76, 86, 90, 93, 96–7, 102–3, 107, 109, 111, 117–18, 120, 124–5, 137–8, 156–7, 273, 275, 296, 308–9

   American readers willingness to accept Anne Perry (a murderer)   90

   Blades, Joe   273–5, 277, 290, 296

   friction with Meg Davis over her management of Anne Perry's state of mind   138

   launches the Monk series   76, 78, 86, 88–92, 96, 100, 103–5, 107–8, 111, 116–17, 139–43, 165–6, 170–1, 191–3, 229–30, 232–4, 241, 258, 260–3, 273, 291–4, 296, 303–5, 310–12

   launches the Pitt series   40, 47, 56, 67, 70–1, 76, 78, 90, 101, 112, 126, 162, 190–1, 258, 276, 304

   Nevler, Leona   15, 76, 88, 100, 102, 128, 134, 193, 228, 263, 273

   offers publishing contracts to Anne Perry   96–7, 117–18

   Susanna, Porter   308, 313

   willing to take a risk with Anne Perry's writings   76

Banyard, Capt. Stanley (Church Army)   280

Barnes, Ray and Chlo (Anne's US neighbours)   17–18

Barnett, Sam (Secretary of Justice and Controller General of Prisons)   246, 316, 318

Barocas, Valari   71

BBC   118, 126, 159, 162–3, 190

Belgium   264–5, 267

Bennett, Dr Francis   180, 182, 197, 208, 215, 217, 219–21

Bible   37–8, 218

Blades, Joe (*see also* Ballantine Publishers)   273–5, 277, 290, 296

Book of the Month Club   160

book reviews   100–101, 108–9, 129, 165, 228, 238, 258, 271, 275, 310–11

Bowen, Trevor   190

British readers   70, 322

Brown, Alan (Crown Prosecutor)   211–14, 216–19, 221, 223, 243, 247

Brown, Sen. Det. Macdonald   200

Browne family   120–1, 148

California   17, 19, 36–7, 39, 305, 323

Cambridge University   50, 206–7, 305

Canada   41, 46–7, 51–2, 63, 204, 276, 308

Canterbury Council of Social Services   150

Canterbury University College   121

capital punishment (*see also* hangings)   244

Capital Punishment Act 1950   244

Cashmere Sanatorium   179–80, 219, 319

Catholicism   315

Catholics, *see* Roman Catholics

censorship   231, 240–1, 281

Christchurch   148, 150, 212, 220, 223, 253, 313

   Cashmere Sanatorium   179–80, 219, 319

   Paparua Prison   205, 208, 221, 243, 246, 315–16

   sensitivity due to the Parker–Hulme story   130

   social mores   150

   St Margaret's College   148, 151, 155, 281–2

   Victoria Park   197, 200, 213

Christchurch Girls' High School   130, 151, 153, 178, 181, 206, 282

Christie, Agatha   31, 48, 89

Christmas   62, 82, 98, 107, 188, 277

Church of Jesus Christ of Latter-Day Saints (*see also* Mormon Church)   18, 21, 37, 79

churches   18, 21, 28–9, 36–7, 40, 47, 61, 80, 89, 153, 216, 227, 229, 242, 269, 295

classmates, memories of   154–5, 173, 180, 182

Colbert, Nancy   41, 44–7, 51, 283, 289

Collins Publishing Co.   24

Crimes Amendment Act 1941   245

Darnton, John   137, 145–7, 156

Darsham   16–17, 19–21, 23, 36–7, 52, 61, 63, 66

Davis, Meg   66, 68, 75, 88, 93, 99, 118, 120, 124, 131, 134, 156, 159, 190, 193, 226, 239, 264–5, 270, 272–3, 290, 298, 308, 324–5

expedition to Ypres with Anne Perry   264–5

introduction to Anne Perry   62–3

London book trade specialist   124

monitors media interviews for Anne Perry   156–7

offers *Cardington Crescent* to St Martin's Press   68–9

death penalty (*see also* hangings)   244–5, 286, 305

Deaver, Jeffery   259–60, 294

Dellon, Hope   31–2, 40–1, 45, 47, 51–3, 55, 62, 69, 76, 97, 162

depression   24, 181, 248, 320

Deseret (Mormon publisher)   194

diaries   184–6, 202, 204, 215, 218, 247

Hulme, Juliet
records 'the most conceited opinions'   222–3

not used as trial evidence against   207

Parker, Pauline
changes of attitude emerge during 1954   182

describes diary as 'a companion and a confessional'   177–8

records mood swings   181

records plans 'for moidering Mother'   187–8

writes first diary in 1953   177

D'Inverno, Peggy   14, 325

Dixon, Vivien   280, 283

Down's Syndrome   151, 219, 249

Dumont Publishers   95

Elliott, Maggie   24, 54

executions, *see* hangings

faith   14, 17, 23, 79, 172, 227, 229, 242, 263, 269, 300, 306

feminism   31, 90, 105, 170, 191

Ferguson, Lin   11–12, 130–1, 168

films and documentaries   15, 71, 84, 112–13, 129–30, 143–5, 147, 158, 164, 189–90, 239, 253, 286, 296, 302–6

Foggitt, Eben   189

Fountain, Lora   239, 241

Fox Cottages   19, 88

France   119, 236, 239–41, 267, 302

Freer, Janet   24–5, 27, 30–1, 34, 36, 40–1, 45–7, 61

French readers   241

French Revolution novels   23, 47, 53, 119, 141, 239

Giles, Phillippa   189

Gillies, Det. Gordon   200, 203

God   18, 21, 23, 38–9, 68–9, 93, 135, 171, 193, 225–8, 270

Gorman, Mary Alice   157

Gresson, Terence Arbuthnot   207, 208, 211, 214, 217, 222–3, 243, 253

Griffiths, Audrey   200

Gristwood, Sarah   131–3

hangings   286–7

HarperCollins   120, 124, 135–6, 163, 312–13

Haslam, Dr Alec   207, 211, 214, 243

Hawes, Keeley   190

Haywood, Supt. Horace   255, 287, 316

Headline Publishing Co.   120, 272–3, 297, 300, 303, 308

Heasman, Frances   71

Heath, Hilary   101–2, 113

Heavenly Creatures   128–9, 153, 138, 143–5, 156, 190, 298

   Academy Award nominations   158

   casting   158

   special effects by Weta Workshop   158

   Toronto International Film Festival (1995)   158

Heurtebise, Emmanuelle   119, 239–41, 310

Hinds, Diane   297, 312

Hinton, Helen   155

Hollywood   15, 19, 112, 147, 183–4, 209, 306, 323

Holmes, Helen   150

homophobia   58

homosexuality   56, 58, 90, 192, 210, 217, 221–2, 248

Hope, Sgt. Robert   199

Hovey, Kim   15, 112, 118, 134, 137–8, 140, 147, 156–7, 272, 274

Hulme, Dr Henry   19, 50, 64, 82–3, 99, 149–50, 154, 165–6, 174, 179, 184–5, 196, 199–201, 216, 219, 236, 249, 254, 270, 280, 282–3, 316

   Cambridge University   50, 206–7, 305

   debriefs (Nazi) Admiral Dönitz   83

   Director of Naval Operational Research   83

   Rector of Canterbury University College   121

   Scientific Adviser to the Air Ministry   85

   University of Leipzig   50

   University of Liverpool   50

Hulme, Hilda (*see also* Perry, Marion)   83–5, 120, 174, 179, 181, 201–4, 208, 214–15, 217, 220, 224, 249, 254

   abandons Juliet and leaves New Zealand   254

   admired for her social charm and generosity   150

   agrees to nurse Juliet after discharge from sanatorium   180

   becomes tired and ill after the birth of her second child   84

   born Hilda Marion Reavley   50

   changes her name by deed-poll to Marion Perry   253, 283

   commits adultery   184

   conducts arrangements for Juliet's defence   207

   divorces Henry Hulme   216

   grants Henry custody of Jonathan   283

   lives in a *ménage à trois*   204

   personal life disclosed in trial   216

   relationship with Bill Perry   184

   shelters with Juliet in air-raid shelters during bombing   82

   society's post-trial attitude to   150

   subpoenaed by the Crown   206

   tells husband about her affair with Bill Perry   184

   testimony at trial   200

   vilified in the media   252

Hulme, Dr Jonathan (Jonty) (Juliet's brother)   84, 206, 236, 264–5, 270, 272, 276, 283, 290–2, 295–6, 305, 310, 313, 325

   childhood relationship with sister Juliet   85

   impact of news of Anne's 'discovery' on his wife and young children   13

   Medbury School   151

   researches material for Anne's books   238, 264

   returns to the United Kingdom in 2000   234

   settles in Scotland near Anne and Marion   234

   studies medicine at St John's College, Oxford   235

   works in Matabeleland North, Zimbabwe   235

Hulme, Juliet (*see also* Stewart, Anne and Perry, Anne)   11, 129–30, 135, 173, 190, 314, 321

   bouts of depression   24, 181, 248, 320

   Cashmere Sanatorium   179–80, 219, 319

   changes name on leaving prison   318

   Christchurch Girls' High School   151, 153, 178, 181, 206, 282

   convalesces in the Bahamas with the Browne family   85, 120–1

   legal arrangements for trial   207

   Mt Eden Prison   74–5, 104, 208, 221, 223, 246–7, 254–7, 277, 279–80, 284–8, 314, 316–17

   murders Honorah Rieper   198, 203

perceived attitude 154
release from prison 317–18
removed from parents' care 85
St Margaret's College 148, 151, 155, 281–2
tuberculosis 132, 167, 179, 256, 282
Hulme, Margery (Henry Hulme's second wife) 82, 283
Hunter, James 223

Ilam homestead 110, 149, 151, 175, 178, 183–5, 187, 199, 201–3, 205–7, 218, 220, 313
Ilam School 149
incest 48, 90, 106, 116
insanity, issues concerning 135, 207–8, 211, 219–21, 223
interviews 13, 131–3, 136–7, 143–4, 147, 156, 160, 163–4, 166–7, 201–2, 220, 222, 272–3, 288, 297–8, 313, 324, 326
Invergordon 14
Italy 95, 282, 301–2, 318

Jackson, Peter (see also Heavenly Creatures) 128–30, 143–5, 158, 190
journalists 11, 13, 15, 133–4, 138, 145, 212, 240–1, 253, 272

Kirwin, Lynne 13, 131–2, 135–7

La Plante, Lynda 101–2, 113, 118, 126, 159, 162
Leslie, Darron 163
Leventer, Lisa 69
Linkiewicz, Dana 302, 312
Los Angeles 17–19, 112, 118, 147, 159, 306, 323
Lowestoft 16, 21–2, 37, 66

Maass, Don 15, 94–5, 97, 117, 126, 134, 138, 145, 167, 232–3, 263, 267, 273, 275, 295, 313
MacDonald, Meg 29–30, 37–9, 61, 66, 80–2, 86–8, 92–3, 98, 123, 238, 264–5, 272, 313
enjoys Anne's company 29
humane reaction to Anne's disclosure 39
MacDonald, Simon 122

Magistrates' Court 205, 208, 214
Mahon, Peter 212, 221
Maidment, Kenneth and Felicity 255–6, 280
Malice Domestic Convention 119
Marsh, Ngaio 31, 48, 150, 190, 313
Mason, Hon. Rex (Minister of Justice) 317
MBA Literary Agents 24–5, 45–7, 52, 54–5, 62, 66, 77, 113, 131, 133–4, 137, 314, 326
Freer, Janet 24–5, 27, 30–1, 34, 36, 40–1, 45–7, 61
Park, Christine 47, 52–5, 61–2, 71
parts company with St Martin's Press 46, 51–2
Taylor, Diana 55, 62–3, 65
McArthur, Louise 152
McClelland, Brian 207, 212, 219, 221, 253
McCormack, Tom 27, 30, 41
McCrum, Robert 18, 141, 143, 166–8, 289
McIlroy, Eric 199
McKenzie, Don (psychologist) 287–8, 316
McKenzie, Insp. Duncan 200
Medbury School (Christchurch) 151
Medlicott, Dr Reginald Warren 208–11, 217–21, 247, 283, 322
Mellor, Vicki 300–301, 303, 308–9, 313
memories of classmates 154–5, 173, 180, 182
Merrow, Jane 190, 296, 305
Milne, Miss (teacher) 153–4
Miramax Co. 145, 147, 156–7
Molyneaux, Const. Donald 199
Mondadori Publishers 76, 95
Monk novels 76, 78, 86, 88–92, 96, 100, 103–5, 107–8, 111, 116–17, 139–43, 165–6, 170–1, 191–3, 229–30, 232–4, 241, 258, 260–3, 273, 291–4, 296, 303–5, 310–12
Moraga (Oakland) 17
Mormon Church 18, 23, 43, 58, 75, 226
in America 17–18, 21, 40
in East Anglia 21
in Scotland 14, 22, 29, 39, 68, 98, 107, 326
Mormons 18, 21, 44, 62, 226–7
Morpeth, Jane 273, 297

Mt Eden Prison   74–5, 104, 208, 221, 223, 246–7, 254–7, 277, 279–80, 284–5, 288, 314, 316–17

  'brutal Victorian fortress'   255

  hangings   286–7

Muirson, Diane   155

murderers   23, 26, 38, 48, 67, 72, 78, 88–91, 103, 128, 230, 239, 242, 267, 292, 299, 307

Nathan, Hilary (*see also* Parker, Pauline)   171–2

  found living in Hoo (near Rochester)   171

Nazis   83, 130, 210

NBC (morning news programme)   137

Needham, Ruth   12, 133

Nevler, Leona   15, 76, 88–90, 93, 95–6, 100, 102, 107–9, 112, 114, 118, 125, 128, 134, 140, 160, 164, 193–4, 228, 263, 273

New Zealand   11, 14, 49, 87, 99, 106, 120, 128, 130, 132, 134, 136, 151–2, 158, 163–4, 171, 206–8, 212, 244–5, 252–4, 268, 281–2, 313–14, 321–2

New Zealand National Radio   137, 163

Newcastle-upon-Tyne   320, 322

North American readers   44, 70, 75, 90, 232, 272

Ormskirk (near Southport)   50

Oxford   75, 235

Paparua Prison (Christchurch)   205, 208, 221, 243, 246, 315–16

paranoia   210, 217, 221–2, 322

Paris   118–19, 239, 242

Park, Christine   47, 52–5, 61–2, 71

Parker, Amy (Pauline's grandmother)   152, 208

Parker, Honorah, *see* Rieper, Honorah

Parker, Pauline   11, 129, 132, 145, 151–2, 155, 158, 167–8, 171, 173–4, 177, 181–2, 187, 196–205, 207–8, 210, 213, 215–16, 218–19, 243–6, 249–51, 313, 316, 321–2

  buys a pacer, 'Omar Khayyám'   175

  changes name to Hilary Nathan   171

  converts to Catholicism   315

  diaries   181, 184, 186, 188, 209, 215, 217–21, 223, 247, 251

  holidays at Port Levy   178–9

  infatuated with Juliet   175

  nocturnal activities   184, 219

  prison life   314

  rejects both her parents   185

  retreats into bouts of depression   24, 181, 248, 320

  sees Juliet as a door to another world   175

  visits Juliet in the sanatorium   180

  visits shipping companies enquiring about fares to New York   183

Parker, Robert William (Honorah Parker's father)   152

Parker, Wendy   152, 172, 197, 208, 313

Parker–Hulme story   11, 130, 136, 272, 321–2

  compared with the Leopold and Loeb case   210

  publication in 1991 of *A Lesbian View*   130

  release of movie *Heavenly Creatures*   128–9

  suggestions of homosexual behaviour   56, 58, 90, 192, 210, 217, 221–2, 248

  Supreme Court Trial   208, 212, 223, 243

  teenage component in the   250

  Television New Zealand proposal for documentary   296

Perry, Anne   11–12, 17, 20–1, 26, 39, 41, 45–6, 70–1, 80, 113, 126–7, 134–6, 146, 157, 164, 167, 228, 294–5, 298, 308, 312–14, 323, 326–7

  author's tours   43–5, 64, 96–7, 112, 118, 128, 134, 138, 144, 147, 157, 159, 179, 240, 272, 298

  California   305

  Canada   41, 46–7, 51–2, 63, 204, 276, 308

  contracts   27, 54, 64–5, 93, 96, 102, 117, 120, 313

  crime books   46, 48–9, 52, 62, 70–1, 102, 113, 119, 126, 140, 239, 241, 272, 275, 302

  films and documentaries   15, 71, 84, 112–13, 129–30, 143–5, 147, 158, 164, 189–90, 239, 253, 286, 296, 302–6

  First World War series   239, 263, 265, 267, 269–71, 273, 282, 296, 298, 300–301, 304

  foreign-language market   40, 119, 275

  French Revolution novels   23, 47, 53, 119, 141, 239

  German Jewish refugees   83, 114

Hollywood   15, 19, 112, 147, 183–4, 209, 306, 323

influence of other crime writers   258–9

literary agents   55, 71, 156, 238

love of poetry   202–3, 257, 278, 280–1, 283, 326

Malice Domestic Convention   119

meets her father (Henry) in secret   82

memories of classmates   154–5, 173, 180, 182

mix-ups with agents   51–2

Monk novels   76, 78, 86, 88–92, 96, 100, 103–5, 107–8, 111, 116–17, 139–43, 165–6, 170–1, 191–3, 229–30, 232–4, 241, 258, 260–3, 273, 291–4, 296, 303–5, 310–12

Mormon attitudes to marriage   68

negotiations with the BBC   118, 126, 159, 162–3, 190

Newcastle-upon-Tyne   320, 322

Pitt novels   40, 47, 56, 67, 70–1, 76, 78, 90, 101, 112, 126, 162, 190–1, 258, 276, 304

Portmahomack   12–14, 92–3, 96, 98–9, 107, 110–11, 124, 131, 133, 138, 140, 142, 147, 167–8, 236–7, 241, 264, 270, 298, 302, 312, 325–6

publications

  Acceptable Loss   312

  Angels in the Gloom   269, 271

  Ashworth Hall   168–9

  At Some Disputed Barricade   298

  Bedford Square   229

  Belgrave Square   109–12

  Bethlehem Road   78, 80, 101, 120

  Betrayal at Lisson Grove   312

  Bluegate Fields   52–6, 58–9, 71

  Brunswick Gardens   191

  Buckingham Palace Gardens   306–8

  Cain His Brother   142

  Callander Square   31–2, 39, 59

  Cardington Crescent   66–9, 71–2

  The Cater Street Hangman   25, 27, 30–2, 39–40, 43, 53, 163, 190–1

  A Christmas Grace   303

  A Christmas Guest   296

  A Christmas Journey   277, 303

  A Christmas Promise   304

  Come, Come Ye Saints   40

  Come Armageddon   193, 195, 227–8

  A Dangerous Mourning   103, 107–8

  Dark Assassin   293–4

  Death in the Devil's Acre   55, 58–60, 71

  Death of a Stranger   260

  A Dish Taken Cold   239

  Execution Dock   310

  The Face of a Stranger   76, 78, 88, 90, 92, 100–101, 111–12, 119–20, 296, 304

  Farriers' Lane   113–14, 116, 120, 126

  A Funeral in Blue   260, 263

  Half Moon Street   230, 232, 260

  Highgate Rise   94, 96, 109

  The Hyde Park Headsman   126–8, 138

  Long Spoon Lane   290

  'Lower Than the Angels'   53

  'Most Violent Ways'   53

  'My Eagle Comes'   77

  The One Thing More   242, 260

  Paragon Walk   34–6, 39, 41, 43–4, 46, 49, 67

  Pentecost Alley   160

  Resurrection Row   41–2, 45, 49, 67

  Rutland Place   47–9, 51–2

  Sadokhar   69, 193, 195–6, 225–6

  Seven Dials   42, 170, 275

  The Shifting Tide   291–2

  Shoulder the Sky   267, 271

  Silence in Hanover Close   72–3, 75, 77

  The Silent Cry   170

  The Sins of the Wolf   138, 140

  Slaves of Obsession   232

  Southampton Row   273–4

  A Sudden Fearful Death   116–17

  Tathea   193–5, 225–9

  'Thou with Clean Hands'   69, 77, 113, 119

  Traitor's Gate   119, 134, 138, 156, 159

  Twisted Root   229

  We Shall Not Sleep   300–301

  Weighed in the Balance   165

  The Whitechapel Conspiracy   258–9, 274, 306

  Whited Sepulchres / A Breach of Promise (USA title)   191–2

Queenswood School, Hawke's Bay   148

re-structures the plots of the non-detective novels   65–6

reacts explosively during Bible studies   37–8

receives her first contract   27

receives regular rejection slips   23

relationship with father   82–3, 99, 174, 282

restores the stone barn   122–4

sells reprint rights for *Rutland Place* to Fawcett   51

sells the Italian rights for *The Cater Street Hangman*   40

sends a profile for publicity purposes   35

settles in Darsham   16–17, 19–21, 23, 36–7, 52, 61, 63, 66

short story collections   239, 263

Suffolk   16–17, 22, 63, 80–2, 87, 99, 107, 171

visits Guernsey   75

World War II memories   82–4

Perry, Marion (*see also* Hulme, Hilda)   19, 49–50, 54–5, 234, 236–9, 252, 284, 290–1, 320, 325

   Anne warns of forthcoming publicity   14

   delighted at son Jonathan's return to the UK   234

   moves to Portmahomack and buys a cottage   98

   reads Anne's scripts   49

   takes up her old role of copyeditor   30

Perry, Walter Andrew Bowman (Bill)   19, 24, 50, 55, 183–4, 196, 200–201, 204, 206, 215–16, 224, 236, 249, 254, 284, 320

   begins a relationship with Hilda   184

   close to death   54–5

   conducts arrangements for Juliet's defence from Port Levy   207

   departs from New Zealand two weeks after the trial   252–4

   diaries (in trial) expose the affair with Hilda Hulme   215

   interviews with the police   201, 203

   introduced to Hilda Hulme   184

   the last officer to leave Dunkirk Beach   54

   marries Marion Hulme   320

   provides background evidence on the girls   214

   recommendations to Anne on her writing   23, 30

   relationship begins with Hilda   183

   subject to blackmail by Juliet and Pauline   184

   subpoenaed by the Crown prosecutor   206

   tenant at the Hulme homestead in Ilam   183

   visits Juliet and Pauline after the murder   200

Port Levy (Banks Peninsula)   178–9, 206–7, 218

Porter, Susanna   308, 313

Portmahomack   12–14, 92–3, 96, 98–9, 107, 110–11, 124, 131, 133, 138, 140, 142, 147, 167–8, 236–7, 241, 264, 270, 298, 302, 312, 325–6

Powell, Grace   256, 288–9, 316

Prince Edward   141, 162–3, 189

prisoners   243, 255–6, 285–9

publishing agents   11, 36, 41, 51–2, 63, 75, 88, 95, 97, 112, 159, 239, 263–4, 270, 275–6, 303, 308

Queenswood School, Hawke's Bay   148

Ramage, William (police photographer)   200, 214

rape   35, 37, 90, 105, 116, 170

readers   48, 79, 94, 100, 138, 228–9, 300, 310, 322

   British   70, 322

   French   241

   North American   44, 70, 75, 90, 232, 272

Reavley, Hilda Marion (later Hulme, Hilda and later Perry, Marion)   50

Relief Society   37

Rieper, Herbert   151–3, 175, 178–9, 181–2, 185, 187–8, 196, 198, 200, 202–4, 208, 214, 219, 243

   accused of having 'defective stock'   219

   de facto status of marriage to Honorah revealed during trial   204

   Dennis Brothers' Fish Shop   153

   discovers money 'stolen' from his fish shop   184

   discovers Pauline's diaries   202

Down's Syndrome daughter in care   249

identifies Honorah's body   203

introduces Pauline to craft-modelling in wood and plasticine   152

learns wife has been involved in an 'accident'   199

Rieper, Honorah   151–3, 179–82, 188, 196–205, 213–14, 249, 251, 313

   Birmingham origins   204

   buried Bromley cemetery, Christchurch   205

   elopes with Herbert Rieper   152

   murdered by Juliet and Pauline   198, 203

   opposes the friendship between Juliet and Pauline   185

   postmortem findings   214

   rigidity of attitude   249

   tries different techniques for handling Pauline's behaviour   182

Ritchie, Agnes   197–9, 201, 214

Ritchie, Kenneth   198–9, 214

Salt Lake City   44, 112

Savill, James   223

Sayers, Nick   120, 124, 135

Scotland   80–2, 86–7, 92, 99, 114, 139–40, 156, 167, 229, 234, 236, 264, 302, 326

Scottish Highlands   22, 81–2, 88

Sealey, John   304

Second World War   81–2, 212, 219

sexualities, women's   116

Shelton, Gilbert   239

Sherman, Ken   15, 112–13, 118, 126, 137, 141, 147, 159, 296, 304–6, 312

Smith, Joseph (prophet)   21, 37, 226–7

South Africa   185, 197, 203, 214

Spain   302–3

Spencer, Caroline   173

St Margaret's College   148, 151, 155, 281–2

St Martin's Press   27–8, 30–2, 41, 44–6, 51–5, 65, 69–72, 76, 86, 94, 96–7, 102, 162–3, 302

Stallworthy, Kenneth   221–3, 288

Stewart, Anne (name selected on leaving Mt Eden Prison and later changed to Perry, Anne by deed-poll)   318, 320

Stewart, Jean (headmistress)   153

Suffolk   16–17, 22, 63, 80–2, 87, 99, 107, 171

suffrage movement   35, 67, 78, 120

Sugarman, Robert   126

Supreme Court trial   208, 212, 223, 243

Sutherland, Nancy   234, 278, 280–3, 288

Talese, Nan   40

Tarbat Ness Lighthouse   92, 238, 325

Tarbat Ness Peninsula   98, 124

Tate, Det. Archie   200–201, 203, 205, 207, 322

Taylor, Diana   55, 62–3, 65

Taylor, Imogen   120, 124, 135–6

Toronto   44, 47, 49, 52, 112, 118

tuberculosis   132, 167, 179, 256, 282

Tyler, Diana   12, 24, 47, 54, 62, 71, 112

Tyndall, Margaret   155, 183, 205

Victoria Park   197, 200, 213

Walsh, Fran   129, 144

Watford   19, 49

Webb, Hon Clifton (Minister of Justice)   245–6

Webb, Marjorie   155, 174

women's sexualities   116

Yentob, Alan (BBC)   159, 162

Yorkshire Television   102, 113, 190

Young, Stephanie (headmistress)   148, 281–2

Ypres   264–8, 301

Zimbabwe   236, 264